K

Women in the Discourse of Early Modern Spain

Florida A&M University, Tallahassee
Florida Atlantic University, Boca Raton
Florida Gulf Coast University, Ft. Myers
Florida International University, Miami
Florida State University, Tallahassee
University of Central Florida, Orlando
University of Florida, Gainesville
University of North Florida, Jacksonville
University of South Florida, Tampa
University of West Florida, Pensacola

Women in the Discourse
of Early Modern Spain

Edited by Joan F. Cammarata

University Press of Florida
Gainesville · Tallahassee · Tampa · Boca Raton
Pensacola · Orlando · Miami · Jacksonville · Ft. Myers

08 07 06 05 04 03   6 5 4 3 2 1

Library of Congress Cataloging-in-Publication Data
Women in the discourse of early modern Spain /
edited by Joan F. Cammarata.
p. cm.
Includes bibliographical references and index.
ISBN 0-8130-2578-8 (alk. paper)
1. Spanish literature—Classical period, 1500–1700—History and criticism.
2. Women in literature. 3. Spanish literature—Women authors—History
and criticism. I. Cammarata, Joan, 1950–
PQ6066 .W56 2002
860.9'352042—dc21   2002033371

The University Press of Florida is the scholarly publishing agency
for the State University System of Florida, comprising Florida A&M
University, Florida Atlantic University, Florida Gulf Coast University,
Florida International University, Florida State University, University
of Central Florida, University of Florida, University of North Florida,
University of South Florida, and University of West Florida.

University Press of Florida
15 Northwest 15th Street
Gainesville, FL 32611–2079
http://www.upf.com

Contents

Acknowledgments vii

Introduction 1
Joan F. Cammarata

Part I. A Woman's Self-fashioning: The Private Gendered Spaces of Feminine Authority

1. Authorizing the Wife/Mother in Sixteenth-Century Advice Manuals 19
   Carolyn Nadeau

2. Identity, Illusion, and the Emergence of the Feminine Subject in *La Lozana andaluza* 35
   John C. Parrack

3. Skepticism and Mysticism in Early Modern Spain: The Combative Stance of Teresa de Avila 54
   Barbara Mujica

Part II. Appropriation and Authenticity of Feminine Identity

4. The Price of Love: The Conflictive Economies of *La gitanilla* 79
   William H. Clamurro

5. The Problematics of Gender/Genre in *Vida i sucesos de la monja alférez* 91
   Rainer H. Goetz

6. *Relaciones de fiestas:* Ana Caro's Accounts of Public Spectacles 108
   Sharon D. Voros

Part III. Cultural Constructs of the Feminine Psyche: Body, Mind, and Desire

7. Masquerade and the *Comedia* 135
   Anita K. Stoll

8. Dreams, Voices, Signatures: Deciphering Woman's Desires in Angela de Azevedo's *Dicha y desdicha del juego* 146
   Frederick A. de Armas

9. Galatea's Fall and the Inner Dynamics of Góngora's *Fábula de Polifemo y Galatea* 160
   Joseph V. Ricapito

Part IV. Power Stratagems of the Feminine Word: Constraints of Silence and Authority of Discourse

10. *De voz extremada:* Cervantes's Women Characters Speak for Themselves 183
    Sara A. Taddeo

11. Silence Is/As Golden . . . Age Device: Ana Caro's Eloquent Reticence in *Valor, agravio y mujer* 199
    Monica Leoni

12. Woman of the World and World of the Woman in the Narrative of Mariana de Caravajal 213
    Louis Imperiale

Part V. Transforming Literary Conventions: Feminine Aesthetics and Gender Norms

13. A Cry in the Wilderness: Pastoral Female Discourse in María de Zayas 235
    Deborah Compte

14. Zayas's Ideal of the Masculine: Clothes Make the Man 253
    Susan Paun de García

15. Desire Unbound: Women's Theater of Spain's Golden Age 272
    Lisa Vollendorf

Contributors 293

Index 297

Acknowledgments

At a time when the complex subject of women's writing was just coming to the fore in Spanish literature, the Northeast Modern Language Association and the South Atlantic Modern Language Association provided much needed forums for the exchange of research and methodology on women in the literature and history of Early Modern Spain. In the nearly one decade of sessions that I have organized on this topic, the ample attendance and the lively discussion that they generated proved the growing focus on this area of Spanish scholarship. The research and ideas voiced in these panel presentations have been expanded and emerge as the essays assembled in this collection.

This book is a collaborative work and I express my deepest appreciation to the contributors of this volume. Their willingness to refine their contributions to achieve coherence in the volume and their unfailing cooperation, patience, and friendship made my work possible. Their commitment to meticulous scholarship and the scope of their investigations will make this volume appealing to a range of readers beyond those of Spanish literary studies. I am very grateful to Susan Fernandez, senior acquisitions editor of the University Press of Florida, who envisioned the possibilities of this volume many years ago. I thank her for her consistent support and encouragement at every stage. She and the staff of the University Press of Florida are to be commended for the efficiency with which they have handled all aspects of the publication of this work.

My deepest gratitude to Dr. Mary Ann O'Donnell, dean of the School of Arts at Manhattan College, and to Dr. Rodney Rodríguez, chairperson in Modern Foreign Languages, who together have encouraged my scholarly interests earnestly and consistently with both moral and material support, without which this project could have been neither initiated nor completed in a timely manner. And finally, to acknowledge that one's love for learning is nurtured in childhood, I give special thanks to my Mom. And to my husband Richard, a special expression of gratitude for his love, understanding, humor, and steadfast support of my professional life.

Introduction

Joan F. Cammarata

Over the past two decades, literary scholars of Early Modern Spain have come to recognize the issues of feminine identity and gender asymmetry as integral components of their critical explorations. It is relevant to acknowledge that during the historical period of the sixteenth and seventeenth centuries, European scholars of theology, ethics, law, and medicine continue the medieval debate over the issue of woman's inferiority to man. Concepts of gender difference derive from classical philosophical and medieval attitudes toward the soul and body. The assumption of mental and physical deficiencies in the female sex leads scholars to concede that woman is not a monster, but they still puzzle over the question, "Is woman a human being?" Upon what data did these male scholars base their assumptions of female inferiority? Ian Maclean, who explores these perceptions in his study *The Renaissance Notion of Woman*, observes:

> [W]oman is considered to be inferior to man in that the psychological effects of her cold and moist humors throw doubt on her control of her emotions and her rationality; furthermore, her less robust physique predisposes her, it is thought, to a more protected and less prominent role in the household and in society. Although apparently not bound by the authority of the divine institution of matrimony, doctors nonetheless produce a "natural" justification for woman's relegation to the home and exclusion from public office, and provide thereby, as well as coherence with a central tenet of theology, an important foundation on which arguments in ethics, politics and law are based. (46)

In the legal codes of Castile, first collected in the Laws of Toro in 1369 and promulgated in 1505, woman is categorized as *imbecilitas sexus* [imbecile sex], along with children, invalids, and delinquents (Formica 179). The rationale for interpretations of female physical weakness as an index of moral weakness stems from Aristotle's postulation that a female is by nature a defective male. A female's natural passivity and cold and moist humors make her unfit for any activity that is not a response to a man's command. Sociological functions are dictated by this natural law that inscribes the rational male element as ruler in a public sphere over the passionate female element contained in the private sphere.

The scriptural seeds of woman's inferiority are planted in the Old Testament and blossom in the social subjugation of women proclaimed throughout the New Testament. In his epistle to the Ephesians, St. Paul, echoing the Aristotelian concept of the natural submission of women, recommends, "Let wives be subject to their husbands as to the Lord; because a husband is head of the wife just as Christ is head of the Church, being himself savior of the body. But just as the Church is subject to Christ, so also let wives be to their husbands in all things" (5:22–24). The justification for woman's traditional subordination is found in the Pauline injunction for woman's silence, which was originally intended to avoid possible scandals in the early Church, "Let women keep silence in the churches, for it is not permitted them to speak, but let them be submissive, as the Law also says. But if they wish to learn anything let them ask their husbands at home, for it is unseemly for a woman to speak in church" (Corinthians 14:34–35). This dictum, which formerly prohibited that women teach the catechism, is perpetuated by the patriarchy during Spain's sixteenth and seventeenth centuries to justify the silencing of the inferior sex and women's exclusion from the public sphere.

The common belief in women's weak nature and in their natural inclination to sin is reinforced by Juan Luis Vives in his influential *Institutio feminae christianae* [*The Instruction of a Christian Woman*] (1523). Vives favors learning for women as the path to acquiring wifely virtues, but he concludes with a condemnation of women in public life and women's public display of learning. Baldassare Castiglione, the enlightened social commentator of the sixteenth century whose work was widely read in Spain, recounts similar arguments for and against the inferiority of woman in his *Il cortegiano* (*The Book of the Courtier*, 1528, book 3, 201–82). While he claims that man and woman have an identical capacity for virtue, he also reaffirms accepted social conventions of the legal and marital subservience of women. As twentieth-century scholars investigate the status of Early Modern women, they are apt to agree with Derrida when he defines the place of woman as a "non-place"; to write from it or in it is to situate oneself in the realm of the "undecidable" (111–13).

This present collection of essays, contributed by scholars of Spain's Early Modern literature, addresses questions related to the artistic production by and about women in sixteenth- and seventeenth-century peninsular Spain. The volume reflects the vibrant, energetic research now taking place in the study of Early Modern women as it analyzes textual and intertextual authority in the creation of feminine discourse. In addition, the historical framework that determines women's identity and cultural roles in their private domain has become an essential component of much scholarly inquiry. Insights into the male social, economic, political, and authorial dominance, which restricted women's active involvement and visibility in the public sphere, explain how cultural practices work to articulate social, political, or artistic boundaries, while opening up channels of communication across those same boundaries. Scholars examine this public/private dichotomy to explain both the cultural devaluation of women and the gender-based allocation of power. Even when an atypical woman ventures successfully into the public sphere, this does not preclude her subordination to men because the exercise of public authority by women is always viewed as illegitimate in the unspoken social codes that govern women's public and private roles. It is not surprising then that men have been, by default, the spokesmen for women marked by cultural silence.

The essays written for this volume seek to restore women to the complexity of their unique cultural contexts and to destroy simplistic notions about women's passivity or activity. The cross-disciplinary collaboration between literature and history indicates that both these disciplines afford a vision of culture as they interpret it. Literature shapes a culture's sense of itself in a historical moment. Early Modern woman's distinctive historical experience finds expression in this volume through analyses of women as literary subject matter and women as the creators of literature in works by both male and female authors. In reproducing the exclusions, dominations, resourcefulness, and oppositions of gender asymmetry, the authors of this volume share a common conception of a complex process that includes the consideration of the formal content of the texts but also of the circumstances of their writing and reading.

The first of the five sections of this collection examines the theme of gendered spaces and the ways in which feminine identity is shaped by women as agents who challenge or redefine their placement in the elite male paradigms of Early Modern society. The narrowing of female boundaries contributes to the erosion of women's public status and leads to the restriction of women to a privatized domestic realm. The image of the ideal female offered to women vilifies participation in the public realm while it extols the private role or cult of domesticity that encompasses wifely or motherly tasks. In her essay "Authorizing the Wife/Mother in Sixteenth-Century Advice Manuals," Carolyn Nadeau explores how Spanish treatises identify the mother as an authority figure during the early stages of a child's development. Her essay focuses on the contributions of Antonio de Guevara's treatise *Relox de príncipes* [*Dial of Princes*] to discuss the ties between breast-feeding, parental roles in raising a family, and public policy on the family in sixteenth-century Spain. She also examines the treatises of two other writers, Pedro de Luján's *Coloquios matrimoniales* [*Marriage Colloquia*] and Fray Luis de León's *La perfecta casada* [*The Perfect Wife*], to show consistencies in the primacy of the mother throughout the century. Within the sociopolitical context of the reign of Charles I, Guevara's ideas mesh with current issues and the state's efforts to centralize power. The essay begins by contextualizing Guevara's work both within the literature on breast-feeding and wet-nursing in Early Modern Europe and within the literature on family/state connections. Although few historical studies on breast-feeding and child development have been done with a focus on Early Modern Spain, Nadeau draws from historical studies in other European countries and from prescriptive Spanish works in an effort to understand the importance of Guevara's treatise. At a time when Spain is striving to become a modern, centralized state, the writers corroborate that the male is the authority figure who rules every facet of the family. However, while Guevara acknowledges the mother's power and independence, he cannot fail to locate the father in an equally important role during the child's breast-feeding years. Notwithstanding their political, social, or spiritual motives, Nadeau establishes that all three writers allude to the legitimate authority of women in areas of the private domain.

Social and economic class remains a fundamental factor in the reconciliation between the patriarchal ideal of the enclosed woman and the everyday reality of participation in the world. The lives of Spanish women differ according to their civil status, class, religion, and locale. There are women who, by virtue of the conditions of their material life and social needs, use their personal experience as a mechanism to devise their own, new structures of authority. John Parrack explores the unique developments in the representation and emergence of Early Modern feminine subjectivity in his essay, "Identity, Illusion, and the Emergence of the Feminine Subject in *La Lozana andaluza*." Within the context of Early Modern Spain, a cultural period in which women such as fictional Celestina and the historical Queen Isabel emerge to confront misogyny, Francisco Delicado's *La Lozana andaluza* [*Portrait of Lozana*] constitutes a significant advance in the (self-)representation of women. In contrast to Celestina, Lozana is able to fully confront the masculine systems of authority, construct and articulate her own identity, and use illusion in order to fashion multiple subject positions through which to advantage herself.

Parrack's essay examines the emergence of Lozana as a self-fashioning female subject, as well as the representation of female authority and interaction within private gendered spaces. Unlike previous female characters, Lozana experiences a dramatic transformation as a youth of only twelve years when she ceases to be defined passively as the Other, the object of mistreatment by authority figures such as Diomedes or her family. In the end, Lozana is not killed or married in accordance with the phallogocentric order of sixteenth-century Spain. Rather, she dies a natural death after having traveled through Europe, explored the subconscious world of dreams, and constructed her own identity (Aldonza>Lozana>Vellida). Lozana and the other female characters exercise their own free will through the devices of manipulation of language and control over sexuality. These decidedly modern developments in the representation of gender occur in a text that stands at the margins of the literary world because of its treatment of eroticism and language and its failure to fit neatly within the trajectory and parameters of Early Modern literature. Parrack confirms that, notwithstanding its often marginal status, *La Lozana andaluza* both reveals and anticipates subsequent developments in the representation of gender in the *comedia,* as well as in the novellas of women writers such as María de Zayas and Ana Caro.

Early Modern women have rarely written their own history but those that did write find that this very status also demands that they maintain their modesty or acknowledge their intellectual inferiority. In defiance against the sole identity of females as obedient wife or nun, women make use of religion and community to embrace the misogynistic image of the ignorant woman and have it work for them. From positions of apparent weakness women begin to distinguish themselves in the first decades of the Early Modern era, but formulaic authorial self-deprecation to mark exterior events is essential in their writings. Feminine literary history becomes comprehensible with the provision of texts by women such as Teresa of Avila, who reveals deliberate communicative strategies to gain acceptance from the male authoritative structure.

The revival of skepticism in the sixteenth century reaches Spain through both primary and secondary sources, among them Erasmus who adopts a skeptical defense of faith, arguing against the intellectualism that had come to pervade theology. Historians disagree on whether or not Teresa of Avila, whose works delineate the road to inner spirituality, actually read Erasmus or not. However, it is generally agreed that she was familiar with the Erasmian thought that permeates the intellectual discourse of her age as she submits her experiences to meditation, scrutiny, and skepticism. In her essay, "Skepticism and Mysticism in Early Modern Spain: The Combative Stance of Teresa de Avila," Barbara Mujica notes that, like Erasmus, Teresa draws heavily on skeptical argumentation, which she uses to disarm her detractors and bolster the feminine sphere. She defends mental prayer by discrediting the intellect while emphasizing personal experience. Although she praises certain intellectual activities such as *lectio divina* [divine reading] as beneficial for the soul, she maintains that it is not through human understanding that spiritual union is achieved. Mujica explores Teresa's use of skepticism as a tactical weapon in her battle to make herself understood and believed. She concludes that Teresa undermines her seemingly submissive position by adopting a skeptical stance with respect to intellect and erudition as part of her combative strategy, thereby subverting the authority of her superiors.

The second section of this volume provides insights into the issues of identity and social conflict in women who make their way by adapting and improvising. The essays reflect the centrality of the questions concerning the formation of identity at the intersection of various social and cultural processes and affirm that even private life, the feminine province, is created in culture. The authors explore the liminal quality of the roles of women as they generate their own place in the intellectual and material world. Feminine identity is perceived as multiple and derived from conditions that limit or expand women's options, such as membership in a family and ethnicity, residence in a geographic locale, or participation in a social class. In the politics of gender-specific experience, women legitimize their actions and achieve self-definition by rejecting family standards, circumventing forms of societal control, and appropriating access to public power.

In Miguel de Cervantes's *Novelas ejemplares* [*Exemplary Novels*], women are often objects of amorous desire and are, at times, independent and strong. But women are also objectified as both the social element of family honor and as the markers of material value. The ways in which they are "valued" reveal much about the patriarchal real world. In his essay, "The Price of Love: The Conflictive Economies of *La gitanilla*," William Clamurro examines the material dimension of the portrayal of the young gypsy girl, Preciosa, who serves as both object of value and as intermediary of desires.

Clamurro shows that *La gitanilla* [*The Little Gypsy Girl*] deals with seemingly antagonistic "economies." Money in its role as language and intermediary between the woman Preciosa and others is most significant as it pervades the story in language, gesture, and plot and as it reveals the problematic interaction of social classes, ethnicities, and economies. Preciosa's gypsy realm and respectable society are parallel and connected economies that allow a certain questioning of the accepted norm, which Clamurro argues is not consciously intended by the author. Cervantes's creation of the female so often involves the journey of a woman whose identity resists conventional social roles.

The tension between the terms "woman" and "writer"—categories that can be simultaneously contradictory and complementary—appears as a subtext in almost all women writers as they mark their presence in the male territory of authorship. Women's self-writing, like all autobiographical narratives, springs from a vital impulse to bring órder to a life lived. The notion of genre plays a vital role in ordering the subject matter of any narrative and can help explain why, how, and with what effects female autobiographers of Early Modern Spain enter the public sphere. At a time when women are commonly excluded from public life and its representations, Catalina de Erauso becomes the first Spanish woman to write an experiential, or secular, autobiography or memoir. This exclusive male genre relies on a linear and pseudohistorical account of the author's achievements in a certain public capacity, that is, in the Church, the military, or government. Rainer Goetz in his essay, "The Problematics of Gender/Genre in *Vida i sucesos de la monja alférez* [*The Life and Adventures of the Lieutenant Nun*]*,*" explores how Catalina de Erauso is able to force her way into this genre only by becoming a man and living a man's life in the Americas.

On the surface, Erauso's life-story reflects this change of identity in the use of masculine pronouns and masculine adjective endings. Yet, the most visible effect of the transformation is the story itself. The author overcomes the social tenet against female self-expression to claim authority in her field of expertise, which is survival in a violent male-dominated world. Catalina de Erauso leaves her convent home to participate in the conquest of the Americas dressed as a man. Only after many years is it revealed that she is a woman and she returns to Europe. She surmounts gender limitations when she receives papal permission to go back to the Americas as a mule driver in male dress. In his study of Erauso's autobiography, Goetz illustrates the process by which she identifies more and more with the patriarchal code that is based on deception and violence. In order to survive and be allowed a voice, she has to abandon her female body and her identification with the Mother. Overcoming the genre barrier does not resolve the tension of gender and the tension between male and female identity in her life and in her life-story. Thus, the autobiography is not only a document of personal achievements that ought to be applauded; beneath the surface, it is also a document of feminine repression and the loss of feminine identity when gender is the dominant signifier for power relations.

In the complex relationship between women's writing and the male-centered canon of Spanish literature, many tenth muses have for many years been denied a place in literary history. Authorship and patronage are means of cultural power. It is not surprising that women writers seek protection and access to the world through connections with wealthy patrons, often noblewomen who have access to a network of well-connected decision makers. Celebrated in her time, Ana Caro Mallén de Soto, a formal poet and dramatist who enters the public world through her chronicles of public events, redefines the category of woman writer. Sharon Voros's essay, "*Relaciones de fiestas:* Ana Caro's Accounts of Public Spectacles," focuses on the only documented professional woman writer of Spain's seventeenth century who begins her public career with her accounts of public spectacles in both Seville and Madrid. Caro's verse account of 1637, *Contexto de las reales fiestas que se hizieron en palacio del Buen Retiro* [*Text of the Royal Festivities Held in the Palace of the Buen Retiro*], is the topic of Voros's essay.

The argument that Caro writes on command as a servant of the powerful, not on her own initiative, reveals the constraints on those women who venture into the public sphere. Voros explores the relationship between discourse and power and shows how Caro inscribes herself within the ideological frame of her own historic period and struggles with her identity as a female writer. Seeking the sponsorship of a wealthy patron as did her contemporary male writers, Caro dedicates the first part of her account to Agustina Spínola, wife to the Genoese banker Carlos Strata who sponsored this event at the Buen Retiro, while she dedicates the second part to the Count Duke of Olivares; the third part of this poetic description is dedicated to the officials of the city of Madrid. Little is known of Caro's personal life outside of her written production. Voros notes that more than a tenth of Caro's poetic description of the festivities involves her struggle as a woman writer and her personal circumstances of arriving in Madrid in winter from her native Seville. While not full participants in the public sphere, women nevertheless develop the expertise to describe events, even those that glorify Spanish imperialism and the monarchy. Voros proves that these accounts should not be dismissed as mere propaganda for the patriarchy since they give testimony to Caro's historical situation as a woman writer, to the system of patronage, and to her feminine identity and authority as a woman writer.

The essays in the third section of this volume explore the feminine body, mind, and desires in relation to the cultural constructs of Early Modern Spain. In a highly misogynistic age, writers warn of women's intellectual and moral weaknesses. By emphasizing the sexually provocative, inconstant, and fragile nature of women, women are viewed as unstable creatures moved by willfulness and emotion and in need of protection. The legal rights of women are undercut by formal and informal laws that relegate their bodies to male domination to the extent that early charter laws authorize husbands to kill adulterous wives. This right is reinscribed into Spanish law when the charter laws are largely superseded by the centralized national law of 1567, the Nueva Recopilación de las Leyes de España [New Recompilation of the Laws of Spain]. Spanish literature and theater, far from ignoring the debate about the role and place of women in society, reflect it, with all the ambiguity and complexity of a codified message. Females are represented as artifice, cosmetic, and adornment and are caught between scorn and misogyny, shame and guilt. The spheres in which women can act are socially limited and the accesses for manipulating their environment are circumscribed. Spanish women have to define their own space of liberty against the diminishing vision of themselves that social and literary discourse projects. In a patriarchal society, all eyes are focused on women's talk, body, image, sexuality, faith, and even their dreams and visions.

It is a commonplace that costume designates social class, time frame, and physical condition. In Spanish theater, costume creates gender in instances of the *mujer vestida de hombre* [woman in male dress]. The veil or shawl, an ancient device used for disguise or protection, is the costume of choice of the *tapadas* [veiled women] in seventeenth-century Spain. Anita Stoll, in her essay "Masquerade and the *Comedia*," illustrates how the figure of the female *tapada* is at the root of the visual deception, although this theme of deception is played out in several ways in its recreation in Early Modern drama. She examines how Tirso de Molina's play, *El amor médico* [*Love the Doctor*], serves to underscore the role of male imagination in the figure of the seductive, veiled woman who only reveals her left eye and hand. Stoll traces how these multiple-identity characters of visual deception endure in Calderón de la Barca's plays, which are variations on the *tapada* theme. In *Mañanas de abril y mayo* [*Mornings of April and May*] (1634), Calderón includes the *tapada* in a case of misidentification by a married man who falls in love with a stranger later revealed to be his own wife. An inquiry into an explanation for the prominence of the veiled figure in seventeenth-century society leads Stoll to investigate the psychological grounds for its popularity in the theories of

Freud and Lacan. The baroque emphasis on the problematic relationship of reality and fantasy corresponds well with the psychoanalytic concept of subjective reality. Stoll concludes that through the placing of an adornment, the female identity in masquerade, the veiled woman represents for the male what he desires, thereby also reinforcing his sexual identity. The *tapada*'s masquerade fits well into this system since the adornment denotes the woman. Stoll confirms that it is the insights of Early Modern dramatists into feminine behavior and the feminine psyche that explain today's re-emerging interest in these plays.

Frederick de Armas, in his study "Dreams, Voices, Signatures: Deciphering Woman's Desires in Angela de Azevedo's *Dicha y desdicha del juego* [*Good and Ill Fortune in Gaming*]," addresses how women playwrights in Early Modern Spain modify female characters to challenge the misogyny of accepted social practices. Azevedo's *comedia* critiques the dowry system, arranged marriages, the economic excesses of patriarchy, the "objectification" of the female body, and the overall inhumanity of male power. Azevedo's play challenges the theatrical practices that seek to contain theater space and, by extension, the patriarchy's efforts to limit and contain women. In this essay de Armas illustrates how men contain women through theories of passion and demonic dreams, while women display their desires through the theory of signatures and the phenomenon of kledonomancy, casual utterances that have dramatic significance. In his examination of these four elements, de Armas discloses how male containment can be amended through the secret writings of female desire.

Addressing the consequences of desire and temptation, Joseph Ricapito's essay, "Galatea's Fall and the Inner Dynamics of Góngora's *Fábula de Polifemo y Galatea* [*Polyphemus and Galatea*]," analyzes a series of poetic elements that deal with images of movement that serve a baroque function: metaphors, allusiveness, hyperbaton, auditory references, and opposite bipolarity. Ricapito traces Góngora's principal techniques as a prelude to the representation of the female protagonist Galatea. Although there are numerous views on the fall of Galatea, Ricapito observes that the liaison between Acis and Galatea is a register of the morality and theology of Góngora's age. Góngora recalls the tragedy of the Garden of Eden, as he equates the cult of beauty with temptation and the fall. Góngora uses the contemporary view of woman as fragile as Galatea succumbs to the persistence of Acis and physical love. Typically baroque, Góngora's eloquent poetry serves to censure the defiant sexuality as a model not to be emulated. He acknowledges his century's moral view of feminine identity and human sexuality.

The fourth grouping of essays addresses the power stratagems of feminine discourse that establish authority and overcome the constraints of silence. These essays are fundamental for this volume inasmuch as they make explicit the ways in which social constructs determine female authorial voice in history and in literature. Silent and silenced by their exclusion from the patriarchal institution of literacy, women speak from a marginal status. The lack of culturally accorded space for feminine expression leads literary critics to continue to explore the significance of the silences historically surrounding feminine sexuality.

In her essay, "*De voz extremada* [Of consummate voice]: Cervantes's Women Characters Speak for Themselves," Sara Taddeo examines the feminine domain in Cervantes's early drama, *El laberinto del amor* [*The Labyrinth of Love*], and in the exemplary novel, *La española inglesa* [*The English Spanish Girl*]. Cervantes explores the nature of language and feminine identity by having women navigate a metaphorical labyrinth. Representing neither Eve, who lost paradise, nor sinless Mary who reopens it, the woman who errs must find her self and her voice. The women of *El laberinto del amor* surmount difficulties through their power of articulation. Similarly, in *La española inglesa* Isabela's *voz extremada* is heard in her domain of requisite silence. Isabela's bilingualism, her power to translate, gives her the power to shape her own story, despite the many setbacks she faces while trapped in a labyrinth of deceit, envy, and desire. Taddeo illustrates that Cervantes's female characters have in common the skillful command of the spoken language in their refusal to be silenced. Their journey of self-discovery in the labyrinth of language leads to a discernible control over their own destinies.

The study of feminine authorship illuminates the cultural images of gender politics, as well as the social and intellectual obstacles to women's writing. In her essay "Silence Is/As Golden . . . Age Device: Ana Caro's Eloquent Reticence in *Valor, agravio y mujer* [*Valor, Offense, Woman*]," Monica Leoni uses Ana Caro's play as a critical base to focus on the communicative and expository power of the silences found on the stage. Leoni argues that Caro skillfully uses a "rhetoric of reticence" to comment on the constraints surrounding women in an honor play whose female protagonist sets out to avenge her own honor, typically lost through seduction. Her analysis of the character Flora shows how this maid's silence, which is not absolute but selective, is meant to be heard by the audience. With this character, Caro subverts the misogynistic tradition of the silent female by saturating her silence with meaning. Leoni portrays Caro as a female writer cognizant of masculine dominance of the written word, which has silenced women. This understanding requires a com-

plex approach to the challenge Caro faced in giving absence and silence a feminine identity.

The act of writing for women differs from the canonical or conventional
manner. Gender difference in writing finds its expression in "writing the
body" or "writing the self." Through self-referentiality, women authors establish their own authority and reject the literary and social conventions that
exclude them. By writing their own lives and citing themselves as authorities,
women create their own subjects and inaugurate their own traditions. They
also subvert the genres they appropriate by writing about themselves. Mariana
de Caravajal appropriates a literary power that allows her to forge an intellectual place for herself through a literary structure of self-examination. In his
essay, "Woman of the World and World of the Woman in the Narrative of
Mariana de Caravajal," Louis Imperiale analyzes the world of fiction in which
Mariana de Caravajal y Saavedra presents her *Navidades de Madrid y noches
entretenidas* [*Christmas in Madrid and Enjoyable Nights*] (1663). While the
female narrative voice does not manifest verbal aggression against the opposite
sex, the act of literary production is rebellion against the authority of the official patriarchal voice. In a calm and serene narrative voice, Caravajal presents
a woman as the uncontested protagonist in a silent revolution against the mental biases of the time, while subscribing to male communicative stratagems.

Imperiale shows how Caravajal systematically eliminates useless husbands
capable of causing displeasure. It is clear that several husbands die early leaving
their widows to venture into areas they never would have transgressed as "perfect wives" protected by phallogocentric power. The husband's death is the
splendid occasion that causes the new widow to arrange for parties and entertainments. Caravajal's self-referential characters make the reader aware of
their life of enclosure. Although relegated to the home, strategies and schemes
to circumvent limitations are put into place by the author. Imperiale also
evaluates the narrative options of the Other sex that contrast with the intolerant attacks of a misogynist writer such as Quevedo. Caravajal observes and
portrays Madrid's society in the process of changing as the traditional family
has been substituted in a cultural initiative that permits women to mediate
their marriages more for their own personal affinities than for collective obligations. Throughout Caravajal's narration, Imperiale notes the presence of the
bourgeois class through the emphasis on dance, fashion, music, cuisine, and
etiquette. In a society in which rites that were reserved for nobility are extended to the middle class, the status of women gathers more and more relevance although not more significance nor autonomy.

In the last section of this volume, the authors contemplate the textual relations between male and female while exploring the misogyny and power of the
traditionally male-centered structures of perception. Inscribing their texts
with their own authority and writing from their own experience, women writers contradict the misogynistic tradition, modify it, dismiss it in defiance, or
engender new forms. Writing out of gender difference, women conform to,
but reverse, accepted models and values to subvert the dominant tradition. In
stories that follow the novella model used by Cervantes, María de Zayas addresses herself to both men and women in her admonitions that men ought to
improve their treatment of women and women ought to avoid the perils of
love. As a writer who laments the lack of women's education, she criticizes
men for denying their daughters a classical education and women themselves
for rejecting their humanist legacy.

The popularity of María de Zayas's books endures through the seventeenth
century, with translations into English and French, and well beyond her death
though her critics branded her writing as pornographic. In two complex and
intriguing collections of short stories, *Novelas amorosas y ejemplares* [*The
Enchantments of Love*] (1637) and *Desengaños amorosos* [*The Disenchantments of Love*] (1647), María de Zayas weaves a female perspective as she
works within traditional literary genres expanding their focus and recreating
the conventions to which they respond. While very few of Zayas's works deal
directly with the pastoral tradition, Deborah Compte in her essay, "A Cry in
the Wilderness: Pastoral Female Discourse in María de Zayas," shows how
"Aventurarse perdiendo" ["Everything Ventured"], the opening tale of Zayas's
first collection, very clearly experiments with the conventions of the genre and
articulates a definitive female voice within a pastoral setting. Venturing into
the traditionally "male" domain of pastoral narrative, Zayas offers the reader
a pointed examination of the genre through a woman's eyes as she inverts and
alters conventional poetic devices.

Compte compares male and female patterns of heroic development in the
pastoral and reveals that in Zayas's tale the traditional male model is inverted
in creating female pastoral protagonists. Standard bucolic themes such as the
shepherd-poet's humility and its application to the female narrator and to the
author herself, as well as the inconstancy of love, point to the clear articulation
of a female voice within the pastoral. Moreover, Zayas's inversion of the bucolic topos of the "retreat" is striking, particularly in relation to the male and
female patterns of development. While the male heroes retreat temporarily to
an idyllic pastoral oasis, they eventually return fully integrated to an urban

society restored and renewed. Compte observes that the female characters, in contrast, eventually abandon society and withdraw to a welcoming female refuge, the convent. Curiously, the retreat to a "woman's space" anticipates the closing of the frame narrative of Zayas's *Desengaños amorosos,* in which the female narrators find sanctuary in the convent. Compte establishes that Zayas is very clearly responding to particular literary traditions and reveals the author's remarkable inventiveness in transforming literary conventions to give voice to a female perspective.

Continuing the discussion on culturally determined identity, Susan Paun de García investigates how María de Zayas expresses a feminine viewpoint on the nation and national identity in her essay, "Zayas's Ideal of the Masculine: Clothes Make the Man." Zayas equates changes in men's fashion with the decline of the nation and a society in peril of extinction. After a very brief historical overview of the national/warrior identity, García turns to changes in men's fashion from the end of the sixteenth century to the first half of the seventeenth century as an explanation of the selected invectives found in the novellas of María de Zayas. García highlights Zayas's chastisement of her male contemporaries who are far from the novelist's ideals in comportment or fashion. For Zayas, the adoption by Spanish noblemen of French-inspired "feminine" costume suggests the deterioration of heroism, power, and virility. García discloses how Zayas condemns the nobility of her day, asserting that they are not worthy of the military insignias they wear, which are now solely a fashion statement. With no warriors to defend damsels, the changes of fashion insinuate a devaluation of women. García establishes that, as always, Zayas's writings are ultimately about issues concerning feminine identity.

In the concluding essay, "Desire Unbound: Women's Theater of Spain's Golden Age," Lisa Vollendorf reminds us that Spain remains on the margins of Early Modern women's studies. She urges that we seek out the huge body of Spanish women's texts still so neglected by scholars and teachers. Vollendorf chooses three women dramatists who supersede patriarchal restrictions through female protagonists who subordinate male desire to female desire. Angela de Azevedo's *El muerto disimulado* [*The Feigned Death*] depicts the patriarchal boundaries that repress female sexuality. Both María de Zayas in her *La traición en la amistad* [*Friendship Betrayed*] and Ana Caro in her play *Valor, agravio y mujer* present the potentialities of women's relationships. Through intrepid women characters these three female dramatists accentuate the vulnerability of female sexuality in the dominant culture.

Vollendorf reveals that women's friendship and desire enable a female homoerotic code that challenges cultural intolerance. She suggests that we look to women dramatists as a source of a larger feminine aesthetic in which a feminized view of the world is articulated where validation of friendship, cooperation, women's freedom of choice, and nonviolence prevails. On a broader scale, her discussion formulates the argument that, to better understand women's writing in the period and to enrich our current perceptions of gender, sexuality, and creative production in Early Modern Europe, we need to acknowledge that these texts not only delineate women's role in literature but also in history.

We have much to learn from one another's questions and the scholarship of many voices. The intellectual diversity and range of experience and knowledge of these essays illuminate important methodological and conceptual issues in feminine discourse and identity. Their analyses show how Early Modern Spanish literature reaffirms the existent ideology about women in texts that align with a symbolic system that contributes directly to the repression of real women. The profound transformations in understanding and interpretation advance the achievements of the last two decades of feminist scholarship. The reconstruction of the lives, works, and representations of women in the Early Modern period offers a framework for moving the discussion forward to decode the voices, texts, and images of women in the past. The innovative analyses of this collection have ramifications beyond the theme of women and literature in Early Modern Spain, urging us to reassess the economic, legal, political, and religious systems that articulate the parameters of women's access to power and self-determination in the past, as well as in the present.

Works Cited

Castiglione, Baldassare. *The Book of the Courtier.* Trans. Charles S. Singleton. Garden City, N.Y.: Doubleday, 1959.

Derrida, Jacques. *Writing and Difference.* Trans. Alan Bass. Chicago: University of Chicago Press, 1970.

Formica de Careaga, Mercedes. "Spain." *Women in the Modern World.* Ed. Rafael Patai. New York: Free Press, 1967.

Maclean, Ian. *The Renaissance Notion of Woman.* Cambridge: Cambridge University Press, 1980.

Vives, Juan Luis. *Obras completas.* Ed. Lorenzo Riber. Madrid: Aguilar, 1947.

Part I

❦

A Woman's Self-fashioning

The Private Gendered Spaces of Feminine Authority

1

Authorizing the Wife/Mother
in Sixteenth-Century Advice Manuals

Carolyn Nadeau

In Early Modern Spain manuals abound that offer guidelines for women's morals, behavior, and sense of identity. In these "how to be a good woman" treatises we find in great detail the qualities toward which a woman should strive and how she should act as a wife. Yet in relatively few works authors discuss how she takes on her authoritative role as mother. Rather the father appears as a persuasive force in determining the child's best interests. But how is he able to govern the family politic even at the stage when the child is nursing and his or her needs can only be fulfilled by the mother, either blood mother or milk mother (a term used to designate the relationship between wet nurse and child)? Is it possible that breast-feeding forced men to concede at least some of the child-rearing authority to women and extend to them an independence that in other developmental stages was not granted? In the sixteenth century, three Spanish writers address this issue: Antonio de Guevara in the *Relox de príncipes* [*Dial of Princes*] (1529), Pedro de Luján in *Coloquios matrimoniales* [*Marriage Colloquia*] (1550), and Fray Luis de León in *La perfecta casada* [*The Perfect Wife*] (1583).

The first and most substantive work of the three is Antonio de Guevara's *Relox de príncipes* in which he lays down rules for marriage, pregnancy, the child's education, and how the wife/mother figures into these stages. Some twenty years later in *Coloquios matrimoniales,* Luján draws extensively from Guevara's writing as he presents his own version of the woman's role in the domestic space. Finally, nearing the close of the century, Fray Luis includes a chapter on the mother's role in caring for children in his essay, *La perfecta casada.* My purpose here is to explore how these writers treat the mother as authority figure during the early stage of a child's development, that is, while a child is nursing. Although all writers clearly designate the male as the authority figure whose decisions are incontestable at most stages of the family's development, the three writers differ in structure, audience, and agenda.

Bishop of Guadix in Granada and later of Mondoñedo in Galicia, commissioner for the Inquisitor General, official chronicler and traveling companion of Charles I (Charles V of the Holy Roman Empire), Antonio de Guevara (1481–1545) formed part of the main political circles of the day.[1] Guevara was also a prolific writer whose writing played an important role in the development of Castilian literature in the sixteenth and seventeenth centuries and was admired and translated all over Europe in his lifetime. In 1529 *Relox de príncipes,* which is an expanded version of his already famous *Libro áureo de Marco Aurelio* [*Golden Book of Marcus Aurelius*], is published and immediately becomes the favorite book of Charles I and later of his son, Philip II. The *Relox* is divided into three books. The first explains how to be a successful Christian prince; the second illustrates how the male reader should interact with his wife and raise his children; and the third describes the virtues of a prince. Located between two books dealing with the prince's role in governing the state, book 2's position within the text points to Guevara's attempt to link the needs of the state with the needs of the family. Of the fourteen chapters (chaps. 18–31) that are dedicated to the influence of the wet nurse in the child's life, seven of these directly deal with breast-feeding either from the blood mother or the milk mother. Guevara divides his discussion into four parts: why mothers should breast-feed their children, what characteristics a wet nurse should have, how long one should nurse the child, and the detrimental effects that witchcraft and superstition have on nursing. The latter seven chapters deal with issues of language learning and women's intellectual capacity.

Generally book 2 of *Relox* follows the Renaissance tradition of manuals for constructing the perfect family. Guevara, like other humanists such as Erasmus (*De pueris*) [*The Education of Children*], Antonio de Nebrija (*De liberis educandis*) [*The Education of Children*], Juan Luis Vives (*Institutio feminae christianae*) [*The Education of a Christian Woman*], Francesco Patrizi (*De institutione reipublicae*) [*The Establishment of the State*], supported the idea that the wife should be subject to her husband in every way. Guevara's passage on the relationship between man and woman captures the tone of these treatises: "En nuestra sagrada religión christiana no ay ley divina ni ay ley humana que en todas las cosas el varón a la muger no se prefiera" (434) [In our holy Christian religion there is no divine nor human law that does not give preference to man over woman in all matters].[2] This attitude makes the breast-feed-ing stage of a child's development all the more intriguing because here Guevara creates an authoritative space for the mother. Like other humanists and priests and physicians, Guevara advised mothers to nurse their own children yet, unlike others, he also recommends that the mother take charge of certain de-cisions that need to be made on behalf of the child.

Pedro de Luján and Fray Luis also signal the mother as authoritative figure during a child's early years. For Luján these issues are handled in only a slightly different way.[3] For most of the fourth colloquium of his *Coloquios matrimoniales,* Luján liberally borrows from Guevara's chapters on preg-nancy and child development and generally reaches the same conclusions re-garding the mother-child relationship. This portion of his dialogues can be divided into four sections: roles of both husband and wife during the preg-nancy (175–90), nursing and choosing a wet nurse (191–200), raising children (201–9), and a conclusion (210–14). Like *Relox, Coloquios* enjoyed enormous popularity in its day and beyond. Bataillon records that Luján's work had no less than eleven editions in forty years (650 n. 17). A generation later Fray Luis also takes a stand on the mother's authoritative role in the household. *La perfecta casada,* which saw four editions in the four years following its initial release (Etreros 34–35), differs from the previous works in that he allows no space for a wet nurse. Rather he insists that only the blood mother care for the child at least for the first two years. In fact for Fray Luis the mother's role in keeping the house in order—both in terms of the physical structure and in terms of its inhabitants—was vital to its success: "en las casadas hay otras que, como si sus casas fuesen de sus vecinas, así se descuidan dellas. . . . y piérdese entre tanto la moza, y cobra malos siniestros la hija, y la hacienda se hunde, vuélvese demonio el marido" (80) [among married women there are those who act as if their homes belonged to others, so grievously do they neglect them. . . . The serving maid goes to the bad, the daughter is up to all sorts of naughti-ness, finances go on the rocks, and the husband turns into a veritable demon] (Hubbard 6–7).

In terms of audience and agenda, the three authors also differ. The rubric for Guevara's book 2 of *Relox* states his goals: "Y tracta el auctor en el presente libro de la manera que los príncipes y grandes señores se han de aver con sus mujeres y de cómo han de criar a sus hijos" (401) [In this present book the author deals with the manner in which princes and noblemen should treat their wives and raise their children]. Guevara focuses on internal family behavior and, although he directs his manual to "príncipes y grandes señores" [princes and noblemen], virtually the whole book is dedicated to the duties of the wife and child-care supporter who at times is the wife, and at other times is the wet nurse or the tutor. Apart from this rubric Guevara does not distinguish between different social classes when referring to the family or the wife, yet his text is specifically directed to aristocrats and his notions of the family are defined by certain sixteenth-century class assumptions that must be taken into account when discussing his text.

Luján in *Coloquios* chooses a very different structure from Guevara's *Relox.* First, his treatment of this theme is framed within a dialogue between a married couple and another woman. In this fourth colloquium Doroctea advises Eulalia and her husband Marcelo on issues concerning matrimony. Unlike Guevara's text, which offers advice for nobility and royalty, Luján directs his work toward a wider audience of upper-class and well-to-do families. The friendly dialogue also creates a more personable atmosphere in which women share personal stories and express fears associated with nursing and in which the husband expresses interest in sharing responsibility for caring for the infant both during the pregnancy and as a newborn.

Fray Luis's *La perfecta casada* is epistolary, a wedding gift for María Varela Osorio in which he glosses verses 10–31 of *Proverbs 31* and advises her in her new role as wife. Like Guevara and in turn Luján, Fray Luis acknowledges sources that range from sacred and secular texts to his own observations in contemporary society. Different from Guevara's structure that reveals a political agenda to join the needs of the family with the needs of the state and from Luján's "friendly dialogue" that pushes a more social agenda of maintaining strong family bonds, Fray Luis's underlying theme as seen in virtually all of his writing is the search for Christian harmony. In *La perfecta casada* this harmony is sought in the domestic space between man and wife. Surprisingly, only one chapter, seventeen, focuses on the wife as mother. But here, as seen in the previous advice manuals of the sixteenth century, very concrete guidelines are laid out.

Returning to *Relox de príncipes,* in the beginning of book 2 Guevara explains that women have a natural instinct to want things, "Infinitas son las cosas que naturalmente dessean las mugeres, y entre las otras son muy essenciales quatro o cinco dellas" (505) [Infinite are the things that women naturally desire, and among them four or five are essential]. He then turns to the first responsibility a woman has after giving birth, breast-feeding her child, and extensively defends why women should choose this source of nourishment for their children.[4]

[Y]a que Dios permitió se hiziessen preñadas, ya que Dios permitió se viessen alumbradas; ¿por qué las mugeres son tan ingratas que, en pariendo los hijos, los echan de sus casas y los embían a criar por las tristes aldeas? . . . Deve assimismo la muger, en acabando de parir a la criatura, darle a mamar de su leche propria; porque parece cosa muy monstruosa aver parido ella el niño de sus entrañas y que le críen y den a mamar mugeres estrangeras. (506)

[As God has allowed them to become pregnant, as God has allowed them to give birth, how can women be so ungrateful that, after giving birth to their children, they throw them out of their house and send them off to the poor villages to be raised? The woman herself, after giving birth to the child, should nurse him with her own milk, because it seems to be a very monstrous thing for a woman to give birth to her child from her own womb and let strange women raise and nurse him.][5]

Guevara immediately turns to the animal kingdom, using wolves and pigs who can feed up to ten offspring at once, monkeys who never let leave of their babes until they have fully weaned, and birds who, in their own nests and without milk to feed their offspring, take care of them themselves. Guevara's use of animal imagery to explore women's natural behavior is not uncommon among Renaissance writers and artists.[6] In fact, both Luján and Fray Luis also draw on the animal kingdom to argue in favor of the natural instinct the female species has for caring for and nursing her offspring.

There are many reasons a woman should want to nurse. First, Guevara explains in *Relox* that the child has great need after being born: "pues al madre le parió con tan malas condiciones de sus entrañas, no es justo en tiempo de tan gran necessidad le fíen de otras personas" (509) [since the mother gave birth from her womb, under such difficult conditions, it is not fair that in time of such dire need she entrust him to others]. Second, Guevara argues that through nursing, not birth, the child will take on the mother's qualities: "porque mamando el niño leche de mujer agena, impossible es que tome la condición de madre" (510) [by nursing from a strange woman, it is impossible for the child to take on the mother's disposition]. In his third point, he explains that to be a complete mother one must fulfill two halves of the whole task: "ca la muger es media madre por el parir y es media madre por el criar" (511) [a woman is half a mother when she gives birth and half when she nurses/raises the child]. Here, Guevara's use of the word *criar* is ambiguous and takes on a meaning that implies both nursing and general care of the infant. Because a wet nurse was often a woman who lived out of the home and in many cases out of town, the wet nurse often raised the child for the first two or three years.

Guevara's intercalated tale of a milk sister who convinced her milk brother to pardon soldiers condemned to death, after he had denied the same requests made by his blood brother, exemplifies the overlapping of breast-feeding and raising the child. As he explains to his blood brother: "Hágote saber, hermano, que yo tengo por más madre a la que me crió y no me parió, que a la que me parió y, en pariendo, me dexó; y, pues aquélla tuve por madre verdadera, justo es tenga a ésta por hermana muy cara" (513) [Let it be known, brother, that the one who nursed/raised me is more a mother to me than the one who gave birth to me and left me, and since the former is my real mother, it is only fair that I appreciate this woman as my dear sister]. In this tale, *criar* like the English verb *to nurse* refers both to breast-feeding and to caring for the child. Guevara's use of a political military account to illustrate family bonds is not a singular case. His text is filled with many such examples; thus, in this descriptive way, he again joins the needs of the family with the needs of the state.

While Luján's six reasons why a mother should nurse her own child are taken directly from Guevara's text, anecdotes and all, the way Luján frames the discussion between the two friends sets up a different tone. Chapter four of *Coloquios* begins with a discussion of Eulalia's reformed husband, Marcelo. Eulalia confides in Doroctea his changed behavior: "El, que antes era jugador, ya es tornado enemigo de jugadores. . . . él, que antes era amigo de alcahuetas, agora es enemigo de ellas" (176) [He, who previously was a gambler, has now become the gambler's enemy. . . . he, who previously visited procuresses, is now their enemy]. After Doroctea and Eulalia consider ways to avoid a miscarriage, Marcelo returns home and enters into the discussion, asking Doroctea what both of them can do in order to have a successful pregnancy. Because Luján sets up this type of dialogue and because the husband directly enters the conversation, the advice that Doroctea gives, while drawn directly from Guevara's book 2, takes on a more personal tone. In addition, no character in Luján's text discusses women's "natural instinct" to want things as Guevara so emphatically states in his advice manual, but rather they directly discuss the roles of both husband and wife while the baby is in the womb.

Of the three texts, *La perfecta casada* takes the strongest stand on the importance of the mother's two roles of giving birth and nursing. While Guevara and Luján discourage procuring a wet nurse, they allow for exceptions, for example, if the mother is physically unable to nurse a child herself. In contrast, under no circumstances does Fray Luis allow for a wet nurse. Instead he offers a series of passionate arguments against hiring a wet nurse. He begins by stating that "lo que se sigue después del parto es el puro oficio de la madre. . . . Por lo cual, téngase por dicho esta perfecta casada que no lo será si no cría a sus hijos" (162) [(a)ll the care which comes after birth is the true function of the mother and of no one else. . . . Therefore, it goes without saying that the perfect wife cannot, indeed, be perfect unless she herself suckles her children] (Hubbard 77). He continues by calling the children sent to wet nurses "bastardos" [bastards] and accuses the mothers who choose to hire a wet nurse of "un género de adulterio poco menos feo y no menos dañoso que el ordinario" (163) [a species of adultery little less odious, and no less harmful than the real one] (Hubbard 79).

Obviously, then, Fray Luis feels strongly about this issue. One cannot separate birthing from nursing; together they form a whole: "Es trabajo parir y criar; pero entiendan que es un trabajo hermanado, y que no tienen licencia para dividirlo. Si les duele criar, no paran, y si les agrada el parir, críen también" (165) [(I)t is work to bring forth children, and work to nurse them, but let a woman understand that the two are bound up together, and that she has no permission to divide them. If it is too irksome to nurse them, then let her not have children. If she longs for children, then let her suckle them] (80). He goes so far as to say that only a coward, afraid of pain, chooses not to nurse her children. He emphasizes that while the child's body is nurtured in the womb, his spirit is nurtured while nursing: "la madre, cuando el parto, era un tronco sin sentido ninguno, y el ama, cuando comienza ya a sentir y reconocer el bien que recibe; la madre influye en el cuerpo, el ama en el cuerpo y en el alma" (163) [the mother gave while her offspring was a form without consciousness, the foster mother gives when the baby begins to feel and to respond to the benefits received; the mother's influence has shaped the body, the nurse's influence has fashioned both the body and the soul] (Hubbard 79).

Despite the different stance Fray Luis presents from Guevara and Luján, in all three texts these ideas on the prenatal and neonatal stages of life raise questions about the child's relation with the father. If the womb stage becomes second to nursing and if the mother jeopardizes passing on her qualities to her child by giving that child to a wet nurse, then how does the child receive the father's characteristics, wet nurse or not?

In his section in *Relox* on how to choose a wet nurse, Guevara laments grown children who do not love their parents and gestures to the father as the responsible source: "y esto que haze el hijo con el padre y la madre justo juyzio es de Dios, en que assí como *el padre* no quiso críar a su hijo en casa quando era niño, que el hijo no reciba a su padre en casa quando es ya viejo" (524; my emphasis) [and what the son does to his father and mother is fair judgment from God because the *father* in refusing to raise his child at home when he was a boy, now the son does not receive his father in his home when he is old]. Guevara attempts to write the father into a significant role in the child's early development in spite of possible judgment errors. Keeping the child close to the hearth would allow the father more control in the child's upbringing and greater benefits when he is old.

Luján attempts to write the father as an authoritative figure in the child's early life with the character Marcelo, who listens attentively to Doroctea's advice and asks for ways in which he can participate in caring for the child. Fray Luis has a much more direct response to the question of the father's influence on the child:

> [L]a madre en el hijo que engendra no pone sino una parte de su sangre, de la cual la virtud del varón, figurándola, hace carne y huesos. Pues el ama que cría pone lo mismo, porque la leche es sangre, y en aquella sangre la misma virtud del padre que vive en el hijo hace la misma obra. (163)

> [(T)he mother who begets a child gives him only a portion of her blood, out of which the vital force of the father forms flesh and bone. In the same way, the foster mother who nurses the child gives him her blood, for her milk is the same as blood, and out of this blood the living force of the father performs the same work, since the father lives again in the child.] (Hubbard 78)

In demonstrating the father's biological influence on the baby's formation, it is the only moment in the text that Fray Luis concedes the use of a wet nurse, or "foster mother."

For hiring a wet nurse, Guevara gives seven conditions in *Relox* that a *mother* must review.[7] He first takes the opportunity to scold the mother on her decision not to breast-feed: "ya que se determina la muger de cerrar y secar las fuentes de la leche que le dio naturaleza, deve poner muy gran diligencia en buscar una muger para ama" (524) [since the woman is determined to close and dry up the fountains of milk that nature gave her, she should take careful measures in looking for a wet nurse]. Implicit in these instructions on how a blood mother should choose a milk mother is Guevara's concession, or perhaps recognition, that women do enjoy some independence in making child-care decisions.

In order to hire the right wet nurse, mothers should know their child's constitution, whether choleric, phlegmatic, sanguine, or melancholic. They should also look for a wet nurse who is healthy—physically, mentally, and spiritually—has a sound disposition, eats moderately, and does not drink. Overconsumption of food leads to poor quality of blood, and as white milk, Guevara explains, is nothing more than cooked blood, it will affect the baby (531). Wine works in the same way. Because of its warm characteristic, wine mixed with the cooked blood will produce bad milk: "no es otra cosa bever vino la muger que cría sino para cozer poca leche poner mucho fuego a la caldera, do la caldera se quema y la leche se assura" (534) [a nursing woman drinking wine is nothing more than putting a high flame under a shallow pot of milk, where the pot will burn and the milk will spoil]. Although he does not raise the issue of religious-ethnic status, Guevara writes that the skin color of the wet nurse is not an issue "porque si la leche que tienen es dulce y blanca, poco haze al caso que el ama tenga la cara negra o hermosa" (525) [because if their milk is sweet and white, little difference it makes if the face is black or beautiful]. He continues by citing an authoritative source: "Dize Sexto Cheronense en el libro *De criar niños* que assí como la tierra negra es más fertil que no la blanca, por semejante la muger que tiene la cara baça siempre tiene la leche más sustanciosa" (525) [Sextus Cheronense states in his book *On Raising Children* that as dark soil is more fertile than light soil, by extension, the woman whose face is dark always has more substantial milk]. Finally, the wet nurse should not conceive while breast-feeding, and she should be well-mannered, that is, not envious, proud, evil, et cetera.

In *Coloquios matrimoniales* Luján borrows from Guevara the qualities a mother must look for in a wet nurse. One of the few differences in content between Guevara's text and Luján's is the latter's insistence that the mother continue to nurse the child even if the quantity of milk is small. When Eulalia worries about not having enough milk to nurture properly her child, Doroctea responds, "[N]o dejes de darle tú alguna leche, que más le aprovecha una gota de la madre que ciento del ama" (195) [Don't stop giving (the child) your own milk, for (the baby) will receive more benefits from one drop of mother's milk than from 100 of the wet nurse's]. Another difference between the two texts is that Luján includes a section on the quality of breast milk, something that Guevara does not. First, he proposes a detailed description of what nursing women should and should not eat in order to produce excellent milk for their offspring:

Cosas hay que hacen buena leche y la multiplican . . . caldos de buenas carnes, polvos de cristal, vino muy mucho aguado, carnes frescas y buenas, anís, mucho dormir, pan no muy blanco, y pocos enojos; las cosas que dañan la leche son éstas: vino puro, comer o beber con otra mujer que críe quita la leche, mucha pimienta, simiente de romero, comer mucha sal o cosas saladas, comer pan seco, o comer mucho queso, vinagre. (199)

[There are things that make good milk and increase its quantity: broth made from good meat; powdered crystal; watered-down wine; good, fresh meat; anise; a lot of rest; bread that is not too white; and infrequent annoyances. Things that harm the milk are: pure wine, eating or drinking with another woman who is nursing lessens milk, a lot of pepper, rosemary seed, a lot of salt or salty food, eating dry bread, or eating a lot of cheese, vinegar.]

Luján also writes on how to recognize good milk: that it look like a pearl when a drop is placed on a mirror, that it taste sweet and not salty, and that it be white with a bluish contour and not yellow (199). These details as well as the omission of Guevara's many examples from erudite sources contribute to the different tone that Luján achieves in approaching this material. Not only the structure of the text, but also his selection of content from Guevara's *Relox* makes the *Coloquios* a more intimate text.

Both Guevara and Luján insist that a wet nurse not become pregnant while she is breast-feeding. Luján writes: "[C]omo la leche se haga de la sangre y el men[i]struo se detenga en la mujer preñada para alimento de lo que está en el vientre, pensando criar al niño con leche mátanlo con la ponzoña que a las tetas viene" (197) [As milk is made from blood and menstrual blood stays in the pregnant woman to nurture what is in the womb, thinking she is nursing the child with milk, she is killing him with poison that goes to her breasts].[8] The separation of nursing and pregnancy leads to the discussion of how long a woman should breast-feed and when she should begin to wean the baby. In her investigation of nursing in Castile during the Middle Ages, Heath Dillard found that most wet nurses were hired for a period of three years by which time the child would be fully weaned (156–57). Throughout book 2, Guevara alludes to a time period of two to three years (515, 527, 529). However, after citing a variety of cultures and classical texts, he concludes that although methods of nursing and weaning vary depending on time, place and culture, he agrees with Aristotle that "el niño deve mamar a lo más dos años, y a lo menos año y medio" (548) [a child should nurse at most two years and at least a year and a half].

In *Coloquios matrimoniales* Luján is more relaxed about how long a child should breast-feed. Doroctea suggests that there should be no firm rules regarding length of time: "[E]n eso no se puede dar regla cierta, porque según la calidad o fortaleza, o debilitamiento de la criatura ha de mamar o no mamar; niño hay que un año le sobra y otro que en dos no tiene harto" (199) [On this matter there cannot be fixed rules, nursing or not nursing depends on the quality and strength or weakness of the child. For some a year is more than enough, for others two years is not enough]. In *La perfecta casada* Fray Luis only indirectly addresses the issue when he weighs the nine months of prenatal care with the twenty-four months of neonatal care. In this discussion he implies that two years is sufficient for a child to breast-feed.

Although Fray Luis does not discuss how long a woman should nurse her child, one of the most interesting points of contrast among the advice manuals of Guevara, Luján, and Fray Luis is the latter's radical stance on family planning. He closes his chapter on the woman's role as primary caregiver to her children by stating that it is better to have few children and raise them well than to have many: "y no ponga su hecho en parir muchos hijos, sino en criar pocos buenos" (166) [not spending herself in bearing many children, but in rearing a few to be truly good] (81). Neither Guevara nor Luján broach this subject apart from stating that a woman should not conceive while she is nursing.

In his last section of *Relox* on nursing the child Guevara warns against the bad effects of witchcraft. Drawing from histories of Egyptians, Peloponnesians, and other cultures, he describes how women channeled the influences of planets, elements, and idols to improve their milk. Guevara explicitly warns against these practices because they are offensive to God and the Christian religion:

> Todas estas antigüedades de la gentilidad he querido contar para que las princesas y grandes señoras huelguen de las leer y saber, pero no para que por ninguna manera las ayan de imitar; porque según la fe de nuestra religión christiana, quan ciertos somos de la ofensa que hazían a Dios en hazer tales supersticiones, tan ciertos somos del servicio que hazemos nosotros en dexarlas. (548)

> [I have told all of these gentile stories so that princesses and noblewomen may enjoy themselves reading them and getting to know them but not, under any circumstances, to imitate them because, according to the faith of our Christian religion, we are as certain at how much they offended

God by doing such superstitious acts as we are of the service we do by
not doing them.]

Sorcery and witchcraft were frequently associated with minority women,
both Moors and Jews. For example, in 1258 at the Court of Valladolid, Muslim
and Jewish women were prohibited from wet-nursing Christians and vice
versa (Fildes 39). But later in the century Luján scarcely mentions the issue in
Coloquios, and when he does it is only in reference to weaning the child and
not to the entire project of breast-feeding. Later, in *La perfecta casada* Fray
Luis makes no mention of these kinds of "offensive" acts neither for milk
production nor for weaning.

Of all three authors Antonio de Guevara most makes the family a subject of
public policy as he seeks to offer guidance on the proper roles of mothers and
fathers within an idealized family. However, in his section in *Relox* on the early
childhood and breast-feeding stage, Guevara hesitates to authorize either the
father or the mother as having more responsibility than the other parent for
the child's early stage of development. Book 2 is written for men and deals with
how they should treat their wives and raise their children yet the language
within these chapters is directed to mothers and wet nurses. He argues that
women should make the decision to breast-feed yet distrusts their ability to
make sound decisions. He repeatedly states that women have the responsibility to secure a sound wet nurse yet he fills his prose with examples of political
and military male leaders, with father's misfortunes, and sons' traits inherited
from their wet nurse. He admonishes women's decisions to send their child to
a wet nurse or to practice superstitious home remedies, yet again, suggests that
the mother be responsible for employing a proper wet nurse. Clearly, Guevara
is suspicious of women's capacity to make good decisions. Distrustful of her
body, skeptical of her intentions, he cannot endorse the power and independence that is appropriately hers, yet, neither can he fully yield that control to
the father. While Luján in *Coloquios* extensively draws on Guevara for issues
regarding the mother's role in early childhood, this struggle to authorize is
diminished in his text. Rather naturally he confers upon mothers many of
these crucial decisions without the crossed signals that underlie Guevara's
Relox. He also makes more clear the father's role through the character Marcelo who, with his wife, inquires about parents' roles in caring for the infant.
Finally, in *La perfecta casada* Fray Luis never hesitates on who is responsible
for what. Clearly women must strive for perfection, and in order to attain that
goal they must breast-feed their children. Undoubtedly the father's influence
is guaranteed because his virtue is carried through from conception.

Guevara's uncertainty as to how both father and mother fit into an authoritative role in this decisive developmental stage is echoed by his incertitude when he claims himself as a reliable source. Several times in these seven chapters of *Relox* on breast-feeding Guevara seeks to legitimize his authority on the subject. In discussing how women should act he begins with a disclaimer:

> Escusado me sería hablar en este caso, pues soy religioso y no he sido casado, mas (por lo que he leydo lo uno, y por lo que he oydo lo otro) osaré tomar licencia de dezir una palabra; porque muchas vezes da mejor cuenta un sabio de una cosa que ha leydo que no la da un simple aunque la haya experimentado. (447)

> [I would be excused from such topics as I am a religious man and have never been married; however (based on what I have read on the one hand and what I have heard on the other), I dare to take license and say a word. Often a wise man tells a better story of what he has read than a simpleton who has experienced it.]

Later, when giving examples from the animal kingdom on why women should nurse their own children, he again qualifies his information: "Hallarán por verdad todos los que leyeren esta escritura, y si quisieren lo verán como yo lo vi por experiencia" (507) [All who read this writing will find it to be the truth and, if they want to, can see it as I have seen it with my own eyes]. These mixed signals, validating himself because he is a wise man who reads or validating himself because he experienced firsthand a specific incident, suggest that when he claims to be an authoritative voice, he is reassuring not only the reader, but himself as well.

In Luján's *Coloquios matrimoniales*, Doroctea also validates her authority: "[A]sí yo hablaré en esto según lo que he visto, oído, y aun leído" (178) [So, I will speak on this matter according to what I have seen, heard, and read]. However, as a married woman herself this type of disclaimer is superfluous. As Rallo Gruss has rightly noted, Doroctea's claim as a reliable source reveals both her as a spokesperson for the author and Guevara as Luján's main source (*Coloquios* 215 n. 2). Fray Luis, on the other hand, has no need to assert his authority in *La perfecta casada*. Rather he extends guidance and admonitions without hesitation. Guevara's need to legitimize his authority compared to Luján's less significant claim and Fray Luis's nonexistent assertion, reveals again that Luján and Fray Luis have very different projects. Their focus is not as connected to state authority as Guevara's yet respectively centers on familial and spiritual stability for the mother.

However, as writers, all three do emphasize a need to authorize themselves in the very structure of their manuals. As sixteenth-century Spanish writers following the traditions of imitation theory, they attempt to rewrite texts, both classical and contemporary, by placing them in a new context. Guevara's *Relox* is to a great degree a rewriting of his earlier work *Libro áureo de Marco Aurelio;* Luján's *Coloquios,* a rewriting of Guevara's *Relox;* and Fray Luis's *La perfecta casada,* an exegetical reading of part of *Proverbs 31.*[9] By exposing oneself to the strength of classical texts, each writer finds his own identity among the sources. And regardless of their underlying projects—whether political, social, or spiritual—all three writers signal an authoritative direction for women as they take on their maternal role during the breast-feeding stage of a child's life.

Notes

1. For an extensive and scholarly study on Antonio de Guevara see Redondo, and for more on his influence in both the political and literary spheres see Grey, Jones, and Rallo Gruss (*Antonio*). For a more extensive study on Guevara's advice on breast-feeding, see Nadeau.

2. All translations in this essay are my own unless otherwise noted.

3. For the most exhaustive study of Luján's *Coloquios matrimoniales* see Rallo Gruss's edition. Also see Bataillon.

4. Fildes's study on wet-nursing discusses the influential writings of the Persian physician Avicenna (980–1036), Rhazes (850–932), Haly Abbas (d. 994), and Moses Maimonides (1135–1204), a Spanish Jew and pupil of the Spanish Muslim physician Averroes (29–30). All wrote instructions on health, diet, milk production, weaning, and general concerns for nursing women. Fildes also describes the restrictions put on wet nurses that aimed to segregate minority women.

5. Although the masculine singular *niño* could refer to the generic child—either boy or girl—I have chosen to translate the word as *child* but its corresponding object pronoun as *him* because I think in Guevara's overall project of advising women how to raise their children he is mostly concerned with sons.

6. Bergmann points out the ambiguous nature of the comparison of women to animals: "On one hand, women's 'natural' tendencies toward nurturing and affection were viewed as dangerous to civilization and detrimental to the production of citizens to serve the modern state. On the other, it was 'monstrous' for them to conform to certain cultural norms, in particular sending infants to wetnurses, which diverged from exemplary maternal behavior among the other animals to which they were compared" (41).

7. Guevara's stance that the mother choose the wet nurse differs radically from practices in Early Modern Florence where the father negotiated the appointment of

a wet nurse with the wet nurse's husband (Klapisch-Zuber 139–53). However, even there sometimes women, not men, located wet nurses for wealthy Florentine families, as is the case with Margherita Datini who would also supervise the nurses once they were hired (Gies 202).

8. Fildes notes that writers on education, such as Sir Thomas Elyot, and physicians and surgeons, such as, Bartholomaeus Metlinger and Eucharias Roesslin in Germany, Felix Wurtz in Switzerland, and Ambroise Paré and Jacques Guillemeau in France, noted the importance of the wet nurse not becoming pregnant because the best blood would go to the fetus first (69–70).

9. While critics have discussed Guevara's borrowing of material from his previous work, *Libro aúreo de Marco Aurelio*, most of this transferal occurs in book 3. Comprising forty chapters, book 3 contains approximately ten chapters from *Marco Aurelio*. However, none of this borrowed material treats the subject of the mother and wet nurses as primary caregivers for children. For the influence of *Marco Aurelio* in *Relox*, see Blanco's edition of *Relox* (chaps. 13–32), Grey (8–17), Rallo Gruss (*Antonio* 296–98).

Works Cited

Bataillon, Marcel. *Erasmo y España.* México: Fondo de cultura económica, 1966.

Bergmann, Emilie. "Monstrous Maternity in Fray Antonio de Guevara's *Relox de príncipes.*" *Brave New Words: Studies in Spanish Golden Age Literature.* Ed. Edward H. Friedman and Catherine Larson. New Orleans: University Press of the South, 1996. 39–49.

Dillard, Heath. *Daughters of the Reconquest: Women in Castilian Town Society, 1100–1300.* Cambridge: Cambridge University Press, 1984.

Etreros, Mercedes, ed. *La perfecta casada.* By Fray Luis de León. Madrid: Taurus, 1987.

Fildes, Valerie. *Wet Nursing: A History from Antiquity to the Present.* New York: Basil Blackwell, 1988.

Gies, Frances, and Joseph Gies. *Women in the Middle Ages.* New York: Crowell, 1978.

Grey, Ernest. *Guevara, a Forgotten Renaissance Author.* Hague: Martuhnus Nijhoff, 1973.

Guevara, Antonio de. *Relox de príncipes.* Ed. Emilio Blanco. Madrid: ABL, Confres, 1994.

Hubbard, Alice, trans. *The Perfect Wife.* By Fray Luis de León. Denton: Texas State College Press, 1943.

Jones, Joseph R. *Antonio de Guevara.* Boston: Twayne, 1975.

Klapisch-Zuber, Christiane. *Women, Family, and Ritual in Renaissance Italy.* Trans. Lydia Cochrain. Chicago: University of Chicago Press, 1985.

León, Fray Luis de. *La perfecta casada.* Ed. Mercedes Etreros. Madrid: Taurus, 1987.

Nadeau, Carolyn. "Blood Mother/Milk Mother: Breastfeeding, the Family, and the State in Antonio de Guevara's *Relox de príncipes* (*Dial of Princes*)," *Hispanic Review* 69.2 (Spring 2001): 153–74.

Rallo Gruss, Asunción. *Antonio de Guevara en su contexto renacentista.* Madrid: Cupsa, 1979.

———. *Coloquios matrimoniales del licenciado Pedro de Luján.* Madrid: Anejos del Boletín de la Real Academia Española, 1990.

Redondo, Augustín. *Antonio de Guevara (1480?–1545) et L'Espagne de son temps.* Geneva: Droz, 1976.

2

Identity, Illusion, and the Emergence of the Feminine Subject in *La Lozana andaluza*

John C. Parrack

Although critical evaluations of *La Lozana andaluza* [*Portrait of Lozana*] have finally emerged from Menéndez y Pelayo's condemnation of the text as "inmundo y feo" (cxciv), studies of the text's eroticism, genre, and use of language have continued to overshadow unique and revolutionary developments in its representation of the feminine subject in this text and Golden Age Spain.[1] In contrast to the female protagonists in *La Celestina*, the *comedia*, or even the novellas of María de Zayas, Lozana escapes the confines of phallogocentric society by neither dying nor getting married, which are the traditional completions of a feminine narrative (García Verdugo 14). In fact, Lozana fully confronts and rebels against the masculine systems of authority, constructs her own identity, and fashions to her advantage multiple subject positions through the use of illusion and female space.

This revolution in the female subject is not surprising in Early Modern Europe, a period characterized by crises (and revolutions) in religion, science, and literature. In fact, as Alice Jardine has suggested, this historical time of transition "was a period when 'woman' was at the height of discursive circulation: a circulation in which women came to play a decisive part" (93). More clearly than the rest of Early Modern Europe, the culture and literature of Golden Age Spain reveal the startling degree to which Jardine's assertion is true. Following the ascendance of Queen Isabella to the throne of Castile in 1474, literary texts increasingly confronted and questioned the medieval tradition of misogyny by exploring and testing the limits of female conduct.

The increased cultural tension surrounding the role of women in Golden Age Spain can be observed in several texts of the 1490s such as Diego de San

Pedro's *Cárcel de amor* (1492), which attacks the misogynist tradition, and Fernando de Rojas's *La Celestina* (1499), which represents its female characters and societal traditions in crisis. A closer look at the former text reveals a critique of the medieval tradition of misogyny. In *Cárcel de amor,* this critique centers on the protagonist Leriano's response to his friend Tefeo's ungrounded criticism of women. The inscribed author anticipates Leriano's subsequent attack on misogyny and undermines the misogynist tradition by failing to develop or enumerate the details of Tefeo's diatribe, portraying it as lacking in foundation—"quién la causava él ni nadie lo sabía" (155) [neither he nor anyone else knew who had inspired it] (66)—and characterizing it as invention—"y para favorecer su habla truxo todas las razones que en disfamia dellas pudo pensar" (155) [and to strengthen his case he adduced every argument that he could think of to slander women] (66).[2] In contrast to the brief description of Tefeo's ill-defined critique, Leriano presents fifteen attacks on those who criticize women, twenty reasons why men are obligated to them, and proofs of their inherent goodness (*Cárcel* 155–71). The text serves fundamentally, therefore, as a defense of women against the existing tradition of misogyny.

Apart from serving as a basis for parody in *La Celestina, Cárcel de amor* recognizes the historical currency of Queen Isabella's reign and contributes to it by framing and increasing the visibility of the debate on women. The best example of this elevation of gender issues centers on the reception of the *Arcipreste de Talavera,* or *Corbacho,* written in 1438 by Alfonso Martínez de Toledo. In the aftermath of San Pedro's sentimental novel, the *Arcipreste* is marketed as a misogynistic text through the explicit allusion to female vices in the title of the 1498 Seville edition: "El Arcipreste de Talavera que fabla de los vicios de las malas mugeres e Complexiones de los hombres" (*Arcipreste* 31) [The Archpriest of Talavera who speaks of the vices of evil women and the Dispositions of men].[3] This practice of privileging the second part of the *Arcipreste* on female vice over the three other parts that address the nature of men, love, astrology, fortune, and fate continues through the five subsequent complete editions that are published between 1500 and 1547 (*Arcipreste* 33–34). Clearly, this shift in the self-representation of the *Arcipreste de Talavera* contributed substantially to the reception of the text as misogynistic and the subsequent attribution of the title *Corbacho* that further positions the text within the misogynist tradition of Boccaccio's *Corbaccio.*[4] As a result, we must conclude that demand existed for texts that confronted the role of women in Golden Age Spain.

The other seminal text that informs the representation of women in *La*

Lozana andaluza is *La Celestina*, published initially in 1499. Similarly, *La Celestina* confronts the position and function of women in Golden Age society through the protagonist Celestina and her personal struggles within a society divided over the decline of rural feudalism and the rise of urban mercantilism. For the construction of feminine identity, the most significant implications of this transition center on the construction of interpersonal relations and the individual subject. The importance of loyalty and society diminishes with the emergence of money and the individual as new forces in Golden Age Spain. Celestina capitalizes on this shift by privileging money over personal loyalty and using sexuality as a means to gain power. Ultimately, however, she is unable to navigate safely through the conflicts surrounding the dissolution of medieval order and the transition to the Early Modern period. Indeed, it is her selfish desire to advantage herself at the expense of Pármeno and Sempronio that leads to her murder in the twelfth *auto* (274–75). As we will see later, Lozana lives in a similar world, where money, sex, and ingenuity are central to individual success. But unlike Celestina, she controls her own destiny and gains complete autonomy within the text.

It is into this male-authored tradition of female protagonists that *La Lozana andaluza* is published in 1528. The importance of both *Cárcel de amor* and *La Celestina* to an informed reading of *La Lozana* is confirmed by both the professional activities of Francisco Delicado and the text itself. From even the most superficial reading of *La Lozana andaluza,* the reader finds frequent allusions to Spanish humanism, literary production, and popular culture. Delicado makes allusion to Spanish humanists such as Antonio de Nebrija (205)[5] and Antón de Montoro (154), and such classical humanists as Seneca, Lucan, Martial, and Avicenna, to whom he refers in chronological order (154).[6] With regard to popular culture, Delicado foreshadows the development of picaresque discourse when he alludes to the popular figures of Lazarillo de Tormes (151) and Pedro de Urdemalas (198), who do not appear in published form until much later.[7]

Most important, however, Delicado makes frequent reference to *Cárcel de amor* and *La Celestina,* the two foundational texts for *La Lozana.* In the *portada* [preface] to the first edition, Delicado situates his text within the textual tradition of *La Celestina:* "Retrato de la Loçana andaluza en la lengua española muy claríssima. Co[m]puesto en Roma. El qual Retrato demuestra lo que en Roma passava y contiene munchas mas cosas que la Celestina" (31) [Portrait of Lozana the Lusty Andalusian Woman. Composed very clearly in the Spanish language at Rome, showing what happened there and containing a great deal more than La Celestina] (1).[8] In accordance with Renaissance tradition, Delicado positions his text to compete with and overshadow its predecessor just as Quevedo or Góngora will later compete with Garcilaso de la Vega. Allusions to *La Celestina* follow in the "Dedicatoria," which makes ludic reference to the "tiempo de Celestino Segundo" (33) [(time) while Celestine II reigned] (2), and continue throughout the text. For example, Lozana herself describes a woman she knew in Rome as "peor que Celestina" (138) [worse than Celestina] (138), a reference that is not a condemnation but a compliment since the comparison is predicated on this woman's ability to misrepresent herself and defraud others. The ability to alter one's subject position in order to deceive was central to the development of female subjectivity in Golden Age Spain and Delicado frequently valorizes it in *La Lozana andaluza*.

As we see in *mamotreto* [chapter] 36, the citizens of Rome recognize Lozana's own abilities in love and deception as superseding those of Celestina. In the course of a conversation between the Embajador and the Caballero, the Caballero describes Lozana as "la más excelente mujer que jamás vido" (153) [the most excellent woman he's ever seen] (159) and the Embajador compares her to her compatriot Seneca (154). Having officially met Lozana, the Embajador is so impressed with her amorous abilities that he seems to suggest that his own love interest has shifted from Angélica, purported to be "la más acabada dama que hay en esta tierra" (154) [the most perfect woman in all the land] (160), to Lozana herself:

> EMBAJADOR. ¡Qu'piu bella la matre que la filla!
> CABALLERO. Monseñor, ésta es Cárcel de amor; aquí idolatró Calisto, aquí no se estima Melibea, aquí poco vale Celestina. (155)

> [AMBASSADOR. Why, the mother is much more beautiful than the daughter!
> GENTLEMAN. My lord, welcome to Love's Prison: here Calisto is idolized; here Melibea is shown no respect; here Celestina is worth very little.] (162)

As we can see, apart from the Embajador's praise for Lozana, it is the Caballero's response, however, that positions Delicado's text within the literary tradition of *Cárcel de amor* and *La Celestina*. By alluding to these texts, the Embajador, and, by extension, Delicado, explicitly acknowledge their role as subtexts to be subverted. Like San Pedro's sentimental novel, *La Lozana andaluza* is structured around a narrative device in which the Author functions both as a character that participates in the narrative and as the scribe who monumentalizes these events. However, in contrast with their role in *Cárcel,* these authorial interventions serve a comedic function in *La Lozana* because the Author must now witness intimate sexual acts that do not occur in San Pedro's sentimental novel.[9] Similarly, the theory of love that emerges from *Cárcel* and *La Celestina* is decidedly different from that in *La Lozana.* Whereas both San Pedro and Rojas describe love as an emotional sickness that afflicts Leriano and Calisto, resulting in their final destruction, love is a purely physical act in *La Lozana andaluza.*

Likewise, Delicado structures his text around the use of dialogue, a device present in both *Cárcel de amor* and *La Celestina.* The subversion of this device in *La Lozana andaluza* occurs through the nature of language. Unlike its subtexts, *La Lozana* employs the explicit use of erotic imagery and the presence of multiple linguistic traditions (Italian, Portuguese, and Catalan, for example). The text confirms the importance of these subtexts and offers insight into Lozana's process of self-fashioning when she describes her own literary taste. On this occasion, Lozana declares *La Celestina* to be one of the literary texts she enjoys as a literary consumer (190). Her affinity toward *La Celestina* is not surprising because it is fundamentally this text whose protagonist inspires her own behavior and that forms the basis for invention or subversion in her own narrative.[10]

Like the author himself, Lozana emerges as an avid consumer of literary texts that test the boundaries of expression and monumentalize the shift in epistemological systems. Both her self-fashioning of subject positions and her subversive response to these texts epitomize the growth of individuality in the aftermath of standardized printed editions. As Eisenstein notes, the standardization of print culture served to promote the development of the individual: "Concepts pertaining to uniformity and to diversity—to the typical and to the unique—are independent, they represent two sides of the same coin. In this regard one might consider the emergence of a new sense of individualism as a by-product of the new forms of standardization. The more standardized the type, indeed, the more compelling the sense of an idiosyncratic personal self. No period was without some sense of the typical and of the individual but concepts pertaining to both were, nevertheless, transformed by the output of standard editions" (84). As we will see later, Lozana responds to this shift from the manuscript culture, agrarian economy, and corporate society of the feudal Middle Ages to the urban individualism and print culture of the Early Modern period through the self-fashioning of subject positions and the exercise of free will (Bouwsma 223–25).

Such allusions to humanists and literary texts such as *La Celestina* and *Cárcel de amor* should not be surprising because Delicado was himself a humanist and an editor of literary texts. After moving to Venice and publishing *La Lozana andaluza* in 1528, he edited chivalric romances such as *Amadís de Gaula* (1533) and *Primaleón* (1534), in addition to two known editions of *La Celestina* (1531, 1534), and a possible edition of *Cárcel de amor* (*Lozana* 11–13; Menéndez y Pelayo cxciv). Delicado's familiarity with these literary texts, therefore, extends beyond that of most sixteenth-century Spanish humanists to encompass real editorial expertise. If the author already had lived in Italy for many years (*Lozana* 11), what suddenly would have prompted the publication of *La Lozana andaluza* and his literary editions between 1528 and 1534? The crucial event, I believe, is the sack of Rome itself in 1527. Delicado's inability to exercise his talents as both editor and author within the Spanish community in Italy prior to the sack may indeed be predicated on the existence of established literary circles and his position as an outsider.

As Kenneth Gouwens has recently suggested, the sack of Rome disrupted literary production within the circle of curial humanists associated with the papacy and shattered their construction and inauguration of a golden age for the Renaissance papacy (6–19). Much of this ideological collapse or fragmentation centers on the increasing divide during the decade preceding the sack between their collective efforts to embellish the image of the papacy and the reality of the increase in Hapsburg power, the exhaustion of papal revenue, and the spread of Lutheranism (Gouwens 2–4). As a result of both this hypocrisy and the moral corruption in Rome, the sack in May 1527 destabilized the literary establishment of curial humanists and attenuated the position of the Spanish as outsiders, making Delicado increasingly free to exercise his literary craft. It is this moral justification, manifested through prophetic allusions to the fate of Rome, that charges the text with a didactic function and overshadows the transgressive developments in female subjectivity and literary language. Delicado added a recurring prophetic device and an "Epílogo" when he revised the text between the sack of Rome and its publication in Venice (*Lozana* 13, 20). This device positions *La Lozana andaluza* within the developing exegetical tradition that sought to explain the cause of the sack and the destruction of the "official narrative" elaborated by the curial humanists (Gouwens 3). Much like the *Diálogo de las cosas ocurridas en Roma*, written by Charles V's Latin secretary, Alfonso de Valdés, Delicado's narrative attributes the sack to the immorality and corruption in Rome (Gouwens 170). In *mamotreto* 15, for example, Rampín refers to a popular saying that describes Rome as: "triunfo de grandes señores, paraíso de putanas, purgatorio de jóvenes, infierno de todos, fatiga de bestias, engaño de pobres, peciguería de bellacos" (81) [glory of men of power, a paradise for whores, a purgatory for the young, a fraud for the poor, a drudgery for the beast of burden, a market place for swindlers and a hell for all] (63).

On other occasions throughout the text, such characters as Rampín, the Author, an Escudero, and Lozana (178) each allude to the punishment and destruction of Rome. Rampín blames the arrogance of the Cardinals for the future suffering of the city (62–63). On a tour of Rome, Lozana and Rampín observe a man preaching its impending destruction (82). Lozana describes Rome as lacking in conscience (134) and predicts the transformation of Rome into a "gran carnecería" (178) [gigantic butcher shop] (190), while the Author advises flight from the city "[p]orque será confusión y castigo de lo pasado" (120) [(b)ecause disorder and punishment will repay the past] (114). Even a lowly Escudero anticipates that in 1527 courtesans will be reduced to mistresses, and mistresses to maids (147). This didacticism also appears in the "Epílogo" (252–54) that attributes the destruction to the "gran pestilencia" (252) [great pestilence] (284) of the city. However, unlike the prophetic allusions throughout the text, this aspect of the text's presumed didacticism is admittedly subsequent to *La Lozana andaluza*'s composition since the "Epílogo" was added just prior to publication in 1528.

Delicado insists on this illusion of didacticism again at the end of the "Epílogo" where he implores the reader to ignore his lack of knowledge and recognize his "sana intención" (254) [good intentions] (286). This projection of intentionality is profoundly ironic and serves to legitimate a text that explores the boundaries of literary expression and female conduct by subsuming it within the existing exegetical tradition that sought philosophical explanations for the sack after the fragmentation of the humanist consensus in Rome (Gouwens 26–29). Behind this false didacticism and the political and literary instability that followed the sack, Delicado elaborates a literary work that is revolutionary for its use of language and its development of the female subject.

The most significant inspiration for female subjectivity in *La Lozana andaluza* comes from the conduct manuals, or handbooks of self-making, that appeared between 1500 and 1530: *Enchiridion militis Christiani* [*Handbook of the Militant Christian*](Erasmus, 1501), *Obedience of the Christian Man* (Tyndale, 1527), the *Prince* (Machiavelli, 1513), and the *Courtier* (Castiglione,

1528) (Greenblatt 84–87). Like the authors of many of these Early Modern handbooks, Delicado recognizes that order does not emerge from nature, as suggested by Aristotelian philosophy, but rather that it is "constructed and manipulable" (Parker 125). Lozana represents one of the first literary manifestations of this shift from what Baron has called the centralized, finite, and static system of Aristotle to the decentralized, infinite, and dynamic epistemology of the sixteenth century (34–35). Apart from being a literary text, *La Lozana andaluza* also differs from these handbooks in that it provides a specifically feminine model of self-fashioning at the margins of official culture. This should not be surprising because, as Rebhorn suggests, literature enjoys a unique freedom to explore and rebel from existing cultural mores:

> Literature does, in other words, what rhetoric treatises and handbooks are prevented from doing, except intermittently, by their form: it presents a direct modeling of rhetorical situations. Literature is a privileged discourse, in a sense, for it opens up the equivalent of a liminal space, a site adjacent to but separate from the space of the real world, in which authors can represent that world in such a way that while often merely rehearsing conventional ideas and arrangements, they also have the freedom to analyze, refine, and critique them. (18)

It is also worth noting that since these handbooks did not, or could not, originate under the climate of cultural control and imperial expansion in Spain during the first half of the sixteenth century, revolutionary developments in literary expression such as *La Lozana andaluza* also may not have been possible had Delicado not been living outside his homeland during this time period.

Now that we have set the stage, let us turn to Lozana and the representation of female subjectivity. As the narrative opens, Lozana typifies the female "Other," the object of authority figures such as her aunt, Diomedes (her purported suitor), or his father. After leaving her aunt as a girl of perhaps only twelve years (de Vries 62), her actions are governed by these men just as her identity—Aldonza—is defined by her physical resemblance to her grandmother (38). Although she will not fully emerge as an autonomous, self-fashioning subject until the fourth *mamotreto*—when Diomedes's father orders her killed—the seed of her future transgression of the literary boundaries of the female subject reveals itself when she first sees Diomedes. On this occasion, Lozana assumes the male role of subject and objectifies Diomedes—an act that both subverts the order of Golden Age gender relations and foreshadows her control over Rampín (see *mamotreto* 14). We see this objectification when Lozana tells her aunt:

Señora tía, ¿es aquél que está paseándose con aquél que suena los órganos? ¡Por su vida, que lo llame! ¡Ay, cómo es dispuesto! ¡Y qué ojos tan lindos! ¡Qué ceja partida! ¡Qué pierna tan seca y enjuta! ¿Chinelas trae? ¡Qué pie para galochas y zapatilla zeyena! Querría que se quitase los guantes por verle qué mano tiene. Acá mira. ¿Quiere vuestra merced que me asome? (40)

[Aunt, tell me at once! Is he the man strolling with that organ-grinder over there? Upon my soul, call him over, do! Such a handsome frame! What beautiful eyes! What a noble brow! Such well-turned legs! Is he wearing slippers? By rights he should be shod in the finest shoes. I wish he would take off his gloves so I could see his hands. He's looking this way. Should I show myself at the window?] (10)

Having met Diomedes, Lozana offers herself to him—"seré siempre vuestra más que mía" (42) [I shall always be more yours than mine] (12)—and leaves her aunt in Seville. The seminal event, however, which provokes Lozana's definitive emergence, is the attempt, orchestrated by Diomedes's father, to kill her secretly. It is this plan, ultimately leading her to Rome, that destroys the passive innocence of her "fantasía y triunfo" (44) [dreams and aspirations] (14). Her innocence and willing subjection to the social control of the male order ends here. This rebellion and the resulting freedom from the controlling influence of Diomedes and his family within the narrative are paralleled by Delicado's subversion of literary norms concerning language and the female subject. Lozana, unlike Celestina, survives the attempt on her life. The freedom gained by Lozana is especially symbolic because her oppressor, Diomedes, shares his name with the fourth-century grammarian who attempted to impose order on literary expression by organizing their genres (Fowler 219–20).

Due to the trauma of this initial episode as a young girl, Lozana discards the passive objectivity that characterized all but her first interaction with Diomedes and takes control of her life, assuming multiple subject positions through the use of illusion. Such an alteration of the female subject is possible because Early Modern European culture tended to define women in terms of their fathers, husbands, or religious orders. In other words, the female identity was always unstable, defined by its shifting relations to systems of cultural authority such as the family, the Church, or the state. Lozana's aunt confirms the instability of the female subject when she bemoans Lozana's departure with Diomedes: "El hombre deja el padre y la madre por la mujer, y la mujer olvida por el hombre su nido" (42) [A man leaves his father and his mother for a woman; a woman forsakes her home for a man] (12). The passive effacement of female identity to which the aunt refers, however, can also be inverted by the emerging female subject whose objective is, in Lozana's case, the active creation of illusions that benefit her.

Similarly, Edward Friedman has alluded to the possibility of illusion in *La pícara Justina* in which women are credited with "the invention of false stories and stratagems" (120).[11] Despite the overtones of misogyny, *La pícara Justina* reveals that illusion is a characteristic of the emerging female subject that is perceived as evil, much like the evolution from object to subject that it subsumes in *La Lozana andaluza*.[12] In other words, Lozana transforms this misogynistic attack on women into the basis for subject formation. The most obvious manifestation of this self-fashioning is the cross-dressing of the *comedia*, but unlike most of those female protagonists, it constitutes a truly inherent aspect of Lozana, the individual. She does not use self-fashioning as a device designed solely to facilitate free movement in the masculine world, but rather as a mode of life after her disillusioning experience with Diomedes.

Although Lozana's emergence as a self-fashioning individual is predicated on her mistreatment at the hands of Diomedes, it is emblematic of the anxiety and instability of Early Modern Europe, a world in which the limits of lateral and vertical mobility through physical space and social class have broken down (Bouwsma 230). The result of this breakdown of the compartmentalized medieval order is the destabilization of the individual. As Bouwsma aptly states: "The needs of survival in a problematic world have tended to alienate the public from any true self or, worse, to require the annihilation of the true for the sake of a social self. Thus, the relation between the boundaries of self-definition and any stable center of the personality have tended to become themselves problematic, and this has been the source of a peculiarly burdensome kind of anxiety in the modern world" (240).

Throughout the narrative of her life, Lozana's own evolution of identities from Aldonza (in Sevilla), to Lozana (in Rome), to Vellida (in Lípari) thoroughly exemplifies this self-fashioning of the subject. It is significant to note, however, that the impetus for her easy movement through space is not her family or social class but her own free will. As Lozana declares when she contemplates her new life in retirement:

Vamos con ella [Guiomar López], que no podemos errar, al ínsula de Lípari con nuestros pares, y mudaréme el nombre, y diréme la Vellida. . . . . Estarme he reposada, y veré mundo nuevo, y no esperar que él me deje a mí, sino yo a él. Ansí se acabará lo pasado, y estaremos a ver lo presente, como fin de Rampín y de la Lozana. (245)

[Let's go with her to the island of Lípari with our peers, because we can't go wrong, and I'll change my name and call myself Vellida. . . . I'll stay quiet, and I'll see a new world and not wait for it to leave me behind, but for me to leave it. Thus, the past will be finished, and we'll consider the present as the end of Rampín and Lozana.] (276–77)

This plan centers on Lozana's resistance to the gender roles that objectify and limit her. She has decided to alter her identity, explore the world, and objectify men. Apart from symbolizing the instability and self-fashioning of female subjectivity, these name changes also allow Lozana to create illusions for her own benefit and to control other characters such as Rampín.

The use of illusion is central to the creation of both female power and subjectivity in Early Modern Europe. Frequently, the locus for the deconstruction of these illusions is a female space in which gender solidarity overshadows differences in language and culture. Teresa de Lauretis describes the value of these differences in twentieth-century feminist writing: "What is emerging in feminist writings is . . . the concept of a multiple, shifting, and often self-contradictory identity, a subject that is not divided in, but rather at odds with, language; an identity made up of heterogeneous and heteronomous representations of gender, race, and class, and often indeed across languages and cultures; an identity that one decides to reclaim from a history of multiple assimilations, and that one insists on as a strategy" (9). What de Lauretis observes in the development of feminism in the twentieth century is also central to the construction of the female subject in *La Lozana andaluza*. In the twelfth *mamotreto*, for example, the *lavandera* [washerwoman] discards the illusion of being Italian when Lozana reveals herself to be Spanish (65). Her use of Italian, in effect, forms the basis for an assumed subjectivity, revealed to a compatriot. Later, when the *lavandera* speaks to a neighbor, she combines Spanish and Italian in the same response (68). The differences in language, race, culture, and profession that separate female characters such as Lozana and the *lavandera* do not preclude communication or the creation of a common female space. They are, to some degree, only a pretext.

As this effacement of differences among female subjects suggests, female space in *La Lozana andaluza* also serves as what Danielle Régnier Barthélemy has termed a *gynaceum*—a sacred female space characterized by the transmission of gendered advice and the transgression of social and cultural boundaries.[13] Ironically, it is the Caballero who alludes to this function of female space and Lozana's abilities within it: "y como las tiene en plática, sabe cada una en qué puede ser loada" (153) [(a)nd by speaking with her, each woman learns her (own) wonderful qualities for herself] (159). The sixth and seventh *mamotretos* constitute such a space not only because they transpire in the enclosed space of the *camisera*'s [shirtmaker] house but also because women discuss such intimate subjects as social deception, illness, sexuality, and even urination. As Lozana herself declares to four other women: "¡Ay, señoras! Contaros he maravillas. Dejáme ir a verter aguas que, como eché aquellas putas viejas alcoholadas por las escaleras abajo, no me paré a mis necesidades" (50) [Ladies, I have wonders to tell you. But first let me go to make water. I was so busy kicking those old painted whores downstairs, that I didn't attend to nature's call] (22). Likewise, when Lozana reveals that she has syphilis, Sevillana's response demonstrates her acceptance of and solidarity with Lozana: "No será nada, por mi vida. Llamaremos aquí un médico que la vea, que parece una estrellica" (49) [It's not really that bad. Let's call a doctor now and have him look at it. Why it looks like a tiny scar] (20).[14] The honest confrontation of such themes demonstrates, as Jardine and others have observed, the tendency toward the representation of female discourse as "unclean" (98). In the case of texts such as *La Lozana andaluza* or *La Celestina*, this unseemliness serves as a discursive mask that the emerging female subject fashions in order to control her own existence, often through the creation of pleasure.

Not surprisingly, a significant aspect of Menéndez y Pelayo's denunciation of *La Lozana andaluza* in his introduction to the *Orígenes de la novela* [*Origins of the Novel*] centers on its eroticism and exploration of the limits of literary and cultural control over the female subject. Much like Celestina, Lozana actively controls the creation of pleasure, and, therefore, she exerts power. In her encounter with the Embajador and Caballero in *mamotreto* 36, Lozana receives the promise of significant financial compensation in exchange for helping the Embajador gain entrance to Angélica's house:

A vuestra señoría metelle he yo encima, no debajo, mas yo lo trabajaré. Esperen aquí, que si su merced está sola, yo la haré poner a la ventana, y si más mandaren, yo verné abajo. Bien estaré media hora, paséense un poco, porque le tengo de rogar primero que haga un poco por mí, que estoy en gran necesidad, que me echan de la casa, y no tengo de qué pagar, que el borracho del patrón no quiere menos de seis meses pagados antes. (154–55)

[I'll take your lordship in openly, not hidden away, but first I'll have to arrange your visit. Wait here, and I'll ask her to come to the window, if she is alone. Then, if you wish, I'll come back for you. Stroll around a little. It will take me at least half an hour, for I must beg her to attend to me first. I am in great need of money and am being thrown out of my house as a result. The drunken swine who owns the place won't accept less than six months' rent paid in advance.] (160–61)

In this passage, Lozana confirms her ability to exert power within a closed female space like Angélica's house in exchange for financial reward. She gets the Caballero to pledge financial support for her by threatening to delay the Embajador's access to Angélica. Parker refers to this device of *dilatio,* or delay, as typical of feminine rhetoric during this period (9–10). It must be noted, however, that Lozana exercises her free will in order not only to employ but also to subvert rhetorical "dilation." Although Parker refers to erotic dilation, or the postponement of coitus, as a significant feminine strategy (16), Lozana clearly rejects this device during her orgy with Rampín in *mamotreto* 14 (73– 79). Notwithstanding the propensity of Early Modern women toward *dilatio,* the only constant for Lozana is the instability of her subject positions and her reliance on illusion.

Much later in the narrative, the power of illusion in the formation of the female subject is confirmed when Lozana advises Coridón on how to recover his lost love, Polidora, who was forced to marry a wealthy old man. Lozana advises Coridón to use the illusion of female subjectivity in order to penetrate the female space that surrounds Polidora:

Amor mío, Coridón dulce, récipe el remedio: va, compra un veste de villana que sea blanca y unas mangas verdes, y vayte descalzo y sucio y loqueando, que todos te llamarán loca, y di que te llaman Jaqueta, que vas por el mundo reprehendiendo las cosas mal hechas, y haz a todos servicios y no tomes premio ninguno, sino pan para comer. Y va munchas veces por la calle d'ella, y coge serojas, y si su marido te mandare algo, hazlo, y viendo él que tú no tomas ni quieres salario, salvo pan, ansí te dejará en casa para fregar y cerner y jabonar. (213)

[My dear, sweet Coridon, here's the remedy: go and buy a peasant woman's clothing—it should be white—and with green sleeves, and go around barefooted and dirty and speaking foolish nonsense so that everyone will call you a crazy woman, and say that your name is Jaqueta who goes around the world reprimanding evil deeds, and do services for everyone and take nothing in payment except bread to eat. And walk down her street many times and gather withered leaves, and if her husband asks something of you, do it; and when he sees that you neither take nor want any salary except bread, he'll let you in his house to scrub and sift and wash.] (234)

What this elaborate illusion demonstrates is the control that the masculine social order attempts to exert over female space, a space that men cannot enter and in which their discourse is powerless. In this privileged female space, Coridón must, as Jaqueta, expand on the illusory identity by creating a narrative that parallels the sad events in Polidora's own life.

The episode reinforces the function of illusion, multiple subject positions, and private space in the creation of the female subject and discursive power. Even the young and inexperienced Coridón recognizes that Lozana lives, as he says, by "*arte e ingenio*" (214) [art and ingenuity] (236). Lozana is a paragon of this illusive self-fashioning, a fact that is stressed by Teresa soon after Lozana's arrival in Rome: "Antes de ocho días sabrá toda Roma, que ésta en son la veo yo que con los cristianos será cristiana, y con los jodíos, jodía, y con los turcos, turca, y con los hidalgos, hidalga, y con los ginoveses, ginovesa, y con los franceses, francesa, que para todos tiene salida" (56) [Before eight days have passed, she'll know everything there is to know about Rome. I can easily see what ruse she will use: to be a Christian among the Christians, a Jew among the Jews, a Turk among the Turks, among gentlemen a lady of breeding, a Genoese among the Genoese, and French among the French: why, she'll have a trick to hoodwink each and every one!] (30). Much later, the Embajador also perceives this illusive ability when he recognizes that Lozana "es astuta, que cierto 'ha de la sierpe e de la paloma.' Esta mujer sin lágrimas parará más insidias que todas las mujeres con lágrimas" (155) [seems quite clever, and it's obvious that she takes after both the serpent and the dove. That woman can clearly get her way dry-eyed a great deal better than all your grand ladies with their buckets of tears] (161). On one of the few occasions that Lozana reveals her true self, she readily admits to being a knowledgeable woman (193).

The final motif that informs Lozana's construction of illusion and female subjectivity is dreams. Despite their frequency and importance as framing devices in medieval fiction (Régnier Barthélemy 385–86), dreams in *La Lozana andaluza* center instead on the protagonist's unconscious. They serve as a means to gain psychological penetration beyond the surface of the illusive subject positions that Lozana projects. Delicado's use of this device may be predicated on the rediscovery and publication of the *Oneirocritica* [*The Interpretation of Dreams*] by the Daldianus Artemidorus. A Greek edition was published in Venice in 1518 with the first Latin edition following in 1539 (Ruiz Garcia 55). As a result, it is certainly possible that the increased cultural currency of dreams in some way impacted *La Lozana andaluza*.[15] Through the dreams that Lozana describes and analyzes, the reader gains access to her most intimate private space. In the first dream episode at the beginning of *mamotreto* 31, Lozana reveals both the frequency and disturbing truth of her dreams:

> Agora me libre Dios del diablo con este soñar que tengo, y si supiese con qué quitármelo, me lo quitaría. Querría saber cualque encantamiento para que no me viniesen estos sobresaltos, que querría haber dado cuanto tengo por no haber soñado lo que soñé esta noche. . . . Mas munchas veces he yo soñado, y siempre me ha salido verdad. (137)

> [May God deliver me from the devil and this dream I just had! If only I knew how to rid myself of it, I would indeed! If only there were some incantation to keep these nightmares away! I would give all I own not to have had such a dream! . . . I have often had dreams, and they have always come true.] (137)

Although the validity of Lozana's dreams remains unclear, her claim, if true, provides her with valuable foreknowledge. However, even if it is false, the illusion of foreknowledge that she fosters is nevertheless a catalyst to her discursive power. This ambiguity is apparent in *mamotreto* 58 in which Lozana tries to exert her influence over Garza Montesina in order to preclude the fulfillment of a dream:

> LOZANA. Señora, llévemela el mozo, porque no vaya yo cargada; no se me ensuelva el sueño en todo, que esta noche soñaba que caía en manos de ladrones.
> MONTESINA. Andá, no miréis en sueños que, cuando veníades acá, os vi yo hablar con cuatro. (224)

[LOZANA. Madam, let the servant take it for me because I shouldn't walk around loaded down with things. May my dream last night not come true for I dreamed that I fell into the hands of bandits.
MONTESINA. Goodness; that was no dream. When you were coming here, I saw you talking to four of them.] (249)

Montesina is not alone in questioning the veracity of Lozana's dreams. The author himself denounces Lozana's premonitions as "alimañas o aves que vuelan" (177) [vermin or flying birds] (189). In response, she seemingly admits to declaring "la mentira con ingenio, por sacar la verdad" (178) [each lie with extreme care in order to bring forth the truth] (190). She concludes her answer by predicting the destruction of Rome in 1527, a prediction she again makes through allegory in *mamotreto* 66 (Acebrón Ruiz 190). As a result, the nature of Lozana's dreams remains an unstable discursive space within the text.

Nevertheless, Lozana confers much value to her dreams. During her final dream at the end of the narrative, she contemplates her retirement to Lípari and her transformation into Vellida. As Lozana's description of the dream suggests, her decision to leave Rome and re-fashion her subjectivity is motivated by the inner world of her unconscious. She tells Rampín:

Ya vistes que el astrólogo nos dijo que uno de nosotros había de ir a paraíso, porque lo halló ansí en su arismética y en nuestros pasos, y más este sueño que yo he soñado. Quiero que éste sea mi testamento. Yo quiero ir a paraíso, y entraré por la puerta que abierte hallare, pues tiene tres, y solicitaré que vais vos, que lo sabré hacer. (244)

[You already saw that the astrologer told us that one of us would go to Paradise because he found it this way in our horoscope and in our conduct and even more in this dream I had. I want this to be my testament. I want to go to Paradise, and I'll enter whichever one of the three gates I find open, and I'll plead for you to go, because I know how to do it.] (275–76)

This affirmation in the final *mamotreto* completes Lozana's emergence as an autonomous female subject. She is not the Other, the object of masculine subjects. Rather, she is the subject who objectifies Rampín and imposes her subjectivity on him. In the "Apología," Delicado removes any doubts about the value of women and the revolutionary development of Lozana by praising her as more valuable than a diamond for her wisdom and intelligence (248). While such developments may not seem dramatic in the twentieth century, they are profound in a historical period characterized by misogyny and the objectification of women.

Notes

1. Central to these new readings of *La Lozana andaluza* are Damiani's edition of the text and book-length studies by Imperiale on the dramatic context of the work.

2. All citations from *Cárcel de amor*, hereafter *Cárcel*, are from the edition by Whinnom. The English version is from the translation by Whinnom.

3. All citations from the *Arcipreste de Talavera*, hereafter *Arcipreste*, are from the edition by González Muela. The translations are my own.

4. The misogynistic reception of the *Arcipreste de Talavera* is further proven by the isolated publication of the second part of the text that specifically attacks women. Such a publication occurred in 1499 under the title "Tratado contra las mugeres que con poco saber mezclado con malicia dicen e facen cosas no devidas" (*Arcipreste* 31) [Treatise against women who with little understanding mixed with malice say and do improper things].

5. All citations from *La Lozana andaluza* are from the edition by Damiani.

6. In addition to these, there are literary references to figures such as Juan del Encina (*mamotreto* 11, p. 59), El Cid (*mamotreto* 18, p. 92), and Apuleius (*mamotreto* 47, p. 187).

7. *Lazarillo de Tormes* first appears in printed form in 1552–53 (Rico 129), while *Pedro de Urdemalas* is printed in conjunction with Cervantes's *Ocho comedias* in 1615 (Canavaggio 61).

8. The English citations from *La Lozana andaluza* are from the translation by Damiani.

9. See *mamotreto* 14 in which the Author suddenly appears at the orgy between Lozana and Rampín in order to describe her snoring (*Lozana* 77). As Beltrán has insightfully suggested, this authorial intervention is visually highlighted typographically in the first edition so as to insist upon the transgression of an intimate discursive space (92).

10. It is worth noting that, like Don Quijote, Lozana's literary awareness encompasses the narrative of her own life's story (190).

11. See *La pícara Justina*, 345, for the narrator's extended diatribe on women and their ability to dissemble.

12. For further discussion of the misogynistic association between women and the deceptive use of rhetoric, see Rebhorn, chapter 3, especially 148.

13. Régnier Barthélemy discusses the concept of *gynaceum* throughout "Imagining the Self," but see especially 314, 336, and 344.

14. Elements of a closed female space also appear in *mamotretos* 51, 54, and 63.

15. In his thoughtful analysis of dreams in *La Lozana andaluza*, Acebrón Ruiz notes a number of interpretive coincidences between Delicado's narrative and the *Oneirocritica* (190–91).

Works Cited

Acebrón Ruiz, Julián. "A propósito de los sueños en *La Lozana andaluza*." *Actas Irvine-'92. Asociación Internacional de Hispanistas. III: Encuentros y desencuentros de culturas desde la edad media al siglo XVIII*. Ed. Juan Villegas. Irvine: University of California, 1994. 3:190–99.

Anonymous. *Lazarillo de Tormes*. Ed. Francisco Rico. Madrid: Cátedra, 1992.

Artemidorus, Daldianus. *La interpretación de los sueños*. Ed. and trans. Elisa Ruiz García. Madrid: Gredos, 1989.

Baron, Hans. "Towards a More Positive Evaluation of the Fifteenth-Century Renaissance." *Journal of the History of Ideas* 4 (1943): 21–49.

Beltrán, Luis. "The Author's Author, Typography, and Sex: The Fourteenth Mamotreto of *La Lozana andaluza*." *The Picaresque: Tradition and Displacement*. Ed. Giancarlo Maiorino. Minneapolis: University of Minnesota Press, 1996. 86–136.

Bouwsma, William. "Anxiety and the Formation of Early Modern Culture." *After the Reformation*. Ed. Barbara C. Malament. Philadelphia: University of Pennsylvania Press, 1980. 215–46.

Cervantes, Miguel de. *Los baños de Argel: Pedro de Urdemalas*. Ed. Jean Canavaggio. Madrid: Taurus, 1992.

Delicado, Francisco. *La Lozana andaluza*. Ed. Bruno Damiani. 1969. Reprint, Madrid: Castalia, 1984.

———. *Portrait of Lozana, The Lusty Andalusian Woman*. Ed. and trans. Bruno Damiani. Potomac, Md.: Scripta Humanistica, 1987.

de Lauretis, Teresa. "Feminist Studies/Critical Studies: Issues, Terms, and Contexts." *Feminist Studies/Critical Studies*. Ed. Teresa de Lauretis. Bloomington: Indiana University Press, 1986. 1–19.

de Vries, Henk. "¿Quién es la Lozana?" *Celestinesca* 18 (1994): 51–73.

Eisenstein, Elizabeth L. *The Printing Press as an Agent of Change. Vol I: Communications and Cultural Transformations in Early-Modern Europe*. Cambridge: Cambridge University Press, 1979.

Fowler, Alastair. *Kinds of Literature: An Introduction to the Theory of Genres and Modes*. Cambridge: Harvard University Press, 1982.

Friedman, Edward H. "Man's Space, Woman's Place: Discourse and Design in *La pícara Justina*." *La Chispa '85: Selected Proceedings: The Sixth Louisiana Conference on Hispanic Languages and Literatures*. Ed. Gilbert Paolini. New Orleans: Tulane University Press, 1985. 115–23.

García Verdugo, María Luisa. *"La Lozana andaluza" y la literatura del siglo XVI: La sífilis como enfermedad y metáfora*. Madrid: Pliegos, 1994.

Gouwens, Kenneth. *Remembering the Renaissance: Humanist Narratives of the Sack of Rome*. Leiden: Brill, 1998.

Greenblatt, Stephen. *Renaissance Self-Fashioning: From More to Shakespeare*. Chicago: University of Chicago Press, 1980.

Imperiale, Louis. *Contexto dramático de "La Lozana andaluza."* Potomac, Md.: Scripta Humanistica, 1991.

————. *La Roma clandestina de Francisco Delicado*. Intro. Tatiana Bubnova. New York: Peter Lang, 1997.

Jardine, Alice. *Gynesis: Configurations of Woman and Modernity*. Ithaca: Cornell University Press, 1985.

López de Úbeda, Francisco. *La pícara Justina*. Ed. Bruno Damiani. Potomac, Md.: Studia Humanitatis, 1982.

Martínez de Toledo, Alfonso. *Arcipreste de Talavera o El Corbacho*. Ed. Joaquín González Muela. Madrid: Castalia, 1970.

Menéndez y Pelayo, Marcelino. "Introducción." *Orígenes de la novela. III: Novelas dialogadas*. Biblioteca de Autores Españoles 14. Madrid: Bailly Baillière, 1910. Clxxxviii–ccii.

Parker, Patricia. *Literary Fat Ladies: Rhetoric, Gender, Property*. London: Methuen, 1987.

Rebhorn, Wayne. *The Emperor of Men's Minds: Literature and the Renaissance Discourse of Rhetoric*. Ithaca: Cornell University Press, 1995.

Régnier Barthélemy, Danielle. "Imagining the Self." *A History of Private Life. II: Revelations of the Medieval World*. Ed. Georges Duby. Cambridge: Harvard University Press, 1988. 311–95.

Rojas, Fernando de. *La Celestina*. Ed. Dorothy S. Severin. Madrid: Cátedra, 1992.

San Pedro, Diego de. *Obras completas, II: Cárcel de amor*. Ed. Keith Whinnom. Madrid: Castalia, 1985.

————. *"Prison of Love," 1492: Together with the Continuation by Nicolás Núñez, 1496*. Trans. and intro. Keith Whinnom. Edinburgh: Edinburgh University Press, 1979.

3

Skepticism and Mysticism in Early Modern Spain

The Combative Stance of Teresa de Avila

Barbara Mujica

Saint Teresa of Avila lived in a period that threw into question centuries-old assumptions on the validity of Church dogma. Central to the dispute ignited by Luther was the legitimate standard of religious knowledge. The skeptic revival of the sixteenth century deeply influenced both Catholics and Protestants and played a significant role in the approach to spirituality adopted by Saint Teresa and other Catholic reformers. Yet, the relevance of Christian skepticism to Teresian spirituality has been virtually overlooked.

The Skeptic Revival

Broadly described, skepticism is a philosophy that casts doubt on the possibility of knowledge. In the Hellenistic period, two currents of skepticism developed. Academic skepticism held that no knowledge was possible because human intellect, reason, memory, and the senses—that is, the means by which cognition is achieved—are imperfect; the faculties therefore convey unreliable information on which faulty judgments are made. Furthermore, appeals to authority are gratuitous, since precepts are created by human beings and interpreted by other human beings. Therefore, no means exist of ascertaining whether or not our determinations are true or false. The Pyrrhonian skeptics held that the Academics purported to know too much, since, by asserting that nothing could be known, the Academics claimed to know *something*. The Pyrrhonians saw Academic skepticism as a form of reverse dogmatism. Basing their system on the texts of Sextus Empiricus, they argued that insufficient evidence exists to determine whether or not anything can be known. Therefore, all judgment must be withheld, and man must function in a suspended state of doubt. Thus, skeptical doubt is not denial, but suspension of judgment (Hallie 9).

From antiquity to modern times religious thinkers have seen philosophical skepticism as antithetical to faith. And yet, during the Reformation, faith and skepticism were not viewed as incompatible. Indeed, both Catholics and Protestants exploited skeptical arguments to their own advantage. Although several texts of Sextus Empiricus existed in Europe during the Middle Ages, he was generally unknown until he was rediscovered in the mid-fifteenth century through manuscripts brought from Byzantium (Popkin, "Sceptical Crisis" 329). The Italian humanists Marsilio Ficino (1433–1499) and Giovanni Pico della Mirandola (1463–1494) read Sextus, and the latter owned two of his texts in Greek (Copenhaver 316). Ficino and Pico della Mirandola were two of Italy's leading Neoplatonists with far-reaching influence in Spain.[1] Significantly, one of the accusations that the Inquisition made against Saint Teresa was that she espoused doctrines similar to those of Giovanni Pico della Mirandola (Swietlicki 78).

Girolamo Savonarola, the leader of the Florentine religious reform movement, ordered a translation of Sextus's works for the purpose of combating pagan philosophies (Popkin, "Sceptical Crisis" 329). One of the judges at the trial that resulted in his excommunication and execution had borrowed a Vatican manuscript of Sextus, which suggests the Church suspected that skepticism was the source of Savonarola's unorthodox ideas (Copenhaver 316). Gianfrancesco Pico della Mirandola, Giovanni's nephew, wrote a laudatory biography of Savonarola in which he maintained that the Florentine reformer had ordered a translation of Sextus to combat the ignorance of those who defended the worth of erudition. In 1520 Gianfrancesco wrote a long treatise, parts of which consist of translations of Sextus's works, to "undercut any claims for secular knowledge" (Copenhaver 316).

The Reformation brought the issue of the possibility of knowledge to a head, with both Catholics and Protestants employing skeptical arguments to bolster their cause. Catholic reformers such as Erasmus adopted a skeptical defense of faith, challenging the intellectualism that had come to pervade theology (Popkin, *History of Scepticism* 1–5). In *De libero arbitrio* (1524) Erasmus states that in the theological controversies that are currently raging, he prefers "the views of the sceptics wherever the inviolable authority of Scripture and the decision of the Church permit" (6). He censures dogmatists who "are so blindly addicted to one opinion that they cannot tolerate whatever differs from it" and notes that individuals can distort Holy Scripture "to serve the opinion to which they have one and for all enslaved themselves" (6). Erasmus held that since we cannot know the Truth any other way, we must rely on the Church. Rather than try to decipher what is not accessible to us, he argues, we should contemplate and venerate God "in mystic silence" (Penelhum 294).

Luther, responding to Erasmus in his *De servo arbitrio* (1525), rejects skepticism, arguing that "the Holy Spirit is no skeptic, and what He has written into our hearts are no doubts or opinions, but assertions, more certain and more firm than all human experience and life itself" (103). However, other Protestant thinkers embraced skepticism as a form of argument in order to undermine the authority of the Church. Dialecticians such as Jean La Placette and David-Renaud Boullier contended that before acceding to the authority of the Church, one would have to discover the validity and truth of Church doctrine. This would require a judge, but since the Church cannot be the arbiter of its own infallibility, the whole process disintegrates into Pyrrhonism (Popkin, *History of Scepticism* 15). Reformers such as Calvin insisted on the substance of the Word of God as revealed through Scripture, holding that by means of divine illumination, the elect—that is, those whom God favors with grace—could examine Scripture and grasp its meaning without the need for Church intervention. Catholics countered by unleashing still more skeptical arguments: since it would be impossible to judge the validity of the diverse interpretations of Scripture proposed by persons claiming to have received divine illumination, an independent authority is needed. That authority must necessarily be the Church, founded by Christ himself and headed by the recipient of God's Word.

The kind of skeptical approach Gianfrancesco Pico della Mirandola embraced was called fideism; it posited that no knowledge was possible except through divine grace, which reveals the truth through Scripture—a stance perilously close to the Protestants'. However, not all fideists adopted such a radical—and potentially heretical—stance. Fideism encompassed a gamut of views, from blind faith to the conviction that in matters of religion reason is subordinate to faith. What all forms of sixteenth-century fideism have in common is the fundamental belief that the existence of God is a matter of faith, not reason. Rational argument might induce belief, but cannot prove the existence of God. Michel de Montaigne (1533–1592) defends Catholicism in his *Apologie de Raimond Sebond* by using Sextus to reduce human knowledge to opinion, thereby depriving the Protestants of any criterion for their claims to knowledge (Screech xxiv). He does not deny completely the rational basis for Christianity, but argues that reason, unaided by divine illumination, cannot by itself discover Truth. Both Man and his circumstances are ever changing, argues Montaigne, and therefore Man's perception of reality is relative. Only God is unchanging, and so Man can rise above his natural limitations only with God's grace ("Apologie" 268).

The skeptical revival of the early sixteenth century had profound effects throughout Europe, where religious thinkers studied Sextus in an effort to deal with the problems of faith and knowledge. It reached Spain through both primary and secondary sources. Of the two extant medieval manuscripts of Sextus's *Pyrrhonian Hypotyposes,* one is a fourteenth- or fifteenth-century translation discovered in Spain (Popkin, *History of Scepticism* 19). An important secondary source was Erasmus, widely admired among Spanish reformers and actively promoted by Cardinal Francisco Jiménez de Cisneros (1436–1517), Isabel the Catholic's confessor. In June 1524, Juan Luis Vives (1492–1540), an exiled *converso*[2] living in Brussels, wrote to Erasmus about the great interest Spaniards were showing in Erasmus's works. Although Vives's claim may have been hyperbolic, Erasmus was without doubt hotly debated in intellectual circles. His works deeply influenced Juan de Avila, whose educational reforms would affect the intellectual and spiritual environment of Teresa's native city, and Gaspar Daza, who would later become one of Teresa's spiritual directors. Daza's disciples included Francisco Salcedo, another of Teresa's spiritual directors, and Julián de Avila, who accompanied the saint on her journeys and would eventually become her chaplain and biographer.

In Paris, where many Spanish ecclesiastics taught at universities, the Jesuit theologian Juan Maldonado (1534?–1583), availed himself of skepticism to undermine Calvinism by using its own skeptical arguments against it. He and other Church reformers, such as the French Catholic Gentian Hervet, adapting "the pattern of argument of the sceptics to the issue at hand, . . . constructed a 'new machine of war' to reduce their opponents to a 'forlorn scepticism' in which they could be sure of nothing" (Popkin, *History of Scepticism* 68). Since Luther and Calvin had challenged the Church's criteria in determining doctrine, Maldonado's group countered that Luther, Calvin, and Zwingli could hardly be thought to possess the key to Truth, since they could not agree among themselves with regard to the meaning of Scripture (Popkin, *History of Scepticism* 69). If the Church could err, argued the Catholics, then so could the Protestant reformers. Applying skeptical methods, Maldonado calls into question the efficacy of reason. He denies the presumptions of the rational man in trying to determine the Truth, and adheres instead to the authority of Church, Scripture, and tradition: "[W]e are Christians, not philosophers. The Word of God is our stay; and while we have this clear and plain, we lay little stress on the dictates of natural reason" (*A Commentary on the Holy Gospels*, quoted by Popkin, *History of Scepticism* 79). Such arguments were perfectly consistent with Jesuit thinking since Ignatius himself repeatedly stresses the limits of reason.

A friend of Montaigne's and an influential leader of university reform in France, Maldonado, like Vives, spent much of his life outside of Spain. However, his work at the Collège de Clermont, where he taught philosophy until he was censured in 1574, and his participation in the reform of the study of theology at the University of Paris, kept him in close contact with Jesuit communities in Spain and Italy.[3] The enormous importance Jesuits placed on correspondence as a means of achieving "union of hearts" ensured that Maldonado's ideas reached an audience far beyond the university (O'Malley 62). The kind of argumentation advanced by Maldonado was common among thinkers trained at Jesuit colleges well into the 1600s.[4] (It is significant that in 1553 the Jesuits opened a college in Avila that provided Saint Teresa with several spiritual directors.) Montaigne's influence on Maldonado is difficult to assess. Paul Schmitt points out similarities between their opinions and suggests that it was probably the Spaniard who influenced the Frenchman. Montaigne, who had a number of friends and relatives among the Jesuits, may well have consulted Maldonado when undertaking his translation of Raymond Sebond, who was Catalan (Schmitt 502).

One of the most influential skeptics was Francisco Sanches, a teacher of philosophy and medicine in Toulouse, whose book, *Quod nihil scitur* [*That Nothing Can be Known*] (1576), is a critique of the Aristotelian concept of knowledge. Sanches demonstrates that all means of determining truth are faulty, partly because the tools at our disposal—reason and the senses—are imperfect, partly because the external world is subject to change. Of Portuguese-Jewish origin and perhaps a distant cousin of Montaigne,[5] Sanches was read in Spain and is quoted by Quevedo at the beginning of "El mundo por de dentro" ["The World Inside Out"].

Skeptical influences are also evident in the *Disputationes metaphysicae*, by Francisco Suárez (1548–1617), the eminent Jesuit theologian whose works were used as textbooks in Jesuit schools. Of particular interest are the sections on reason, judgment, and the interpretation of evidence, in which Suárez discusses the ways in which the mind distorts evidence conveyed by the senses. Suárez explains that because sense perception is unreliable, people are often confronted with signs that conflict with reason or with one another, making it impossible to ascertain the truth. Furthermore, reason is easily swayed by the will and by personal interest, causing people to see as good certain things that are evil (2:286–87).

Two more authors merit mention here: Juan Huarte de San Juan (1533–1592) and Pedro de Valencia (1555–1620). Huarte stresses the unreliability of the senses and of reason in *Examen de ingenios* (1575), a book that may have influenced both Montaigne and Pierre Charron. Valencia, a highly respected Doctor of Law and Royal Historian to Philip III, displays knowledge of skepticism in his *Academica sive de judicio erga verum* (1576), a clarification of Cicero's *Academica,* in which he examines various approaches to truth. Valencia places considerable stress on the skeptics, leading some critics to conclude that this was his preferred point of view (Ihrie 24). Like Montaigne, he asserts that true knowledge is not accessible through the natural light of reason, but is a gift from God. Valencia laments that the unavailability of original texts obstructs his exposition of Sextus Empiricus's ideas, apparently distrusting the Latin translations that were available to him (Ihrie 24).

Skepticism and Apophaticism

The spread of skepticism coincided with new approaches to spirituality that flourished in the fifteenth and sixteenth centuries, in particular the *devotio moderna*—a movement originating in Holland that stressed the inner life and downplayed the role of the intellect and sensory perception in the spiritual process. Rather than rites and formalities, the *devotio moderna* emphasized meditation and prayer. Christian skepticism complemented and nourished this trend toward mental prayer, which had been practiced in certain monasteries from the late Middle Ages.

The *devotio moderna* drew on the tradition of apophatic spirituality, defined by a late-fifth-century monastic writer known as the Pseudo-Dionysius. Deeply influenced by Neoplatonism, the apophatic, or negative, approach denies to God all "qualities of the creatures, until it reaches 'the super-essential darkness'" (Copleston 110). The goal is to obliterate all anthropomorphic notions of God (that is, the idea that God "sees" or "thinks" in human terms), not in order to understand God rationally, which is impossible, but in order to confront the unknowable: "When the mind has stripped away from its idea of God the human modes of thought and inadequate conceptions of the Deity, it enters upon the 'Darkness of Unknowing,' wherein it 'renounces' all the apprehension of the understanding and is wrapped in that which is wholly intangible and invisible . . . united . . . to Him that is wholly unknowable" (Copleston 110). This annihilation of self, this complete yielding, is the "mystical marriage" between the soul and God, characterized in some mystics such as Teresa de Avila, by raptures, visions, or other altered states.

The melding of the philosophical and spiritual is manifest in Erasmus, for example, who used skeptical arguments to justify allegiance to the Church and advocated mental prayer as a means of transcending the intellect to embrace God fully. His *Modus orandi Deum* (1524), which was translated into Spanish as *Tratado de la oración* [*Treatise on Prayer*] in 1546, won instant popularity among Spain's growing population of contemplatives—even though Erasmus had lost favor in official circles and several of his works would soon be on the Index. Another book on mental prayer, *Tercer abecedario espiritual* [*Third Spiritual Alphabet*] (1527), by the Franciscan reformer Francisco de Osuna, was Saint Teresa's introduction to the *devotio moderna*. At the core of Osuna's system is *recogimiento* [recollection], a method of prayer based on inward focus on the presence of God achieved through benumbing the senses and reason, which leads to negation of the self in order to attain pure and direct reception of God's will. Because recollection bypasses the senses and makes no use of reason, in matters of mystical theology, experience is understood as the only real authority.

Saint Teresa's Combative Stance

Teresa de Avila, whose works constitute one of the most moving depictions of inner spirituality of the sixteenth century, probably never heard of Sextus Empiricus, but the skeptical and apophatic movements converged in her world. Although Christian skepticism and apophaticism were surely not the only philosophical and theological approaches to influence Teresa, circumspection with regard to the intellect and the senses are key elements in Teresian spirituality. Carol Lee Flinders suggests that *conversos* may have been drawn toward mental prayer because they felt more comfortable in the "church within a church" of the soul than in an institution centered on ritual and run by priests (168). Of *converso* background—as were Vives, Montaigne, Sanches, and many proponents of the *devotio moderna* (all of whom were adamant about their orthodoxy)—Teresa ultimately finds in the anti-intellectualism of Christian skepticism and apophatic spirituality a weapon against the learned men of the ecclesiastical hierarchy.

It is unlikely that Teresa read Erasmus, although Marcel Bataillon places her among his spiritual heirs. Rather than a conscious skeptic—one who, like Montaigne or Sanches, uses skeptical argumentation in a conscious and deliberate way—Teresa appropriates the language and rhetorical devices of skepticism to cast doubt on the efficacy of reason and the senses. Joan Cammarata has referred to Teresa's discourse as a *retórica de la incertidumbre* [rhetoric of incertitude] that avoids claims to knowledge and renders all assertions as opinions. Many critics have seen Teresa's use of expressions such as *paréceme, podrá ser, será así* [it seems to me, it could be, it might be so] as a strategy against Church authorities who suspected her of heresy (Flasche, Weber, Ahlgren, Cammarata, Slade). Cammarata points out that in conjunction with the *retórica de la incertidumbre,* Teresa uses a *retórica de la abyección* [rhetoric of abjection] by means of which she belittles her own intellectual capacity in order to appear less contumacious, insubordinate, and unorthodox to her accusers. Carole Slade shows that Teresa's writing follows the plan of the judicial confession, which was designed to elicit a self-condemnation on the part of the penitent, but that she undermines her own admission of guilt by inserting elements of the penitential confession, which was designed to elicit forgiveness; thus, Teresa uses the rhetoric of incertitude and abjection to construct a "dialogized heteroglossia that disputes the condemnation inherent in judicial confession" (17). Although these critics are correct in asserting that Teresa's methods of discourse served her well in her efforts to fend off charges of unorthodoxy, we must remember that the language of incertitude and abjection were not her invention, although she clearly used them to her own advantage.

The rhetoric of incertitude reflects the basic premise of Christian skepticism and permeates the work of religious and secular writing alike. Likewise, the *retórica de la abyección* is common in the writing of the sixteenth century and not particular to Teresa. Since antiquity, rhetoricians stressed the importance of putting the audience in a favorable state of mind by affecting modesty. Orators routinely stressed their own inadequacy, their uneducated and rude speech, their artlessness, and their intellectual defects. The topos of *mediocritas,* derived from the Bible as well as from the classics, was common in writers from the Middle Ages into the Early Modern period (Curtius 83–85).

For Christian writers, the rhetoric of self-disparagement often reflected a sincere awareness of the individual's flaws and the evil in all human souls. As Carole Slade and others have pointed out, Teresa incorporates many elements of the autobiographical confession. She read Saint Augustine and identifies the

Confessions as one of her primary inspirations in her *Vida* [*Life*]. In Augustine's verbalization of the alterations of the inner self realized through introspection Teresa found a vehicle for the expression of her own sinfulness. Also of importance were Ignatius's *Spiritual Exercises,* which offer a meticulous method of self-examination through which one is forced to confront one's failings. Michel Foucault points out that in the sixteenth century the development of procedures of spiritual direction and examination of conscience, along with the refinement of a language of transgression, facilitated the verbalization of sin (119). This, asserts Georges Bataille, made it possible for mystics such as Saint Teresa to dismiss the physical sensations associated with ecstasy as not sexual and therefore not sinful, and so to give reign to their mystical flights (225).

In her battle to make herself understood and believed, Teresa, more often than her male contemporaries, identifies her flaws as intellectual. She refers to herself as an ignorant woman and disparages the cerebral capabilities of her sex. However, she often carries her laments even further, demeaning human intellect in general. For example, she begins her discussion of prayer in *Fundaciones* [*Foundations*] by asserting her own fallibility, then universalizing the notion of intellectual fallibility. In her hands, skepticism ultimately becomes a tactical weapon that allows her to undermine the ecclesiastical authority she claims to support.

Sextus argues in *Outlines of Pyrrhonism* that our perception of reality is necessarily distorted by our "constitutional peculiarities" (54), state of mind (wishes, fears), health, age, culture, place, et cetera (59), arguments repeated by all the major Renaissance apologists for skepticism. Similarly, Teresa adopts the skeptical premise that in worldly matters, knowledge is problematical because individuals' perception is necessarily colored by their motives and desires. A person's reason is easily clouded, she explains, by "bodily humors," such as melancholy. Once that occurs, the passions take over: "lo que más hace este humor es sujetar la razón, ésta oscura, ¿qué no harán nuestras pasiones?" (*Fundaciones* 96) [since this humor can subdue reason, what won't our passions do once reason is darkened?] (*Foundations* 134). When our reason has been impaired, explains Teresa, the Devil tempts and deceives us by playing on our emotions and making it difficult for us to discern the true from the false.

Teresa also adopts a skeptical position with regard to memory and imagination, both of which delude. She complains repeatedly about her own poor memory and asserts that both memory and *imaginación* [runaway thought] cloud human judgment by misrepresenting phenomena. Teresa often uses the expression *era imaginación* [it was an imagination] to refer to a malformation of fact. For example, she describes as an *imaginación* the obsession of a nun who thought she would die if she failed to take communion daily (*Fundaciones* 89).

Teresa's constant use of expressions such as *paréceme, puede que, a mi parecer* [it seems to me, it's possible that, in my opinion] is the bulwark of her skeptical discourse. However, they attest not only to her own uncertainty, but to the universal inadequacy of human intellect as well. Teresa asserts repeatedly that the mind is incapable of grasping God's workings: "Apenas deben llegar nuestros entendimientos, por agudos que fuesen, a comprenderla. . . . no hay para qué nos cansar en querer entender" (*Moradas* 838) [(H)owever acute our intellects may be, they will no more be able to attain to a comprehension of this than to an understanding of God. . . . there is no point in our fatiguing ourselves by attempting to comprehend] (*Interior Castle* 29). In describing spiritual experiences, Teresa rarely affirms that a particular event happened, but describes instead *what seemed* to have happened. She often uses expressions to describe visions such as *se me representó* [it appeared to me]—precisely the same kind of language that Miguel de Cervantes uses to describe Don Quijote's fantasies. By using such language, Teresa, like Cervantes, takes her narratives out of the realm of objective reality and creates a deliberate ambiguity. She repeatedly affirms that she relates events *as she experienced them* and invites her confessors to judge their authenticity for themselves, since she, an ignorant woman, cannot.

In *Moradas* Teresa describes the stages of the soul's journey to God as a process of interiorization that consists of definite stages. Teresa envisions the soul as a castle made of diamond or the purest crystal that consists of seven mansions, each of which contains many rooms. The castle is perfectly circular, which, as John Welch has pointed out, is significant because the circle is a Jungian symbol of "self" (35–36).[6] In the center of the castle resides the King—God—to whom the spiritual path leads. The goal is to travel through the rooms until reaching the innermost chamber, where perfect union or the "mystical marriage" can take place. However, the journey is difficult and perilous. Outside the castle live insects and serpents, the impediments (distractions, enticements) to a successful journey. Some of these make their way into the outer rooms and attempt to prevent our progress. The "serpents within" (fear, anger, jealousy, et cetera) are more numerous in the outer rooms, in which we are still strongly attached to the outside world, but sometimes make their way into the inner mansions, where they haunt us even as we approach our goal.

During the first phase, imaged in the first three mansions of the "interior castle," the traveler struggles. The initial—or "meditative"—stages require a conscious effort to detach oneself from the outside world; this one accomplishes through reading, praying, listening to sermons, conversing with spiritual people, or reflecting on religious images. That is, the intellect is active, although not always fully effective, for as one attempts to direct one's attention to God, distractions (random thoughts, sensorial stimuli, worldly matters) constantly threaten to drag one backward. It is only through God's loving grace that the traveler manages to struggle onward. The fourth mansion is transitional. There, the traveler begins to relinquish the active role and enter the state of recollection. In the last three—or "contemplative"—stages, the traveler surrenders to God and is carried forward by God's will. Visions or raptures—signs that one is no longer in control of one's faculties—sometimes characterize these stages.

In *Vida* Teresa describes the same phenomena using different images. Here, she compares the soul to a garden that must be carefully tended so that it can flower and bear fruit. In the initial stages the gardener must weed and fertilize diligently, images that suggest the intense soul-searching, praying, and other active steps one must take in order to enter into the spiritual life. Watering the garden requires that the gardener bring water up from a well, a task that requires intensive manual labor. But as one matures spiritually, the watering process becomes easier and easier, until it is taken over entirely by God, who sends down a nourishing rain.

In both books Teresa maintains that in spite of our limitations, we can labor to prepare our souls for God's grace. Although the activities of the meditative stage require use of the intellect, it is not through the intellect that we attain truth. In the early stages of prayer, cerebral activities can stimulate religious experience; thus, for beginners, reading can lead to spiritual advancement, not because it imparts any real knowledge, but because it acts as fertilizer for the garden that is the soul. Yet, Teresa explains, any benefits she derived from reading Saint Augustine's *Confessions,* for example, came not from her own intellective efforts, but from God, who appreciated her efforts and rewarded her (*Vida* 181; *Life* 69). In this sense, her readings brought her closer to God, although her understanding was unable to grasp the reality of God's love until she had fully experienced it (*Vida* 181; *Life* 69). Teresa does not discount the intellect altogether, but asserts that true knowledge requires divine enlightenment. Without it, reading and other intellectual activities bear no fruit: "Hartos años estuve yo que leía muchas cosas y no entendía nada de ellas. . . . Cuando Su Majestad quiere, en un punto lo enseña todo, de manera que yo me espanto" (*Vida* 204) [For many years I read a great deal, and understood nothing. . . . When His Majesty wishes, he teaches us everything in a moment in the most amazing way] (*Life* 86).

Once God produces the spark—*la centillita*—thereby initiating the process, the faculties become a hindrance. The soul must retreat into silence in order to lay itself open to the divine presence. It must block out the noise, which distracts and obstructs. Teresa defines "noise" as the clamor of the intellect, which wants to thank God for these mercies, "ordenar pláticas y buscar razones" (*Vida* 227) [to compose speeches and draw up arguments] (*Life* 107).[7] But the noise of the intellect stirs up the memory and the imagination, thereby preventing recollection.

The learned are less likely to experience the divine presence than simpler people, argues Teresa, because they tend to intellectualize, to apply passages from Scripture, to explicate and debate. By engaging the understanding, they thwart the surrender of the will. Any consolations that come from the understanding are like water running over the ground, she explains. They cannot be drunk from the source, and they are full of impurities (*Camino* 722; *Way of Perfection* 139). To arrive at the highest state of prayer, individuals must empty their minds to make way for God's saving power. True wisdom is to understand—to the extent that humans can understand anything—that "todo es no saber nada" (*Camino* 736) [to know nothing is everything] (*Way of Perfection* 160). The learned employ their intellects propitiously for preaching and scholarship, but in prayer, "quédense las letras a un cabo" (*Vida* 228) [learning should be put on one side] (*Life* 107–8). Teresa encapsulates this idea in one of her best-known maxims: "[E]l aprovechamiento del alma no está en pensar mucho, sino en amar mucho" (*Fundaciones* 76) [(T)he soul's progress does not lie in thinking much but in loving much] (*Foundations* 117).

Like the classical and Christian skeptics, Teresa argues that experience, intuition, and tradition are better guides than the intellect. While Teresa insists on her intellectual limitations and lack of learning, she nevertheless asserts her authority by affirming her own experience not only in spiritual but also practical matters. Certainly, *Fundaciones* portrays a woman of extraordinary business acumen, administrative talent, political savvy, and psychological penetration—all of which Teresa acquired, she insists, through experience (*Fundaciones* 167; *Foundations* 195). Although experience usually collaborates with intellect to impose common sense, human reason is so fragile that any fixation, preoccupation, or passion can confound it. Teresa offers the example of a nun who was intelligent, yet carried her vow of obedience to such an extreme that when she, Teresa, gave her a rotten cucumber and told her to plant it, the woman—instead of using her experience and reason to figure out the vegetable would dry up if put under the ground—asked her if she wanted it sown upright or horizontally!

Like Sextus and Montaigne, Teresa asserts that reason cannot be trusted because disease can incapacitate it. In her discussion of melancholia in *Fundaciones* she identifies unreasonableness as the disorder's primary symptom. The best cure is busyness. Melancholic women must be kept occupied to prevent their minds from wandering, argues Teresa. Otherwise, they will give free reign to the imagination and do themselves great harm (*Fundaciones* 99; *Foundations* 138).

Both classical and Christian skepticism argue that individuals necessarily judge from their own perspectives, so that two people examining the same situation may arrive at radically different conclusions. Likewise, Teresa, recognizing the inevitable diversity of opinion, often considers her adversaries' views and sometimes admits that they may be right (*Vida* 392; *Life* 241). However, because she believes human judgment to be flawed, she tends to disregard others' opinions and look to God for guidance. And once she has made her decision, she is usually able to find allies in the Church hierarchy![8]

The unreliability of the senses is the skeptics' key argument. Since the intellect acts on information conveyed by senses, the defective nature of sensory perception leads necessarily to faulty judgments: "If the senses do not apprehend external objects, the intellect cannot apprehend them either" (Sextus 59). Regarding the senses, Montaigne writes that "ausquels gist le plus grand fondement et preuve de nostre ignorance" ("Apologie" 252) [they are the proof as well as the main foundation of our ignorance] (*Apology* 170). Although Teresa does not deny outright the trustworthiness of the senses, she cautions against them. She notes that if she were blind or in the darkness, she would be less readily able to identify a person than if she could actually see him. On the other hand, when one perceives an object with the physical eyes, one often wonders whether one has actually seen it or just imagined it (*Vida* 327; *Life* 229). Teresa views the physical senses as guides rather than conveyors of Truth. She distinguishes between them and the spiritual or supernatural senses, which transmit Truth unerringly.

Apophaticism coincides with Christian skepticism in its view that the physical senses distance Man from Truth. For the apophatic, the physical senses distract, while for the skeptic, they misrepresent. Teresa integrates these two concepts when she describes the physical senses as the handmaidens of the intellect that convey information to the mind, which the understanding then interprets. In *Moradas* she calls the senses servants who live in the first mansion—the one farthest from the divine presence enshrined in the core of the soul—whose task it is to mediate with the outside world. The senses, which receive information from the external world—the world of appearances— constitute a danger because they can sway the will inappropriately. As one penetrates the interior castle through meditation and prayer, one leaves behind these minions and approaches the King.

Apophaticism creates a dualism between intellect/sense and spirit that requires that the former be deadened in order for the mystic union to take place. Teresa repeatedly warns against the distracting power of the senses, which must be benumbed for spiritual progress to be made. Enticed herself by the sensorial world as a young girl (*Vida* 124; *Life* 165), she is aware of the senses' ability to distort reality and elicit injurious thoughts, thereby obscuring Truth. She stresses that spiritual novices must learn the art of recollection—an inward focus on the presence of God that requires withdrawing attention from the external world perceived through the senses. In *Moradas* Teresa compares the soul with a sea urchin or a turtle, animals that retract into their shells. These images connote retreat, interiority, shutting out.

This concept of spirituality, fundamental to the *devotio moderna* and to apophaticism in general, gives rise to a contradiction with the notion, basic to Christianity, of divine revelation through sensation, for at the heart of the New Testament is the appearance of God's self-revelation in the humanly visible form of Christ. Through Christ, the divine (by definition, nonsensate) becomes knowable by means of evidence mediated by the senses (Fields 227). Teresa clearly felt the need to conciliate the apophatic and kataphatic (image-driven) approaches to spirituality. In chapter 22 of *Vida* she censures those who reject Christ's humanity as revealed through the senses. She then goes on to describe the importance that paintings, corporeal visions, and imaginative visions have played in her own spiritual development. She explains, however, that representations of Christ are not the same as other images perceived by the physical senses, since the revealed Christ cannot be conceived of in the same way as other corporeal things. With regard to visions, she argues that these are not seen with the physical eyes, but in ways that transcend the corporeal.

Teresa seems to advance and retreat constantly, first asserting the *realness* of her visions, then arguing that she has not actually seen them. The constant backtracking and revising in Teresa's discussion of visions may stem, at least in part, from her discomfort with the inconsistencies of her position on the senses. Her tendency to restate, clarify, and explain evinces a struggle not only with the yearning to express the inexpressible, but also with the desire to reconcile contradictory concepts of the validity of sensory perception. Expressions such as *por mijor decir, eso debe ser, paréceme* [rather, it must be, it seems to me] suggest that Teresa is rethinking the issue as she writes.

Teresa classifies visions according to how they are perceived: *visiones corpóreas* [corporeal visions], images distinguished with the eyes; *visiones imaginarias* [imaginary visions], images seen in the mind or fantasy; and *visiones intelectuales* [intellectual visions], images perceived, but not with the eyes. In chapter 27 of *Vida*, she describes an intellectual vision of Christ at her side: "[V]i cabe mí, u sentí, por mijor decir, que con los ojos del cuerpo ni del alma no vi nada, mas parecióme estaba junto cabe mí Cristo y vía ser Él el que me hablaba, a mi parecer" (*Vida* 325) [I saw Christ at my side—or, to put it better, I was conscious of Him, for I saw nothing with the eyes of the body or with the eyes of the soul. He seemed quite close to me, and I saw that it was He. As I thought (to me it seemed), He was speaking to me] (*Life* 187–88). Teresa insists not only on the authenticity of this vision, but also on its incorporeal, insensate nature: "Parecíame andar siempre al lado Jesucristo; y como no era visión imaginaria, no vía en qué forma; mas estar siempre al lado derecho, sentíalo muy claro" (*Vida* 325) [All the time Jesus Christ seemed to be at my side, but as this was not an imaginary vision I could not see in what form. But I most clearly felt that He was all the time on my right] (*Life* 188). The senses with which she "sees" this vision transcend those of the body:

[Mi confesor] preguntóme en qué forma le vía. Yo le dije que no le vía. Díjome que cómo sabía yo que era Cristo. Yo le dije que no sabía cómo, mas que no podía dejar de entender que estaba cabe mí y le vía claro y sentía, y que el recogimiento del alma era muy mayor, en oración de quietud y muy continua, y los efetos que eran muy otros que solía tener, y que era cosa muy clara. (*Vida* 326)

[(My confesor) asked me in what form I had seen Him, and I replied that I had not seen Him. He asked me how I knew it was Christ, and I replied that I did not know how, but that I could not help being aware that He was beside me, that I had plainly seen and felt it, and that when

I prayed my soul was now much more deeply and continuously recol-
lected. I said that the effects of my prayer were quite different from those
I had experienced hitherto, and that this was perfectly evident to me].
(*Life* 188)

In perfect recollection, with the senses and intellect benumbed, Teresa experiences a vision that transcends the sensory, but that she can describe only
through sensorial terms. First she calls it a vision, then insists, *no es visión*
(*Vida* 327) [it's not a vision] (*Life* 189). Neither is it simply a feeling: "No es
como una presencia de Dios que se siente muchas veces" (*Vida* 327) [It is not
like the presence of God, which is often experienced] (*Life* 189). This kind of
experience—unlike the image-based visions Teresa describes elsewhere—impresses one with an acute awareness of God's favor. In the physical world, one
sometimes doubts one's own eyes, she explains, but the intellectual vision is so
powerful that it leaves no room for doubt. Likewise, when God speaks to the
soul through that language that bypasses the senses, *la habla sin hablar* (*Vida*
189) [speech without speaking] (*Life* 68), reaching it not through pictures or
words, *sin imagen ni forma de palabras* (*Vida* 190) [without image or words]
(*Life* 68), but through an intellectual vision, the soul understands great truths
and mysteries in a way that surpasses purely human means. Thus, the further
away one leaves the senses, the closer one comes to Truth.

Numerous critics have commented on the profusion of metaphors that
enrich Teresa's writing. Elizabeth Teresa Howe has studied the wealth and
complexity of her metaphors, which are taken from flora, fauna, warfare,
games, hunting, the elements, the human body, the social body, and everyday
activities. Certainly, this abundance of metaphors is a testimony to Saint
Teresa's struggle to bridge the abyss between experience and utterance, but it
is also something more.

The goal of mystical writing is not really to make the reader "understand"
the mystical experience, since the soul's union with God defies understanding and, therefore, verbal description. This notion seems incongruous with
Teresa's stated pedagogical intent. After all, language is the fundamental tool of
teaching. However, as Steven T. Katz explains, mystical pedagogy uses language not to communicate information, but to revolutionize the disciple's
consciousness (6). The chanted "nonsense" syllables or mantras that are fundamental to many Oriental meditative techniques have the purpose of causing
practitioners to break free and transcend "the regulative categories of knowing" (6). This opens them up to "new forms of awareness" that are conducive
to, and permit a more intense awareness of the divine. Teresa accomplishes

something similar by using language in such a way that it often overwhelms and confuses. By amassing unrelated and sometimes contradictory metaphors, she overburdens the mind and causes an erosion of logical connections that in effect deconstruct all rational notions of God.

Much has been made of the spontaneity of Teresa's writing. Víctor García de la Concha shows how Teresa casually combines diverse narrative forms and imbues her text with the energy and the unpremeditated quality of spoken language. Elias Rivers writes: "She seems to have wanted to transcribe her experiences as directly as possible into the Spanish sounds and the rapid, but irregular, flow of speech that an intelligent woman would come out with spontaneously, with no thought of constructing a well-written text" (121). Teresa's chaotic style has the effect of shocking and shattering and deconstructing what Katz calls the "standard epistemic security of 'disciples'" (7). In mystical writing, language thus becomes part of the process by which mystical knowing becomes possible.

In addition to instructional, much of Teresa's work is confessional or explanatory, composed at the command of confessors and spiritual directors for the purpose of clearing her of suspicions of unorthodoxy. Throughout her writing Teresa lauds obedience as the most perfect virtue, and she does, in fact, acquiesce constantly to her superiors' directives. However, for Saint Teresa, as for Saint Ignatius, obedience signified mastery of the ego rather than servile submission to authority. If Teresa obeyed the command to write, she did so without compromising her convictions.

Judicial confession, as Carole Slade has stressed, is a highly conventionalized sphere of written language designed to lead to self-incrimination, but Teresa undermines the genre by introducing elements of penitential confession, which serve to soften and contradict potentially ruinous evidence (13). However, the chaotic, antirational language of mysticism is not necessarily an effective tool for this purpose. Teresa's spiritual directors and confessors have commanded her to *explain* and *describe* her spirituality, and so she has recourse to the one thing that her interrogators cannot question: her own experience. Frustrated by her inability to elucidate that which cannot be subjected to rational explanation, she appeals repeatedly to the validity of knowledge acquired experientially. Only those who have had the experience will understand, she explains, with the unarticulated corollary that those who have not had such an experience will not understand (*Vida* 323; *Life* 186).

As Alison Weber, Joan Cammarata, and Gillian Ahlgren have shown, by adopting a posture of humility, Teresa was able to diminish the perception that she represented a threat to the authority of the ecclesiastical hierarchy. The rhetoric of self-deprecation, through which Teresa belittled her lack of erudition, became part of her defensive strategy. Teresa cleverly subverts her expression of modesty by ranking experience over intellect and erudition. She suggests that, while it is true she has no learning, true knowledge derives not from information conveyed through words, but from personal experience. With respect to her own reading, she says: "Aunque he leído muchos libros espirituales . . . decláranse muy poco, y si no es alma muy ejercitada, aun declarándose mucho, terná harto que hacer en entenderse" (*Vida* 220) [Even though I had read many spiritual books . . . if the soul has not a great deal of experience, it will have as much as it can do to understand its state, however much they (the books) say] (*Life* 100). That is, Teresa not only discredits her own book learning, but also that of the *letrados* [men of letters] she claims to hold in high regard: "[S]i no tiene experiencia de estas cosas, por letrado que sea, no bastará para entenderlo" (*Fundaciones* 104) [If he doesn't have experience of these things, his learning however great will not suffice for him to understand them] (*Foundations* 142). Thus, Teresa reinforces her own position and even discreetly sets herself above those who judge her. By arguing that men should not feel disgraced because they cannot understand what only *otro mayor Señor* [another greater Lord] can impart, she allows her detractors to save face (since they can hardly expect to compete with God!) while forcing *them* into a position of humility. Furthermore, by maintaining that the *letrado* should not feel mortified that "hace el Señor en esta ciencia a una viejecita más sabia" (*Vida* 408) [the Lord is perhaps giving to some little old woman a deeper knowledge of this science than to himself] (*Life* 254), she attacks from a position of modesty.

This is precisely the approach she takes in her discussion of an unidentified priest, *persona muy principal* [a very important person], probably Father García de Toledo, in chapter 34 of *Vida*, in which she criticizes clerics who presume to understand spirituality without themselves being spiritual, simply because they have studied. She explains how she herself guides this learned man, convincing him to adopt an attitude of humility rather than to attempt to understand what is beyond him. She asserts her authority over him by asseverating the supremacy of Knowledge received through divine enlightenment over knowledge received from letters, that is, words. Yet, by relying so heavily on personal experience, Teresa was taking a risk, as Ahlgren shows, because by the second half of the sixteenth century experiential authority was rapidly eroding within the Church (67). In order to present herself in a nonthreatening way, Teresa adopts a strategy of subordination. She could then affirm herself as an intercessor before God (Ahlgren 68).

One means Teresa used to carry out this strategy of subordination was to second the Church's skeptical position with respect to visions, voices, and other such divine intervention while defining herself as a recipient of God's grace rather than as an active participant in the spiritual encounter. In a period in which convents were full of women claiming to have had supernatural experiences, Teresa had to be cautious about appearing to give credence to phenomena expressly discredited by the Church. In *Fundaciones* she warns against nuns starving or abusing themselves, thereby inducing spurious mystical experiences. She notes that inexperienced persons who lack the proper criteria for judgment readily allow their imaginations to invent counterfeit visions: "[E]s posible que . . . les parezca que ven lo que no ven" (104) [(I)t is possible for such persons to think that they see what they do not see] (*Foundations* 141). By recognizing that those susceptible to suggestion often "see what they don't see," Teresa uses skeptical arguments to situate herself within Church orthodoxy.

But Teresa adopts a skeptical position not only toward visions in general, but also toward her own in particular. Having asserted her authority based on personal experience, she subjects that experience to scrutiny. Referring to her visions, she repeatedly interjects a note of caution: "Ya puede ser yo sea la engañada; mas diré lo que me acaeció" (*Vida* 284) [Of course, it may be I who am mistaken—but I will describe what happened to me] (*Life* 134); "no sé si sé lo que me digo" (*Camino* 680) [I'm not sure if I know what I'm talking about] (*Way of Perfection* 67); "ni creo sé cuál es espiritual, ni cuándo se mezcla sensual, ni sé cómo me pongo a hablar en ello" (*Camino* 680) [I am not sure that I know when (love) is spiritual and when there is sensuality mingled with it, or how to begin speaking about it] (*Way of Perfection* 68). Teresa asserts that she is not truly qualified to evaluate her own experiences and therefore will leave judgment to the Church. Her skeptical stance anticipates and quells criticisms by showing her to be duly humble and as orthodox as the investigating officials. At the same time, she insists that her visions must come from God because she lacks the intellectual and imaginative wherewithal to invent them.

Christian skepticism provided a method of argumentation appropriate for the defense of contemplative spirituality and apophatic mysticism through its repudiation of reason and the senses as sources of true knowledge. Saint Teresa uses skeptical arguments—albeit unsystematically and fortuitously—to call into question the wisdom of her superiors by challenging the efficacy of the faculties. In her hands, skepticism became an arm against the *letrados* whose exalted intellectualism she strives to undermine. Skepticism nourished the Catholic reform, providing spiritual leaders such as Teresa de Avila with an efficacious tool with which to defend their spirituality against a stultifying mind-set within the Church.

Notes

1. Renaissance Neoplatonists were suspect in large part because they preached a spirituality that bypassed ecclesiastic intermediaries and the rational process. Commencing from the Platonic premise that all that exists in the world is a simulacrum of a supreme Idea, the Neoplatonist seeks the divine through the contemplation of physical beauty and esthetic harmony, which are reflections of absolute Beauty and Harmony—that is, God.

2. A term applied to Catholics of Jewish origin.

3. Like Erasmus, Maldonado was a fierce opponent of Scholasticism; his methods focused on meditations on Scripture, the writings of the Church Fathers and the councils, canon law, ecclesiastical history, and, in the humanistic tradition, the study of languages (Prat 171).

4. With the advent of scientific rationalism in the early seventeenth century, Jesuits frequently had recourse to skeptical arguments to oppose scientists' claims to knowledge. Jesuits were among the most vociferous and influential of Galileo's opponents, for example (Sobel 191). Their arguments rested on the premise that outside of Doctrine, everything is mere opinion, a position that astronomers such as Galileo, who based their scientific beliefs on observation, could not accept. See Sobel 250, 254, 263.

5. Limbrick points out that there is no concrete evidence of Sanches's Jewish background. She also notes that although he was called *le grand Pyrrhonien* [the great Pyrrhonist] his position was actually closer to that of the Academic Skeptics than to Pyrrho's (5).

6. Welch, in his Jungian analysis of *Moradas,* sees the castle as a mandala figure, a circular symbol of the self in which the conscious and the unconscious are integrated. The journey into the castle is therefore a journey into the self that permits the individual to get in touch with his or her innermost depths.

7. The English citations of Teresa's *Life* are taken from Cohen's translation; Kavanaugh's translation was also consulted.

8. St. Ignatius expresses a similar view in his letter to Francisco de Borja, who was being considered for cardinal. Ignatius says that he has decided to oppose the election of Borja, but that if Borja is elected he will support him. Others may see Borja's candidacy differently than he does, Ignatius says, because the same Good Spirit can move people to see things in different ways.

Works Cited

Ahlgren, Gillian T. W. *Teresa de Avila and the Politics of Sanctity.* Ithaca: Cornell University Press, 1996.

Bataille, Georges. *Erotisme: Death and Sensuality.* Trans. Mary Dalwood. San Francisco: City Lights, 1986.

Bataillon, Marcel. *Erasmo y España.* Trans. Antonio Alatorre. Mexico: Fondo de Cultura Económica, 1950. [*Erasme et l'Espagne,* 1937].

Cammarata, Joan. "El discurso femenino de santa Teresa de Ávila, defensora de la mujer renacentista." *Actas Irvine–'92. Asociación Internacional de Hispanistas. II: La mujer y su representación en las literaturas hispánicas.* Ed. Juan Villegas. Irvine: University of California, 1994. 2:58–65.

Copenhaver, Brian P. "Doubt and Innovation." *The Columbia History of Western Philosophy: The Renaissance.* New York: Columbia University Press, 1999. 315–27.

Copleston, Frederick, S.J. *A History of Philosophy: Vol. 2., Part I.* Garden City, N.Y.: Image, 1962.

Curtius, Ernst Robert. *European Literature and the Latin Middle Ages.* New York: Harper and Row, 1963.

Erasmus, Desiderius. *Concerning the Immense Mercy of God. The Essential Erasmus.* Trans. John P. Dolan. New York: New American Library, 1964. 226–70.

———. *An Inquiry Concerning Faith: The Essential Erasmus.* Trans. John P. Dolan. New York: New American Library, 1964. 205–21.

Erasmus, Desiderius, and Martin Luther. *Discourse on Free Will.* Trans. Ernst F. Winter. New York: Continuum, 1997. (Includes Erasmus's *The Free Will* and Luther's *The Bondage of the Will.*)

Fields, Stephen, S.J. "Balthasar and Rahner on the Spiritual Senses." *Theological Studies* 57 (1996): 224–41.

Flasche, Hans. "El problema de la certeza en el *Castillo interior.*" *Congreso Internacional Teresiano: 4–7 octubre, 1982.* Ed. Teófanes Egido Martínez, et al. Salamanca: Universidad de Salamanca, 1983. 2:447–58.

Flinders, Carol Lee. *Enduring Grace: Living Portraits of Seven Women Mystics.* New York: HarperCollins, 1993.

Foucault, Michel. *The History of Sexuality.* Trans. Robert Hurley. Vol. 1. New York: Vintage, 1990.

Hallie, Philip P. "A Polemical Introduction." *Selections from the Major Writings on Scepticism, Man and God.* By Sextus Empiricus. Trans. Sanford G. Etheridge. Indianapolis: Hackett, 1985.

Howe, Elizabeth Teresa. *Mystical Imagery: Santa Teresa de Jesús and San Juan de la Cruz.* New York: Lang, 1988.

Ihrie, Maureen. *Skepticism in Cervantes.* London: Tamesis, 1982.

Ignatius of Loyola. *Obras de san Ignacio de Loyola.* Ed. Ignacio Iparraguirre, S.J.,

Cándido de Dalmases, S.J., and Manuel Ruiz Jurado, S.J. Madrid: Biblioteca de Autores Cristianos, 1991.

———. *Personal Writings.* Trans. Joseph A. Munitiz and Philip Endean. London and New York: Penguin, 1996.

Katz, Steven T. "Mystical Speech and Mystical Meaning." *Mysticism and Language.* Ed. Steven T. Katz. Oxford: Oxford University Press, 1992. 3–41.

Limbrick, Elaine. Introduction. *That Nothing is Known.* By Francisco Sanches. Ed. Elaine Limbrick and Douglas F. S. Thomson. Cambridge: Cambridge University Press, 1988. 1–90.

Luther, Martin. *The Bondage of the Will.* Trans. Ernst F. Winter. New York: Continuum, 1997.

Montaigne, Michel de. "Apologie de Raimond Sebond." *Essais, Livre II.* Paris: Flammarion, 1979. 105–268.

———. *An Apology for Raymond Sebond.* Trans. M. A. Screech. London and New York: Penguin, 1993.

O'Malley, John W. *The First Jesuits.* Cambridge, Mass.: Harvard University Press, 1993.

Osuna, Francisco de. *The Third Spiritual Alphabet.* Trans. Mary E. Giles. New York: Paulist Press, 1981.

Penelhum, Terence. "Skepticism and Fideism." *The Skeptical Tradition.* Ed. Myles Burkyeat. Berkeley and Los Angeles: University of California Press, 1983. 287–318.

Popkin, Richard. *The History of Scepticism from Erasmus to Spinoza.* Berkeley and Los Angeles: University of California, 1979.

———. "The Sceptical Crisis." *The Columbia History of Western Philosophy: Seventeenth-Century Philosophy.* New York: Columbia University Press, 1999. 329–36.

Prat, J. M., S.J. *Maldonat et l'Université de Paris au XVIᵉ siècle.* Paris: Julien, Lanier et Cᵉ, 1856.

Rivers, Elias. "The Vernacular Mind of Saint Teresa." *Carmelite Studies* (Special issue: *Centenary of Saint Teresa*). Washington, D.C.: Institute of Carmelite Studies, 1984. 113–29.

Sanches, Francisco. *Que nada se sabe.* Madrid: Espasa-Calpe, 1972.

Schmitt, Paul. *La Réforme Catholique: Le Combat de Maldonat (1534–1583).* Paris: Beauchesne, 1985.

Screech, M. A. Introduction. *An Apology for Raymond Sebond.* By Michel de Montaigne. London and New York: Penguin, 1993.

Sextus Empiricus. *Selections from the Major Writings on Scepticism, Man and God.* Ed. Philip P. Hallie. Trans. Sanford G. Etheridge. Indianapolis: Hackett, 1985.

Slade, Carole. *St. Teresa de Avila: Author of a Heroic Life.* Berkeley and Los Angeles: University of California Press, 1995.

Sobel, Dava. *Galileo's Daughter.* New York: Walker, 1999.

Suárez, Francisco, S.J. *Disputaciones metafísicas.* Trans. Sergio Rábade Romeo, Salvador Caballero Sánchez, and Antonio Puigcerver Zanón. 7 vols. Madrid: Gredos, 1960.

Swietlicki (Connor), Catherine. *Spanish Christian Cabala.* Columbia: University of Missouri Press, 1986.

Teresa de Jesús. *The Book of Her Life. The Collected Works of St. Teresa of Avila.* Trans. by Kieran Kavanaugh, O.C.D., and Otilio Rodríguez, O.C.D. Vol. 1. Washington, D.C.: Institute of Carmelite Studies, 1987.

———. *Camino de perfección. Obra completa.* Ed. Enrique Llamas, et al. Madrid: Espiritualidad, 1994. 516–809.

———. *Castillo interior o las moradas. Obra completa.* Ed. Enrique Llamas, et al. Madrid: Espiritualidad, 1994. 829–997.

———. *The Foundations. The Collected Works of St. Teresa of Avila.* Trans. Kieran Kavanaugh, O.C.D., and Otilio Rodríguez, O.C.D. Vol. 2. Washington, D.C.: Institute of Carmelite Studies, 1985. 95–309.

———. *Interior Castle.* Trans. E. Allison Peers. New York: Image, 1989.

———. *Libro de las Fundaciones.* Ed. Víctor García de la Concha. Madrid: Austral/ Espasa-Calpe, 1991.

———. *Libro de la vida.* Ed. Dámaso Chicharro. Madrid: Cátedra, 1993.

———. *The Life of Saint Teresa by Herself.* Trans. J. M. Cohen. London and New York: Penguin, 1957.

———. *The Way of Perfection.* Trans. E. Allison Peers. New York: Image, 1991.

Vives, Juan Luis. *Tratado del alma. Obras filosóficas.* Trans. Lorenzo Riber. Madrid: Aguilar, 1948.

Weber, Alison. *Teresa de Avila and the Rhetoric of Femininity.* Princeton: Princeton University Press, 1990.

Welch, John, O. Carm. *Spiritual Pilgrims: Carl Jung and Teresa de Avila.* New York: Paulist Press, 1982.

Part II

✿

Appropriation and Authenticity
of Feminine Identity

4

The Price of Love

The Conflictive Economies of *La gitanilla*

William H. Clamurro

Throughout his fiction, Miguel de Cervantes's representations of women manifest far too much variety for neat generalizations. Women are often idealized to an improbable degree, and they also are sometimes portrayed as figures of low comedy and the grotesque.[1] But even limiting our view to the more idealized portrayals of the women found in the putatively serious, unironic tales of love, loss, trials, and restorations of the *Novelas ejemplares* [*Exemplary Novels*], there is a subtle and various range—in the development of the women as characters or in the manner of their description and of the events that they provoke or to which they fall victim—that reveals a larger system of social and material values. In the *Novelas ejemplares,* Cervantes's women are often objects of sincere and admirable amorous desire. They are at times (for a while, at least) surprisingly independent and strong. But they are also, first and last, objectified as both the social element of family continuity, honor, and possession and also as the markers of material value.

In effect, as each woman's story unfolds, the ways in which they are "valued" and the manner in which they act and are represented reveal much about the unideal, socially plausible, and patriarchal, orderly world within and beyond that of Cervantes's ostensible fictions. Although the "materialization" of the female is found, to a greater or lesser degree, in all of Cervantes's *Novelas ejemplares* where love is a factor, in *La gitanilla* [*The Little Gypsy Girl*] the material dimension is most pervasive and complex. The portrayal of the young gypsy girl as both the object and focus of attention and desire and also as the "medium" or negotiator between individuals, between separate and contending yet connected segments of society, and ideological values makes this text an especially telling object of reconsideration.

In *La gitanilla* the concept of romantic love seems to overwhelm for many critics the ability to read the unromantic irony of the story's materiality.[2] The obvious love interest and the familiar narrative pattern—the lost or stolen child who is ultimately found and restored, the episodes of disguising and adventure on the part of the male protagonist, and so on—all conspire to lead many readers to see the *novela* as an affirmative love story.[3] In at least one case (Forcione), the idealizing tendency of the reader prompts the conclusion that *La gitanilla* embodies the ideals of Christian marriage, as filtered through an Erasmian optic.[4] It would be perverse for me to deny that *La gitanilla* is a love story framed within a tale of loss and restoration. The *novela* does contain a narrative that expresses the "romance ideal" of the affirmation and redemption, of a microcosmic society first "disturbed" but finally restored and raised to a higher level of virtue. Indeed, the romance pattern is the core upon which Cervantes works his variations in this *novela* and also in *El amante liberal* [*The Generous Lover*], *La española inglesa* [*The English Spanish Girl*], and *La ilustre fregona* [*The Illustrious Kitchen-Maid*]. Something of this same romance tendency, with the disordered world being corrected and raised to a higher level of harmony, can also be dimly perceived (with some heavy forcing of the argument) in *La fuerza de la sangre* [*The Power of Blood*].[5] *La gitanilla* could thus be seen as a fitting introduction to the collection as a whole, or for much of it.

There is, however, something not quite right about a reading of *La gitanilla* that so heavily privileges love, loss, and recovery, and final, affirming restoration and resolution, at the expense of a more inclusive consideration of the evident undercurrents of the ironies of social class and ethnic difference, and the peculiar role of material and money in their many forms.[6] Noble sentiments are indeed present in the story. But there is also the complex interplay and development of individual identity and material wealth in its many dimensions, especially in the presentation of the female character. As always, we are dealing with what we could call the objectification of the woman. But most unusual and revealing is the manner in which Preciosa (who is clearly the central, unifying figure of the story) serves as both object of value and as negotiator or intermediary of values, desires, and sociocultural boundaries.

The heroine's name, Preciosa, with its rich overtones of the beautiful and the valuable, underscores the notion of value. Likewise, the verb *preciarse* (used in the sense of "to present, value, or pride oneself as" a certain sort of person) appears on a couple of key occasions in which the concept of identity is stressed.[7] Finally, the role of money, in its strategic entries into the story and its equally significant moments of absence, is central to both the action and the semiotic system of the text. What is the price of love in the Cervantine world? And what are the values, both ethical and material, that undergird this world? In Preciosa's initially independent, fluid, and negotiatory movement through both mainstream and marginalized social levels, and in her final restoration— or resignation—to her proper aristocratic identity, Cervantes gives us a hint of the complexity of such questions.

Initial and integral to the issue of money and how the characters are linked to money and other "objects of wealth," is the question of theft. The *novela* begins and ends with explicit articulations of this problem. For example, the gypsies, as introduced at the beginning, are defined as nothing more nor less than congenital thieves. Yet both the act of thievery and the general "lawlessness" that one would expect from such a group is curiously absent, not only from the central actions of the female protagonist, Preciosa, but also largely from those around her, at least insofar as the narrative presents it.[8] There is, however, an implicit "theft" with which the narrative (the extradiegetic story prior to the opening paragraph) begins: the theft of the beautiful young girl. Long before her true identity is revealed at the end of the story, the sensitive reader intuits that Preciosa has been "displaced" from her true world. The central problem of identity is thus implicitly framed as the result of an act of theft. Similarly, a crucial "theft" happens at the end of the story, an incident that concerns material but that is not in fact a theft: I refer to the frame-up perpetrated by the rejected Juana Carducha, when she plants her own jewels in Andrés's saddlebags.[9] The initial theft—the kidnapping of Preciosa—deprives the girl of her true identity, or rather, it allows her to exist or operate within another identity, one that in many ways seems more authentic in terms of her self-expression than the one to which she will return. By contrast, the trumped-up theft near the end of the story prompts the crisis that reveals the true identity of the nongypsy, Andrés Caballero, as Don Juan de Cárcamo. Under the relevant yet richly ambiguous and sometimes misleading sign of theft, *La gitanilla* begins and ends with a complex ensemble of ironies and dissonant reversals of conventional expectation.

La gitanilla is less a story about theft, however, than it is a subtle narrative system that deals with seemingly antagonistic "economies" that finally prove to be troublingly related. For, while theft is a crucial structural element of the text, it is only one of the many ways in which Cervantes develops and utilizes money and material wealth in this *novela*. Money, both as fact—and especially in its form as coinage—and metaphor pervades the story, in language, gesture, and plot. Love (both the higher, ideal sentiment, and the "process" of court-ship) itself is not exempt from the swirl of terms denoting material value and exchange. If language is a medium of exchange, is not money (coinage, a prime example of objects whose primary function is exchange and representation of material value) also a language? From the perspective of the ideal, love is sup-posed to transcend such base, material concerns; and in Cervantes's world it would appear to. But love and the overcoming of all obstacles to the lovers' union always occurs within an implicitly privileged world—a world of the aristocracy and/or of the wealthier (merchant) classes.[10] In *La gitanilla*, the question of wealth has been settled, implicitly and in an a priori manner. Cer-vantes's virtuous and admirable, sincere lovers are always endowed with much more than (mere) physical beauty and metaphysical, moral grace.

Yet before this ultimate reunion and replacement of Preciosa back into the social sphere of the aristocratic class from which she was stolen, the young girl, as the improbably beautiful and inexplicably mobile, autonomous gypsy, is able to act and interact as a voice and a presence that negotiates and judges. She views her own ostensibly gypsy world and is able to modify its harshest rules. Preciosa also enters the nongypsy, mainstream Spanish society and renders similar commentary. She even appears to debunk the poetic conventions and more romantic assumptions of love, or that view of love that would seem indifferent to wealth and social rank. For example, in a moment of apparent, out-of-character satire, Preciosa herself, in commenting upon one of the *paje-poeta*'s [page-poet] poems, says, with as much prescience as satire: "En *pobre* acaba el último verso.... ¡mala señal! Nunca los enamorados han de decir que son pobres, porque a los principios, a mi parecer, la pobreza es muy enemiga del amor" (1:76) ["The last verse ends in 'poor,'" Preciosa observed. "A bad sign! Lovers must never say they are poor, because at the outset, it seems to me, poverty is a great enemy of love"] (30). The final quatrain of the poem to which this statement refers reads as follows: "Preciosa joya de amor, / esto humil-demente escribe / el que por ti muere y vive, / pobre, aunque humilde amador" (1:76) [Jewel of love, my Precious one, / these lines are humbly penned for you, / by one whose love, though poor, is true; / who, humbly poor, loves you alone] (30).

At this moment in the *novela*, Preciosa is the witty, outspoken, free-spirited gypsy, and *not* (or not yet) the "constant," obedient, aristocratic woman Costanza.[11] Moreover, at this moment in the story, she is about to go from the place where the idle, wealthy gentlemen are gambling and where this poem is discovered by one of them, to the home of Doña Clara and the *teniente* [government official], where it will turn out that no one has any money to pay the gypsies for their palm reading (1:78). In this light, Preciosa's put-down could be seen as the sort of gratuitous satire that Cervantes allows this highly verbal, mobile woman—but only during the time prior to her restoration to her authentic aristocratic rank and identity. As she says to the *teniente*, when he too is unable to come up with payment, "Coheche vuesa merced, señor tiniente; coheche, tendrá dineros, y no haga usos nuevos, que morirá de hambre" (1:81) ["Take bribes, lieutenant, take bribes, and you'll have money, and don't try to change the customs or you'll die of hunger"].[12] The satiric point of this passage is both obvious and highly conventional, echoing the final words of condemnation of the court (and thus of government service, in general) spoken by the once again sane but rejected Tomás Rueda near the end of *El licenciado Vidriera* [*The Glass Graduate*].[13] Equally pertinent, however, is the simple but unremarked fact that this pair of lovers (like all the admirable lovers in Cervantes's stories) will indeed realize their united, family oriented love within that part of a harmonious world where wealth and material security accompany the aristocratic rank to which, in Cervantes's "romance" world, the beautiful and virtuous always ultimately belong and return.

Preciosa's not-really-gratuitous satiric remark about the incompatibility of love and poverty is also tied to a larger pattern of materialization. As the structure of the first line of the cited quatrain reminds us—"Preciosa joya de amor"—the woman is both "Preciosa, the jewel of love," and also that "precious jewel of love" that the woman traditionally is. Both from the conventional poetic perspective and given the exigencies of Cervantes's story, the young woman must to some extent fulfill her role as exemplar of beauty and as vessel of the honor (through chastity) that both determines the object of a suitor's desire and that, once attained through Christian marriage, becomes the symbol of family continuity and collective *honra* [honor]. The final lines of the *paje-poeta*'s poem are, of course, a curious and artificial pose. This is no impoverished poet, as we will find out. But even here, we are struck by this shadowy figure's strange and disconcerting tactic of slipping a gold coin into the folded paper on which he has written his "gift poem" to and about the gypsy girl. Preciosa accepts the coin the first time, but on a second occasion, she turns it down. Nowhere in the text is it stated, nor is it clear by implication, what is really intended by the *paje-poeta*, and his later confession that he was never in love with Preciosa does not help. What does emerge is a subtle and disturbing sense that it is appropriate for female beauty to be associated with and to attract the tokens of material wealth.

Returning to the moment in which the gold coin is discovered folded into the paper upon which the poem is written, we recall that Preciosa, unaware of its hidden content, has placed the paper into the bosom of her dress. The included coin is only revealed when one of the gambling *caballeros* [gentlemen] notices the paper and, unbidden and certainly unwelcomed, snatches it out of Preciosa's dress—in effect, reaching his impertinent hand into a zone where it has no business going and would not go if the *caballero* were dealing with a woman of his own "respectable class" (which, ironically, Preciosa *is*). We are here reminded that there are thresholds of freedom and familiarity that this self-possessed gypsy girl can transgress while she is living within this identity. But such zones are forbidden and impossible to the woman who (not only beautiful but also aristocratic) she is finally revealed to be. So, as the *paje-poeta*'s coin finds its way secretly into the woman's breast, it embodies its purpose as a token of love, a love later flatly denied by this same man. But this element of coins and bodies cannot avoid the suggestion of the exchange of love *for* money, the transactions of sex.[14]

The ambiguous implications of the *paje-poeta*'s money are reiterated later in the story when the youth reappears at the gypsy camp (1:108). When the suspicious and jealous Andrés takes Clemente aside and questions him about why he has left the city and seems to be fleeing, Andrés also asks about the fugitive's interest in Preciosa in a way that foregrounds the material dimension: "Si la quisiéredes por esposa, yo y todos sus parientes gustaremos dello; y si por amiga, no usaremos de ningún melindre, *con tal que tengáis dineros,* porque la codicia por jamás sale de nuestros ranchos" (1:113; my emphasis) [If you want her as your wife, I and all her family will be delighted, and if as a mistress, we shall make no fuss, provided you have money, for greed is never far from our camps] (63). Andrés feigns a certain indifference, but when the *paje* answers "Dinero traigo" (1:113) [I have money] (63), the narrator relays Andrés's thoughts as follows: "Este fue otro susto mortal que recibió Andrés, viendo que el traer tanto dinero no era sino para conquistar o *comprar* su prenda [Preciosa]" (1:113; my emphasis) [This was another mortal shock for Andrés, who saw all this money as being intended simply to conquer and purchase his prize] (64). In effect, the *paje* appears (to Andrés) to be doing exactly what the disguised nobleman himself had done in his first appearance in the story, the moment on the road when he backed up his declaration of love with a purse full of gold. Andrés's fear—that Clemente's money reflects a love interest (and the more money, the more intense the love)—is justified more by its recapitulation of his own tactic and mentality than it will prove to be by Clemente's later revealed, true motives.

Money in its role as language and intermediary between Preciosa and others is most significant in the case of her real suitor, Don Juan de Cárcamo. Here we find a curious and dissonant conflict of intention and expectation. Don Juan is unquestionably in love with Preciosa, enamored in the most authentic, chaste, generous, and self-sacrificing manner. Yet for this aristocratic youth, money also speaks loud and clear. The reader is struck by the man's first appearance, nearly a third of the way into the narrative. As the aristocratic Don Juan de Cárcamo that he is, he wants to make a striking first impression. He thus enters the story dressed in his finest attire, and the text gives special emphasis to the richness of the clothes and his gold-adorned sword and dagger, elements that symbolize his rank and underline personal, or at least *family,* wealth. Although too young (we presume) to have won on his own merits the title of a chivalric order, he stresses his belonging to this rank.[15] The youth declares his love and stresses his family's rank and wealth. Finally, he backs up the sincerity of his declaration by offering a considerable sum as a kind of "earnest money." As he states, "Cien escudos traigo aquí en oro para daros en arra y señal de lo que pienso daros; porque no ha de negar la hacienda el que da el alma" (1:84) [I have a hundred golden crowns here to give you as an earnest and indication of what I intend; because he who gives his soul won't withhold his property] (37). This offer occasions a small conflict between Preciosa and her gypsy grandmother. For, after Preciosa replies to Don Juan's declaration of love by imposing her own conditions of test and deferral, and after she stresses her sense of personal and sexual integrity in the conventional semimaterialized terms ("Una sola joya tengo, que la estimo en más que a la vida, que es la de mi entereza y virginidad, y no la tengo de vender a precio de promesas ni dádivas" [1:85] [Only one jewel I possess, and to me it is worth more than life itself; that jewel is my integrity and virginity, and I shall not sell it in exchange for promises or gifts, precisely because then it will be something you can get for money; and if it can be purchased it will be of very little value] [38]), when the young woman tries to reject the proffered earnest money (1:88), the *gitana vieja* [old gypsy] steps in and overrules the girl.

The old gypsy's arguments do not merely reflect greed and general material interest, but also include the rationale that for the gypsies, as a socially marginal and often oppressed group, money is a powerful defensive weapon in their often contentious interactions with the mainstream Spanish society. As she asserts, "Y si alguno de nuestros hijos, nietos o parientes cayere, por alguna desgracia, en manos de la justicia, ¿habrá favor tan bueno que llegue a la oreja del juez y del escribano como destos escudos, si llegan a sus bolsas?" (1:88) [And if any of our children, grandchildren or relations should fall, through some misfortune, into the hands of the law, can there be any better favour to reach the ear of the judge or notary than these crowns, if they get to their purses?] (41). Aside from the self-evident logic of this argument—along with yet another sly satiric reflection upon the importance of money and its influences, corrupting and otherwise, on the mainstream social structures—this passage foreshadows an important element of the story's conclusion. For, when Andrés Caballero the apparent gypsy is arrested for his impulsive killing of the insolent soldier, and even after he is revealed to be not the gypsy Andrés, but the nobleman Don Juan de Cárcamo, the family of the victim nonetheless needs to be "bought off." As the text so bluntly puts it, "Recibió el tío del muerto la promesa de dos mil ducados, que le hicieron por que bajase de la querella y perdonase a don Juan" (1:133) [The dead man's uncle received the promise of two thousand ducats which they gave him to make him withdraw his complaint and forgive Don Juan] (83). Thus we see once again manifested the pervasive power of money in and around the edges of the social, legal, and judicial processes, a power that is simultaneously plausible and coldly startling, given the putatively positive, romantic, and virtuous worldview that we would expect and that seems to prevail as the story concludes.

In Don Juan's first entry into the narrative, his money is welcome. Later, the cash that he keeps with him while masquerading as a gypsy allows him to buy things, on the sly, that he can claim to have stolen, thereby convincing the gypsies that he is doing his job while also protecting his aristocrat's virtue from the stain of crime. We might consider the whole underlying issue of "When is a crime *not* a crime, and why?" Is the fraudulent assertion that one has committed a theft perhaps not a transgression of another sort? The more important point, however, is that telling versions of materialism pervade all sectors of the respectable mainstream Spanish society as well as the supposedly lawless and parasitic realm of the gypsies and that money is most emphatically both a tool and a powerful, if ambiguous, language. We come to realize that Don Juan de Cárcamo and his family, their tactics and assumptions, are all of a piece with both the generosity of the idle gambling caballeros and the ironic lack of "available cash" in the home of Doña Clara and the *teniente*. Likewise, the firsthand knowledge of the *gitana vieja* concerning the usefulness of money in buying one's way out of legal trouble proves chillingly consistent with what the "good" aristocrats often do. We also recall Don Juan's remark early in the story that his own father is at the court soliciting a higher government position: "Mi padre está aquí en la Corte pretendiendo un cargo, y ya está consultado, y tiene casi ciertas esperanzas de salir con él" (1:84) [My father is here at court trying to secure an appointment, for which he has already been recommended, and which he is almost certain to get] (37).[16] Thus, in what seems a realistic yet only minor detail, it is again suggested that the young man and his family are more complex than our assumption of an aristocrat's high moral standard and solid wealth might imply. The Cárcamo family is nobility, but it too is, in its own way, parasitic.

Where then do we end up as this deceptively complex love story, which is also the problematic interaction of social groups and economies, comes to its happy end? Cervantes has portrayed the gypsies, and not just the exceptional Preciosa, and their marginal, thieving culture—or as we might now say, "lifestyle"—as not so much the hostile antagonists of a putatively law-abiding, mainstream Spanish society, but rather as a parasitic yet parallel world. Preciosa's complex gypsy realm is one that both shares and yet subtly critiques the assumptions and processes of respectable society. These parallel and connected economies allow a certain questioning of the accepted norm—something, I would argue, not consciously intended by the author.

The narrative use and the descriptive presentation of Preciosa as the self-possessed and free-spirited, mobile critic of both the gypsy world and the mainstream society is Cervantes's artifice for exploring the juxtaposition of their respective economies and values. Preciosa's temporary power is even more significant when we note how she falls silent and submits upon being recognized and restored to her rightful parents—how in that moment she becomes the "possession" of family and patriarchy. Similarly, Don Juan de Cárcamo, while ostensibly an admirable and virtuous figure, is a creature of his rank and wealth, as is graphically shown when the homicidal "gypsy" gets off the hook, merely by being unmasked as a nobleman and when family money can lubricate the mechanisms of reconciliation. *La gitanilla* suggests that, while love cannot be bought outright, neither can it prosper in a situation of misery and oppression. Preciosa herself states that "la pobresa es muy enemiga del amor" [poverty is a great enemy of love]. Likewise, the entirety of the *novela* illustrates in numerous ways—and on a level that is not so much below the obvious, conventional one of the love story, but rather that shadows and is integral to the ostensible main plot—the complexities of individual identity as it contends with one's social role and position.

Cervantes's creation of the female so often involves this improbable excursion of the woman armed with and armored by a resolute will and a surprising autonomy. Yet it is only a temporary freedom or mobility, and even at its greatest extent, during no moment of the adventure or excursion of feminine possibility is either the desired, principal woman or her noble male suitor—or any of those around them—free of the weight and pervasive implications of the power and burdens of material wealth. Ironically, in the creation of his most liberated and transcending heroine, Preciosa, Cervantes also creates his most penetrating, revealing window into the materially determined structures and dissonances of a larger society, one that reaches from the margins of the gypsy world to the seemingly virtuous and stable, aristocratic circle of Don Juan de Cárcamo and the restored Costanza.

Notes

1. One might propose a spectrum of types ranging from the grotesque of the witch Cañizares in the *Coloquio de los perros* [*The Dialogue of the Dogs*] or the comic Maritornes of the *Quijote*, to Sigismunda in the *Persiles*. On the more serious issue of what the female may have meant to Cervantes in and of itself and as a way of "knowing," see especially El Saffar's *Beyond Fiction*.

2. Notable readings that go against the grain of the idealizing tendency and that astutely examine the ironies of this *novela* include those by Gerli and ter Horst.

3. This view is shared by critics as diverse as Casalduero, El Saffar, and Forcione, among others; even the recent study by Zimic argues this interpretation without reservation.

4. See Forcione, especially "Cervantes's *La Gitanilla* as Erasmian Romance" (93–223).

5. The other notable "love story" type *novelas* of the collection—*El celoso extremeño* [*The Jealous Old Man from Extremadura*], *Las dos doncellas* [*The Two Damsels*], and *La señora Cornelia* [*Lady Cornelia*]—while clearly participating in this materialization of the female, represent special and dissident cases, as I have noted in my study, *Beneath the Fiction*.

6. A very incisive reading of the text from this perspective is found in Presberg.

7. See for example Don Juan's statements "porque me precio de decirla [verdad] en todo acontecimiento" (1:93) [because I pride myself on telling it come what may] (45) and "La palabra que yo doy en el campo, la cumpliré en la ciudad y adonde quiera, sin serme pedida, pues no se puede preciar de caballero quien toca en el vicio de mentiroso" (1:94) [The promise I gave you in the country, I shall fulfill in the city or anywhere else, without having to be asked; for one who is in any way untruthful cannot pride himself on being a gentleman] (46). All quotations of the text are from Sieber's edition and are identified by volume and page number; the English translations are taken from C. A. Jones's edition and are identified by page number.

8. The notion that the gypsy world is peculiarly "lawless" and "demonic" is

much stressed, perhaps over stressed, in Forcione's reading. I put it this way because it seems to me that the gypsy world is not so much lawless as it is ruled by contrary, conflictive laws of its own—some being of a seemingly idyllic, communitarian sort, and others clearly grim; see the exposition of the gypsy elder at Don Juan's initiation ceremony (1:100–103).

9. While this is done in order to prevent his leaving, it also represents an act of angry retaliation at the youth's rejection of her advances. In any case, the concept of a trumped-up theft has a symbolic appropriateness, given the masquerade essence of Don Juan/Andrés's actions and temporary existence in this gypsy world (1:123).

10. The slightly unconventional example of this cross of class lines, further complicated by a union across cultures or national identity, is given in *La española inglesa,* as I have noted in *Beneath the Fiction,* chapter 4.

11. It is worth noting that the true name of the ostensible gypsy Preciosa is Costanza, the same as the "ilustre fregona" [illustrious kitchen maid] in the *novela* of that name; the latter woman, however, is not so much "misplaced" as she is the temporarily abandoned, unacknowledged product of an act of sexual violence.

12. The rest of her comment is worth considering: "Mire, señora: por ahí he oído decir (y aunque moza, entiendo que no son buenos dichos) que de los oficios se ha de sacar dineros para pagar las condenaciones de las residencias y para pretender otros cargos" (1:81) [Look, my lady, I've heard it said round here (and although I'm young, I realize that it's not just a saying) that one has to extract money from one's office to make good the claims at the end of one's term of service and to secure new appointments] (35).

13. As Tomás states, "¡Oh Corte, que alargas las esperanzas de los atrevidos pretendientes y acortas las de los virtuosos encogidos, sustentas abundantemente a los truhanes desvergonzados y matas de hambre a los discretos vergonzosos!" (2:74) [Oh court, you who build up the hopes of bold office-seekers, and cut short those of them who are virtuous and bashful; who keep shameful rogues in prosperity and starve modest and discreet men to death] (146).

14. As I have noted, "Although . . . these generous gestures and the tokens involved (the coins) may be ideally both an intensifier and an objectification of their purer sentiments, the latent suggestion of the devaluing objectification of women and of the 'commerce' with them—prostitution—persists and works to undermine the idealism and simplicity of the message" (*Beneath the Fiction* 22).

15. As he states, "[S]oy caballero, como lo puede mostrar este hábito—y apartando el herreruelo, descubrió en el pecho uno de los más calificados que hay en España" (1:84) [I . . . am a gentleman, as this insignia will show—and unfastening his cloak he revealed on his breast one of the most distinguished in Spain] (37).

16. See especially Maravall.

Works Cited

Casalduero, Joaquín. *Sentido y forma de las "Novelas ejemplares."* Madrid: Gredos, 1974.

Cervantes, Miguel de. *Exemplary Stories.* Trans. C. A. Jones. Harmondsworth, England: Penguin, 1984.

———. *Novelas ejemplares.* Ed. Harry Sieber. 2 vols. Madrid: Cátedra, 1984.

Clamurro, William H. *Beneath the Fiction: The Contrary Worlds of Cervantes's "Novelas ejemplares."* New York: Peter Lang, 1997.

El Saffar, Ruth. *Beyond Fiction: The Recovery of the Feminine in the Novels of Cervantes.* Berkeley and Los Angeles: University of California Press, 1984.

———. *Novel to Romance: A Study of Cervantes's "Novelas ejemplares."* Baltimore: Johns Hopkins University Press, 1974.

Forcione, Alban K. *Cervantes and the Humanist Vision: A Study of Four Exemplary Novels.* Princeton: Princeton University Press, 1982.

Gerli, E. Michael. "Idealism and Irony in *La gitanilla.*" *Cervantes* 6.1 (1986): 29–38.

Maravall, José Antonio. *Poder, honor y élites en el siglo XVII.* Madrid: Siglo XXI, 1979.

Presberg, Charles D. "Precious Exchanges: The Poetics of Desire, Power, and Reciprocity in Cervantes's *La gitanilla.*" *Cervantes* 18.2 (1998): 53–73.

ter Horst, Robert. "Une Saison en enfer: *La gitanilla.*" *Cervantes* 5.1 (1985): 87–127.

Zimic, Stanislav. *Las "Novelas ejemplares" de Cervantes.* Madrid: Siglo XXI, 1996.

5

The Problematics of Gender/Genre
in *Vida i sucesos de la monja alférez*

Rainer H. Goetz

In the Hispanic world of the seventeenth century, at a time when women were commonly excluded from public life and its representations, Catalina de Erauso, nicknamed "la monja alférez" [Lieutenant Nun], gained widespread recognition after it became known that she had run away from a convent and spent twenty years living as a man. Her secret may have remained undiscovered, had she not revealed herself to the Bishop of Guamanga, who brought the story to light. The news of the real identity of the woman soldier spread rapidly and Erauso became a local and regional celebrity. The autobiographical account of her life, presumably begun in 1624,[1] further spread the fame of the Lieutenant Nun throughout the Americas and Spain. Even after she retreated from public view, she and her life story continued to generate interest in literary circles: her exploits became part of the history of the Spanish conquest,[2] spawned several contemporary pseudohistorical treatises, and provided the material for a play that blends and dramatizes some of her experiences.[3]

In recent years, in the wake of growing critical interest in autobiographical and women's writing, Catalina de Erauso's life story has been rediscovered and made available to a wider audience, both in Spanish and in translation.[4] The *Vida i sucesos de la monja alférez* [*The Life and Adventures of the Lieutenant Nun*] occupies problematic critical territory at the intersection of genre and gender—a text of uncertain generic characteristics, assumed to have been written by a person whose gender identification is equally suspect. Doubts about the text's authorship, about its historical authenticity, about its position within the framework of Golden Age genres, and, most important, about the impact of biological sex and gender on the text and on its reception, continue to add to the critical controversy.

To many scholars of autobiography, Early Modern life stories present themselves as rather clumsy and unpolished pieces of writing. At their worst, they are considered failed or incomplete attempts at autobiographical writing; at their best, they might be prehistoric side shoots or mere precursors of the true masterpieces of modern autobiography. Since most definitions of the modern autobiographical genre are exclusive, Early Modern life stories usually do not play an important role in its discussion.

In mapping the history of attempted definitions of autobiography, Philippe Lejeune describes the two general approaches to the task; he considers them equally flawed because they are based on what he calls "optical illusions"—on one extreme the illusion of eternity, on the other the illusion of the birth of a genre. The latter assumes that the genre was "born all of a sudden, [and] would last in accordance with its essence" (145). Lejeune admits that French historians of autobiography are particularly tempted to consider Jean-Jacques Rousseau's *Confessions* the origin and model of modern autobiography; however, he argues convincingly that this assumption "disqualifies the past and closes off the future. We are thus led to underestimate the factors of continuity with the past and to overestimate the coherence of the modern development of the genre" (145–46). The illusion of birth, then, results in a restrictive normative definition that excludes all autobiographical forms and manifestations that do not conform to the chosen model.[5]

The alternative approach is based on the concept of a unified autobiographical genre whose eternal existence can be documented from the very beginning of writing itself, based on the erroneous assumption that a single determining feature—the use of the first person singular by the narrator—is always present and has always had the same relevance. Spengemann echoes Lejeune's objections by affirming that definitions of autobiography are generally stipulative, utilitarian, and ahistorical; in other words, they are formulated a priori, correspond to the intended use to be made by the respective commentator, and are believed "to hold true for autobiographical writing of all periods." He also observes a "shift of emphasis from the biographical and historical facts recorded in autobiography, to the psychological states expressed in the text, to the workings of the text itself"; this process, even though it is far from unilinear, has further contributed to the number of existing definitions (186–87).

Complicating the situation even further, Sidonie Smith justifiably asks "where in the maze of proliferating definitions and theories, in the articulation of teleologies and epistemologies, in the tension between poetics and historiography, in the placement and displacement of the 'self' is there any consideration of woman's *bios,* woman's *aute,* woman's *graphia,* or woman's hermeneutics?" (7). Leigh Gilmore argues that "much of traditional autobiography studies has been formulated in such a way as to exclude or make supplemental a discussion of gender. The order of analysis has gone something like this: 'First we'll figure out what autobiography is; then we'll figure out what women's autobiography is'" (21). Establishing the law of genre in this way, the woman writer as the protagonist of her cultural narrative becomes an oppositional figure, an outlaw. Gilmore echoes the earlier argument by Smith, who points out that the critical theorists and literary historians of autobiography have largely failed to take into account the life stories of women, promoting all too common attitudes and themes. Among the faults are:

the articulation of "normative" generic definitions that in their very conceptualization preclude both aesthetic appreciation and sophisticated reading of works by women; the omission or neglect that follows from the devaluation of works by women; the impoverishment of a history of autobiography that silences women and their contribution to the genre; the facile and unexamined assumptions about gender-appropriate content, structure, style, and narrative perspective; the failure to consider gender a relevant factor in either the configuration of identity or the institution of literature itself; the unselfconscious ignorance of the relationship of ideologies of gender to ideologies of selfhood. (15)

Clearly, in view of the critical landscape that surrounds autobiographical writing, the appreciation and study of Erauso's *Vida i sucesos* is hampered on two fronts: the author is female, and her text does not easily fit into existing definitions of the autobiographical genre.

The problems of definition and the concomitant problem of a critical approach are reflected in the history of the text's critical reception. Manuel Serrano y Sanz, one of the genre's earliest commentators, groups Spanish life stories according to the gender, civil status, profession, or lifestyle of the respective authors. He also privileges the so-called secular autobiographies over spiritual life stories, based on the belief that the secular autobiography is a historiographical form that presents facts in their complete historical dimension, from their conception until their final realization (i, ii). Serrano y Sanz acknowledges the existence of Erauso's *Vida i sucesos,* yet he considers it plagued by anachronisms and absurdities. Since the story does not meet the primary prerequisite of a historiography—the verifiable authenticity of the information—it has to be a fictional pseudoautobiography, not acceptable as a source of historical information, and therefore unworthy of serious discussion (clxi).[6]

The *Vida i sucesos* does not fare any better in the traditional realm of literature. A critical reading in search of literary or fictional attributes reveals that this life story lacks the traditional aesthetic values, the narrative characteristics, and the rhetorical perfection one associates with a novel.[7] The lack of an obvious plot structure, the virtual neglect of character development, and other perceived shortcomings have led to highly unflattering characterizations that continue to spread the impression of imperfection and underscore the perceived hybrid character of the *Vida i sucesos.*[8] Even Vallbona, in her evaluation of the manuscript, is unable to confirm the generic status of the *Vida i sucesos,* describing it instead in reference to contemporary genres such as the picaresque novel, the chronicle, the adventure novel, and the popular tale (9). Indirectly, in choosing these points of reference, critics privilege them as literary manifestations that are more complete, more elaborate, more valuable, than Early Modern life stories. A similar process of privileging occurs when a contemporary literary theme, for example that of the manly woman or *mujer varonil,* common in Golden Age drama, is used as a backdrop for critical commentary (Martin 39–41).[9]

The only way out of the limitations imposed by the tenuous position of Early Modern life stories between history and fiction is the continued attempt to carve a critical niche for the genre, beginning with a viable working definition. Hans-Robert Jauss proves that even texts that do not readily conform to an existing literary genre—like Early Modern autobiography—can be placed within a context of genres if the particular genre theory allows the possibility of transgression and transformation and takes into account shifts in the reception of historical texts (76–109). Alongside Jauss's genre theory, the intertextual approach to literature postulates that writers are first and foremost readers, and that "texts are . . . not structures of presence but traces and tracings of otherness. They are shaped by the repetition and the transformation of other textual structures" (Frow 45). The process of repetition and transformation affects all levels of the text, from its basic components to its genre. In fact, Laurent Jenny considers intertextuality "the defining condition for literary readability. . . . We grasp the meaning and structure of a literary work only through its relation to archetypes which are themselves abstracted from a long series of texts of which they are, so to speak, the invariants" (34).

The archetype of the introspective confession is clearly Augustine's *Confessions*. Yet the long interval between the two traditional cornerstones of the genre—Augustine's late-fourth-century and Rousseau's late-eighteenth-century *Confessions*—leaves a critical gap that needs to be bridged. After Augustine, autobiographical writing continues sporadically throughout the Middle Ages, but the *Confessions* do not become a recognizable generic model until the sixteenth century. At that time, two distinct types of self-representation have crystallized in European literature: the introspective confession, and the experiential and documentary memoir or *libro de la vida*, which is a product of the Renaissance (Goetz 13–66).[10]

The best-known example of a Golden Age confessional autobiography, the *Vida* of Teresa of Ávila, shows a structure similar to that of Augustine's *Confessions;* both life stories are divided into a before and after that hinge on an experience of conversion. In the first part of her *Vida,* Teresa emphasizes her self-proclaimed sinfulness that culminates in being sent to a convent at age sixteen. Short on conviction, unable to renounce the attractions of secular life, and plagued by serious doubts about the legitimacy of her visions, Teresa comes across Augustine's account of his conversion. The chance encounter has a definite impact on her life and on her written life story. Before, she was hampered by the very focus on her sins; now she is writing with new self-confidence the story of God living within herself (294). Saint Teresa must have been one of the first readers of Augustine's autobiography in the vernacular, and the first to recognize and apply the generic features of the *Confessions,* thus initiating the tradition of confessional life stories in Spain.

The second form of the Early Modern life story, the memoir or *libro de la vida* of the sixteenth and seventeenth centuries, is an exclusive male genre mostly tied to careers and accomplishments in the Church and in Church politics[11] and in the military.[12] In Italy, similar life stories document the authors' success in business affairs or in the mastery of a trade. For the most part, women were excluded from the political, administrative, and theological arenas and the professions, so they were unable to lead public lives or pursue careers that could be recorded. Consequently, "[T]here are very few women writers in Spain in the period, even fewer than elsewhere in Europe. The Spanish obsession with domestic privacy often prevented the publication of memoires [*sic*] and personal letters" (Paul Julian Smith 221).

In contrast to the introspective confessional autobiography, the *libro de la vida* avoids any reference to the author's inner life or personality. Equally absent is a plot structure—experiential autobiographers present a chronological string of actions and events and try to avoid the impression of having interpreted or manipulated the historical facts. The *libro de la vida* shares many generic features with the historiographical genre of the chronicle. Whereas modern historiographical writing eschews the use of the first person, the empirical *I* is a common element in late medieval historiography and in self-referential narratives found as part of private and official documents (Goetz 31–42). The pure form of the chronicle presents a series of events in the order of their occurrence, but neither connected by causality or logic, nor structured or otherwise modified; the absence of rhetorical embellishment or a plot structure further enhances the perception of authenticity and truthfulness.

The fact that experiential life stories are without an ending or a satisfactory conclusion establishes another analogy to historiographical writing: like the chronicle, a life story does not provide closure. Since the *libro de la vida* is seen literally as a story of the author's whole life, it terminates when that life comes to an end, or when the author chooses to stop writing. The fact that most *libros de la vida* lack one of these necessary elements of a true narrative may be an ironic confirmation of their intended historicity.[13] Conversely, it is one of the first modern novelists, Miguel de Cervantes, who provides us with an example of this unusual characteristic. During Don Quijote's encounter and conversation with Ginés de Pasamonte, the protagonist inquires of his fictional interlocutor, self-professed author of a memoir, whether he has finished his *libro de la vida:* "How can my life story be finished," responds Pasamonte, "when my life is not over yet?" (1:265).

The memoirist's intention in writing and circulating this type of autobiography is to foster his fame and to ensure the memory of his heroic and often marvelous accomplishments, whose authenticity is supported by verifiable historical information.[14] One must assume that these facts were not simply preserved in memory; soldiers are known to have kept detailed records, which were used mainly to claim rewards for years of service.[15] Erauso's own petitions contain the names and background of her commanders, list military appointments, and mention memorable exploits, all of which can be cross-referenced and compared to other available records. Naturally, these and similar documents kept by soldiers could have provided excellent assistance in the redaction of memoirs or *libros de la vida*.

Regarding the social status of the authors of *libros de la vida,* one must assume that the literary practice undergoes a process of democratization. The sixteenth-century aristocrat Alonso Enríquez de Guzmán writes his life story in order to entertain and instruct his readers, handing down to young noblemen the ideals of their social class and teaching them their future duties through his own example. Less than a century later, when Erauso redacts her *Vida,* writing one's life story has become a mere convention, open to memoirists from all walks of life. Indeed, it was Benvenuto Cellini who claimed that "all men of whatsoever quality they be, who have done anything of excellence, or which may properly resemble excellence, ought if they are persons of truth and honesty, to describe their life with their own hand" (1). The existence of a large number of memoirs and other forms of autobiographical writing has been confirmed recently; James Amelang, in his overview of the popular autobiography—life stories written by European craftsmen, peasants, and workers—refers to a wide range of explicit and implicit motives, chief among them "inscribing, and ensuring, the author's sense of value, of being worth something" (194).

Catalina de Erauso's choice of a title suggests that the reader can expect to find an experiential autobiography or memoir.[16] In the account itself there is no mention of a motive or an addressee; furthermore, it is not known whether the original manuscript included a dedication that could have indicated a motive or purpose other than the ones outlined in the description of the genre. However, the nature and presentation of the author's experiences confirm the generic characterization of the text.

After a brief reference to her family background, the narrator immediately launches into the story of her astonishing experiences. The daughter of a Basque aristocrat and officer, Catalina de Erauso grows up in a convent in San Sebastián. At age fifteen, during her year as a novice, she gets into a heated argument with an older and much stronger nun; the confrontation turns into a tussle, and Catalina has to suffer a beating at the hands of her adversary. She deeply resents this humiliating experience and soon finds an opportunity to escape from the convent and to transform herself into a man, cutting her hair and fashioning some male clothing out of her nun's habit. Her disguise and behavior are so convincing that none of her future employers becomes in the least suspicious; not even her father and mother recognize her in several chance encounters. Catalina spends three years in northern Spain, and then travels to the New World, where she lives more than fifteen years unrecognized, working as a shopkeeper, a soldier, and a cowhand, among other professions, or roaming the vast territory trying to elude an ever-tightening net of victims in search of revenge and law enforcement officials.

If she is not involved in the war against the natives, she is involved in quarrels and sword fights throughout South America. The temerity she shows in the war against the Araucanians also governs her life in general; Catalina is surrounded by men who gamble, drink, womanize, quarrel, and kill, and the account of her exploits proves that she fits into this male world. During one of the many duels she is pitted against her own brother, Miguel de Erauso, also a military officer, without recognizing him. In the course of the sword fight Catalina ends up wounding him mortally. This episode is one of the few where she allows herself to express any personal feelings, mentioning the pain she felt at his burial (65).

The narration of actions and experiences typical of the *libro de la vida* briefly ventures into the territory of the confessional autobiography. The author's encounter with the Bishop of Guamanga, who offers Catalina safeguard in his residence, leads to an interview in which she reveals her status. The memory of the saintly bishop's presence and influence during this episode, and the nature of the experience itself, results in a shift from Catalina's objective way of narrating to an emotionally charged passage:

> I fue en esto desmenuzando tanto, i mezclando buenos consejos, i los riesgos de la vida i espantos de la muerte i contingencias de ella, i el asombro de la otra, si no me coge bien: procurándome socegar i reducir a quietarme, i arrodillarme a Dios, que yo me puse tamañito, i descúbrome viéndolo tan santo varón i pareciendo estar yo en la presencia de Dios. (109)

> [And he continued to ask about so many details, while throwing in pieces of good advice, and talking about the risks of life and the horrors and uncertainties of death, and about the bewilderment of the afterlife, if it catches me unprepared: trying to calm me down and bring me to reconcile myself and humble myself before God to such a degree, that I ended up feeling very small. Seeing that he was such a godly man and under the impression of being in the very presence of God, I revealed my secret.]

After the private conversation with Catalina, the bishop demands a proper confession, based on a self-examination of her life—an easy task, since she has already confessed once (110). The news of her having lived in disguise causes astonishment and raises doubts, but Catalina offers to prove the factuality of the information; indeed, two matrons confirm that she is a woman and that she has preserved her virginity.

The conversion appears to be complete when Catalina takes off her disguise, again dons a nun's habit, and enters the Convent of St. Clare in Guamanga. After the sudden death of the Bishop of Guamanga in 1620 she relocates to Lima, where she stays at the Convent of the Most Holy Trinity for the next two years and five months. At that time, notification arrives from Spain that she had never professed as a nun; the consequent release from the convent marks a reversal of what could have been the effect of her conversion experience. During her preparations to return to Spain, when the Archbishop of Bogotá urges her to remain at a convent of her choice, she flatly refuses the offer; she tells him that she does not have an order nor a religion, and that she will do on her own what is best for her salvation (115). The deliverance she envisions is a secular one, namely to apply for a pension and to continue living as she had before.

In 1624 she embarks on her voyage to Spain and—according to one manuscript mentioned by Vallbona (32)—she begins writing down her life story. The brief account of the voyage and of her subsequent adventures underscores Catalina's return to male clothing, a male lifestyle, and a masculine point of view as the narrator of her life story. She mentions that she was treated well aboard the ship, until she became involved in a knife fight with a fellow gambler and was branded a troublemaker (117). Upon her arrival in Spain she causes a stir because of her attire, and many people congregate to see her dressed as a man (118). Her first attempt to travel to Rome proves unsuccessful, but she is granted a state pension for the services she performed as a soldier. Finally, she succeeds in reaching the Holy City and is granted an audience with Pope Urban VIII, to whom she tells her life story and experiences, her sex and virginity. The pope gives her permission to continue wearing man's clothing, urging her to live honestly and to avoid insulting her neighbors, for fear of God's vengeance (122–23).

The account of her life ends with a further affirmation of her masculine identity. In Naples, when two damsels address her as "Lady Catalina" and ask where she is going, she responds in true fashion, threatening to punish the two prostitutes with a hundred slaps and give another hundred slash wounds to whoever would try to prevent it (124). According to a historical treatise published in Mexico in 1653, Erauso stayed in Europe only long enough to settle her affairs. After returning to the New World in 1630, she spent the last twenty-four years of her life in Mexico under the assumed name Antonio de Erauso, working as a muleteer (Vallbona 170–75).

In spite of a brief interlude, the *Vida i sucesos* largely presents itself as a manifestation of the secular and experiential autobiographical genre of the Spanish Golden Age. The confessional element is limited to a brief episode that does not influence the course of the narration—the account is conceived as a memoir or *libro de la vida*, and is executed in accordance with its generic characteristics. Therefore, from this particular perspective, more than a tension of genre, the account projects a tension of gender that remains unresolved. In her life, Catalina de Erauso struggled to find her place and her identity as a person and as an author, and this struggle manifests itself on several textual levels in her life story. Traditionally, she has been considered a cross-dresser or transvestite—a person who adopts the habits and clothing of the opposite sex temporarily and for external motives. According to Rudolf Dekker and Lotte van de Pol, "[P]assing oneself off as a man was a real and viable option for women who had fallen into bad times and were struggling to overcome their difficult circumstances." The authors also argue that "the pressures which led to the decision of cross-dressing could be both material, such as poverty, or emotional, such as patriotic fervor or love for another woman, or a combination of these" (2). In view of the many examples of women who lived as men most of their lives or who steadfastly refused to end their disguise, among them Erauso, it may be more advantageous to introduce the concept of transsexuality, and to separate biological or sexual identity from gender identity. This would mean the distinction between primary and secondary sexual identification, in other words, the assumption that being biologically male or being female is different from being masculine or being feminine.

On the text's surface, the autobiography reflects Erauso's dominating gender identity in the predominant use of masculine pronouns and adjective endings.[17] One could argue that if it were not for the knowledge of the author's biological sex, the overwhelming majority of the experiences narrated in the *Vida i sucesos* could have been written by a man. The author admits, for instance, that on various occasions she entered relationships with women who were unaware of her true biological sex. She reveals that her first employer tried to arrange marriage between the young shopkeeper Catalina and his mistress, Doña Beatriz de Cárdenas; Catalina appears to be willing to agree to the deal—until Doña Beatriz attempts to seduce him/her, which dooms the relationship (47). On another occasion, Catalina is fired when her second employer observes her frolicking with one of his sisters-in-law (51). Even when the relationship with women is not of the amorous kind, a masculine perspective prevails: when Catalina narrates the episode of helping Doña María Dávalos escape her abusive husband, she cannot resist the temptation to belittle the plight of the powerless woman, referring to her contemptuously as "mi afligida" (90) [my distressed one].

According to psychoanalytic theories about the construction of identity, gender identification is tied intimately to the drama of the child's separation from the mother. In boys, the identification with the father constitutes the model of socialization and entry into the culture, whereas girls' identification with the mother leaves them in a state of cultural exclusion. In classical Freudian theory, the father is instrumental in breaking the boy child's symbiosis with the mother, thus allowing for the positive—but nevertheless painful—resolution of the Oedipus complex, which results in the formation of the autonomous male subject and of culture itself. The formation of female identity follows a more tortuous path, by which the girl becomes detached from her mother as a result of her envy for the penis. In Lacanian terms, the male or female subject is formed as a result of the intervention of the Symbolic order between the Imaginary and the Real. The process of identification is complete when the infant becomes aware of the laws of organization and exchange within his or her group and accepts society's rules and restrictions. In other words, gender identification occurs through the construction of a socially and sexually defined image in relation to what Lacan has called the phallic signifier, which identifies the male as complete and the female as incomplete. The identification with the mother leads to woman's exclusion from the symbolic order and prevents her from participating in patriarchal society.

The *Vida i sucesos* reveals that instead of following the gender identification process expected of a young woman, Catalina separates from the mother and begins to identify with the father world and its code, based predominantly on violence and deception. In essence, it is as if she were following the psychosexual development of a male child. Given the fact that the autobiographer provides very few details about her childhood years, the memory and mention of the circumstances of her flight from the convent assume greater importance. Being overpowered in the fight with a fellow nun appears to be the trigger for the decision to abandon her life as a female. Erauso's definitive separation from the mother world and from the abbess as her surrogate mother happens shortly after her escape from the convent, when she finishes converting her skirt into a pair of pants and her petticoat into a jacket and gaiters. She exchanges the sewing needle for the sword and embarks on the road toward success and rise in a male-dominated society. This is achieved by serving and observing those who are in positions of power—a university professor in Vitoria, the king's secretary in Valladolid, a knight of Santiago, the captain of a ship—and by imitating their behavior. In remembering this apprenticeship she unabashedly admits that, upon leaving service, she rewarded herself by stealing her employers' money.

In the New World, Catalina soon finds her place in the male hierarchy and in positions of control that are highly representative of the Symbolic order. Not without pride, she remembers that she was very effective as a shopkeeper: "Yo me quedé en Sana con mi tienda: fui vendiendo conforme a la pauta que me quedó: fui cobrando i asentando en mi libro, con día, mes i año, género, varas, i nombres de compradores y precios, i de la misma suerte lo fiado" (45) [I stayed in Sana with my store, and kept selling according to the guidelines that I had: I collected the money and wrote down in my book, with day, month, and year, the kind and the measurements of the cloth, and the names of the buyers and the prices, and followed the same procedures with purchases on credit].

As a soldier she joins the fight against the native Araucanians to help impose civilization and religion. In one of the many battles, Catalina distinguishes herself by rescuing the very symbol of nationalistic and military pride, the flag: "Viéndola llevar, partimos tras ella yo y dos soldados de caballo por medio de grande multitud, atropellando i matando, i recibiendo daño. . . . Maté al cacique que la llevaba i quitésela, i apreté con mi caballo, atropellando, matando i hiriendo a infinidad" (58) [Seeing it carried off, two other soldiers on horseback and myself went after it through a multitude of people, knocking them down and killing them, and getting wounded ourselves. . . . I killed the chieftain who was carrying it and took it away from him, and charged with my horse, running over, killing and wounding countless numbers]. Upon her return to Europe, she is equally quick in defending her pride as a Spaniard; on her way to Rome, when an Italian soldier offends the Spanish, she returns the insult and provokes a sword fight. Needless to say, she defends herself well and underscores her nationalistic pride (122).

The masculine gender identification is reflected in Catalina's appearance. Cutting her long hair is not the only way to purge her female physical features; Stephanie Merrim quotes a contemporary commentator who describes her as "tall and robust in figure, basically masculine in appearance, with no more bust than a young girl. She told me that she had employed some kind of remedy to make it disappear" (178). The psychological identification goes far beyond her choice of professional activities and appearance; in her autobiography, she presents herself as a stereotypical Golden Age male whose masculinity surpasses that of most of her male contemporaries. The majority of her violent altercations with other men originate from a seemingly overzealous preoccupation with male honor: she is quick to feel insulted or slighted, and equally quick to prove her manliness with the sword. The results of these gestures of male power are violence, wounds, death, and the need to live the life of a fugitive.

If Erauso had been a man, her life story would be a brilliant example of the positive resolution of the Oedipus complex, in which a subject achieves independence and accedes to the father's power. However, since she is female, it is easy to see the problems that result from the clash between her masculine gender identification and her biological sex. Catalina seems to be unable to stop running, unable to find a place of stability in which she as a subject can engage in both love and work. The relationship with fellow human beings is based primarily on competition in dealing with men and frustration in dealing with women. Even though Catalina is attracted to other women, especially those who are good-looking, and encounters women who are attracted to him/her as a possible husband, she has to deny herself the satisfaction of a sexual relationship and is condemned to live a life of chastity. There is one instance when Catalina appears willing to return to the mother world and to the relative security of the convent, but her "conversion" is temporary.

Both Saint Teresa and Catalina de Erauso succeed in overcoming the social injunction against female self-expression to the point of claiming authority in their respective fields—that of spirituality and personal experience of the supernatural and that of survival and success in a violent world. Yet, neither form of self-expression is without its problems. In Saint Teresa's life story the reader is confronted with the tension of conflicting genres and is disconcerted by the resulting ambivalence of the *Vida*. The underlying organizing principle of the spiritual autobiography, the experience of a conversion, is almost hidden from view. What is visible is the seemingly chaotic combination of many other texts and genres, which has also been attributed to the author's natural, intuitive (as opposed to literarily conscious), feminine, approach to writing.[18]

In Erauso's life story there is an ambiguity of gender as a result of conflicting male and female identities. Her autobiography mirrors her adopted status as a member of the dominant male hierarchy; her text does not have to be sanctioned by anybody, and she can write without the fears that characterize Teresa's story. Being an independent author, she is able to convey experiences and knowledge in a self-assured tone and manner; in fact, she mentions only one instance in which she lost control of a situation—the "conversion" experience brought about by the Bishop of Guamanga, a man of God and a moral authority, who succeeds in making her feel small and weak (110). In her auto-biography, Erauso constructs her self in a typical masculine fashion. Whereas Teresa's life story presents itself as feminine—unconstructed, sensuous, and defiant of chronology—the *Vida i sucesos* is strikingly different in its linearity, objectivity, and its chronological forward drive.

Both autobiographers succeed in entering the public sphere, but only one lives to see her efforts bear fruit in a man's world. Most of Teresa's writings are not published until after her death in 1582, and the *Vida* will not gain its due critical acceptance until five hundred years after it was written. Catalina de Erauso, on the other hand, makes a name for herself—Lieutenant Nun—which reflects the antithesis of biological sex and true gender identification. To reward her exploits in warfare and her contributions to the conquest of Chile she is granted a prize worthy of a male warrior and servant of the empire; she receives an *encomienda* of her own, with full authority over a tract of land in Mexico and over the Indians who live on it.

Notes

1. According to Vallbona, the original manuscript of *Vida i sucesos de la monja alférez* is lost. The first printed edition, prepared by Joaquín María Ferrer in 1829, is based on a handwritten copy that dates from 1784. All references to the text in Spanish are from the 1992 edition of *Vida i sucesos* by Vallbona. All translations in this chapter are my own.

2. See chapter 37 of Fray Diego de Rosales's *Historia general del reino de Chile*, reproduced in Vallbona, 177–83.

3. For a thorough discussion of *La monja alférez*, a Golden Age *comedia* commonly attributed to Juan Pérez de Montalván, see Perry.

4. See *Lieutenant Nun: Memoir of a Basque Transvestite in the New World*, trans. Michele Stepto and Gabriel Stepto.

5. Feminist critics concur; Gilmore charges that autobiography as a genre has become identified exclusively with "master narratives of conflict resolution and development" by Western white males (17). The same interpretive grid has been applied to the *Vida i sucesos;* Juárez concludes that the story reflects the development of Erauso's personality and the resolution of her gender conflict (193).

6. Vallbona mentions similar critical opinions based on the lack of historical accuracy in Erauso's life story (1–30).

7. The picaresque novel is a common point of comparison. For instance, Anderson Imbert, referring to the 1828 edition of the *Vida i sucesos,* calls it "picaresca Historia de la monja alférez" [picaresque history of the Lieutenant Nun] (67). However, memoirs or *libros de la vida* were written long before the publication of the first picaresque novel; indeed, *La vida de Lazarillo de Tormes* can be read as a parody or carnival version of the aristocratic *libro de la vida* (Goetz 121–35).

8. Earlier critics' opinions of the *Vida i sucesos* range from the charge of being a dull novel ("novela escrita sin ingenio") to that of being a literary fraud ("superchería literaria") (Vallbona 10).

9. See Dekker and van de Pol's study of female transvestism in Early Modern Europe, which mentions the literary inspirations provided by female cross-dressers (92–95).

10. Gusdorf argues that experiential life stories existed long before the term "autobiography" itself was coined; until then, their authors used analytical titles like *Vie de M. Un Tel, écrite par lui même, Eigene Lebensbeschreibung,* or *De vita propria* (963). Amelang's bibliography of popular autobiographies (258–350) confirms that numerous such life stories were written in Early Modern Europe.

11. See the life stories of Archbishop Martín Pérez de Ayala of Valencia and Bishop Diego de Simancas of Zamora, both published in Serrano y Sanz's *Autobiografías y memorias.*

12. Published life stories by Spanish soldiers include those by Alonso Enríquez de Guzmán, Alonso de Contreras, Diego Duque de Estrada, Jerónimo de Pasamonte, to mention a few.

13. See the *libros de la vida* by Alonso Enríquez de Guzmán and Alonso de Contreras, in addition to the *Vida i sucesos* of Erauso.

14. One could cite the fact that Erauso gives precise information on the number of churches, clerics, and ecclesiastical dignitaries in some cities she visited.

15. Vallbona's edition of the *Vida i sucesos* includes Erauso's memorandum to King Philip IV, in which she summarizes her activities as a soldier of the Crown (appendix 2).

16. The titles of Early Modern autobiographies alone can be misleading as an indication of their generic affiliation; in accordance with the description of the two contrasting genres, Saint Teresa's life story ought to be titled *Confesiones* rather than *Vida* or *Libro de la vida.*

17. Even in writing her life story retrospectively, the author quite faithfully uses masculine and feminine pronouns and adjective endings in accordance with the respective sex/gender she projected to the outside world: feminine until her flight from the convent, masculine until her confession to the Bishop of Guamanga, feminine for the next three years, masculine for the rest of the autobiography.

18. Since she writes outside the dominant male culture, for female readers who are virtually excluded from the written word, Teresa's style is closer to *parole* than to *écriture.* This results in a text that is dialogic and multidimensional, tailored to the abilities of her female readers (Cammarata 59).

Works Cited

Amelang, James S. *The Flight of Icarus: Artisan Autobiography in Early Modern Europe.* Stanford: Stanford University Press, 1998.

Anderson Imbert, Enrique. *Historia de la literatura hispanoamericana.* 2d ed. México: Fondo de Cultura Económica, 1957.

Cammarata, Joan. "El discurso femenino de Santa Teresa de Ávila, defensora de la mujer renacentista." *Actas Irvine–'92. Asociación Internacional de Hispanistas. II: La mujer y su representación en las literaturas hispánicas.* Ed. Juan Villegas. Irvine: University of California, 1994. 2:58–65.

Cellini, Benvenuto. *The Autobiography of Benvenuto Cellini.* Trans. John Addington Symonds. New York: Scribner's, 1896.

Cervantes, Miguel de. *El Ingenioso Hidalgo Don Quijote de la Mancha.* Ed. John Jay Allen. 2 vols. Madrid: Cátedra, 1977.

Dekker, Rudolf M., and Lotte C. van de Pol. *The Tradition of Female Transvestism in Early Modern Europe.* Trans. Judy Marcure and Lotte van de Pol. New York: St. Martin's, 1989.

Erauso, Catalina de. *Vida i sucesos de la monja alférez.* Ed. Rima de Vallbona. Tempe: Center for Latin American Studies, Arizona State University, 1992.

Fernández, James D. *Apology to Apostrophy: Autobiography and the Rhetoric of Self-Representation in Spain.* Durham, N.C.: Duke University Press, 1992.

———. "La *Vida* de Teresa de Jesús y la salvación del discurso." *MLN* 105 (1990): 283–302.

Frow, John. "Intertextuality and Ontology." *Intertextuality: Theories and Practices.* Ed. Michael Worton and Judith Still. Manchester and New York: Manchester University Press, 1990. 45–55.

Gilmore, Leigh. *Autobiographics: A Feminist Theory of Women's Self-Representation.* Ithaca: Cornell University Press, 1994.

Goetz, Rainer H. *Spanish Golden Age Autobiography in Its Context.* New York: Peter Lang, 1994.

Gusdorf, Georges. "De l'Autobiographie initiatique a l'autobiographie genre littéraire." *Revue d'Histoire Littéraire de la France* 75 (1975): 957–94.

Jauss, Hans-Robert. *Toward an Aesthetic of Reception.* Minneapolis: University of Minnesota Press, 1982.

Jenny, Laurent. "The Strategy of Form." *French Literary Theory Today.* Ed. Tzvetan Todorov. Cambridge: Cambridge University Press, 1982. 34–63.

Juárez, Encarnación. "Señora Catalina, ¿dónde es el camino? La autobiografía como búsqueda y afirmación de identidad en *Vida y sucesos de la Monja Alférez.*" *LA CHISPA '95: Selected Proceedings.* Ed. Claire Paolini. New Orleans: Tulane University, 1995. 185–95.

Lejeune, Philippe. *On Autobiography.* Ed. Paul John Eakin. Trans. Katherine Leary. Theory and History of Literature 52. Minneapolis: University of Minnesota Press, 1989.

Martin, Adrienne. "Desnudo de una travestí, o la autobiografía de Catalina de Erauso." *Actas Irvine–'92. Asociación Internacional de Hispanistas. II: La mujer y su representación en las literaturas hispánicas.* Ed. Juan Villegas. Irvine: University of California, 1994. 2:34–41.

Merrim, Stephanie. "Catalina de Erauso: From Anomaly to Icon." *Coded Encounters: Writing, Gender, and Ethnicity in Colonial Latin America.* Ed. Francisco

Javier Ceballos-Candau, et al. Amherst: University of Massachusetts Press, 1994. 177–205.

Perry, Mary Elizabeth. "La monja alférez: Myth, Gender, and the Manly Woman in a Spanish Renaissance Drama." *LA CHISPA '87: Selected Proceedings.* Ed. Gilbert Paolini. New Orleans: Tulane University, 1987. 239–49.

Santa Teresa de Jesús. *Libro de la vida.* Ed. Dámaso Chicharro. Madrid: Cátedra, 1994.

Serrano y Sanz, Manuel, ed. *Autobiografías y memorias.* NBAE 2. Madrid: Bailly-Baillière, 1905.

Smith, Paul Julian. "Writing Women in Golden Age Spain: Saint Teresa and María de Zayas." *MLN* 102 (1987): 220–40.

Smith, Sidonie. *A Poetics of Women's Autobiography: Marginality and the Fictions of Self-Representation.* Bloomington: Indiana University Press, 1987.

Spadaccini, Nicholas, and Jenaro Talens, eds. *Autobiography in Early Modern Spain.* Hispanic Issues 2. Minneapolis: The Prisma Institute, 1988.

Spengemann, William C. *The Forms of Autobiography.* New Haven: Yale University Press, 1980.

Stepto, Michele. Introduction. *Lieutenant Nun: Memoir of a Basque Transvestite in the New World.* By Catalina de Erauso. Trans. Michele Stepto and Gabriel Stepto. Boston: Beacon, 1996. Xxv–xliv.

Vélez, Irma. "Vida i sucesos de la Monja Alférez: un caso de travestismo sexual y textual." *La seducción de la escritura: Los discursos de la cultura hoy.* Ed. Rosaura Hernández Monroy and Manuel F. Medina. México: n.p., 1997. 391–401.

6

Relaciones de fiestas

Ana Caro's Accounts of Public Spectacles

Sharon D. Voros

It is often assumed that women writers, because of their marginality in Early Modern Spain, either developed no real discourse at all (Mariscal 55; Smith 14) or wrote against the oppression of their sex when they did take up the pen.[1] Yet many scholars are calling for a balance between these two critical approaches. For Ronald Surtz, such "received opinions" regarding women writers are in need of reassessment (1) and Deborah Jacobs cautions against "romanticizing marginality" and subversion in women-authored texts (73–84). This study evaluates a style of discourse not usually associated with women but commonplace in baroque Spain and supportive of monarchy and empire—the accounts of public spectacles. Understanding the political ideology becomes further compounded by the lack of information on women, unless they had taken the veil; more is known about the lives of religious women writers than their secular sisters.

When women do not adhere to a politics of feminism and ostensibly support the patriarchy, their work is frequently dismissed. George Mariscal, for example, takes María de Zayas and Teresa of Ávila to task for their conservative notions of women and gender and wonders whether "modern forms of female subjectivity" even exist in Early Modern Spain (56–61). Mary Elizabeth Perry coins the term "patriarchal woman" defined as a female enforcer of male dominance and the suppression of women, especially those deemed "evil" (142). Why then study the *relaciones de fiestas* [accounts of festivals], numerous in baroque Spain says Francisco López Estrada in one of his several studies of Ana Caro ("Flandes" 109), if they only serve as propaganda? If we examine the entire scope of women writing in the baroque era, we arrive at a more accurate account of female participation in the public arena. Female-authored discourse intended for the public becomes problematic since it addresses a general audience for whom convention and tradition are more vigorous than in works designed for private reflection.

Unfortunately, efforts of women who cultivate accounts of public festivals have been met with contempt even by some of their strongest supporters. Georgina Sabat de Rivers observes for Sor Juana Inés de la Cruz that her *El Neptuno alegórico* [*The Allegorical Neptune*], a description of the triumphal arch constructed for the Marqueses de la Laguna in 1680, has been deemed a "vicio de culteranismo" (66) [vice of cultured style]. Further, public spectacles have not been considered high art in the Western World. Aristotle considers spectacle to be the lowest form of drama since the "production of spectacular effects depends more on the art of the stage machinist than on that of the poet" (30–31). In her edition of *El conde Partinuplés* [*The Count of Partinuples*], Lola Luna quotes Jean Sentaurens's study of Seville in which he states that women and children preferred fanfare and spectacle (47), implying that they are less educated than men; this perhaps was a reason for the popularity of such plays in Seville with their use of stage machinery and magic effects. While public festivals by their very nature are more a popular art form, the accounts of these festivals in the hands of Ana Caro become poetic artifacts. The *relación,* not always written in verse, also refers to legal accounts used extensively as petitions or grievances within the Spanish empire (González Echevarría 58). There are also many accounts of public spectacles in prose (Simón Díaz 442–51). The *décima musa* or Tenth Muse, as her compatriot Luis Vélez de Guevara called Ana Caro in his 1669 *El diablo cojuelo* [*The Limping Demon*], composed all her known accounts in verse.

How then do we analyze women's accounts of festive performances, a genre itself discredited? The value of these baroque accounts lies in the evidence they provide regarding the marginalized female voice. Just how much women were in the service of the power elite is certainly difficult to document, even for men. Richard Kagan offers evidence of women in opposition to imperial politics in his analysis of Inquisition records in *Lucrecia's Dreams* as an indication of the consequences of speaking against royal policies (104). This is certainly not the case for Ana Caro in any of her accounts. Both she and Sor Juana, for example, were paid by city officials for their efforts, and documentation exists to attest to this payment. Sor Juana received 200 pesos (Paz 256) and Caro, 1,100 reales (Luna 13; Varey 268). Their accounts are not only part of feminine discourse, but became an opportunity for women writers to make a name and create an identity for themselves in the public arena as well.

While Caro is not the only woman writer to cultivate the *relación* as a poetic form, she certainly has a number of them in print with identifiable authorship. An account of a public festival appears also in Leonor de la Cueva y Silva, who begins her only extant play, *La firmeza en la ausencia* [*Firmness in Absence*], with a description of a tournament. The unknown woman writer Eugenia Buesso gives an account of a bullfight in Zaragoza that found its way into print in 1669; both women used the *octavas reales* [royal octaves] as a metric form for account writing, as does Caro. Thus the corpus of *relaciones* written by women is not large, compared to production by male authors, yet women have similar comments regarding the humble status of the writer who, like Icarus, dares to describe the grandeur of a royal spectacle: "Ícaro ya mi pluma no presuma / bolar al Sol" [Icarus now, my pen does not presume to fly to the Sun], states Juan Francisco Davila in his *Relación de los festivos aplausos con que celebró esta Corte Católica las alegres nuevas del feliz Desposorio del Rey nuestro Señor Don Felipe Quarto* [*Account of the festive applause with which this Catholic Court celebrated the happy news of the wedding of our King Don Phillip the Fourth*] in 1648 (Simón Díaz 504). In a society obsessed with social status and lineage, male writers certainly felt a need to inject a rhetoric of humility into their public discourse, yet when women employ the same rhetorical strategies, they are dismissed as subservient to the patriarchy. How then do we assess this most baroque of literary exercises, written in both prose and poetry, especially when the writer gives us a poetic rendition of events that support the Church and the monarchy?

As the only documented professional woman writer of her era, Ana Caro began her writing career as an observer of public pageantry with four verse accounts:[2] the 1628 *Relación de las fiestas por los mártires del Japón* [*Account of the Commemoration for the Martyrs of Japan*], her first published work (López Estrada, "La relación" 51); the 1633 *Romance por la victoria de Tetuán* [*Ballad for the Victory in Tetuan*] (López Estrada "Tetuán"); the 1635 *Fiesta y octava celebradas con motivo de los sucesos de Flandes en la iglesia de San Miguel* [*Festival and Octave Celebrated for the Events in Flanders, in the Parish of San Miguel in Seville*] (López Estrada "Flandes"), and the 1637 *Contexto de las reales fiestas que se hizieron en el palacio del Buen Retiro* [*Text of the Royal Festivals Held in the Palace of the Buen Retiro*] ("Contexto"), that I will focus on here.[3] This "book," as Caro calls it, is about as long as a *comedia*, 2101 lines: "Yo hice un libro de las fiestas que V.S. hizo por los años de S.A. el

Príncipe nuestro señor, . . . y benida de la Serenissima Princesa de Cariñan" (Varey 268) [I wrote a book of the festivities that your Lordship held for the birthday of his Royal Highness the Prince our lord, . . . and the arrival of the very serene Princess of Carignano]; *El conde Partinuplés* has 2110 lines, and *Valor, agravio y mujer* [*Valor, Offense, and Woman*], 2757 lines. John Varey notes an order for payment of 100 ducats to Ana Caro from the Town Council of Madrid, the same amount paid to Andrés Sánchez del Espejo (268), who also wrote an account of this lavish 1637 event.[4] León Pinelo mentions Pedro Calderón's play *Don Quijote* as part of the festivities on "martes de Carnestolendas" [Shrove Tuesday], February 24, 1637, a dramatic work unfortunately lost to us (311).

For Luna, however, Caro's occasional poetry only proves that she wrote on command as a servant of the powerful, not of her own initiative (13), since she may have been paid by the Count-Duke of Olivares himself or Carlos Strata, a wealthy Genoese banker who had bailed out Philip IV several times (14). Luna does not cite the Varey article with the archival evidence that the Town Council of Madrid paid for Caro's account and other bills for the festivities, not cleared until 1640, three years later (Varey 268). Since Caro's surviving accounts of public spectacles appear to be those she was paid for, this argument imposes a double bind on her writing: if women write at all, they must be subversive in their identity as women, yet if they write according to the ideology of their time, they betray their gender. We expect women to oppose the systems of domination that control them in this postmodern age. When they do not operate according to this expectation, the problematic nature of female discourse becomes evident, as in Mariscal's discussion of María de Zayas and Saint Teresa; he allows Francisco Quevedo and Miguel de Cervantes their "contradictory subjects," while women are not extended the same privilege (61). Yet Marsical's notion of *admiratio*, defined as dominant discourse that seeks control over its readers by imposing a rhetoric of wonder and suspension of the senses, also applies to Caro's accounts of public spectacles (192–94). Is it fair to expect women to ignore the dominant discourse of their own era? Should the exaltation of the Catholic faith or the territorial expansion of the empire be taboo topics for women? A construction of feminine identity should not censor women but take into account the historical circumstances in which women write. Not only do women writers anticipate our own present, but they also include issues of their own time with which they establish their identities as writers.

While I will focus on the 1637 account, some assessment of Caro's earlier accounts of public spectacles is in order. First of all, they all deal with events occurring outside Spain, as do her two extant plays; *Valor, agravio y mujer* takes place in Flanders, and *El Conde Partinuplés,* in Constantinople. Caro then is not limited to a purely peninsular worldview. As a resident of Seville, she is conscious of Spanish imperial expansion and Spain's commitment as defender of the true faith. According to López Estrada ("La relación" 51), Caro's first published work was the account of *Las fiestas por los mártires del Japón,* which took place in 1628 in Seville in what is today the Plaza de San Francisco, to honor the beatification of twenty-three Franciscans martyred in 1597 ("La relación" 54). Caro wrote forty-nine *octavas reales* with a description of the festivities in praise of these martyrs. Three aspects of her writing for the public sphere emerge: plays on words, such as her own name *Caro* [dear], a rhetoric of "false modesty" (Curtius 83), and authorial asides and interventions. "Caro" is an economic term, as in the dedication stanza to Juan de Elossidieta, "Podréis dezir muy bien que a sido treta / el valerme de vos, que os cuesta Caro" ("La relación" 62) [You could say very well that my availing myself of you has been a ruse that has cost you Dear], perhaps a reference to payment from him for her account. References to the topos of "false modesty" (Curtius 83) involve expressions of the writer as overwhelmed with the enormity of the task of describing "glorias tan altas" ("La relación" 61) [such high glories], like Phaeton's fateful flight. According to Sherry Velasco, women writers frequently call attention to themselves as women with "humble apologies" (3) in introductory comments to their works. Women, however, are not the only writers to do so, as Curtius so aptly points out (83).

Caro also inserts her authorial voice into the account:

Mas ¡ay, Dios!, ¿dónde voy, siendo impossible
pintar tanta grandeza mi ignorancia
por lo mucho que tiene de indezible
por lo poco que tengo de elegancia?
("La relación" 64)

[But, oh Lord! Where am I going, since it is impossible for my ignorance to depict such greatness; the ineffable is so great and my elegance so insignificant?]

This aspect of her writing for the public is a means of impressing upon her readers the spectacular nature of the festivities, clearly the rhetoric of *admiratio.* But in the midst of the pomp and circumstance, Caro reveals a deeper concern, for she reflects upon the question of the poor who were given free food, perhaps a way of justifying the expense for such public ostentation, "pues de la misma suerte a comer dieron / a quantos pobres allegar quisieron" ("La relación" 67) [for in the same way, they gave food to as many poor people as wished to come]. She also references the "común miseria y desventuras / en que España se ve" ("La relación" 69) [common misery and misfortune that one sees in Spain], evidence that Caro was not a mere apologist for Hapsburg politics but a sensitive observer of unresolved social issues of her day. Twentieth-century views on these spectacles as mere propaganda are at variance with Caro's own understanding of such festivities as contributing to the common good, not just the "alabança en varones tan famosos" ("La relación" 67) [praise of such famous men].

Caro's second account, the 1633 *Romance por la victoria de Tetuán,* delves into the *romancero* or ballad tradition to describe a "[g]randiosa vitoria" (López Estrada, "Tetuán" 339) [grandiose victory], an event, however, that amounts to little more than Christian cattle rustling in Muslim Morocco. Throughout her account, one cannot help but think that the Spanish aristocracy must have had something better to occupy their time than chasing cattle in Tetuán and scattering their hapless Muslim owners into the hills. An account, printed in Seville by Simón Fajardo ("Tetuán" 345), was widely read at a time when Spain desperately needed good news from abroad, even if that only meant corralling cattle across the Straits of Gibraltar. I agree with Lola Luna (*El conde Partinuplés* 6) and Mary Elizabeth Perry (14) regarding the crisis situation in Seville in the first half of the seventeenth century in which women acquired more responsibility in civic life. War, plague, and poverty were key issues of the day; Spain suffered serious depopulation of up to 20 percent, due in part to the immigration to the New World (Kagan, *Lawsuits* 220). The economics of crisis is perhaps what motivated Caro to take up the pen to comment upon the successes of the empire, such as they were, or at least to provide an income for herself as a writer on a topic of immediate concern.

The majority of the forty-five noblemen who participated in this event were Portuguese ("Tetuán" 346). Was Caro attempting to prove their patriotism to the crown? This was an era of shifting political alliances on the Peninsula with Portugal gaining its independence. John Lynch observes that the relationship between the Portuguese nobility, generally supportive of the union with Spain, became strained over questions on the protection of Portuguese colonies and Spain's inability to defend them from the Dutch and other plunderers during the 1630s (149–57), a moment contemporaneous with

Caro's concern for Spanish victory abroad in the publication of this "mock epic" of the famous Moroccan cattle raid. Caro emphasizes the boldness of the expedition into enemy territory where no Christian had ever set foot before:

Ni de padres ni de abuelos
ni de otras christianas huellas
fue pisado este lugar
donde estampamos las nuestras.
("Tetuán" 342)

[Neither by parents, grandparents, nor any other Christians was this place trod upon where we now imprint our footsteps.]

Apparently the Muslims fled rather than fight, leaving the cattle behind, "Los moros, sin defenderse, / con el miedo y la violencia / dexan el ganado" ("Tetuán" 344) [The Moors, without defending themselves with fear and violence abandon the cattle]. A total of eight hundred head of cattle were rounded up by Portuguese soldiers. While Caro extolls the event as comparable to Roman and Greek exploits, she includes Portugal in the glory along with Castile ("Tetuán" 345). One could argue that her notion of the preservation of empire involved keeping Portugal under the crown of Spain.

Caro's third *relación* deals with a more serious topic, the 1635 massacre in Tillemont, Flanders, during the war with France. Atrocities included burning churches, killing monks, and raping nuns, all this by Spain's Roman Catholic neighbor ("Flandes" 111). According to López Estrada, these events were front-page news in 1635, in the midst of which Ana Caro had a definite role to play as chronicler of the religious festivities in the parish of San Miguel in Seville in the same year. Again, just as Luna takes her to task for a lack of political depth in her version of this festival, she also condemns Caro for supporting Spain's imperial policy (12–13). We as scholars, however, need to exercise caution in evaluating these problematic texts so as not to berate women with the typical double bind. Indeed, Caro takes the stance of a moralist and states that this festival demonstrates to the "Herege atreuido" [bold heretic] that his actions in Flanders were shameful ("Flandes" 136). Caro strongly argues in favor of the importance of public spectacles within seventeenth-century Spanish culture as a means of impacting international policy and protesting injustices.

There are several points about this account that merit comment before we delve into the 1637 account of the festivities at the Palace of the Buen Retiro.

Caro chose the *silva pareada* [seven-syllable and eleven-syllable rhymed couplets] as the principal metric form for her account, also the metric form for the second part of the 1637 account. Thus, she had employed all three metric forms used in the 1637 *Contexto* before its composition: the *octavas reales* in 1628, the *romance* in 1633, and finally the *silva pareada* in 1635. Further, her status as a writer has been well established, as evidenced by the poems dedicated to her at the beginning of this 1635 account. Diego de Ortega Haro wrote three *décimas* [a stanza of ten eight-syllable lines] in her honor, referring to her as "la Musa Sevillana" [Sevillian Muse] and as a "Coronista" [Chronicler]; there is no mention of her theater ("Flandes" 119). María de Haro says in her *décima*, "[C]on que te admiren los hombres / y te embidien las mugeres" ("Flandes" 120) [So men admire you and women envy you]. Francisco Coronel composed a sonnet extolling Caro's "Divino ingenio, soberana pluma" [Divine wit and sovereign pen] and calls her a "deterrent to heretics" ("Freno al sectario soys"). Juan de Mesa composed two *décimas,* also with praise for her as the "Musa española" ("Flandes" 119–21) [Spanish Muse].

Included here also is a feature she continues extensively in the 1637 account, the address to noble patrons. The system of patronage has generated a great deal of concern among us postmodernist scholars critical of colonial/imperial policy. As Kristiaan Aercke has argued regarding the problematic nature of baroque spectacles, "It is difficult to accept that Lotti and Calderón would produce a grandiose spectacle for Philip and his court in order to blame Philip and his court for liking grandiose spectacles; should the king 'reform,' the first people affected adversely would be, precisely, Lotti and Calderón and their colleagues working in various artistic media" (154). Thus, the question of patronage, writers, and artists is not just one involving women, but one of the entire baroque era. If we dismiss Caro as self-serving in writing these accounts, then we have to dismiss just about every major writer or artist of the time.

Here for the first time in her accounts is a dedicatory address to the wife of an important patron, the Count of Salvatierra, organizer of the festivities, whom she calls "mi señor" ("Flandes" 121) [my lord]. In the preface Leonor de Luna Enríquez, Countess of Salvatierra, is Caro's "primer acreedor" [primary creditor]. The writer skillfully employs banking metaphors to explain her relationship to the countess, to whom she owes a debt, her writing. This "epítome de poquísimo valor" [draft of very little value] only acquires value in the hands of its owner, the countess herself. Caro signs, "Menor criada de V. Señoría" [Humble servant of your Ladyship]. Ana, the poor debtor only capable of writing "malos versos" [bad poetry], notes her boldness along with her asking for pardon for such an "atrevido yerro" [daring error]. While public discourse in our twentieth-century culture avoids such expressions, courtly conventions of humility were crucial in seventeenth-century forms of address. As an example of the attention paid to protocol, Antonio de Torquemada's *Manual de escribientes* [*Manual for Writers*] includes an entire section on courteous expressions and the ending of letters ("De las cortesías y de los fines de las cartas") (248–50), which includes using "Vuestra Señoría" [Your Lordship/Ladyship] as an address of courtesy for "gente calificada" (249) [prominent people]. Thus, Caro follows the dictates of conventions of her day for which this form of address and closure are appropriate for the rank of the addressee. Since we know so little about her personal life or even her family (Luna 11), reference here of her in the service of the count and countess place her as a kind of secretary, perhaps similar in vocation to the great Lope de Vega who performed the same function for his noble patrons.

At the conclusion of the poem's 873 lines, however, there is a second address to Leonor de Luna Enríquez in terms that indicate that the countess may have had a hand in commissioning the account. We have no more information about the lady other than that Caro dedicates the poem to her "para cantar tu nombre, / elogios dedicando" ("Flandes" 141) [to sing of your name and dedicate praises], but with no real details on her person or accomplishments. Caro does emphasize another aspect of the account that she includes amply in the 1637 account and that is the focus on a noble woman patron accepting the work of a woman writer, along with the characteristic topos of false modesty: "Y pues nació muger, aunque divina, / acete de muger estos borrones" ("Flandes" 141) [And since you were born woman, although divine, accept from a woman these scribblings]. Caro indicates that it is the grandeur of the event, not just patronage of the countess, that adds worth to the account about it: "Supla, pues, la grandeza, / de materia tan alta, / lo que a la obra, y al estilo falta" ("Flandes" 141) [Then may the greatness of such lofty material make up for what the work and style are lacking]. Thus, the baroque text maintains its ambiguous style that both reveals and conceals the object of its discourse.

This is the same Countess of Salvatierra whom J. H. Elliott discusses in *The Count-Duke of Olivares* (538). She attempted to advise the Count-Duke of Olivares himself who apparently disregarded her warnings about the French attack on Fuenterrabía in 1638, a detail also noted by Luna (23). However, given the rather distant references to the countess in Caro's dedication and the signature as "Menor criada," it appears likely that our Tenth Muse had the social status of a paid employee rather than a person of privilege; there is never even a question of Caro's having equal rank to her patrons. Such is the world in which this woman author functioned as a writer. To dismiss her attitude as unnecessarily obsequious and subservient to the nobility, oversimplifies the difficulties of women writers in a very limited profession for them, especially as concerns their participation in public life.

Turning to the *Contexto de las reales fiestas,* I find it interesting to note that more is known about this 1637 festival than Caro's own life. Hers is not the only account of the 1637 festival, although Jonathan Brown and John Elliott consider it a significant source for information about this event (200). Brown and Elliott quote Caro's version of the words spoken by the king as he leaves the house of the Genoese banker Carlos Strata before the festival:

> Reconocido voy, quanto gustoso,
> Carlos, de la lealtad que en vos retrata
> el desvelo mayor, y agradecido
> a lo bien que de vos estoy servido.
> ("Contexto" 11)[5]

> [I am grateful as much as pleased, Charles, for the loyalty that you show in this great effort and I am grateful for how well I am served by you.]

It is not clear from her text, however, whether she was even in close enough proximity to the king to overhear his words. Better known are León Pinelo's *Anales* and Sanchez del Espejo's *relación* (Varey 254), although these accounts do not provide "exact" words for Philip IV.[6] This carnival spectacle at the Buen Retiro lasted for ten days, from February 15th to 24th, staged to honor the coronation of Ferdinand III of Hungary (Philip's cousin) as Emperor of the Holy Roman Empire and secondarily to celebrate the arrival of María de Borbón (the Princess of Carignano), cousin to Queen Isabel and wife to Tomás de Saboya, who managed to secure some victories over the French in Flanders (Varey 266). Caro's account is her first description of a primarily political, rather than specifically religious, baroque festival designed to dazzle the French enemies and Spanish people alike in a very public display of imperial wealth.

Varey notes, however, that the relationship between the Princess of Carignano and the Spanish Crown was a deplorable one, due in great part to the political machinations of the count-duke himself (272); she may even have been more of a hostage than a guest although Caro obviously does not mention this in her *Contexto*. In part 2, Caro notes that the princess was seated next to her cousin the Queen Isabel de Borbón in the "[r]eal balcón" [royal balcony]. Caro's description of them combines the beauty of the two ladies as "candores puros de la Lis Francesa" [pure-white innocence of the French fleurs-de-lis] with emphasis on their country of origin; apparently the princess's children were also present along with Prince Baltasar Carlos ("Contexto" 21). Caro follows with a description of the ladies in waiting, "Las damas de la Reyna . . . / fueron prisión de libres pensamientos" [The ladies-in-waiting of the queen were a prison for free thoughts], an allusion to the competition of Venus who received the golden apple from Paris, thus beginning the Trojan War. Could this be a veiled reference to the virtual incarceration of the princess and her four children that Varey mentions? The juxtaposition of terms and dual referent of Paris as Trojan prince and Paris as the seat of French power tempts the twenty-first century reader to interpret the phrasing as such. The event was costly, designed for the extravagance that the Buen Retiro was meant to provide; it put the aristocracy, not just the king, on display, especially the Count-Duke of Olivares himself. By 1643 both the count-duke, removed from office, and the Genoese banker Carlos Strata, due to illness, would be marginalized from power (Elliott 626), and the count-duke's portrait removed from the Velázquez equestrian painting of Baltasar Carlos at the Buen Retiro Palace (Brown and Elliott 676). Such was the harsh reality for those men in high places who fall from power.

Another established aspect of Caro's public writing style is her address to her patrons; she dedicates part 1 to Agustina Spínola, part 2 to the Count-Duke of Olivares, and part 3 to the Town Council of Madrid. Luna assumes that Caro had a subservient attitude toward her powerful compatriot since she signs "Criada de Vuestra Excelencia" [Servant of Your Excellency] in her dedication to the count-duke in the second part. I find it telling, however, that Caro gives him second billing. In a society obsessed with rank and position, she reserves the dedication of the first part for Agustina Spínola, wife of the wealthy Genoese banker Carlos Strata and daughter of the famous commander of the Flanders campaigns, the First Marquis of Los Balbases, Ambrosio Spínola. Apparently the good general's relationship with the count-duke was not an easy one (Brown and Elliott 346–58). Although Ambrosio Spínola died in 1630, I also find it telling that Caro does not even mention him. Only in passing does she discuss Agustina's lineage with "Claríssima Casa de los Spínolas" (A3) [the very illustrious house of the Spinolas]. As a convention of closure, she signs "Servidora de V. m. [Servant of Your Worship] in part 1,

"Criada de V. Excelencia" [Servant of Your Excellency] in part 2, and "De V. Señoría servidora" [Servant of your Lordship] in part 3. Her identity as "servant" I read as a purely conventional, not descriptive, means of epistolary closure to appeal to noble patrons.[7] The encomium to Agustina Spínola in the 1637 account is probably a plea for support for printing a piece that places the wife of a wealthy banker in such prominence in part 1. Carlos Strata financed at least one *relación* of this event, and it could have been Ana Caro's, although the evidence here shows that the Town Council of Madrid footed the bill (Varey 268).

Just how much access Caro had to the elite circle of the count-duke is doubtful. I disagree with Luna (13) that these accounts prove she capitulated completely to Spanish imperial politics for her own monetary gain. This critical opinion would make sense had Caro dedicated the entire work to Don Gaspar, but she does not. Since the first part of the *Contexto* takes place in the Strata house on the Carrera de San Jerónimo that served as a dressing area for Philip before the procession (he entered the house on February 15), and the second part deals with the procession orchestrated by Don Gaspar, placing women first does obey the dictates of narratological ordering. There appears to be plenty of evidence that the *Contexto* was intended more for the folks back home in Seville and the general reading public than for the inner circle of the power elite; the final, third part deals with additional festivities, plays and masques, with names of local officials and is dedicated to the Town Council of Madrid itself. While Caro and even Sor Juana bring attention to themselves as writers with self-deprecating strategies, they both include praise for wives of noble patrons as part of, although not central to, public events. Still, interpretation of these forms of address and their attendant topics of false modesty remains problematic.

Electa Arenal, for example, sees in these invocations of Phaeton or Icarus an act of literary daring that goes beyond the dominant discourse of power and subsequently challenges royal patronage (127). Curtius, however, reads false modesty as a rhetorical means for garnering favor with superiors through humiliation of the writer (83). Caro's accounts move between both levels of discourse; the discourse of the public event is not undercut or subverted by the personal commentary as one might expect in our own era. The ironic "slippage" between these two levels, public discourse versus private reflection, does not occur as expected and we glimpse very little of her own feelings regarding these events. I do agree with Luna's observations that this woman writer is "ubicada en un espacio mixto entre lo privado y lo público" (11) [located in an ambiguous space between the private and public world], but what writer of this period is not? My argument is that even this space is usually reserved for men, not women, and, therefore, Caro's presence in the public arena merits more attention, not just for her politics but for her perceptions on her own culture and time that we do not frequently see from a woman's point of view.

Ruth Lundelius notes the printed version of Caro's 1637 account was not her first draft (230). Caro claims in her initial statement to her "Lector caro" [Dear Reader] that she did not intend publication of her account: "[P]erdónale este pecado a mi ignorancia, advirtiendo que lo mal razonado dél es averse hecho sin intención de publicarlo, y con diferente asunto, . . . hágolo ya mudándolo el principio" ("Contexto" A3) [Forgive my ignorance of this sin with the warning that the poorly expressed part of it (the poem) is its composition, with different subject matter, and without my intention of publishing it. . . . I write it now having changed the beginning]. With a play on words that recalls the 1628 account, she again brings up the topic of remuneration for her services, with a play on the double meaning of "pagada" as "paid" or "content": "Suplícote le censures como tuyo, y le compres como ageno, que con esso, si tu no contento, yo quedaré pagada" ("Contexto" A3) [I beg you to censor it as yours and buy it as a stranger, for with that, if you are not happy, I will be paid/content]. The dedications to Agustina Spínola (part 1), Olivares (part 2), and the Town Council of Madrid (part 3) were probably added for the printed edition. Caro probably also read these verses in public, for Alonso de Castillo Solórzano places her in Madrid in the company of María de Zayas, and alludes to such a public reading of the *Contexto*, "con sus dulces y bien pensados versos suspende y deleita a quien los oye y lee; esto dirán bien los que ha escrito a toda la fiesta que estas Carnestolendas se hizo en el Buen Retiro" (1549) [with her sweet and well-reasoned verses she suspends and delights those who hear them or read them; this they will affirm those to whom she has written concerning the festival that during Shrovetide was held in the Buen Retiro]. Lundelius also comments on Caro's connections in Madrid and Seville, but notes that she did not remain long in the capital city (230–31).

Can Caro really be condemning this baroque extravagance as she comments on it? Again, I must agree with Aercke in *Gods of Play* who cautions against reading baroque hyperbole as *vituperatio* [censure] (154). I would go a step further, however, and argue that accounts of public spectacles more appropriately belong to the tradition of the *regimiento de príncipes* or advice to princes. Caro's account shares some features with this medieval Castilian tradition (Goldberg 100). While advice to princes was certainly a general European tradition, praise of ruling nobility also involves reminding them of their duties. If we take Fray Martín de Córdoba's *Jardín de nobles donzellas* [*Garden of Noble Maidens*] as an example of this tradition, we see that it also includes an address to a royal personage, Isabel the Catholic, and a tripartite scheme in his treatise, although there is no proof that the queen ever read the treatise (Goldberg 41). The role of adviser to princes gives the writer a kind of moral superiority and protection with which a discourse of virtue can be maintained as a possible criticism toward the discourse of power (Mariscal notes the rivalry of the discourse of class versus the discourse of virtue, 47).

Caro may have intended her address to the count-duke as a reminder of the importance of the Spanish empire in his elaboration of spectacle. Indeed Philip IV himself did not disregard advice from women, to which his correspondence to Sor María de Jesús de Ágreda bears witness; the good nun frequently signs "su menor sierva" (73) [your humble slave]. We have at least one instance to show that the count-duke refused to listen to a woman's point of view when the Countess of Salvatierra warned him about the French (Elliott 538). Perhaps Caro anticipated his reaction and came to the conclusion that the only way to advise Don Gaspar is through praise of his exploits and calumny on his jealous detractors.

Since Caro discusses criticism of these public festivities, one might construe her observations as a way to bring such comments to the notice of her benefactors, if indeed they did contribute to her welfare. In the Tillemont commemoration, she comments on the criticism that the spectacle was excessive, "Unos dizen que excede" (138) [Some say that what one has seen exceeds], as noted earlier. In the *Contexto* she also acknowledges the public outcry regarding the tremendous cost of the 1637 festivities in Madrid as "el veneno de la envidia / y del odio la ponzoña" ("Contexto" 39) [the poison of envy and the venom of hate]. To whom is she referring here? Is this a veiled means of letting the count-duke know about criticism of this lavish event? Both Varey (259) and Deleito (215–19) refer to bills heaped upon the town council, many members of which felt that the festivity should have taken place in the Plaza Mayor or in the Plaza de Palacio. The Buen Retiro's Prado Alto de San Jerónimo, an empty area near the Buen Retiro Palace, required costly leveling to accommodate the area for the procession (Varey 262). Caro discusses the issue with specific references to measurements of the area for the event and the orders given by the count-duke himself:

Mandó el Conde allanar junto al Retiro
una agradable plaza
en cuya grande y espaciosa traza
se vía desde afuera
una Troya murada de madera.
("Contexto" 19)

[The Count ordered that an enjoyable plaza be flattened near the Retiro
Palace. Within its great and spacious area, one saw, from the outside, a
walled Troy made of wood.]

I believe the above comment is even more telling for Caro's own perspective on the events in part 2, for she says "se vía desde afuera" [one saw from the outside]. She never states exactly where she is standing as she observes the procession, but with this comment, she appears to be outside the main festival area. She describes the painted wooden structures constructed for the occasion ("Contexto" 18–19), decorated to imitate silver, bronze, jasper, and marble (Varey 262). This information was readily available in accounts by León Pinelo and Sánchez de Espejo (Varey 262) and Caro could have supplemented her observations from them. She does give specifics, such as the measurements of this new plaza, larger than the Plaza Mayor ("Contexto" 18). Further, in part 3, she heaps praise on the *regidores* [aldermen] of the City of Madrid to whom she dedicates the *romance* in this section, a demonstration of her affection for more popular forms of government. Account writing for the local agencies was an avenue for women not only to enjoy public appreciation but also to get their start as writers. Caro continually emphasizes that the authorship of this account is female and does not apologize for writing at the service of an aristocracy or society of which she is a part. She is, however, more an observer than a participant, as we ascertain from what she actually witnessed.

Ana Caro's narrative discourse moves from the perspective of an insider located inside the Strata house in part 1, to that of an outsider in parts 2 and 3, as concerns royal authority and presence. Like the *comedia*, this 1637 account has three parts. In the first part, *octavas reales,* Caro dedicates the first four stanzas to herself, as aspiring to topics beyond her command ("Aspiro al imposible de más gloria" [I aspire to the impossible of more glory]), with help from Thalia, a teacher of women ("precepto de una clase de mugeres") ("Contexto" 1). Of the sixty-nine *octavas reales,* eight contain information about the author as a female Icarus; she writes that "la acción . . . atrevida en el impulso intima / Buelo fatal de plana, y cera leve" (1) [the action, daring in its impulsiveness, orders a fatal flight of smooth, light wax], and in the conclusion Caro states, "Deja, pluma ignorante, deja el vuelo" (12) [Cease, ignorant pen, cease your flight]. A full 11.5 percent of the text reflects on her own position as a woman writer. Even her appeal to Agustina Spínola conveys a desire to be heard, not for monetary gain but for the honor of service:

Que admita mis borrones le suplico.
Si por muger, como muger me ampara;
No aspiro a premio más grandioso o rico,
pues todo premio es corto a los honores
que ya espero gozar en sus favores. (12)

[That you accept my scribblings I beg you if only because I am a woman, as a woman you help me. I don't aspire to a more grandiose or rich reward, since any reward falls short of the honor that I expect to enjoy in your favor.]

This is a system of patronage at work that even male writers had to solicit. Female-authored accounts all include some panegyric to noble women and thus convey a sense, as Electa Arenal observes, that women are also participants in major cultural evolutions (127).

Caro's description of the interior of the Strata house emphasizes the visual splendors of aristocratic wealth. The Genoese banker had made vast contributions to the crown, "Fue pues, su Magestad, . . . / a la del Noble Strata, casa donde / de su franca riqueza hizo alarde" (4) [Then his Majesty went to the house of the Noble Strata, a house where its evident wealth made an impact], and now lavishes even more gifts on his Royal Highness. Philip took all gifts from Strata and "duly dispatched" them to the Buen Retiro Palace (Brown and Elliott 200). Caro here uses the perspective of an eyewitness, "sin que los ojos puedan mirar tantos" (4) [my eyes could not see so much wealth], to describe jewels, art works, tapestries, and reliquaries as she gives the impression of having witnessed the king's arrival at this house. Yet she does not follow events chronologically, for her own arrival in Madrid does not appear until part 2. With this chronological transposition of events, I suspect that the self-referential sections in part 2 were probably part 1 in her first draft, changed later to reflect the assistance or support of her patroness Agustina Spínola, although there is no documentary proof of any payment.

Despite the *amplificatio* of subject, Caro clearly controls her narrative and directs the reader to what she finds significant with authorial interventions: "Soberbia, desatino, o arrogancia / . . . / es la ponderación de mi ignorancia / quando pintar aun lo menor presumo" (5) [Pride, foolishness, arrogance . . . describe the deliberation of my ignorance when even minor things I presume to depict]. Her insistent commentary on the greatness of events and her failure to capture the magnitude of them serves to emphasize this spectacle. Since the level of detail of precious objects in the Strata house appears high, including urns of gold—"[d]e América las venas más Copiosas" (8) [from America the most abundant veins of gold]—it is tempting to conclude that she was indeed present at these events. There is no secondary independent source known to confirm this presence, however. She concludes part 1 with praise for Agustina in terms of the discourse of virtue—"espejo de virtud, ingenio y arte" (12) [model of virtue, wit, and ability]—and an appeal for her support "si por muger, como muger me ampara" (12) [since I am a woman, as a woman you help me]. No physical description of the lady appears in this part and her final comment leads me to believe that Caro is still expecting some sort of remuneration or recognition, not yet resolved, from Doña Agustina.

In part 2, dedicated to the count-duke himself, who presumably read the account "que escriví a Sevilla y V. Excelencia vio" (16) [that I wrote in Seville and that your Excellency saw], Caro states that she has been encouraged to publish her *borrones* [scribblings] although all the credit for the *asumpto* [subject matter] goes to Don Gaspar. As with her other patrons, these verses are a tribute to the count-duke. She mentions both the "propteción de su Excelentíssima mano" [protection by your very excellent hand] and "generoso amparo" [generous help], giving credence to the notion that she might have had some assistance or recognition from him. In the same breath, however, Caro reminds him of his duty to the nation: "[C]uya vida guarde Dios, para que en ella aumente España felicidades" (13) [May God keep you in long life, so that with it you may increase Spain's happiness]. Here we see evidence of her writing as the *regimiento de príncipes,* or advice to princes, regarding their moral obligations. This dedicatory preface to the count-duke had to be written after the festival when she had returned to Seville, confirmed by Lundelius, since Caro left very shortly after the event to return to Seville (230).

Evidence of a personal sense of deception or oppression on Caro's part (Lundelius 230) is evinced from her statements regarding sadness, such as "triste presagio a las desgracias mías" (14) [sad presage of my misfortunes]. However, no personal issue comes to the fore except for the severe winter conditions in Madrid and the king's absence. The king was at the Pardo Palace when Caro arrived in Madrid (15). Yet, despite her self-effacing rhetoric, the first 111 lines of this *silva pareada,* a total of 993 lines in part 2, again about 11 percent, concern Caro herself and her reasons for coming to Madrid in the dead of winter:

> Guiada del espíritu ambicioso
> o el deseo curioso
> del gusto, que apetece
> lo que en los imposibles desfallece
> quise ver a Madrid, Corte española,
> grandioso mapa donde se acrisola
> el valor y nobleza. (13)

> [Guided by an ambitious spirit or a curious desire for the pleasure, that what is appealing in impossible things grows faint, I insisted upon seeing Madrid, the Spanish Court, a grandiose map where valor and nobility are concentrated.]

As a "mujer determinada" [determined woman], she has come to look the king in the face: "Pisé a Madrid . . . / alentando el deseo (cosa rara) / por verle al Rey la cara" (14) [I came to Madrid . . . bolstering up my desire (a rare thing), to look the king in the face]. Certainly Caro's direct approach in seeking out the king himself is a better example of feminine authorial daring, since Maureen Flynn points out the more dangerous aspects of the female gaze (24). While Caro expresses the desire to look the king in the face, her actual experience is still unconfirmed by this *Contexto.* León Pinelo says the king left for the Pardo on January 8 and returned on February 7 (98). Caro notes he returned about three weeks after his departure, which would place his return closer to the end of January (15), but she gives no specific dates. The closest she comes to the king is in her description of the events in the Strata House.

While in part 1, Caro describes the rich interior of the Strata house, in both parts 2 and 3, she takes the stance of an outsider. I find it particularly telling that Caro points out the location of her *posada* or inn on the Red de San Luis, between the Calle de la Montera and what today is the Gran Vía, not in the Buen Retiro Palace itself (13). It is not clear that she ever saw the king's face up close, though the nobility in procession get their due with descriptions of their mottos or enormous carts pulled by twenty oxen (28). She must have seen the queen, however, since she describes the seating arrangements for her and the

Princess of Carignano (21). She also gives a fairly careful description of the procession that began with the king: "El rey nuestro señor que fue el primero, / en su cartela tuvo por divisa / un claro sol" (23) [The king our lord went first. In his cartouche he has as a device the shining sun]. The count-duke follows with his devices and a retinue of nobles and their mottos. There are fifteen names cited here (23–25). The king appears "con rostro apacible" [with a peaceful face] yet with "gran poder" [great power], or "divinamente humana" [divinely human], hardly *vituperatio* but not necessarily proof of any privileged access to his royal personage (30).[8]

Caro's personal observations, such as her lodging and impressions of winter in Madrid, and comments not related to public events, situate this woman writer with respect to known facts of the royal itinerary and convey a notion of immediacy characteristic of an eyewitness account. Telling also is that the discussion of performances and the symbolism of the pageantry reveal a wealth of detail as with the Strata house in part 1. She is silent, however, on the details of the dramatic works performed during the festivities. Surely plays, authors, and famous names, such as Cosme Lotti and Calderón, would have not escaped her attention, especially since these events were organized by a fellow Sevillian, Luis Vélez de Guevara, who knew her (Varey 266). Did they ignore her in Madrid when they praised her in Seville? One can only conclude that either she was not invited to these court performances or she was an observer, not a participant, and not a very privileged one at that.

In part 3, Caro returns to the topic of poverty in Spain as she addresses "[l]a muy noble, ilustre, insigne, leal, coronada Villa de Madrid" (30) [the very noble, illustrious, famous, loyal, crowned municipality of Madrid]. She feminizes the image of the city as mother, as she did in *Valor, agravio y mujer* when she discusses Don Juan's origins in Córdoba, "madre de los ingenios" (l. 239). Here she returns to her concerns for issues of the poor and praises Madrid for its generosity in helping the disadvantaged, "las grandisoas acciones que V. Señoría cada día exerce con los desvalidos y pobres, de quien es piadosa madre: y principalmente en la bizarría y gallardo ánimo con que en las Reales fiestas del Buen Retiro mostró quan generosamente se corona Reyna de todos los del Orbe" (30) [the grandiose actions that Your Ladyship each day performs with the invalids and the poor, of whom you are a pious mother; and above all in the gallant and brave spirit with which in the royal festivities at the Buen Retiro showed how generously you are crowned queen of everyone on the planet]. Her connection between the issues of poverty and the public festivities is not just a naive one but an expression of her concern that forms a subtext here, not to undercut or subvert public spectacle but to give expression to serious issues in the public forum. In digging deeper into her *Contexto,* we find that these social issues emerge along with her own authorial voice and her self-deprecating terminology, such as the "[p]obre barquilla el ingenio" [a poor little boat is my wit], her image to express the impossibility of depicting the enormity of the festivities (31–32).[9] Here she extends the notion of "pobre" [poor] to herself while she had previously acknowledged the generosity of the Town Council of Madrid.

Given the complexity of the *Contexto,* my final comments on it concern another aspect of Ana Caro's personal reflections. She begins part 3 with forty-six lines of her own commentary in *romance* and then proceeds to discuss once more the purpose of the festivities (Ferdinand and the princess, the king at the Pardo, et cetera), until she begins the description of the participation of the *regidores* of the Town Council of Madrid. Varey includes copies of documents from Claudio de Cos and Gonzalo de Pacheco de la Vega (279–81), both mentioned by name by Caro (34). She also alludes to a poetry competition that took place, according to Varey (266) on February 19. It is unclear whether Caro participated or was simply there, since she says, "[S]e miró . . . / . . . *entre ellos* / Yo, con rústica çampoña, / *sin intentar competencias* / por no hallar afrentosas / victorias de Pam, y Marfias / en mis ambiciones locas" (34; my emphasis) [One observed . . . *among them* I, with my rustic panpipes *without attempting to compete* so as not to encounter insulting victories of Pan and Marfias in my mad ambitions].

Does this mean that she did or did not participate or that she felt her "rústica çampoña" was not on a par with the competition she found in Madrid? Since she has an abundance of names of town council participants in the processions and an enumeration of day-by-day events in this part, but no names of poets or writers, my conclusion is that she was an observer, not a participant, in this event. Her use of the impersonal reflexive "se miró" obscures the identity of the eyewitness. Yet, her affection and praise for the *regidores* both begins and ends part 3, with the prefatory address to Madrid and the concluding address to town council members in their works and successes that "en las noticias del tiempo / vitores y laureolas / le repitan las hedades / a vuestra fama gloriosa" (40) [in the news of the time, victors and laurel wreaths will repeat through the ages your glorious fame]. With this concluding statement, at least members of the Town Council of Madrid knew that someone appreciated their efforts.

To conclude, we know more about the personal life of Sor Juana than we

know about Ana Caro, Eugenia Buesso (the author of the only other published woman's account of a public festival that I have been able to locate), or
Leonor de la Cueva. Yet with the topic of false modesty, a commonplace of
discursive practice of the *relación,* Caro conveys a sense of personal presence
in Madrid as witness to a historical event, with change of climate and humble
dwelling in an inn on the Red de San Luis. Her accounts provide not only
information on her whereabouts but also give a lasting impression of self-
conscious discourse of a woman determined to make her voice heard through
the medium of propagandistic rhetoric. Her status as a writer can be traced
through these *relaciones,* especially her 1635 account, which begins with four
laudatory poems ("Flandes" 120) and thus establishes her cultural authority in
matters of public discourse.

Adding to the difficulty of understanding women's writing is baroque discourse itself that suggests ironic readings in its complexity with contradictions
between *vituperatio* and *laudatio* [praise], or amplification of subject and hyperbole of panegyrics. Is she really praising the Count-Duke of Olivares or
giving him a gentle reminder of his mission to keep Spain prosperous? Elements of the tradition of advice to princes clearly shape her discourse. Further,
access to public events does not imply change in social status for women, although we see an appeal in Caro for support from her noble patrons. While
women were certainly not full participants in the public arena, they still developed the expertise to describe real events, even those that glorify and exalt
Spanish imperialism, and establish their own identity as writers. Caro is not,
however, oblivious to the social concerns of her day, which included poverty
mentioned in both the 1635 and the 1637 accounts.

While the rhetorical apparatus of the account of public festivals with its
baroque style suggests that what is articulated is not to be read at face value,
these accounts should not be dismissed as mere propagandistic discourse, for
they can shed light on the historical era in which Caro wrote and lived with
details of the system of patronage with which she had to contend. So little is
known about Ana Caro that her accounts are one way of documenting her real
life experiences, yet she does not apologize for having authored these texts, but
refers to herself as determined in her propagandistic rhetoric. Resonances of
marginality, however, echo from one account to another. As Buesso says, "Asi
al tomar el vuelo es bien se abata / mi necia pluma que escribir procura" [Thus
upon taking flight, it is good that my foolish pen, that tries to write, desists].
Caro writes, "[D]eja, mi pluma ignorante, deja el vuelo" (12) [Cease, my ignorant pen, cease your flight]. In flying close to the sun, Ana Caro, as do her

sisters, has left a complex historical testimony of public life and private efforts to convey a sense of the grandiose at a time when the Spanish Empire needed all the help it could get.

Notes

I would like to thank my colleagues in the History Department at the U.S. Naval Academy who made comments on an earlier draft of this essay, especially Phyllis Culham who invited me to make a presentation on Ana Caro during Women's History Month, 1998. An earlier version of this paper was presented at the South Atlantic Modern Language Association in 1997.

1. Merrim states persuasively that "Speaking broadly of Golden Age theater, we might assert that whereas the male characters generally function as bearers and defenders of the social (honor) code and order, female characters—'she Devils' of sorts—subvert and disrupt them" (96).

2. Luna uses the term "de oficio" as applied to Ana Caro because of the "official" nature of her discourse in the *relaciones* as the only woman writer for whom documents exist of actual payment.

3. Since López Estrada published two of these accounts in 1983, I will refer to the "Costumbres sevillanas" as "Flandes" for the 1635 account and "Tetuán" for the 1633 account. All English translations in this chapter are my own.

4. See Lynch for an explanation of the monetary system in Spain during the seventeenth century. A ducat was worth 375 *maravedís* while the *peso*, common currency for the American treasure, was 272 *maravedís* (422).

5. I follow the spelling and punctuation of the facsimile edition noted as "Contexto" with folio-style page numbers that are not part of the original printing. There are errors in numbering in the Pérez Gómez edition. He inserts a page 16 for the dedicatory preface to the Count Duke in part 2 in between pages 12 and 13. There are two pages numbered as 34. I also did some minor editing on spelling such as "v" instead of "u" and the inclusion of standard accent marks.

6. As the eminent scholar and Hispanist Shirley Whitaker has pointed out in her numerous presentations at the Golden Age Theater Symposia in El Paso, the public would not have been able to discern Philip IV's voice.

7. My thanks to Joan Cammarata for corroborating the idea that these terms are conventions of the time. Evidence from the epistographical texts abounds in Early Modern Spain. Dr. Cammarata pointed out to me that Teresa of Ávila took great care in her epistolary rhetoric of closure. The count-duke himself uses the rhetoric of humility in a letter dated September 11, 1621, to the Archbishop of Granada, don Garceran Álvarez, who protests "las salidas del Rey de noche" [the night departures of the king] (*Epistolario* 61). The count-duke's reply is signed "B. L. M. de usía ilustrísma su servidor, El Conde de Olivares" (62) [Your servant, the Count of Olivares, kisses the hand of your very illustrious lordship]. The archbishop signs, "B.L.M. de vuecencia su mayor servidor, el Arzobispo de Granada" (61) [The Arch-

bishop of Granada your greatest servant kisses the hand of your excellency]. Yndu-
ráin also comments on such formulaic courtesy (53–79).

8. There are two page 30s in this 1951 edition. The reference here is to the first
page 30.

9. See Lope de Vega's "Pobre barquilla mía," in *Poesías líricas,* vol. 2. Montesinos
gives the date of 1632 for Vega's *barquillas,* so mention of them here would have
some resonance with Caro's reading public.

Works Cited

Aercke, Kristiaan P. *Gods of Play: Baroque Festive Performances as Rhetorical Discourse.* Albany: State University of New York Press, 1994.

Ágreda, Sor María de Jesús. *Correspondencia con Felipe IV: Religión y razón de
estado.* Ed. Consolación Baranda. Madrid: Castalia, 1991.

Arenal, Electa. "Where Woman Is Creator of the Wor(l)d. Or, Sor Juana's Discourses on Method." *Feminist Perspectives on Sor Juana Inés de la Cruz.* Ed.
Stephanie Merrim. Detroit: Wayne State University, 1991. 124–41.

Aristotle. *Poetics: Aristotle's Theory of Poetry and Fine Art.* Ed. S. H. Butcher. New
York: Dover, 1951. 1–111.

Brown, Jonathan, and J. H. Elliott. *A Palace for a King: The Buen Retiro and the
Court of Philip IV.* New Haven: Yale University Press, 1980.

Buesso, Eugenia. *Relación de la corrida de toros que la imperial ciudad de Zaragoza
hizo en obsequio a su Alteza, 1669. Escritoras españolas.* Biblioteca Nacional de
Madrid: Chadwych-Healey España, 1991–92. Microfilm.

Castillo Solórzano, Alonso de. *La garduña de Sevilla y anzuelo de las bolsas: La
picaresca española.* Ed. Ángel Valbuena y Prat, 1526–1618. Madrid: Aguilar,
1966.

Caro, Ana Mallén de Soto. *El conde Partinuplés.* Ed. Lola Luna. Kassel: Reichen-
berger, 1993.

———. *Contexto de las reales fiestas que se hizieron en el Palacio del Buen Retiro.*
Ed. Antonio Pérez Gómez. Valencia: María Amparo y Vicente Soler, 1951. [Fac-
simile ed.]

———. *Valor, agravio y mujer. Women's Acts: Plays by Women Dramatists of
Spain's Golden Age.* Ed. Teresa Scott Soufas. Lexington: University of Kentucky Press, 1997. 163–94.

Cueva y Silva, Leonor de la. *La firmeza en la ausencia. Women's Acts: Plays by
Women Dramatists of Spain's Golden Age.* Ed. Teresa Scott Soufas. Lexington:
University of Kentucky Press, 1997. 198–224.

Curtius, Ernst Robert. *European Literature and the Latin Middle Ages.* Trans.
Willard R. Trask. New York: Harper, 1963.

Deleito y Piñuela, José. *El rey se divierte.* 3d ed. Madrid: Espasa-Calpe, 1964.

Elliott, J. H. *The Count-Duke Olivares: Statesmanship in an Age of Decline.* New
Haven: Yale University Press, 1986.

Epistolario español: colección de cartas de españoles ilustres antiguos y modernos. Ed. Eugenio de Ochoa. Vol. 62. Madrid: Biblioteca de Autores Españoles, 1870.

Flynn, Maureen. "La fascinación y la mirada femenina en la España del siglo XVI." *Historia silenciada de la mujer. La mujer española desde la época medieval hasta la contemporánea.* Ed. Alain Saint-Saëns, 21–37. Madrid: Editorial Complutense, 1996.

Goldberg, Harriett, ed. *Fray Martín de Córdoba: "Jardín de nobles donzellas." A Critical Edition and Study.* Chapel Hill: North Carolina University Studies in the Romance Languages and Literatures, 1974.

González Echevarría, Roberto. *Myth and Archive.* Durham, N.C.: Duke University Press, 1998.

Jacobs, Deborah. "Critical Imperialism and Renaissance Drama: The Case of *The Roaring Girl.*" *Feminism, Bakhtin, and the Dialogic.* Ed. Dale M. Bauer and Susan Jaret McKinstry. Albany: State University of New York Press, 1991. 73–84.

Kagan, Richard L. *Lawsuits and Litigants in Castile, 1500–1700.* Chapel Hill: University of North Carolina Press, 1981.

———. *Lucrecia's Dreams: Politics and Prophecy in Sixteenth-Century Spain.* Berkeley and Los Angeles: University of California Press, 1990.

León Pinelo, Antonio de. *Anales de Madrid (desde el año 447 al de 1658).* Ed. Pedro Fernándes Martín. Madrid: Instituto de Estudios Madrileños, 1971.

López Estrada, Francisco. "Costumbres sevillanas: El poema sobre la fiesta y octava celebradas con motivo de los sucesos de Flandes en la Iglesia de San Miguel (1635) por Ana Caro Mallén." *Archivo Hispalense* 209 (1983): 109–50.

———, ed. "La frontera allende el mar: el romance por la victoria de Tetuán (1633) de Ana Caro de Mallén." *Homenaje a José Manuel Blecua: Ofrecido por sus discípulos, colegas y amigos.* Madrid: Gredos, 1983. 337–46.

———, ed. "La relación de las fiestas por los mártires del Japón de Doña Ana Caro Mallén (Sevilla), 1628." *Homenaje a Antonio Pérez Gómez.* Cieza: Artes Gráficas Soler, 1978. 51–69.

Luna, Lola. "Ana Caro, una escritora 'de oficio' del Siglo de Oro." *Bulletin of Hispanic Studies* 72 (1995): 11–26.

Lundelius, Ruth. "Ana Caro: Spanish Poet and Dramatist." *Women Writers of the Seventeenth Century.* Ed. Katharina M. Wilson and Frank J. Warnke. Athens: University of Georgia Press, 1989. 228–50.

Lynch, John. *The Hispanic World in Crisis and Change 1598–1700.* Oxford and Cambridge: Blackwell, 1992.

Mariscal, George. *Contradictory Subjects: Quevedo, Cervantes, and Seventeenth-Century Spanish Culture.* Ithaca: Cornell University Press, 1991.

Merrim, Stephanie. "'*Mores Geometricae:* The Womanscript' in the Theater of Sor Juana Inés de la Cruz." *Feminist Perspectives on Sor Juana Inés de la Cruz.* Ed. Stephanie Merrim. Detroit: Wayne State, 1991. 94–123.

Paz, Octavio. *Sor Juana Inés de la Cruz o las trampas de la fe.* 4th ed. México: Fondo de Cultura Económica, 1990.

Perry, Mary Elizabeth. *Gender and Disorder in Early Modern Seville.* Princeton: Princeton University Press, 1990.

Sabat de Rivers, Georgina. "*El Neptuno* de Sor Juana: fiesta barroca y programa político." *University of Dayton Review* 16.2 (Spring 1983): 63–73.

Simón Díaz, José, ed. *Relaciones breves de actos públicos celebrados en Madrid de 1541 a 1650.* Madrid: Instituto de Estudios Madrileños, 1982.

Smith, Paul Julian. *The Body Hispanic: Gender and Sexuality in Spanish and Spanish American Literature.* Oxford: Clarendon, 1989.

Surtz, Ronald E. *Writing Women in Late Medieval and Early Modern Spain: The Mothers of Saint Teresa of Ávila.* Philadelphia: University of Pennsylvania Press, 1995.

Torquemada, Antonio de. *Manual de escribientes.* Ed. María Josefa C. de Zamora and A. Zamora Vicente. Madrid: Anejos del Boletín de la Real Academia, 1970.

Varey, John E. "Calderón, Cosme Lotti, Velázquez and the Madrid Festivities of 1636–1637." *Renaissance Drama: Essays Principally on Masques and Entertainments.* Ed. S. Schoenbaum. Evanston: Northwestern University Press, 1968. 253–82.

Vega, Lope de. *Poesías líricas, II.* Ed. José F. Montesinos. Madrid: Espasa-Calpe, 1963.

Velasco, Sherry M. *Demons, Nausea, and Resistance in the Autobiography of Isabel de Jesús, 1611–1682.* Albuquerque: University of New Mexico Press, 1996.

Yndurráin, Domingo. "Las cartas en prosa." *Prosa y pensamiento en la época del Emperador.* Ed. Víctor García de la Concha. Salamanca: Universidad de Salamanca, 1988. 53–79.

Part III

❧

Cultural Constructs of the Feminine Psyche

Body, Mind, and Desire

7

Masquerade and the *Comedia*

Anita K. Stoll

It is a commonplace that costume is of tantamount importance in the theater. Costumes are used to create social class, time frame in period pieces, physical condition when the text calls for a handicap such as blindness, and gender in the frequent use in the Golden Age of the *mujer vestida de hombre* [woman in male dress]. Costume may also be used as a mask for hiding or protection. For example, the use of the veil or shawl was as ancient "como el haber mujeres en el mundo" [as there have been women in the world] (Arismendi 53). Just such a costume was used in Spain in the seventeenth century. Those employing it were known as *tapadas* [veiled women] and appeared in the Golden Age drama's recreation and intensification of aspects of life. Deleito y Piñuela cites a seventeenth-century source description: "El taparse es embozarse . . . de medio ojo, doblando, torciendo y prendiendo el manto de suerte que, descubriendo uno de los ojos, que siempre es el izquierdo, quede lo restante del rostro aún más oculto y disfrazado que si fuera cubierto todo"[1] [This practice is to disguise oneself . . . covering one eye, doubling, twisting and fastening the shawl so that by uncovering one of the eyes, which is always the left, the rest of the face may be even more hidden and disguised than if it were totally covered]. The practice degenerated finally "en disfraz hipócrita del vicio" [in a hypocritical disguise of vice], according to one historian (Arismendi 65).

As a result of the women's use of this disguise to move about freely, in 1560 Philip II decreed that women should always have their faces uncovered under penalty of 3,000 *maravedís* for each offense. This prohibition was renewed several times and the fine raised.[2] However history suggests that they preferred to pay the fine and continue the practice, which only disappeared in the eighteenth century during the reign of Charles III, as he and his prime minister, Esquilache, labored to move Spain into the new European ways of dress (Deleito y Piñuela 287–89). Golden Age dramas that foreground the figure of the *tapada* have useful sociological import for Golden Age scholars as well as psychological relevance for today, as an examination of works by Tirso de Molina and Calderón de la Barca will demonstrate.

Doña Blanca de los Ríos, the editor of Aguilar's *Obras dramáticas completas [de] Tirso de Molina* [*Complete Dramatic Works of Tirso de Molina*] points to *La celosa de sí misma* [*Jealous of Herself*] as the genesis and popularizer of the *tapada* on the corral stage, and playwrights in succeeding generations took up the figure for their comedies of manners (2:1435). Along with Tirso's *El amor médico* [*Love the Doctor*] are the several plays by Calderón demonstrating the adoption of the *tapada: Las mañanas de abril y mayo* [*Mornings of April and May*], *El escondido y la tapada* [*The Hidden Man and the Veiled Woman*], *Casa con dos puertas* [*House with Two Doors*], and *La dama duende* [*The Phantom Lady*].[3]

The initiating play, *La celosa de sí misma* (1621), has elicited much praise from scholars prior to this century, as well as recently. In 1850 Hartzenbush praised it as "el mejor de lo que trazó la pluma de Fray Gabriel Téllez" (11) [the best of what Fray Gabriel Téllez's pen produced]. A more contemporary discussion of it is by P.R.K. Halkhoree, who countered criticism of the play's structure and disproved it by demonstrating unity around a central theme, that of *tropelía*, or visual deception. He calls the play a social satire written to poke fun at court society. The figure of the *tapada* is at the core of the visual deception, although this theme of deception is played out in several ways. This play features a corollary aspect of the disguise also described historically:

> [E]sta costumbre era típica del coqueteo femenino. Solía quedar libre y a la vista una mano y, a veces, algo del antebrazo, que jugaba sutilmente con la parte libre del chal. Y si ese ojo era hermoso y expresaba mucho y bien, si esa mano era un pájaro que revoloteaba con no menor donaire, podía resultar una terrible arma de enardecimento. (Quoted in Arismendi 54)

> [The costume was typical of feminine flirting. Usually a hand, which played subtly with the free part of the shawl, and sometimes part of the forearm, remained uncovered. And if that eye was beautiful and expressed a lot well, if that hand was a bird that fluttered effectively, it could be a strong aphrodisiac.]

Thus the enticing hand added to the charm of the visible left eye. The wide-spread use of the seductive disguise and hand during the seventeenth century is illustrated in Ricardo Palma's "La conspiración de la saya y el manto" ["The Conspiracy of the Cloak and Veil"] in his *Tradiciones peruanas* [*Peruvian Traditions*], where he quotes a poem: "Digo que no eran dedos / los de esa mano / sino que eran claveles / de a cinco en ramo" (196) [I swear that those were not fingers on her hand but rather five carnations in a bouquet].

The very first scene of *Celosa* illustrates the fluidity of appearances, demonstrating Tirso's penchant for pointing the direction of the whole play early on. As the play begins, the poor resident from León, Melchor, and his servant Ventura arrive in Madrid to meet for the first time his wealthy bride-to-be, the daughter of an old friend of his father. Tirso signals the running joke on "unseen" and deceptive viewing as Ventura's comment on women suggests a confusing multiplicity of visual realities and identities: "Dama hay aquí, si reparas / en gracias del solimán, / a quien en un hora dan / sus salserillas diez caras" (1441) [There are ladies here, if you look closely, you'll see the effects wrought by cosmetics; within an hour she produces ten faces from her tiny vials].

Other parts of this opening conversation lead to similar examples of perceptual complications expressed through metonymy and metaphor. Among these is the *gracioso* [comic figure] Ventura's prophetic and metatheatrical reaction to Melchor's wish to enter a church for Mass: "¿Qué va que antes que a tu suegro / ... / veas, tienes de caer / en la red de un manto negro?" (1442) [And thus, before you see your father-in-law, you must be caught in the net of a black veil?]. Thus he metonymically evokes beforehand his master's falling in love with the gloved hand (*red*—the "net" of the previous quote) of a woman well-disguised by a shawl (*manto*). The lady in question, Magdalena, who is really Melchor's intended, is repeatedly referred to as *manto* or *mano,* and the *mano* as the hand-covering *red,* as identified by such various qualities and parts of the hand as *hoyuelos, blancura,* and *dedos* [dimples, whiteness, fingers]: "¡Ay! Qué mano! ¡Qué belleza! / ¡Qué blancura! ¡Qué donaire! / ¡Qué hoyuelos! ¡Qué tez, qué venas!" (1445) [What a hand! What beauty! What whiteness! What dimples! What complexion! What veins!]. There are many other examples of multiple metonymies, such as Melchor's speech: "Dadme por esa merced / a besar la nieve helada / del puerto de mis deseos" (1481) [Allow me the kindness of kissing the brilliant whiteness of the portal of my desires], a word embroidery in the Gongoristic style. What he means, of course, is let me kiss your hand. The trope is underscored for its comic value by Ventura: "¡Que bien del espejo digas, / sin ver no más que la tapa! / ... / ¡De

la tumba por el paño! / ¡De la toca por la lista! / ... / ¡De la espada por la vaina!"
(1461) [Of the mirror you may well say, without seeing more than the surface!
... Of the tomb only the shroud! Of the veil only the ribbon! ... Of the sword
only the scabbard!].

Of course when Melchor meets Magdalena without the disguise of the
manto, he finds her not as attractive or desirable as his *tapada,* pronouncing his
judgment: "Fea mujer" (1457) [ugly woman], and he decides to end the engagement and his chance for wealth in favor of his imaginary love. He shows
his complete blindness, or, we may say, subjective perception carried to comic
extreme, with the following statement as he tries to explain to his cousin the
beauty of his loved one: "[N]o sé yo por qué al amor / le llaman y pintan ciego,
/ pues lo que no ve no estima" (1453) [I don't know why they call and describe
love as blind, since what one does not see one does not esteem]. He has only
seen a *tapada* who shows one eye, and her gloved hand, and so he is a perfect
example of his own unique worldview.[4]

The church where the two encounter each other is famous in the annals of
the period as a place for the women to flirt and the men to pursue. True to this
reputation, Magdalena sees and then entices Melchor with such movements as
the removal of her net glove. (We should not fail to recognize the symbolic
value of the "net.") The text suggests that she did this repeatedly, bringing
Halkhoree to comment: "This is surely the earliest representation on stage of
an embryonic striptease!" (74). From this beginning she continues masquerading throughout the entire play for Melchor, first as this unnamed *manto/red*
and then identified as the fictitious countess.

The figure of the left eye and hand of *El amor médico* serves again to underscore the role of the male imagination and misperception. Gaspar lived in the
home of Jerónima's brother for a month without noticing her. She decides to
pursue him and in doing so she puts herself in his path various times as a *tapada*
with different identities. He falls in love with her as *tapada* twice, once as a
Spanish woman living in Toledo, and once as a Portuguese woman. In each
case he falls in love with her hand. He is so fickle (or, we may say, susceptible
to an image triggering his ideal) that his servant, the *gracioso* Tello, constantly
teases him about his inconstancy: "Tantas quiere cuantas ve" (999) [He loves
as many as he sees]; "¡Bueno es que en un año mudes / tres mujeres! ¿Son
camisas?" (1000) [So in one year you fall for three different women? Are they
shirts?]; "la cuarta / que hemos mudado" (1006) [the fourth that we have
changed]; and "[M]ientras pasa / otra, ... vendrá a ser la dama quinta" (1007)
[When another goes by, she will be the fifth].

These multiple-identity characters leading to visual deception, illustrating the human tendency to perceive subjectively, resurface also in Calderón's plays. These works, dated between 1629 and the mid 1630s, are variations on the theme.[5] The best-known play incorporating the figure of the *tapada* is *La dama duende* (1629). As the play opens, the *dama* protagonist is disguised with her *manto* as she flees from her brother, who happened upon her on the street. She has left her brother's home secretly in this disguise because, as she says, otherwise she is an enclosed prisoner. The *galán* [suitor], Don Manuel, responds to her plea for help and detains the brother, allowing her to escape. This scene underscores the prevalence in the society of the subterfuge. The disguise leads to Don Manuel's giving her an additional identity, that of "La dama duende," exemplifying the baroque period's preoccupation with the nature of reality.

While *La dama duende* contains only this opening scene presenting the *tapada,* the popularity of the figure in the society apparently led Calderón to expand her role on the same pattern in the second play: *Casa con dos puertas* (1632), the beginning of the *refrán* [proverb] that ends "mala es de guardar" [is difficult to guard]. The connection with the earlier play made glaringly obvious as the *gracioso* metatheatrically points out: "La dama duende habrá sido / que volver a vivir quiere," (278) [It must have been the phantom lady, who wishes to come back to life].[6] The paradoxical aspect from Tirso's play of the *galán* who falls in love with a person whom he really doesn't see is repeated here by Lisardo, who admits "que adora lo que no ve" (277). When he discusses the woman's use of the *manto* with Calabazas, this *gracioso* cynically suggests:

Mujer que se viene así
a hablar con quien no la vea,
donde ostentarse desea
bachillera e importuna,
que me maten si no es una
muy discretísima fea,
que por el pico ha querido
pescarnos. (278)

[A woman who shows up this way to speak with someone who can't see her, where she wants to show herself off as learned and importunate— devil take me if she isn't a very clever ugly one who just by showing her beak wants to catch us.]

In yet another play, *Las mañanas de abril y mayo* (1634), Calderón again includes the *tapada* and salutes Tirso's popularizing play with the use of the title "celosa de sí mesma" twice in the work. He takes Tirso's recognition of the role that imagination plays in amorous attachments and adapts it with a twist to one of the story lines of the play, a case of misrecognition by a married man who falls in love with a presumed stranger who is later revealed to be his own wife. The telling passage that underscores the supreme role played by his imagination makes clear that he didn't really see the disguised person:

Bajaba por una cuesta
una mujer. . . .
un encanto, sí, embozado,
disfrazado, sí, un hechizo. (579)

[There coming down the hill was a woman. . . . Really enchanting, disguised, covered up, of course, bewitching.]

Calderón emphasizes the widespread use of the practice, as the lady's servant, Inés, comments to the married Doña Clara:

Si tapadas
estamos y en este traje,
que es en el que todas andan,
¿Cómo te han de conocer? (575)

[If we go veiled and in this get-up, which is what everyone does, how are they to recognize you?]

It is obvious that one of Calderón's strategies in pleasing his public is his clever use of intertextuality in the reference to popular plays and traditions. He again includes in this work the following metatheatrical reference: "¡Vive Dios / que tienen aquestos lances / cosas de la Dama Duende!" (593) [My heavens! These happenings / are just like in *The Phantom Lady!*].

His work *El escondido y la tapada* (1636) also foregrounds the figure even in the title and is cited as the inspiration for Sor Juana Inés de la Cruz's use of the *gracioso* Castaño in *Los empeños de una casa* [*The Cares of a House*] who cross-dresses as a *tapado* in one of the most hilarious scenes in the whole *comedia* repertoire (Weimer; Valbuena Briones "La Particularidad," "Calderón"). The case for grouping these plays around the 1629 *La dama duende* is cemented in this play in yet another reference to the original, as the servant Beatriz comments: "Esto ya es hecho, porque es / paso de la *Dama Duende*" (693) [This is already established, because it's taken from *The Phantom Lady*].

An inquiry into an explanation for the popularity of the *tapada* in seventeenth-century society, beyond its convenience for enclosed women, leads to an investigation of its psychological grounds in the psychoanalytical theories of Sigmund Freud and his followers. The objection has previously been raised that it is improper to apply such twentieth-century theories to seventeenth-century creations. Both Freud and later Jacques Lacan answered this by claiming that human subjects as language users have always had the same psychic structure (Sullivan 84). The baroque emphasis on the problematic relationship of reality and fantasy corresponds well with the view in psychoanalysis of reality as subjective.

Freud's follower, Jacques Lacan, has stated that Woman is masquerade. Lacan's idea of psychic development is based on a child's unhappy discovery, at about the age of eighteen months, that he and mother are really separate persons, despite his greatest wish, partly through the presence of a third person, often the father. This represents the child's entry into the world of language and culture. His accepting this severe blow causes a division in the psyche, initiating subjectivity and sexual difference, the desire for the fantasized ideal m(other). This acceptance carries with it the person's need for a constructed imaginary identity, a precarious, uncertain project, and, therefore, susceptible to uncertainty and alteration and the necessity for reinforcement. The fantasized ideal is Lacan's symbolic phallus, which represents the lack of the desired union with the m(other) and possessed by no one. Each person carries an impossible ideal of what, or who, will fulfill this lack. Love is the label we give to the attempt to fulfill this need.

For the constructed imaginary identity the symbolic phallus is that which is identified as filling the lack. According to Lacan the masquerade for the female serves to show what she does not have by showing through adornment, the putting-on, of something else. She becomes, at least in the mind of the one who desires her, the symbolic phallus, representing for the male what he lacks and desires, thereby also reinforcing his sexual identity. She wishes to put on this adornment in order to stimulate the masculine subject's fantasized ideal with the hope of attracting her own fantasied masculine completion or perfect mate. As Lacan put it, "[I]mages and symbols for the feminine subject cannot be isolated from images and symbols of the woman" (90); only thus can she represent lack, be what is wanted. Adornment *is* the woman. The *tapada*'s masquerade fits well into this system, since she is identified by such adornment. Another of his statements fits perfectly the situation of the *tapada*: lack "is never presented other than as a reflection on a veil" (90).

Thus the nature of femininity is to be the cause of masculine desire. As one of the authors of *Feminine Sexuality,* Jacqueline Rose, rephrases it: "The concept of the symbolic states that the woman's sexuality is inseparable from the representation through which it is produced. For Lacan, masquerade is the very definition of 'femininity' precisely because it is constructed with reference to the male sign" (43). According to the theory, women dress femininely in order to trigger the masculine fantasy of his ideal, and on the chance that the one she attracts may evoke her own fantasy ideal.[7] In order not to leave out the men in a discussion of representation, we should note that the male version is "display," as he attempts to assert "I *have* the phallus," but it is only an imaginary illusion: for example, all the trappings of authority, hierarchy, order, position (such as medals, ties, uniforms), which men use to reinforce their identities and to manifest power. The word "homeovestism" or "macho masquerade" has recently been coined to describe the use of clothing by those men who use exaggeratedly masculine costume (Moorjani 24). The concepts of defending one's honor and the swordplay typical of seventeenth-century Spain also could be seen as serving this purpose.

A look at Sor Juana's *Los empeños de una casa* (1683) (Valbuena Briones "Calderón") returns us to the end of the seventeenth century to observe her genius in carrying the whole idea of the *tapada* to its ultimate farcical moment, illustrating perfectly the role the feminine subject's masquerade and masculine imagination play in male/female relationships. Sor Juana's *gracioso* Castaño is comically played out as he dresses himself as a woman on stage. He tellingly observes:

> ¿Quién duda
> que en el punto que me vean
> me sigan cuatro mil lindos
> de aquestos que galantean
> a salga lo que saliere,
> que a bulto se amartelan,
> no de la belleza que es,
> sino de la que ellos piensan? (685)

[Who can doubt that as soon as they see me I'm pursued by 4000 of those gallants who pay court to any woman they see, heedlessly falling in love, not with the beauty before their eyes, but with the one they imagine they see?]

And now we return to the issue of the relevance of twentieth-century theories as applied to seventeenth-century life.[8] Supporting the assertion of psychoanalysts that the human psyche is essentially the same throughout the ages is an early example of masquerade, found in Aristophanes' play *Lysistrata*. Early in the play the women begin to plan their actions to halt the war by considering their "weapons" as Kleonike speaks, "There's nothing cosmic about cosmetics—and Glamor is our only talent. All we can do is sit, primped and painted, made up and dressed up (carried away by her argument) ravishing in saffron wrappers, peekaboo peignoirs, exquisite negligees, those chic, expensive little slippers that come from the east" (11). They are planning to exert their influence over men by providing the ideal image to evoke desire, then to withhold their attentions until the warriors give up the battle.

Like Aristophanes' timeless play, these Golden Age works demonstrate yet again the bases for the continuing interest of a reading/play-viewing public in seventeenth-century works. Those writers who speak for the ages have comprehended the workings of the unchanging human psyche theorized by Lacan and Freud and have known how to satirize them in an effective and enduring fashion, so that we today, at the beginning of the twenty-first century, can observe again man's unchanging nature.

Notes

1. This is quoted by Deleito y Piñuela (123), citing from *Ilustración de la Real Prematica de las Tapadas, Velos antiguos y modernos en los rostros de las mujeres. Sus conveniencias y daños* (Madrid, 1641). All English translations throughout this essay are mine.

2. León Pinelo's *Anales de Madrid* records these, for example, "año 1639": "Una de doze [prematicas] para que ninguna muger anduviese tapada sino descubierto el rostro de modo que pudiese ser vista i conocida" (316) [One of twelve (royal ordinances) decreeing that no woman would walk around veiled but with her face revealed so that she could be seen and recognized].

3. I have not looked into Lope de Vega's voluminous production, although it seems likely that he also employed this figure.

4. Mitchell and Rose's edition of selected readings of Jacques Lacan's writing provides a discussion of part-objects, which is what Melchor desires in his worship of Magdalena's hand (11; 119–20).

5. The dates are those provided by Valbuena Briones in his Aguilar edition of Calderón's *Comedias*.

6. In the introduction to Calderón's *Comedias,* Valbuena Briones also indicates several other similarities between the two plays (273–75).

7. Additional explanation and commentary can be found in Riviere's "Womanliness as Masquerade" in which she says that womanliness "could be assumed and worn as a mask, both to hide the possession of masculinity and to avert the reprisals expected if she was found to possess it" (38).

8. The validity of applying twentieth-century theories to seventeenth-century products is attested to by the several essays that have appeared recently: Conlon's "Amón: The Psychology of a Rapist," Sullivan's "Love, Matrimony and Desire in the Theater of Tirso de Molina," Welles's "The Anxiety of Gender: The Transformation of Tamar in Tirso's *La venganza de Tamar* and *Los cabellos de Absalón,*" and Stroud's *The Play in the Mirror.*

Works Cited

Arismendi Ariel, María Elena. "Las tapadas." *Revista de Dialectología y Tradiciones Populares* 43 (1988): 53–58.

Aristophanes. *Lysistrata.* Ed. William Arrowsmith. Trans. Douglass Parker. Ann Arbor, Mich.: Ann Arbor Paperbacks, 1969.

Calderón de la Barca. *Obras completas: Comedias.* Ed. Julián Valbuena Briones. Madrid: Aguilar, 1987.

Conlon, Raymond. "Amón: The Psychology of a Rapist." *Bulletin of the Comediantes* 45.1 (Summer 1993): 41–52.

Deleito y Piñuela, José. *La mujer, la casa y la moda.* Madrid: Espasa Calpe, 1954.

Halkhoree, P.R.K. *Social and Literary Satire in the Comedies of Tirso de Molina.* Ottawa: Dovehouse, 1989.

Hartzenbush, Juan Eugenio. *Comedias escogidas de Fray Gabriel Téllez.* Madrid: Rivadeneyra, 1850.

Juana Inés de la Cruz, Sor. *Los empeños de una casa. Comedias, sainetes y prosa. Obras completas.* Ed. Alberto G. Salceda. Vol. 4. México: Fondo de cultura económica, 1957.

Lacan, Jacques. *Feminine Sexuality.* Ed. Juliet Mitchell and Jacqueline Rose. Trans. Jacqueline Rose. New York: Norton, 1983.

León Pinelo, Antonio. *Anales de Madrid (desde el año 447 al de 1658).* Ed. Pedro Fernández Martín. Madrid: Instituto de estudios madrileños, 1971.

Molina, Tirso de. *La celosa de sí misma. Obras dramáticas completas [de] Tirso de Molina.* Ed. Blanca de los Ríos. 3 vols. Madrid: Aguilar, 1946.

Moorjani, Angela. "Fetishism, Gender Masquerade, and the Mother-Father Fantasy." *Psychoanalysis, Feminism, and the Future of Gender Psychology in the Humanities.* Ed. Joseph H. Smith and Afaf M. Mahfouz. Baltimore: Johns Hopkins University Press, 1994. 22–41.

Palma, Ricardo. *Tradiciones peruanas.* Edición publicada bajo los auspicios del gobierno del Perú. Vol. 2. Madrid: Calpe, 1888.

Riviere, Joan. "Womanliness as Masquerade." *Formations of Fantasy.* Ed. Victor Burgin, Donald James, and Cora Kaplan. New York: Methuen, 1986.

Rose, Jacqueline. "Introduction II." *Feminine Sexuality.* Ed. Juliet Mitchell and Jacqueline Rose. Trans. Jacqueline Rose. New York: Norton, 1983.

Stroud, Matthew D. *The Play in the Mirror.* Lewisburg, Pa.: Bucknell University Press, 1996.

Sullivan, Henry W. "Love, Matrimony and Desire in the Theater of Tirso de Molina." *Bulletin of the Comediantes* 37.1 (Summer 1985): 83–100.

Valbuena Briones, Julián. "Calderón y el teatro seglar de Sor Juana Inés de la Cruz." *Archivum Calderonianum. Hacia Calderón. Décimo coloquio anglo-germano.* Ed. Hans Flasche. Stuttgart: Franz Steiner Verlag, 1994. 79–89.

———. "La particularidad de *Los empeños de una casa,* de Sor Juana Inés de la Cruz, ante la tradición calderoniana." *Hispanic Journal* 18.1 (1997): 159–68.

Weimer, Christopher B. "Another Look at Castaño: Sor Juana, Calderón, and the Intertextualities of Comic Cross-Dressing." Paper read at the Spanish Golden Age Theater Symposium, El Paso, Texas, 1997.

Welles, Marcia. "The Anxiety of Gender: The Transformation of Tamar in Tirso's *La venganza de Tamar* and *Los cabellos de Absalón.*" *Bulletin of the Comediantes* 47.2 (1995): 341–72.

8

Dreams, Voices, Signatures

Deciphering Woman's Desires in Angela de Azevedo's
Dicha y desdicha del juego

Frederick A. de Armas

Studying the Elizabethan theater, Sue-Ellen Case asserts: "The female body had become the site for sexuality. If women performed in the public arena, the sexuality inscribed upon their bodies would elicit immoral sexual responses from the men, bringing disorder to the social body" (20). A similar situation is found in the Spanish theater of the Golden Age. As Teresa Scott Soufas declares: "The presence of women in the performance is presented as the source of obscenity" (*Dramas* 25).[1] Women playwrights of the Spanish Golden Age thus strove to modify female characterization on the stage in order to challenge the misogyny of the moralists and to question accepted social practices—thus metamorphosing a site for sexuality and disorder into a place for chastity and reform. Angela de Azevedo, a little-known playwright who served as lady in waiting for Queen Isabel de Borbón, wife of Philip IV, is the author of three *comedias* [plays] that challenge the traditional perception of women's roles.

Studying Azevedo's one play that has a secular focus, *El muerto disimulado* [*The Feigned Death*], Anita Stoll shows how the playwright, through the use of cross-dressing and "the inversion of traditional behavior patterns" (156), is intent on "breaking cultural stereotypes" (161). Stoll concludes that "Azevedo renders a portrait of woman as intelligent and capable of a great deal more than the traditions of domesticity and silence that society of the time regarded as appropriate" (161). Studying her other two plays, *Dicha y desdicha del juego y devoción de la Virgen* [*Good and Ill Fortune in Gaming and Devotion to the*

Virgen] and *La margarita del Tajo que dio nombre a Santarén* [*The Pearl of the Tagus River Who Gave Her Name to Santaren*], Soufas shows how Azevedo actively seeks to transform the female body as seen on stage. *Dicha y desdicha del juego* not only shows the "objectification and commodification of the female" but also presents an extended critique of the dowry system and more generally "of the male supervision of marriage arrangements" (Soufas, *Dramas* 73). While questions of greed and dowry show the economic excesses of patriarchy, the commodification of the female body, when juxtaposed to woman's "virtuous and faithful intentions" (85), portrays the inhumanity of male power and the humanity of feminine behavior.

Angela de Azevedo not only shows the female body as a place for conflicting visions; she also conceives of theater as a site that must be opened to new perceptions. Studying Renaissance social and theatrical practices, Ania Loomba concludes: "The drive to limit and contain theater space was concurrent with and similar to the effort to limit and contain women" (131). This essay will show how Azevedo's *Dicha y desdicha del juego* is a work that challenges both the containment of theater and of women. Through characters' writing and deciphering, Azevedo's *comedia* reveals a dichotomy that privileges women's roles and questions the usefulness of patriarchal power. While men misread and contain women through theories of physiognomy and demonic dreams, women exhibit their hidden desires through the theory of signatures and the phenomenon of kledonomancy. An examination of these four elements, together with astrological prediction, will reveal how male containment can be written off or at least re-written through the secret writings of female desire.

In a cleverly dramatic beginning reminiscent of the works of Andrés de Claramonte,[2] Azevedo's play shows a darkened scene where the spectator hears the disembodied voice of Felisardo who is railing against the person who has invaded the sanctity of his home. He then appears "a medio vestir, de noche, con la espada en la mano" (4) [half dressed, in night clothes, with sword in hand],[3] searching for the interloper. From the opposite door Sombrero comes rushing in. He is Felisardo's servant and *gracioso* [comic figure] who is chasing would-be robbers. In a typical quid pro quo scene,[4] where one person is mistaken for another in the confusion of the night, Felisardo takes his servant Sombrero for an interloper while the *gracioso* believes that Felisardo is a thief. When María, who is Felisardo's sister, and her servant bring in a light, the violence comes to an end. Curiously, both Felisardo and Sombrero had begun their night chase because of a dream. Sombrero admits that he has been afraid of thieves since he was little: "a quien cobré tanto miedo / desde muy niño, señores, / que siempre sueño con ellos" (ll. 128–30) [I had become so afraid of them since early childhood, gentlemen, that I always dream of them]. While Sombrero's dream foregrounds the typical cowardice of the *gracioso,* Felisardo's dream is more poignant and telling. He also dreams of a thief entering the house, but what is to be stolen is his sister's honor:

> cuando de la fantasía
> tuvo unos avisos necios,
> de que en esta casa, que es
> sagrado del honor templo,
> entrando un hombre atrevido,
> profanamente resuelto,
> robar quería (¡que arrojo!)
> la prenda rica (¿dirélo?)
> perdona, hermana querida,
> si te agravio, si te ofendo,
> que son cosas de sueño. (ll. 55–65)

[when fancy gave me the foolish warning that in this house, which is the sacred temple of honor, a daring man had entered, profanely resolved to rob (what rashness!) the rich jewel (can I say it?). Forgive me, beloved sister, if I insult you, if I offend you, but these are things that arise in dreams].

Using a sacred language to refer to his home and his honor, Felisardo evinces his fear that his sister will be the cause of his dishonor. Woman, then, appears as a possession of man, as the weak link in a man's honor. Even though Felisardo admits that his sister's virtue is beyond reproach, and even though he praises her for her devotion to the Virgin Mary, his dream betrays both his commodification of woman and his attempt to contain her desires.

The interpretation of dreams was a common practice from classical times well into the Spanish Golden Age. Lope de Vega, for example, seems extremely knowledgeable concerning oneiric phenomena, using them in a number of his plays.[5] Lope was probably aware of Macrobius's *Commentary on the Dream of Scipio,* a key classical text for the classification of dreams; and he may have also known Achmet's *Oneirocriticon* [*Dream Interpretation*],[6] which was published together with Artemidorus's *Oneirocritica* [*The Interpretation of Dreams*] in 1603 by Nicolaus Rigaultius. Artemidorus, a second-century native of Ephesus, traveled extensively collecting dreams and analyzing them. His treatise is perhaps the most famous classical text on dream interpretation. Michel Foucault explains that, for Artemidorus, there are two types of dreams, the *oneiroi* or prophetic dreams and the *enypnia*.[7] Felisardo's dream seems to belong to this second type. They are, as Foucault explains, "dreams that express the present affects of the individual and 'run their course in proximity to the mind'" (*Care* 10).

Macrobius provides a very apt example: "the man who fears the plots or might of an enemy and is confronted with him in his dream" (88). As Foucault explains: "This kind of dream has a simple diagnostic value. . . . [I]t conveys that which is deficiency or excess in relation to the body, and that which is fear or desire in relation to the mind" (*Care* 10). The diagnosis, then, has nothing to do with María and everything to do with Felisardo. Artemidorus claims that this type of oneiric phenomena occurs when the dreamer has not been able to preserve a balanced physiology, when passions, desires, or fears can easily take over (*Care* 12). Felisardo's cares,[8] his desires, then, have overwhelmed his mind and his physiology to the point that he acts out his dream. That he battles with his own servant who also acts out a dream shows that his lower nature is almost as much out of control as in the fearful *gracioso*. In a subtle manner, Azevedo is utilizing oneiric theories to show Felisardo's fear of losing his honor as a worthless fantasy that corresponds to the imbalances in his constitution. Indeed, as Pedro Ciruelo contends, dreams can be caused by "los humores que se mueuen dentro del cuerpo" (64) [the humors that move within the body].

But there is one more troubling element in Felisardo's dream. The spectator soon discovers that this oneiric phenomenon was inspired by the devil. *El Demonio* [the devil] himself appears, and in a very lengthy *relación* confesses his role: "moví la fantasía, imaginando / que fuera una desdicha sucediendo" (ll. 524–25) [I moved their fancy, hoping that a calamity would take place]. While the devil hoped to create a *desdicha* [misfortune] from the dreams, he failed, he thinks, because of the Virgin's protection for her devotees Felisardo and María. This demonic explanation does not conflict with the general theory of the nightmare. Macrobius points to the popular belief in the incubus as affecting such dreams.[9] The *Malleus Maleficarum* [*The Hammer of Witches*], the most important treatise on witchcraft of the period, shows how the devil can affect the human being through disposition: "[B]y a similar admonition of the disposition and humours of men, he renders some more disposed to anger, or concupiscence or other passions" (51). Indeed, the devil can "stir up and

excite the inner perceptions and humours, so that ideas retained in the reposi-
tories of their minds are drawn out and made apparent to the faculties of fancy
and imagination" (50). In fact, the devil is particularly attracted to the noxious
or diseased humors in the person. For example, adust or unnatural melancholy was often referred to as a *balneum diaboli* [the devil's bath] (McCrary
122), since the devil enjoyed plunging into these liquids. Thus, the devil uses
Felisardo's physiological imbalances to insinuate himself into his disposition,
perceptions, and humors creating vivid dreams through the fancy and imagination.

Although Felisardo is the male protagonist of *Dicha y desdicha del juego*
and is portrayed in many ways as an admirable figure, he falls short when
contrasted with his sister María. While Felisardo's humoral imbalance leads
him to have demonic dreams where he suspects and pursues his sister, thinking
of her as a site for lustfulness that must be contained, she is portrayed in the
play as chaste and devoted to the Virgin Mary, to whom she constantly prays.
María's light (both María and her servant Rosela bring in a light to the darkened room) brings clarity and order to the darkness and violence of Felisardo's
demonic nightmare visions.[10]

A similar contrast between male and female desires and actions can be
found in Violante (Felisardo's beloved) and Don Nuño (Violante's father).
Nuño wants to marry his daughter to a rich young nobleman, Don Fadrique,
although he realizes that Felisardo is a better person. Felisardo, although
noble, is very poor. Nuño also realizes that his daughter is in love with Felisardo and that she is saddened by the new arrangement: "Muy triste a Violante
veo / desde el día que la he hablado / en su casamiento, indicio / del amor de
Felisardo" (ll. 2057–60) [I have seen that Violante has been very sad since the
day I spoke to her about her marriage, which points to her love for Felisardo].

Nuño's attitude shows how he views his own daughter as a commodity that
he can sell to the highest bidder. It also evinces his cruelty and insensitivity to
his daughter's desires. Nuño is able to ascertain Violante's feelings through
physiognomy and the understanding of facial transformations due to an amorous passion. Gian Battista della Porta published in 1586 what was perhaps the
most popular book on the subject, *De Humana Physignomia* [*Human Physiognomy*]. Julio Caro Baroja describes its main thrust: "El fundamento de la
fisiognomía está en la correspondencia de las vicisitudes del alma y del cuerpo;
porque el alma enamorada, envidiosa, atormentada, sorprendida se refleja en
rasgos corporales" (122) [The basis of physiognomy is to be found in the correspondence between the vicissitudes of the soul and of the body; because the

soul that is amorous, envious, or tormented is surprised when it finds itself mirrored in corporeal traits]. Spanish theologians such as Martín del Río considered physiognomy a licit and valid way to judge character, intelligence, passions, and even the future (137). Indeed, in his *Disquisiciones mágicas* [*Treatise on Magic*] Martín del Río stresses the study of the face and the forehead in these matters (Caro Baroja 137; del Río 151).

Having found indications of Violante's love for Felisardo, Nuño, after telling her that she is to marry Fadrique, searches for signs in Violante's face as prescribed in most treatises on physiognomy. He clearly perceives her vexation:

> que aunque por disimularlo
> se ha empeñado su prudencia,
> en el rostro, que es traslado
> de las pasiones del pecho,
> se deletrea a lo claro
> su enojo.
> (ll. 2064–69)

[Even though through prudence she has attempted to hide this, it is clearly written in the anger shown in her face, which is a mirror of the passions of the heart].

Once again, Nuño disregards his findings because he wants to marry his daughter to a rich man (ll. 2080–82). What he does not know is that Fadrique is mutable in both his amorous passion and in his promises. On returning from the Indies, Fadrique's ship capsizes in a storm. He promises the Virgin Mary that if she saves him from this storm, he will marry the poorest but most virtuous woman he will encounter in Oporto. He soon meets María, Felisardo's sister, and expresses his love for her. But, when his father tells him that he is to marry the very rich Violante, he forgets María.

While the leading male characters in Azevedo's *Dicha y desdicha del juego* are cruel, avaricious, suspicious of women, and mutable in their love, the lead women show compassion, unselfishness, and firmness of purpose in their love interests. When Violante learns that her father has betrothed her to Fadrique, her maid attempts to soothe her by telling her that this man may be more handsome than Felisardo. Violante replies that even if he were as handsome as Adonis, Narcissus, or Ganymede (ll. 1614–15), she would still reject him because her heart is satisfied with Felisardo. Indeed, she proclaims that "es imposible el mudarme" (l. 1643) [it is impossible to change my mind]. The only way that Fadrique can win her heart is for her to have a second such organ: "Corazón pues nuevo aguardo / en que don Fadrique escriba, / porque en éste está muy viva / la firma de Felisardo" (ll. 1664–67) [I thus wait for a new heart in which don Fadrique can write, for this one shows too vividly Felisardo's signature].

By expressing that her heart holds Felisardo's signature, Violante may be hinting at the theory of signatures. Explaining the order of things as perceived by the sixteenth-century mind, Michel Foucault considers signatures as a way in which the ordered world of similitude and resemblances makes itself known: "These buried similitudes must be indicated on the surface of things; there must be visible marks for the invisible analogies" (*Order* 26). Foucault then quotes Paracelsus: "It is not God's will that what he creates for man's benefit and what he has given us should remain hidden. . . . And even though he has hidden certain things, he has allowed nothing to remain without exterior and visible signs in the form of special marks—just as a man who has buried a hoard of treasure marks the spot that he may find it again" (*Order* 26).

Felisardo is Violante's treasured love. His signature thus rests upon her heart, showing that the amorous sympathy between these two human beings is of a cosmic nature and part of the book of the world. Thus, the only way Violante can love Fadrique is to have a second heart. Violante, then, can clearly read the prose of the world and cherish the sympathies of nature. While her father can also read these signs (through the science of physiognomy), he rejects them in favor of personal gain. Felisardo is even more unskilled at reading the prose of the world. He is unable to interpret dreams and chases demonic fantasies instead of reading his own shortcomings in the oneiric phenomenon.

Very much like Violante, María shows her firmness in love, her desire for only one man, Don Fadrique. Such is the power of her immutable desire, that the prose of the world is not content to have her hold the signature of her beloved. Instead, the world will actually voice her amorous choice. María tries to confess to her maid the name of the man she loves. But instead of saying this name, she goes on to endlessly describe her feelings. Finally, when she appears ready to name him, it is her brother, shouting from another room, who completes the phrase: "Don Fadrique" (l. 1851). It is not that Felisardo has heard his sister and wants to name her beloved; he is actually shouting Fadrique's name in anger, since he has just found out that Fadrique is betrothed to his own beloved Violante. Thus, Felisardo is unaware that his shout completes his sister's phrase. María has just received an omen known as kledonomancy. Otis

Green defines it as "the interpretation of words overheard by chance as applying to a given critical situation of which the speaker of the words has no idea"
(2:237). Not much interpretation is needed in the case of María. It is as if nature
is shouting back to her the name of her secret beloved—and it is her brother,
who knows nothing of María's passion, who shouts these words. Kledonomancy, then, as Claude Anibal suggests, consists of "words or phrases casually
uttered by persons quite innocent of their dramatic significance" ("*Voces del
cielo*" 57).

The prevalence in the belief in kledonomancy during the Spanish Golden
Age can be attested by Ciruelo's extended discussion of this phenomenon in
his *Reprouacion de las supersticiones y hechizerias* [*A Reproof of Superstitions
and Sorcery*]. He labels it simply as: "Omen: quiere dezir adeuinar por dichos
o hechos que otros los hazen a otro proposito" (63) [Omen: it means to divine
through words or deeds that which others do for another purpose]. After giving numerous examples of how diviners interpret words that are not intended
for them, he prohibits the use of kledonomancy as a mortal sin since the
divination is accomplished "por inspiracion del diablo con quien tiene pacto
secreto" (63) [by the devil's inspiration with whom (the diviner) has a secret
pact]. However, in Azevedo's play, kledonomancy is not to be seen as a demonic moment. First of all, the words are not interpreted by a diviner; and
second, María is not in doubt as to whom she loves—she has merely hesitated
in stating his name. Although Ciruelo condemns this practice, it is very common in the literature of the period. Perhaps the most famous example occurs in
Don Quijote, part 2. As two boys quarrel over crickets, one says: "[Q]ue no la
has de ver en todos los días de tu vida" (2.77.581) [You will never see her again
in your life]. Don Quijote takes it to mean that he will never see Dulcinea
again. As Anibal has noted, the device appears at least seven times in Mira de
Amescua's theater.[11] It also appears in the theater of Claramonte, Lope de
Vega, Tirso de Molina, and Calderón.[12] Azevedo may have taken some of these
works as models (perhaps those by Claramonte) in order to show once again
in her *comedia* how the women understand and are in tune with nature's writings while men ignore, disregard, or misunderstand the signatures of the
world.

Of all the possible ways of reading the world's text, perhaps the most common and the most absorbing for the sixteenth and early seventeenth century
was the art of deciphering the future using the zodiacal signs, stars, planets,
and constellations. Don Quijote is quite emphatic as to the popularity of astrology in the Spanish Golden Age "que tanto se usan ahora en España, que no

hay mujercilla, ni paje, ni zapatero de viejo que no presuma de alzar una figura
. . . echando a perder con sus mentiras e ignoracias la verdad maravillosa de la
ciencia" (2.25.237) [that is so popular today in Spain that there is no woman,
page, or shoemaker, however old he might be, that does not try to cast a horoscope . . . destroying with their lies and ignorance the marvelous truth of that
science].

Indeed, astrology is probably the most common way to predict the future
in the Spanish *comedia*. In Azevedo's *Dicha y desdicha del juego,* it is used by
Felisardo. Realizing that the only way he can marry Violante is to become rich
very quickly, Felisardo decides to gamble. He conveniently recalls that an astrologer had cast his horoscope ("levantándome figura" l. 2263) and told him
that a propitious planet ("afable el astro" l. 2264) would deliver a great finding
("grande hallazgo" l. 2266), which Felisardo interprets as great winnings.
Felisardo's servant, Sombrero, immediately finds fault with this undertaking
calling the astrologer a drunk ("Ese astrólogo borracho" l. 2278). Sombrero
thus reflects Don Quijote's warning that everyone was casting horoscopes,
thus detracting with lies the truth of astrology. More importantly, Sombrero
also reminds Felisardo that one of his father's last commandments on his
deathbed was to admonish him never to gamble (ll. 2259–60). As with the
dream, Felisardo prefers to believe what is false rather than come to an understanding of the flaws in his own character. In the dream, he chooses to suspect
his sister rather than coming to understand his own problems; now, he chooses
to believe an astrologer rather than trusting in his father's last words.

Both the astrologer's words and his father's admonition come into play in
the scene that follows. Challenging Fadrique to a game of cards, Felisardo at
first wins a huge fortune (400,000 *ducados,* l. 2494) and sends Sombrero to
inform Violante of the happy event. Thus, the astrologer's words seem to have
come true. But then, Felisardo rashly decides to keep on gambling and then
loses everything. His gaming frenzy is such that he even gambles and loses his
own sister to Fadrique. Felisardo's father, knowing of the propensity for excessive gambling in the family, had advised his son to refrain from this pursuit.
Felisardo recalls his admonition when it is too late and all is lost. The father's
voice, then, had represented the warnings of Nature.

Having been unable to heed the writings placed by God in the world,
Felisardo feels that his only recourse is to turn to demonic writings. He signs
a pact with the devil, renouncing God and the Christian faith (ll. 2820–24).
He only refuses the devil one thing, to renege on the Virgin Mary. Predict-
ably, the devil takes him up into the air on his way to hell, but the Virgin

Mary, pleased by Felisardo's love for her and by María's piety, stops the devil in midair. Soufas has argued that the "frequent use of extensive stage machinery and props indicates that she [Azevedo] enjoyed the advantages of court sponsorship and perhaps its more elaborate staging opportunities" (*Women's Acts* 1). But, at least in the case of *Dicha y desdicha del juego,* the machines used here to present the celestial battle where the devil, the Virgin, and Felisardo are suspended in the air, are the ones used typically in many of the saints' plays of the period presented in the *corrales* [theaters]. As John Cull has explained, these *tramoyas* or stage machines that took actors up into the air, were much appreciated by the groundlings. These *mosqueteros* [*groundlings*] also watched for any malfunction, which was rather common as one of the servants recounts in Calderón's *El galán fantasma* [*The Phantom Lover*].

The text of the play disallows any malfunctions in the play of the world: the Virgin orders Felisardo to return home where everything will be resolved satisfactorily. The spectator is then treated to the ingenious way in which the plot can be resolved happily, the playwright assuming the role of the Virgin's agent. As Fadrique rushes to María's house in order to possess and dishonor her, the spectator wonders how this can be averted. The scene shifts to María's home where she is asleep under an oratory presided over by the Virgin. As Fadrique bursts in, he first hears and then sees María speaking in her sleep. She is experiencing a nightmare where Fadrique has come to dishonor her, and she admonishes him for acting against her and against the Virgin. Fadrique comes to understand that María's words in her dream are supernatural in origin and meant to warn him of his mistakes. This climactic moment in the play combines two key elements utilized previously, the oneiric phenomenon (which in this case is a prophecy or *oneiroi* of what evils *could* happen if Fadrique did not reform) and a kledonomantic moment where Fadrique hears a voice whose counsel he applies to his own situation. The words uttered by María, who has no idea or knowledge of the real-life situation, are thus truly kledonomantic since they are said in response to a dream event.

Thus, the work begins and ends with a dream. While the first oneiric phenomenon had been experienced by a man whose humoral imbalance had allowed demonic elements to influence him, this second dream is experienced by a woman who can utter not only prophetic words but also kledonomantic advice since she is inspired by celestial power. The recipient of the kledonomancy is Fadrique, a man who has proven to be inconstant in love and in prayer. These words effect his conversion. Now that woman has brought the erring male in line with the celestial will and with nature's wisdom, the play can be brought to an end—a play orchestrated by the Virgin (ll. 3593–94). All ends happily as Fadrique agrees to marry María and as Felisardo, released from the devil's pact, is happy to marry Violante. Together, they restrain the devilish violence of Violante's father, Don Nuño, and convince him of the celestial impetus that has guided these events.

Azevedo's play, then, turns poetic language into the language of the world. Through oneiric phenomena, physiognomic knowledge, the theory of signatures, kledonomantic prophecies, and astrological predictions, *Dicha y desdicha del juego* shows how male figures are inept at interpreting heaven's will as written in the book of the world, turning at times to the mendacious writings of the devil. While men claim that they seek to contain women's passions, it is their own passions, their greed, lust, and suspicious natures that are evinced in their actions. Women, on the other hand, are seen as careful and insightful readers of the prose of the world; their virtue, piety, chastity, and constancy serving to challenge the patriarchal vision of woman as source of obscenity and chaos. As bringers of clarity and light to male confusion, the lead women of the play can be seen as metonyms for Azevedo's own role. And the playwright's role, as inscribed in the *comedia,* comes closer to that of the Virgin. She uses the writings of nature, miraculous interventions, and amazing turns of plot to present a world where heaven's will (and the author's dictates) prevail, and where women are the best interpreters of heaven's will to their society.[13]

Notes

1. Soufas also points to "diatribes against the female presence in the audience for the theatrical performances" (*Dramas* 26).

2. While Lope de Vega often begins his plays with monologues or a dialogue between secondary characters, Claramonte attempts to surprise the audience from the very beginning "con objeto de captar la atención y el silencio de ese público ruidoso que llenaba los corrales de comedias" (Hernández Valcárcel 87) [with the intention of capturing the attention and the silence of the noisy public that filled the theaters]. The beginning of *El valiente negro en Flandes* [*The Brave Black Man in Flanders*] and of *La infelice Dorotea* [*The Unfortunate Dorotea*] recalls the first scene of Azevedo's play. Indeed, *La infelice Dorotea* begins with two men (Mendo and Layn) pursuing Sancho as if he were a thief. Dorotea appears and ends this chase (ll. 1–11). The same elements are found in Azevedo's play where Sombrero is supposedly pursuing a thief and where the female protagonist, María, puts a stop to misguided violence. Since Claramonte's play was composed in 1620, it may be possible to date Azevedo's play toward the beginning of her service to Queen Isabel in 1621.

3. The edition cited is found in Soufas's *Women's Acts.* All English translations are my own.

4. Guichemerre has studied quid pro quo scenes in French comedies (1640–1660), many of which are indebted to Spanish plays of the Golden Age. The most extreme quid pro quo he encounters is the mistaking of a person for a ghost (70–72).

5. See de Armas, Kirschner, and Palley. These plays include: *El caballero de Olmedo* [*The Knight of Olmedo*], *El casamiento en la muerte* [*Marriage in Death*], *Los españoles en Flandes* [*The Spaniards in Flanders*], *El mejor mozo de España* [*Spain's Fairest Son*], *El nuevo mundo descubierto por Colón* [*The New World Discovered by Columbus*], *La Santa Liga* [*The Holy League*], *La tragedia del rey Don Sebastián* [*The Tragedy of King Sebastian*], et cetera. Claramonte was also fond of including oneiric phenomena in his plays. *La infelice Dorotea,* which may have served as model for Azevedo's initial scene, also contains poignant dreams.

6. Achmet's text was well known in the Middle Ages, having been translated into Latin. Achmet is a pseudonym and the work was actually written by a Christian Greek "to project an air of erudite, cosmopolitan learning, which the Arabic scholars at this time quite deservedly possessed" (Oberhelman 12).

7. Macrobius distinguishes five types of dreams, but includes the *enypion* (in Latin *insomnium* or nightmare) (88).

8. Felisardo confesses that such dreams arise from cares: "que un cuidado que tenemos / entre sueños nos dibuja / la fantasía" (ll. 210–12) [that some care that we have, fancy draws it in dreams].

9. Macrobius discusses the incubus when dealing with the *phantasma* or *visum,* the second category of nonprophetic dreams (89).

10. Later in the play, Felisardo will succumb to his humoral imbalances and to the demonic powers, agreeing to a pact with the devil (ll. 2820–23).

11. Anibal asserts: "Mira never allows his characters to accept kledonomantic phenomena at their face value. His protagonists are not superstitious, and not realizing the human sources of the *voces,* never really interpret them as omens" ("Another Note" 252).

12. See, for example, Claramonte's *Deste agua no beberé* [*I Will Not Drink These Waters*]; Lope's *El caballero de Olmedo* and *La inocente sangre* [*Innocent Blood*]; Tirso's *La elección por la virtud* [*Elected by Virtue*] and *Santo y sastre* [*The Tailor as Saint*]; and Calderón's *La gran Cenobia* [*The Great Zenobia*] and *La hija del aire* [*The Daughter of the Air*]. Hernández Araico uses a case of kledonomancy in Calderón's *La devoción de la misa* [*Devotion to the Mass*] to discuss the term "irony" (46).

13. After completing this essay, I encountered the fascinating essay by Gascon. He argues that the play "comes dangerously close to heresy" by enhancing the authority of the Virgin Mary, thus "undermining the authority of God the Father and of the patriarchy that determines Catholic doctrine" (76).

Works Cited

Anibal, Claude E. "Another Note on the *Voces del cielo.*" *Romanic Review* 18 (1927): 247–52.

———. "*Voces del cielo*—A Note on Mira de Amescua." *Romanic Review* 16 (1925): 57–70.

Caro Baroja, Julio. *Historia de la fisiognomica: El rostro y el carácter.* Madrid: Istmo, 1988.

Case, Sue-Ellen. *Performing Feminisms: Feminist Critical Theory and Theatre.* Baltimore: Johns Hopkins University Press, 1990.

Cervantes, Miguel de. *El ingenioso hidalgo don Quijote de la Mancha.* Ed. Andrés Murillo. 2 vols. Madrid: Castalia, 1978.

Ciruelo, Pedro. *Reprouacion de las supersticiones y hechizerias.* Ed. Alva V. Ebersole. Valencia: Albatros/Hispanólila, 1978.

Claramonte, Andrés de. *Comedias.* Ed. María del Carmen Hernández Valcárcel. Murcia: Academia Alfonso X el Sabio, 1983.

———. *La infelice Dorotea.* Ed. Charles Ganelin. London: Támesis, 1987.

Cull, John. "'Este paso está ya hecho': Calderón's Observations on *Corral* Performances." *Forum for Modern Language Studies* 29 (1993): 271–86.

De Armas, Frederick A. "The Allure of the Oriental Other: Titian's *Rossa Sultana* and Lope de Vega's *La Santa Liga.*" *Brave New Words: Studies in Spanish Golden Age Literature.* Ed. Edward H. Friedman and Catherine Larson. New Orleans: University Press of the South, 1996. 191–208.

Foucault, Michel. *The Care of the Self. The History of Sexuality: III.* New York: Vintage, 1988.

———. *The Order of Things.* New York: Vintage, 1973.

Gascon, Christopher D. "The Heretical and the Herethical in Angela de Azevedo's *Dicha y desdicha del juego y devoción de la Virgen.*" *Bulletin of the Comediantes* 51 (1999): 65–81.

Green, Otis H. *Spain and the Western Tradition.* 4 vols. Madison: University of Wisconsin Press, 1964.

Guichemerre, Roger. *La comédie avant Molière (1640–1660).* Paris: Armand Colin, 1972.

Hernández Araico, Susana. *Ironía y tragedia en Calderón.* Potomac, Md.: Scripta Humanistica, 1986.

Kirschner, Teresa J. "La representación del sueño y de la imaginación en el teatro histórico-legendario de Lope de Vega." *Texto y espectáculo: Selected Proceedings of the Symposium on Spanish Golden Age Theater.* Ed. Barbara Mujica. Lanham, Md.: University Press of America, 1989. 35–46.

Loomba, Ania. *Gender, Race, Renaissance Drama.* Manchester, England: Manchester University Press, 1989.

Macrobius. *Commentary on the Dream of Scipio.* Ed. and trans. William Harris Stahl. New York: Columbia University Press, 1952.

McCrary, William. *The Goldfinch and the Hawk: A Study of Lope de Vega's Tragedy "El caballero de Olmedo."* Chapel Hill: University of North Carolina Press, 1968.

Oberhleman, Steven M. *The Oneirocriticon of Achmet: A Medieval Greek and Arabic Treatise on the Interpretation of Dreams.* Lubbock: Texas Tech University Press, 1991.

Palley, Julian. *The Ambiguous Mirror: Dreams in Spanish Literature.* Chapel Hill, N.C.: Hispanófila, 1983.

Río, Martín del. *La magia demoníaca.* Vol. 2 of *Disquisiciones mágicas.* Ed. and trans. Jesús Moya. Madrid: Hiperión, 1991.

Soufas, Teresa Scott. *Dramas of Distinction: Plays by Golden Age Women.* Lexington: University Press of Kentucky, 1997.

———, ed. *Women's Acts: Plays by Women Dramatists of the Golden Age.* Lexington: University Press of Kentucky, 1997.

Sprenger, James, and Henry Kramer. *Malleus Maleficarum.* Ed. and trans. Montague Summers. New York: Benjamin Blom, 1970.

Stoll, Anita. "'Tierra de en medio': Liminalities in Angela de Azevedo's *El muerto disimulado.*" *Engendering the Early Modern Stage: Women Playwrights in the Spanish Empire.* Ed. Valerie Hegstrom and Amy R. Williamsen. New Orleans: University Press of the South, 1999. 151–64.

9

Galatea's Fall and the Inner Dynamics of Góngora's
Fábula de Polifemo y Galatea

Joseph V. Ricapito

The text of Luis de Góngora y Argote's *Fábula de Polifemo y Galatea* [*Polyphemus and Galatea*] offers the reader and scholar a number of challenges. Thanks to the landmark work of Dámaso Alonso and Antonio Vilanova, to mention only two,[1] many of these challenges have been resolved, but there are still other challenges that the reader encounters largely because each generation interprets the Cordovan poet through newer poetic sensitivities.

Every poet faces the challenge of having his words move from the printed page to the living consciousness of the reader. The greatest challenge is the flatness of the verbal creation, and it will rest there until the reader takes these words and assimilates them into his or her own imagination. Poetry occurs when the words of poetical clusters are impressed upon the reader's own imagination. It is then that the poetical transfer occurs, and the process to which all poets aspire takes place. The poet, must, perforce, adopt strategies to have the poetic narrative move forward. But this process is encumbered by the basics of prose narration. The poet, who is forced by the genre to seek an economy of means, must go beyond the basic tools of narrative dynamics. Góngora's challenge is to go from stanza to stanza vertically by using means that themselves go beyond the limitations of mere verbal description.

If poetry is characterized by its compression, how then can the poet create a poetic dynamic that gives greater nuances and contours to the tale of Acis and Galatea? It is the purpose of this paper to study the poetic dynamics that Góngora uses in this work in order to tell a tale poetically in its greatest and fullest contours; and to study the fall of Galatea as a model of unconventional action.

Most basically Góngora depends upon verbs and verb tenses. These form the skeletal background and structure of the poem. Examples are simple verbal actions such as a bird that "pula" [polishes] (st. 2)² or "Treguas al ejercicio sean robusto" [With gentle silence and attentive leisure / At truce with strenuous sports] (st. 3); "el pie argenta de plata al Lilibeo" [Marsala's foot is shod with silver foam] (st. 4); "cabrío / de los montes esconde" [In which as many of the caprine race . . . with their numbers hide] (st. 6); "al viento que lo peina proceloso" [Unkempt it hangs or in disorder streams] (st. 8).³

There are many instances in Góngora's use of verb tenses to give the poem its basic impetus and dramatic movement. This is the most basic level of dynamic action, and Góngora needs these tenses to communicate the action. However, it is in other ways that he is able to give his poem an inner direction and movement. Since my interest is in showing the inner dynamics of the work and its relation to Galatea's fall, I would start with those poetic elements that deal with movement.

The very mention of "purpúreas horas" [encrimsoned hours] implies temporal movement. The images of "peinar el viento / fatigar la selva" [You scour the air or beat the forest's bounds] (st. 1) describe actions that involve movement, metaphorical in the case of both verbs, "peinar" [to comb] and "fatigar" [to tire]. Even the mention of "la caverna profunda" [the murky den] (st. 5) takes the reader downward into the depths of a cave. When the trope is static it can subtly contain suggestions of movement, as in "horror de aquella sierra" [terror of the countryside] (st. 6). In describing Polifemo's abode, the mention of a "redil espacioso" [a pinfold wide] (st. 6) not only creates space but also creates movement within that space. The mountainous environment, described in the sixth stanza as "cumbres ásperas" [the rugged mountains], contains the uplifting statement of the peaks in "cumbres" but also the severity of the terrain in "ásperas" [rugged]. Together the image conveys a rising, vertical sensation. This same spatial and vertical movement can be seen in the verse "un silbo junta y un peñasco sella" [A whistle gathers and a boulder locks] (st. 6); both verbs create a rising sensation. The description of Polifemo as "un monte era de miembros eminente" [of human limbs a lofty mountain made] (st. 7) contains the metaphor of hyperbolic size which, in its superhuman extension, especially by comparing him with "monte" [mountain], gives the impression of a vast physical expansion both vertically ("monte" [mountain]) and horizontally ("miembros" [members]).

The total metaphor *grows* in both directions. When Góngora describes Polifemo's hair as "Negro el cabello, imitador undoso" [His hair . . . To rival Lethe's dark obscurities] (st. 8), the adjective "undoso" [wavy] creates a verbal picture of a waving object, which in Polifemo's hyperbolic size and shape can almost be vertiginous. The verse, moreover, cascades in waving levels before the reader's imagination. It is followed by "vuela sin orden, pende sin aseo" [Unkempt it hangs or in disorder streams] (st. 8). Both these verbs, "vuela" [streams] and "pende" [hangs] function as bearers of movement and recall the floating hair of Venus in Botticelli's *Birth of Venus*. The waving and suspense serve a baroque function of movement and activity within the otherwise static action and description. Similarly, "un torrente es su barba impetuoso" [His beard like an impetuous torrent teems] (st. 8); "barba" [beard] functions as an anchor holding down the verse, around which the noun "torrente" [torrent], which flows outwardly, is further intensified by its adjective "impetuoso" [impetuous]. The description also creates further initial impressions of a negative nature concerning Polifemo: images of overflowing, exaggerated extension, almost explosive in its latent potency, confabulate to attack the reader and dislodge themselves from the otherwise confining effects of the hendecasyllable form.

Góngora's wish to create an expansive narrative can be read in stanza 9: "armó de crüeldad" [Shod with the wind and armed with cruel hate], "calzó de viento" [the wind shod] endows the tropes with a vitality that might otherwise be lacking. The unlikelihood of "armar" [to arm] with "crüeldad" [cruelty] or even the less likely "calzar" [to shoe] with "viento" [wind] challenge the natural rhetoric and diction of language. The very extremeness of these two metaphors explodes through common reality outwardly in a tridimensional manner. Another example of how Góngora creates space-expansion, and thus inner movement descriptively, is to be seen in the following: "su piel manchada de colores ciento" [its skin with many colours maculate] (st. 9). The adjective "manchada" [maculate] fractures space into smaller particles, and the particle comes off the flatness of "piel" [skin], which multiplies, especially when joined with the further detail of "colores ciento" [many colours—literally one hundred colors]. Both "colores" [colours] and "ciento" [many or one hundred] in their plurality and multiplicity go beyond mere description. As in the case of Polifemo's size, the plurality is movement when various linguistic forms are juxtaposed.

Allusiveness creates further suggestive strategies on Góngora's part vis-à-vis his reader: "Cercado es cuanto más capaz, más lleno" [His wallet, ever full however wide] (st. 10). While "capaz" [wide] and "lleno" [full] may be viewed as static, although puffy with their fullness, "cercado" [cradled or closed in] creates the sensation of "circling," "containing," thereby achieving two effects: vertically by growth and fullness, plenty; and horizontally by "cercado" [cradled or closed in] that contains it. This containment is dynamic in as much as one can sense the tension of the fullness of the pouch, wallet "zurrón"; or conversely, the process does flood outwardly when we read in the same stanza, "el zurrón, casi abortada" [the wallet almost emptied] (st. 10). The qualifying "casi" [almost] is insufficient to hold back the pressure and power. The "casi" creates a sensation of resignation, surrender, before a stronger power. In this image, the dynamics or inner pressure and rupture are clear.

One of the most important devices that Góngora uses throughout the poem is the hyperbaton. The classical device can serve many functions. Within the perspective of my paper I cite two illustrative examples: "un monte era de miembros eminente" [of human limbs a lofty mountain made] (st. 7). Góngora obviously wishes to describe Polifemo in his monstrous and gigantic state. Straight description would indicate Polifemo's vastness, but the metaphor impresses the reader affectively with Polifemo's extension. This metaphor, couched in the hyperbaton, opens the field from A ("monte" [mountain]) to the other extreme B ("eminente" [eminent, outstanding]). Within this field "era de" [was] functions as a linchpin between the two extremes of A and B, with a vertical, soaring and searching quality, as extreme A seeks to join with B.

In this same stanza "cíclope, a quien el pino más valiente, / bastón, le obedecía, tan ligero, / y al grave peso junco tan delgado, / que un día era bastón y otro cayado" [like a light staff the stoutest pine obeyed / His mighty grasp, but if he leaned thereon / Under his weight, a crumpled reed, it shook, / One day a staff, the next a shepherd's crook] (st. 7). The placement of words within these verses carries out an acrobatic function, as one bounces off another in synchopative fashion "bastón, le obedecía, tan ligero," et cetera. The hyperbatons can function to retard action, or accelerate it, or as in this case create a gymnastic action with words sparking against each other, almost helter-skelter.

A further example of the effect of hyperbaton can be read in "En carro que estival trillo parece" [her car a threshing mill decrees] (st. 18). "Trillo" [threshing mill] struggles with "parece" [seems] whose natural and normal word order would favor preceding "trillo." "Estival" [summery] and "trillo," being of two different species, create a natural "combat" between them. This incompatibility can only be brought about through the skillful use of the hyperbaton.

Above I have cited several metaphors as belonging to this design of inner dynamic action. I add a few more because they strengthen my thesis. In stanza 18 one reads, "las provincias de Europa son hormigas" [the lands of Europe are ants]. Dámaso Alonso's explanation clearly defines this metaphor "campiñas de cuyas siempre fértiles cosechas las naciones de Europa son hormigas, pues, como hormigas al grano, van allí a abastecerse" [whose ever fertile harvests the nations of Europe are ants, which, like ants go to the grain, they go there to supply themselves] (st. 116). The comparison aims at several levels of understanding. European nations come to Sicily to obtain its natural products, especially grain. For the purposes of my thesis, "hormigas" [ants] is particularly apropos, basically because it indicates movement within the metaphor itself. In choosing "las naciones de Europa" [the nations of Europe], Góngora has "Europe" mean the countries of Europe that, coupled with the image of the busy movement of ants, take sustenance and save it for a rainy day.[4] The line "wriggles" before us, as one would expect a baroque treatment to do.

Another example appears in stanza 45: "que pedazos / la segur de los celos hará aguda" [with trenchant axe would to splinters hew]. The metaphor is naturalistic, with the sickle slashing away. But it is jealousy like the sharp, well-honed edge of the sickle, with its incisiveness that cuts away at Polifemo. The word "segur" [axe or sickle] alludes to its practical function, repetition through which Góngora will achieve his effect of having Polifemo be cut down through jealousy. The metaphor functions on several levels, but the predominant action, using a sickle, creates a movement that enlivens an important stanza.

There is yet another dimension to the poem that Góngora uses skillfully and to good purpose, that is, sound and auditory references.[5] The very "rimas sonoras" [sonorous rhymes] (st. 1) that open the poem are a harbinger of further auditory dimensions of the poem, more than just the sounds of poetry: "que en vano / aun desmentir al cascabel presuma" [although in vain / To hush the witness of his bell presume] (st. 2). "Mudo" [mute] in a previous verse plays against the suggestions of sounds produced by the "cascabel" [bell] on the horse's neck. Sounds, whether explicit or implied, create another dimension to the poem (in this sense Baena's use of the word "estereofónico" [stereophonic] makes perfect sense), and it is an active element in the play between writing, reading, hearing, and listening. Similarly, this process occurs in stanza 3: "silencio dulce, en cuanto / debajo escuchas de dosel augusto" [With gentle silence and attentive leisure / At truce with strenuous sports, listen in state / From your high seat]. The adjective "dulce" [sweet] gives a special nuance to "silencio" [silence], and then "escuchas" [you listen] creates the matrix for an auditory image. In fact, the movement is derived from a pause that occurs after the "silencio dulce" [sweet silence] before introducing "escuchas" to complete the idea.

Within the picture of "lo monstruoso" [what is monstrous] and "lo grotesco" [what is grotesque] of Polifemo, the predominant figure has been the hyperbole.[6] Therefore any association with him must be consonant with this standard. "Que un silbo junta y un peñasco sella" [A whistle gathers and a boulder locks] (st. 6); any sound that emerges from his world must also be huge. As an auditory reference it would create a sound of havoc, this sound going across fields and mountains. This initial suggestion of sound is later verified in stanza 12: "Cera y cáñamo unió . . . cien cañas, cuyo bárbaro ruido" [A hundred pipes with wax and string are joined / A horrid din the vile contrivance makes], the sound emerging from the monster's pipes. This imagery creates a sound that is not relegated to a mere static reference. More echoing and sounding occur in stanza 21: "El céfiro no silba, o cruje el robre" [No more the crack of the resounding sling, / Or, to replace the humble herd they lack, / The breezes whistle and the oak-twigs crack]. Even the negative "no silba" [does not whistle] evokes the suggested sound and the "cruje" [crack] of the oak gives further, wider dimensions to the action and milieu. Silence or "negative sound" in a Gongoristic creation inevitably evokes sound. "Muda la noche el can" [The sheepdog mute by night] (st. 22) in its own linguistic state dismantles the silent reference. Other references to sound carry special connotations and therefore increase the auditory dimension of the poetry: "Bala el ganado; al mísero balido" [The sheep . . . bleating in dismay] (st. 22). "Mísero" [miserably or dismay] creates humanly reflective images.

Some further dimensions of sound are achieved when the poetic narrator says, "¡Revoca, Amor, los silbos!" [Restore the whistles, Love] (st. 22). This can be associated with the initial "rimas sonoras" [sonorous rhymes] (st. 1). The imperative emphasizes a relationship that is extratextual; it steps out of the immediate intrapoetic relationship. It certainly differs from the intrapoetic "Dulce se queja, dulce le responde / un ruiseñor a otro" [(The nightingales) Sweetly complaining, sweetly answering each other] (st. 23). This reference remains within the textual context and is responsible only to the author's need to create an ambiance reinforced by sound. Another reference stresses the presence of sound within the narrative: "La ninfa, pues, la sonorosa plata /

bullir sintió" [The nymph no sooner heard an altered sound / Come from the tinkling silver] (st. 28). The reference here is to the flowing stream. "Sonorosa" [sonorous] gives the clues that "plata" [silver] alone as a simple chromatic reference would not indicate that we are speaking of a river. "Sonorosa" creates the pastoral ambiance, within recognizable classical intertexts. Sound then, is yet another function of the dynamic that Góngora is using in his poem. If the text is to move upward, off the page, sound will move outward, giving deeper contours to the poem.

Góngora's use of other techniques also accounts for the inner dynamic as the action moves from stanza to stanza, not placidly like a Renaissance stream, but painfully and tortuously like the true baroque monument that it is. One of these is the opposition of one thing to another that creates a tension between the opposites: "y al grave peso junco tan delgado" [Under his weight, a crumpled reed] (st. 7).[7] Within the same line "peso" with its implications of weight is juxtaposed to "delgado" of the reed, heightening their differences. The strong comparison that emerges creates a tension as well as an impressive effect, "vuela sin orden, pende sin aseo" [Unkempt it hangs or in disorder streams] (st. 8). The preposition "sin" [without] is the axis between these two binomials. A series of oppositions are juxtaposed: "Vuela" [streams] that signifies movement and "pende" [hangs] that is static; "orden" [order] is control and "aseo," its opposite, is looseness, freedom. Unlike a situation where opposites paralyze a movement, Góngora's contrasts highlight the inner dynamic, and the action keeps moving forward to the next stanza, "redima feroz, salve ligera" [Can save with violence or redeem with speed] (st. 9). Both these adjectives create an aesthetic tension, as they do in "la fuga suspender podrá ligera" [Avails to stay the flying maiden's pace] (st. 17). Quite aside from the skillful hyperbaton, "fuga" [flight] and "suspender" [stay] oppose each other; it is like the runner who is suddenly stopped at the starting line; action is in some way stunted, "Sicilia, en cuanto oculta, / en cuanto ofrece" [Pomona's wealth Trinacria displays / And hides as plentifully Bacchus' spoil] (st. 18).

The range between ingredients is narrow. Structured on two different levels, each level has an active role: one conceals, the other gives. In decoding this dual and opposite structure, the reader is stopped and must decipher the first level of opposite bipolarity; although temporarily arresting the reader, it does not stop the inner structure from moving on. Another part of Góngora's technique in his use of oppositions is to use negatives to detail positives: "a la tierra, poco avara" [Grudged nothing by the soil] (st. 20). "La tierra" [the earth] in a late Renaissance context, certainly in a Gongoristic reference, usually invokes the idea of the earth as the great cornucopia. Earlier in the poem he speaks of the delights nature produces in Sicily (sts. 10, 11). In fact, in the next line Góngora says "el cuerno vierte el hortelano, entero" [Empties his horn of plenty liberally] (st. 20). Consequently, by offering first a self-negating syntax "poco avara," the next line with "cuerno vierte" subverts the inhibiting reaction of both "poco" (even though it is used adverbially) and "avara" [avaricious]; and more so with "entero" that also stands in opposition to "avara." The action through these oppositions moves in fits and starts.

Stanza 39, with its "paces no al sueño, treguas sí al reposo" [Not peace for sleep but truce to all repose], displays the same kind of oppositions, but here where you would normally have two similar terms "paces/reposo" [peace, repose], Góngora dismantles "paces" [peace] by placing the "no" after "paces." This technique has a double function to counterpoise "no paces" to "reposo" and to juxtapose "no" with "sí." Perhaps one way to describe this poetic procedure is to liken it to a barbed-wire fence; it moves along, but it is studded with obstacles, linguistic in this case.

Another technique in Góngora's arsenal is the particular use of adjectives, for example, in the second stanza "pula en la maestra mano / el generoso pájaro su pluma" [Let the noble hawk remain / polishing]. Examine the phrase "Treguas al ejercicio sean robusto" [With gentle silence and attentive leisure] (st. 3). The adjective exudes the quality of fullness that in fact makes the verse itself robust: "el pie argenta de plata al Lilibeo" [Marsala's foot is shod with silver foam] (st. 4). As part of the chromatic reflection of the poetry, this adjective "plata" [silver] joins extremely well with the rest of the environment. When the narrator describes Polifemo's cave as "Guarnición tosca de este escollo duro" [For garniture some rugged tree-trunks grow] (st. 5), Góngora works to present Polifemo in the coarsest terms. These adjectives serve to extend the already established image of magnitude, and the adjectives here accentuate the monstrous contours of Polifemo and his surroundings. The adjectives bring further sharpness to other adjectives describing him; these are abrasive contours. Continuing in Polifemo's description, his hearth is described as "formidable de la tierra / bostezo" [Earth, yawning hugely, leaves a dismal space] (st. 6). To describe the opening of Polifemo's abode as a yawn achieves the qualities of magnitude. The reader could almost sense the opening as growing, enlarging. As for the "bastón, le obedecía, tan ligero, / y al grave peso junco tan delgado, / que un día era bastón y otro cayado" [His mighty grasp, but if he leaned thereon / Under his weight, a crumpled reed, it shook, / One day a staff, the next a shepherd's crook] (st. 7), the double mention of

"bastón" [reed] creates the vertical image of straightness, but he then juxta-
poses these two references with "cayado" [staff], and the vertical images give
way to the curved one.

As a part of the description of Polifemo, the image "obscuras aguas del
Leteo" [Lethe's dark obscurities] (st. 8) appears. Mention of the river Lethe
should conjure up images of darkness, but there are diabolic contours for
which Góngora was striving that other adjectives might not have conveyed.
"Obscuras" [obscurities] here also accentuates depth as well as darkness, and
this depth has further infernal connotations in the pagan figure of Polifemo;
the downward stroke of the adjective is penetrating.

In stanza 15, the narrator states, "inducir a pisar la bella ingrata, / en carro
de cristal, campos de plata" [His love, and beg the thankless nymph to ride /
His crystal car across the silver tide.] The verb "pisar" [step on] carries the
natural stress within the rhyme of the hendecasyllable, and in this position
followed by the same stress on "ingrata" [ungrateful] intensifies the very act
of stepping. The first line emphasizes the act as a physical one. This physical-
ity is then contrasted with the visual adjectivization of "cristal" [crystal] and
"plata" [silver]. Góngora has in effect passed from one mode to another in a
chiasmic way, but also stresses the act as process. Likewise, in stanza 17 the
parallel construction of "a su pie divino, / dorado pomo a su veloz carrera"
[her sacred foot . . . rapid race] (st. 17), the second case where both noun and
adjective stress swiftness, the verse forces a return to the earlier verse that is
abstract, "divino" [divine]. The jump between one and another is readerly
kinetic.

The example of stanza 22 is: "Bala el ganado; al mísero balido" [the flock
bleats; to the miserable bleating]. The adjective "mísero" [miserable] by itself
does not give us any particular clue until in the next verse we read that: "el lobo
de las sombras nace" [wolves steal from the shadowy glade] (st. 22). The adjective serves as a presentiment of the flock's potential demise. Such activity in-
fuses the verse with a special vitality. In the following stanza the adjective
"fugitiva" of "la fugitiva ninfa" [the flying maiden] does more than describe
Galatea's fleeing. She is in part the "belle dame sans merci" [the beautiful
woman without mercy], the "mujer altanera" [the haughty woman] who cannot but flee; "fugitiva" [flying, fleeing] implies not only flight but also conceal-
ment.

An excellent example of the effects of chromatic intensity is in stanza 14.
The lines "Purpúreas rosas sobre Galatea / La alba entre lilios cándidos deshoja"
[Encrimsoned roses mixed with lilies white / On Galatea's beauty Dawn be-

stows] (st. 14), create a mixed and swirling juxtaposition of colors where deep red and white conjoin to paint this scene, and with the verb "deshoja" [defoliates] has created a scene of fluttering colors that affirm Horace's "ut pictura poesis" [poetry like a picture], not just as placid and static description, but as dynamic movement and action.[8]

I have attempted to trace the ways in which Góngora has written his poetry as a challenge to the static page.[9] What has resulted is a poem that is akin to a physical structure (having depth, breadth, transversal diagonals), and the reader's attempt to wend his or her way through this maze creates the dynamic movement that takes the reader from the first verse to the very last.[10]

It is important to have examined the principal techniques that Góngora uses in the poem so that we can see how Galatea functions in the poem. We now arrive at the second point of this paper—Galatea's fall.[11] This fall exists on several levels, but we wish to stress the moral overtones of the episode. Although there are numerous views on this question, I contend that the dénouement of the love affair between Acis and Galatea is suggestive of a moral and theological question very much in the air during Góngora's time.[12]

It is refreshing to find quoted reference to a seminal article by Stephen Gilman published in 1946 that forms the theoretical basis of this part of my paper (Friedman 54). In this article Gilman suggests the effects of the Tridentine presence in literature by surveying the works of sixteenth-century moralists. In these works, Gilman notes, there was a great emphasis placed on the importance of literature exemplifying certain moral and theological principles, the most important question being personal salvation. This was the *only* question, and literature was to bear this purpose. An excellent example is to be found in the *Conversión de la Magdalena* [*The Conversion of Mary Magdalen*] by Pedro Malón de Chaide, wherein a lost woman is converted to the saintly life. Guzmán de Alfarache bears this same purpose (although there may be some question about the "sincerity" or the literary appropriateness of his conversion): the lowliest, most sinful of men or women can, with the help of God's grace, be saved. Don Juan Tenorio is the negative example of someone who has not heeded calls for moral change and therefore perishes in hell. Don Juan is the example, as Gilman explains, of the "confiado en sí mismo," the person who does not become aware of his sinful proclivities and how these tendencies will lead him to hell. On the other hand, Guzmán de Alfarache is the example of the "caído en la cuenta" the person who realizes the error of his ways, and allows God into his life. With Gilman's essay as a model we can study how Góngora replays on one level the tragedy of the Garden of Eden, with the lovers being expelled.

Góngora's treatment of the Polifemo myth will avail itself of a number of attempts, and one of these is the cult of beauty that becomes synonymous with the world of temptation and the road to the fall.[13] In this schema, Polifemo is both a tangible character, used in a physical sense, but he also possesses moral symbolism.[14] In his exaggerated size, in the catastrophic effects of his movement, he is the embodiment of evil, while Acis and Galatea are the embodiment of beauty, but a beauty that covers a vulnerability that is a part of the human condition. Their erotic coupling, seen from Góngora's contemporary, religious perspective represents a challenge to the mores of conventionality. Gilman speaks of the caution to be gleaned in the works of the moralists—that no unconventional act is acceptable—and so Acis and Galatea openly indulge their erotic wishes and by so doing, like Don Juan Tenorio, they distance themselves from God in their sinning. This act will not be without its punishment, for no unconventional act can be accepted or glorified.

Góngora uses pagan, classical characters to play out the scenario, which on the most manifest level seems like a replay of classical, Spanish, and Italian treatments of the Cyclops myth. On the mythical level, one reads in Polifemo's reaction jealousy at seeing Galatea won over by Acis. But one sees to what an extent Góngora is using contemporary views and applying them to his characters. The characters of the *Polifemo* are similar to the mythological characters of Velázquez. Bacchus, Vulcan, Aesop—the Drunkards—are in the paintings of Velázquez characters of flesh and bone realistically depicted. They look like characters that one might have seen anywhere in Spain.[15] Góngora has done the same. He has hung the clothes of his day on characters of yesterday.[16]

Although one can read in the actions of the characters the points of view of Góngora's own temporal reality, we must not forget that Góngora's task is to create poetry qua poetry; that is a challenge to previous poets, especially of the Renaissance.[17] His presentation of the Garden of Eden scenario is an example of the perfect meld between form and content. Góngora's poetry will surpass other attempts at poetically depicting the Cyclops myth by creating a poetry that is devastating in its formal structure and enunciation. Essentially, there is no incompatibility between poetry as aesthetics and as a harsh moral and theological preoccupation, even with the treatment of the love theme that is resolved into a condemnatory resolution. Góngora's treatment of the Cyclops theme is the best not only because it is aesthetically beautiful, but also because in the extremeness of its baroque expression it destroys its competitors, which I take to have been one of Góngora's purposes.

Galatea as Eve

Stanza 13 brings Galatea to the reader, depicted as she is, a product of the sea. But Góngora telegraphs to the reader some early indications of a sexual, erotic dénouement by saying "vio el reino de la espuma" [seen in Ocean's kingdom yet] (st. 13).[18] "La espuma" [foam] here contains sexual symbolism that may be brought to bear later; here it is an anticipation. Her eyes are depicted as "Son una y otra luminosa estrella / lucientes ojos de su blanca pluma" [Bright stars, both one and other, are the pair / Of shining eyes in snow-white plumage set] (st. 13). This initial stanza underscores her greatest assets that are also described in terms of color and light. "Blanca" [white] is stated and indirectly alluded to. Stanza 14 stresses the contrast between red and white ("Purpúreas rosas / lilios candidos"; "púrpura nevada, o nieve roja" [Encrimsoned roses or white lilies / rosy snow, or snowy rose]). The stress on the color red hints at further erotic suggestions.[19]

The introduction of the god Palemon serves to suggest an early hint of Acis yet to come, but Galatea is still bathing in a type of innocence. The rejection of Polifemo and Palemon are part of the defense of her innocence. The pose of the disdaining woman is in reality a rationalization of her own innocence. Further erotic signs are seen in stanza 17 when the poet relates "ya que no áspid a su pie divino" [eager less / To be an aspic to her sacred foot] (st. 17). The "áspid" [serpent] here is the menace of Palemon's sexuality. This sexual note is further restated by the "delfín que sigue en agua corza en tierra" [The dolphin strives in vain / To match by sea the deer that runs the plain]. The dolphin amidst the waves is symbolic of phallic power and further, there is the admonition of the dolphin who seeks out, as Alonso says, "¡Oh, cómo se equivoca quien trata de perseguir lo inalcanzable, quien, como delfín que nada por el mar, pretende seguir a una ninfa que huye, veloz cual corza, por la tierra!" [What a mistake it is for one who tries to pursue the unattainable who, like a dolphin that swims in the sea, claims to follow a maiden that flees, as far as a deer on the plain!] (st. 112). There is a constant attempt and assault on Galatea's sexuality as is seen in the phallic symbols of the snake and the dolphin. The following two stanzas describe the great abundance of Sicily, and this too is a reflection of Galatea's fullness of beauty, a beauty that attracts all the youths of the island. Galatea's resistance is under continuous attack.

In stanza 23 further presentiments are revealed through the nightingales:

"Dulce se queja, dulce le responde / un ruisenor a otro, y dulcemente / al sueño da sus ojos la armonía" [Sweetly complaining, sweetly answering, / The songbirds with their mingled harmony / Bring slumber no less sweetly to her legs]. The variations on "dulce" [sweet] prefigure what will happen with Acis, but it also reveals a particular quality of this love, a languorous sweetness that receives an equal amount of languorous response in return. The phrase "Dulce se queja" [Sweetly complaining] is a strong example of a mixed sexual desire that is sweetly painful.

The arrival of Acis in his splendid beauty sets the stage. His arrival is also framed in terms of human and animal dimensions: "Era Acis un venable de Cupido" [Acis, a shaft from Cupid's bow] (st. 25). The "venablo" [dart] is usually used in a hunting context. Acis is out stalking a prey, and the prey will be Galatea. The intensity of his erotic desire is to be seen further in the fact that he is described as "un fauno, medio hombre, medio fiera" [a faun, half human and half beast]. His gifts, products of nature's bounty, will be offered to Galatea. This is not a situation that functions exclusively on a mental or intellectual level, following perhaps Platonic suggestions. His gifts are of a material nature.

Galatea's response to Acis and his gifts is ambivalent as is to be read in the verb "Huyera" [she would have fled] (st. 28). There is a tentative element here: "She would have fled, but. . . ." And the ambivalence is further seen in the fact that she is overcome by "mas tan frío se desata / un temor perezoso por sus venas" [but sluggish torpor bound / Her limbs, and all her blood ran chill with dread], and the "tan frío" [so cold] is later intensified by "grillos de nieve fue, plumas de hielo" [With snowbound feet and wings that freeze with fright]. In stanza 29 she will be depicted as "aunque estatua helada" [although a frozen statue]. Her "temor perezoso" [lazy fear] is a form of sexual ambivalence in the face of her lover's desires.[20] "Perezoso" also reveals her own positive sexual wishes, as her reserve and defenses weaken. Strictly from a moral point of view—and I believe Góngora has structured and articulated this—Galatea responds dutifully by fleeing, just as she rejected other solicitous lovers, but her weakness is tested before the beauty of Acis.

When he reviews the ideas of the moralists, Gilman notes that visual perception is the first step in what may ultimately result in a fall. In beautiful Renaissance landscapes, Nature is pictorially represented with lush and full colors—greens, reds, blues—yet the eye could not discern snakes and scorpions hidden therein. Essentially, one should not trust what one sees, and Acis is the tantalizing object that she should reject or at least be cautious about; but vulnerable as she is to physical love, she hesitates, and that hesitation represents a key step in her fall.

Góngora wishes to have her attention fixed on Acis's beauty and therefore reiterates his description of him as "El niño Dios . . . / ostentación gloriosa . . . alto trofeo" [The little blindfold love-god will take / Her captive, and adorn his mother's tree / With the high spoils of glorious victory] (st. 30). Once again, the act of falling in love is described through the "arpón dorado" [golden dart] as piercing "su blanco pecho" [her ivory bosom] (st. 31). She pauses to admire the gifts that Acis has brought. As we assign "blame" in a moral way, we must highlight the fact of Acis's deception. He is "fingiendo sueño" [feigning sleep] (st. 32). This relieves Galatea of a certain amount of blame since she comes upon him fortuitously, but Acis, whose passion is anticipated in various sexual symbols earlier, is using this strategy to cause her to pause.

It is not purely accidental that in the first two verses of stanza 36 we find "el áspid" [the serpent]. The "áspid" is a sign of the presence of sin, as interpreted in the theology of the time, and is also reminiscent of the Genesis tale of Adam and Eve. To be sure, the beauty of the *locus amoenus* [the pleasant place] where the lovers meet is comparable in ways to the Garden of Eden. A series of images add to the erotic content of the encounter with phrases such as:

en el lascivo, regalado seno:
en lo viril desata de su vulto
lo más dulce el Amor, de su veneno;
bébelo Galatea, y da otro paso
por apurarle la ponzoña al vaso. (st. 36)

[So it is with the virile countenance, / Where now his sweetest poison Cupid blends, / Which drinking, Galatea longs to seize / The venomed cup and drain it to the lees.]

"En lo viril desata de su bulto" [in his virile countenance] and love as erotica is restated in terms of "dolce amore" [sweet love], "lo mas dulce el Amor, de su veneno" (st. 36). While "dulce" [sweet] recalls the earlier depiction of love (sweetness) as pain ("dolor"), it also points to the sinful content of the love with the use of "veneno" [poison] as part of Cupid's nefarious instigation. Moreover, the response, suggested by the poisoned arrow, finds its continuation in the next two verses, "bébelo Galatea, y da otro paso / por apurarle la ponzoña al vaso" (st. 36). Acis feigns sleep but is all eyes ("Argos es siempre atento a su [Galatea's] semblante" [Intent as Argos, scans the maiden's face] [st.

37]); that is, he is carefully measuring her defense against the poisonous darts of love to see if she will defend herself or give herself up to passion.

Acis emerges from his feigned sleep, and the passionate intention is clear. His first line of offense is his good looks ("El sueño de sus miembros sacudido, / gallardo el joven la persona ostenta" [His limbs now shaken free from sleep, reveal / His youthful comeliness to fuller view] [st. 38]). The ivory color of Galatea's feet and shoes is a chromatic indication of innocence and purity, and his attempt to kiss them is clearly erotic ("y al marfil luego de sus pies rendido, / el coturno besar dorado intenta" [He hastens at her marble feet to kneel / And kiss the golden buckle of her shoe] [st. 38]). As Alonso transcribes the last few verses of the stanza "Menos asusta al marinero el rayo que puede ser previsto; menos le turba la tormenta prevenida o pronosticada: bien lo puede testimoniar Galatea, que no esperaba la súbita acción del mozo" [The lightning that the sailor can anticipate he fears less, the anticipated storm bothers him less: Galatea can bear witness to it, who did not expect the sudden action of the young man] (st. 192). Clearly Galatea is taken aback by his sudden wakefulness and may not be able to defend herself. Rather, as Alonso comments regarding stanza 39, that Galatea, "dulcemente risueña, no paces para que volviese a dormir, sino treguas al descanso, es decir, que interrumpiese su descanso para estar con ella" [sweetly smiling, (offers) not peace to go to sleep again, but rather a truce to repose, that is, that he might interrupt his rest in order to be with her] (st. 196).

The description of the *locus amoenus,* the "sitio de amor," further accentuates a perfect natural place for lovemaking. The Edenic quality of the *locus amoenus* [the pleasant place] is continued in stanza 40 and serves as the introduction to the lovemaking of the doves that clearly precedes that of Acis and Galatea themselves: "reclinados, al mirto más lozano, / una y otra lasciva, si ligera, / paloma se caló, cuyos gemidos / —trompas de amor—alteran sus oidos" [They see two doves alight on gentle wing / And, from the lustiest myrtle, in the thrill / Of passion, moaning soft laments to move / Their hearers with the clarion—call of Love] (st. 40). Acis's strategy reaches its final conclusion. The "gemidos" [moans] of the doves prefigure those of the two lovers. True to the pose of the "belle dame sans merci," Galatea has her own pose: "El ronco arrullo al joven solicita; / mas, con desvíos Galatea suaves, a su audacia los términos limita" [The husky cooing stirs the youngster's veins / But gently she eludes his hot desire, / Sets limits to his boldness and restrains / All but the plaudits of the feathered choir] (st. 41), but the mention of Galatea's breasts— "fugitivo cristal, pomos de nieve" [The crystal flees, the apples turn to snow] (st. 41)—merely indicates that the sexual act will follow. Especially when in the following stanza Góngora describes the kiss of the lovers: "No a las palomas concedió Cupido / juntar de sus dos picos los rubíes, / cuando al clavel el joven atrevido [Acis] las dos hojas le chupa carmesíes" [Scarcely had Cupid let the doves unite / Their ruby bills before the stripling dares / With his own lips to suck the sweet delight / which, like two crimson petals, blooms on hers] (st. 42).

But the erotic part of the poem ends here. The figure of evil or sin in the form of Polifemo appears. Now the sinful act must receive its due, although the human and emotional aspects of Polifemo's lament temporarily conceal the author's punishment motif.[21] The quick exit of the lovers repeats the motif of the flight or expulsion of the lovers from their paradisiacal garden. Acis is smashed by a rock and metamorphosed into a clear stream. The moral dimensions of the poem are complied with. The erotic element of the gods, although pagan, are seen through the eyes of a poet of Spain's seventeenth century, moreover, under the influence of Tridentine moral exigencies.

The frame of the myth of Polifemo and Galatea, although of classical origin, bears the covering of a modern Spanish approach. In his sonnet ("Mientras por competir"), Góngora gives us a picture of another aspect of Golden Age morality: the beauty of today will end up in the grave tomorrow; therefore one must not place all of one's hopes and wishes on it. Similarly, the audacity of the sexuality of Acis and Galatea cannot be left to stand as something positive or acceptable; it cannot serve as a model for any reader. Typically baroque, Góngora wraps the beautiful poetry around what is an admonitory act.

In writing his *Polifemo*, Góngora turned to all the classical and contemporary Spanish and Italian versions of this myth in order to go beyond, in what could be termed a Bloomsian, "anxiety of influence."[22] He is determined to best all other versions both poetically and morally—even Ovid's to which he obviously is the closest—in an attempt to present a contemporary view of the age-old problem of sexuality and its concomitant repercussions morally, religiously, and theologically.

Notes

1. I think of Dámaso Alonso and Antonio Vilanova, both of whose contributions to the understanding of Góngora are unsurpassed. Citations from the *Polifemo* are taken from Alonso's text. See Orozco for authoritative views of the baroque. For comments concerning the baroque see Alonso; Cascardi, 130; Cruz Cortado, 52; Foster and Foster, passim; Jammes, passim; Read, ix; C. C. Smith,

"Approach," 236; Young, 57; Parker, 8 passim, although, in spite of Parker's many perceptive comments, some might find objectionable his idea that "[t]his fact, together with the standpoint of the theoretists, indicate that Wit is the basic baroque style" as well as his statement that "the baroque style in *Polifemo*, highly mannered and elaborate though it is, has no strain or tension to it" (79); the reader should consult Spitzer on the question of tensions in the text. Vilanova's study of sources and comparisons with other Polyphemic texts covers all ground. For other critics that study the relation between Góngora's composition and earlier treatments of the myth and texts see Cruz, 170; Guyler, 240; Jammes, 565; Lehrer, 2, 3; P. J. Smith, 224; C. C. Smith ("Musicalidad" 139; "Rich Rhyme" 110; "Theoretical" 165; "Approach" 236–37); Young, 57. For Góngora and his epigones see Cruz Cortado, passim; Dolan, "Figures," for comparisons with Andrew Marvell.

2. Translations of "Polyphemus and Galatea" are taken from Cunningham's verse translation in Parker.

3. See Baena, 90, for the interesting study of language and of verb tenses. For other treatments of style and language see Dolan, "Ground," 232, 244; Caldera, 233, and his view of how Góngora compresses the Polifemo figure into 24 verses; Cortázar, 136; Foster and Foster, passim; Gates, 503 passim; Raulston, 25; P. J. Smith, 224; Young, 57. Although he deals with Góngora's *Soledades,* McVay offers perceptive insights into the linguistic features that can be applied in some ways to the *Polifemo.*

4. See *El conde Lucanor,* story 23, for a graphic example.

5. The musicality of Góngora's poetry and its association with sound in general has been noted by Baena, a "texto estereofónico," 90; Jammes, 543; Ruster, 113; Selig, 217.

6. Within the concept of hyperbole in Nature, see Carenas, 309; see also Cascardi for baroque, "apparent symmetries are unbalanced; grotesque exaggerations and hyperbolic contrasts prevail," 130; Dolan, "Ground," 228; conversely, silence (and absence) has also been studied in the poem. See Cancelliere, 793; Friedman, 69; Roldán, 125; Ruster, 116; C. C. Smith, "Approach," 236–37; P. J. Smith, passim.

7. See Spitzer on this subject.

8. The theme of color and painting in *Polifemo* have been closely studied. See Cancelliere; Dolan, "Ground," 225, 229; Roldán, 128; Selig, 216–18. For light imagery, see Friedman, 68; for the specularity see Cruz, 179; for Góngora as visual poet, see Ruster, 112. See also Dolan, "Figures," 245.

9. Admittedly, there are other tropes and techniques that Góngora uses, but I want to focus on those that create a view of the poetry as dynamic and not static.

10. Critics have commented cogently on different aspects of Góngora's creation. I wish to call attention particularly to Friedman's view of his poetry as a puzzle to be solved, 55; Góngora's care in identifying objects and his vision of the world as possibility (Paiewonsky Conde 63); uses of mutability and ambiguity (Raulston 25); and uses of "enargeia, evidentia, illustratio" (P. J. Smith 224); Worren, 27.

11. The Fosters deal with the problem of the fall with their usual acuity, although

there are some points of difference between their views and mine on this question (118–24).

12. See Ruster, 113, for metaphysical complications in the poem. See Foster and Foster, 118, for observations on the fall but not in a Christian context. We read "Rather we are referring to the implications of Góngora's approach to human nature, an approach which completely bypasses Christian, religious contexts. . . . Góngora can refer to phenomena of human nature and experience that could be formulated in Christian terms of the Fall; the deliberate suppression of explicit religious references can be taken as indication of his desire to dwell on human nature outside the context of religious myths" (118).

13. For the Fosters, the characters embody different symbols. They say: "The 'classic' setting of the *Polyphemus* (Sicily) is superficially standard pastoral, only to be shattered by the terrible dark forces of Nature/human nature as personified by the enraged Polyphemus" (98); and "Thus, when we speak of Galatea as an Eve figure, as a temptress, it is not so much in terms of a Christian context. Rather, she possesses an immediate level, ideal human beauty, which is completely abandoned to itself (the Spanish word is here precise: Galatea evinces an unconcerned *ensimismamiento*)" (118). See also C. C. Smith, "Approach," 236, for observations that can be read as more abstract aspects of the poem.

14. See Cruz, 179, for pertinent statements on this theme, as well as Foster and Foster, 119; Lehrer, 3; C. C. Smith, "Approach," 224.

15. See Cancelliere, 791, for other remarks on Velázquez, sight, and painting in Góngora.

16. In trying to see a link between Góngora's life and time and his creation, Lehrer broaches the question of how the *limpieza de sangre* [purity of bloodline] questions may have affected Góngora, 77.

17. See Garcilaso's and Góngora's "Mientras por competir con tu cabello" [Meanwhile to compete with your hair].

18. Ciplijauskaité observes the "amor carnal" aspect of stanzas 40–42 as does Cortázar, who focuses on verses 23–42 and their "sugerencias eróticas" (133). The Fosters aver "Góngora devotes considerable space to detailing the awakening of passion between Galatea and Acis, and his concentration on the erotic constitutes a valuable advancement over earlier treatments of the encounter" (98–99). See Read's interesting: "Góngora came the closest to achieving a balance between the masculine and feminine. His sublimated forms are constantly infused from below by surges of erotic energy whose source is the polymorphously perverse body of childhood" (ix).

19. While these verses might recall Petrarch's "Chiare, fresche e dolci acque," Navarrete, in his excellent book, *Orphans of Petrarch,* sees in the *Polifemo* "perhaps the most effective upending of Petrarchism [by Góngora] in the Spanish Golden Age" (198). For discussions on the role of color in the poem, see Cancelliere, 790–91; Roldán, 128.

20. It would do well to interpret Galatea's ambivalence in terms of Spitzer's

belief that the Spanish Golden Age literature that was called "barroco" was characterized by a tension between opposites, and that the tension in the author was behind the literary presentation. For Galatea, there is the one pole of virginal innocence, and the other pole is the indulgence in the love act with Acis.

21. Guyler comments on the giant Cyclops as lover as a comic absurdity (245), and Cascardi says: "While there is an unbridled parodic reevaluation of the pastoral in Góngora, there is also a creation to be put in its place" (135). I do not agree that Polifemo in love is a comic absurdity, nor do I believe that there is a parodic intent in the *Polifemo.*

22. One can legitimately see Góngora in his competition with contemporary and classical poets as working under an anxiety to surpass their creations.

Works Cited

Alonso, Dámaso. *Góngora y "El Polifemo."* 4th ed. Madrid: Gredos, 1961.

Baena, Julio. "Tiempo pasado y tiempo presente: de la presencia a la estereofonía en *La fábula de Polifemo y Galatea.*" *Calíope* 2.1 (1996): 79–99.

Caldera, Ermanno. "En torno a las tres primeras estrofas del *Polifemo* de Góngora." *Actas del Segundo Congreso Internacional de Hispanistas, celebrado en Nijmegen del 20 al 25 de agosto de 1965.* Ed. Jaime Sánchez Romeralo and Norbert Poulessen. Nijmegen: Instituto Español de la Universidad de Nijmegen, 1965.

Cancelliere, Enrica. "Dibujo y color en la *Fábula de Polifemo y Galatea.*" *Actas del X Congreso de la Asociación Internacional de Hispanistas.* Ed. Antonio Vilanova. Vol. 1. Barcelona: Puvill, 1992. 789–98.

Carenas, Francisco. "Reflexiones sobre el *Polifemo.*" *Romanische Forschungen* 86 (1974): 301–13.

Cascardi, Anthony J. "The Exit From Arcadia: Reevaluation of the Pastoral in Virgil, Garcilaso and Góngora." *Journal of Hispanic Philology* 4 (1980): 119–41.

Ciplijauskaité, Biruté. "Lectura de *Polifemo* en 'Salvación de la primavera' de Jorge Guillén." *Hommage à Robert Jammes* (Anejos de Críticón, 1). Ed. Francis Cerdan. Vol. 1. Toulouse: PUM, 1994. 231–38.

Cortázar, Celina S. de. "Sobre los versos 201–202 del *Polifemo* de Góngora: 'El celestial humor recien cuajado. . . .'" *Cuadernos del sur* 11 (1972): 133–36.

Cruz, Arnaldo. "Exclusión y afirmación en Góngora." *Dispositio* [Notes] 9.24–26 (1984): 167–82.

Cruz Cortado, Antonio. "Secuelas de la *Fábula de Polifemo y Galatea:* versiones barrocas a lo burlesca y a lo divino." *Críticón* 49 (1990): 51–59.

Dolan, Katherine Hunt. "Figure and Ground: Concrete Mysticism in Góngora's *Fábula de Polifemo y Galatea.*" *Hispanic Review* 52 (1984): 223–32.

———. "Figures of Disclosure: Pictorial Space in Marvell and Góngora." *Comparative Literature* 40 (1988): 245–58.

Foster, David William, and Virginia Ramos Foster. *Luis de Góngora.* New York: Twayne, 1973.

Friedman, Edward H. "Creative Space: Ideologies of Discourse in Góngora's *Poli-*

femo." Cultural Authority in Golden Age Spain. Ed. Marina S. Brownlee and Hans Ulrich Gumbrecht. Baltimore: Johns Hopkins University Press, 1995. 51–78.

Gates, Eunice Joiner. "Sidelights on Contemporary Criticism of Góngora's *Polifemo." PMLA* 75 (1960): 503–8.

Gilman, Stephen. "An Introduction to the Ideology of the Baroque in Spain." *Symposium* 1 (1946): 82–107.

Guyler, Samuel L. "Góngora's *Polifemo:* The Humor of Imitation." *Revista hispánica moderna* 37 (1972–73): 237–52.

Jammes, Robert. *Etudes sur l'Oeuvre Poétique de Don Luis de Góngora y Argote.* 2 vols. Bordeaux: Institut d'Etudes Ibériques et Ibéro-Américaines de l'Université de Bordeaux, 1967.

Lehrer, Melinda Eve. *Classical Myth and the "Polifemo" of Góngora.* Potomac, Md.: Scripta Humanistica, 1989.

McVay, Ted E. "Góngora's *Soledades* as a Problem of Language and Meaning in Seventeenth-Century Spain." Ph.D. diss., Louisiana State University, August 1989.

Navarrete, Ignacio. *Orphans of Petrarch.* Berkeley and Los Angeles: University of California Press, 1994.

Orozco Díaz, Emilio. *Góngora.* Barcelona: Editorial Labor, 1953.

———. *Manierismo y Barroco.* Madrid: Cátedra, 1975.

Paiewonsky Conde, Edgar. "Góngora y la visión del mundo como posibilidad." *Cuadernos hispanoamericanos* 202 (1966): 62–88.

Parker, Alexander A. *"Polyphemus and Galatea": A Study in the Interpretation of a Baroque Poem.* (With a verse translation by Gilbert F. Cunningham.) Austin: University of Texas, 1977.

Raulston, Stephen B. "Vision, Desire and the Reader of the *Polifemo." Lucero* 1 (1990): 17–27.

Read, Malcolm K. *Visions in Exile. The Body in Spanish Literature and Linguistics: 1550–1800.* Amsterdam: Benjamin, 1990.

Roldán, Juana. "Descripción formal en la *Fábula de Polifemo y Galatea." Proceedings of the Pacific Northwest Conference on Foreign Language* 24 (1973): 124–29.

Ruster, Michael Bradburn. "'Fábula de polifonía': Harmony and Discord in Góngora's *Polifemo." Lucero* 2 (1991): 112–19.

Selig, Karl-Ludwig. "Góngora's *Fábula de Polifemo y Galatea:* Ekphrasis and the Interaction and Competition of the Senses." *Romanische Lyric. Dichtung und Poetik. Walter Pabst zu Ehren.* Ed. Titus Heydenreich, Eberhard Leube, and Ludwig Schrader. Tübingen: Stauffenburg, 1993. 216–19.

Smith, Colin C. "An Approach to Góngora's *Polifemo." Bulletin of Hispanic Studies* 42 (1965): 217–38.

———. "La musicalidad del *Polifemo." Revista de filología española* 44 (1961): 139–66.

————. "On the Use of Spanish Theoretical Works in the Debate on Gongorism." *Bulletin of Hispanic Studies* 39 (1962): 165–76.

————. "Rich Rhyme in Góngora's *Polifemo*." *Bulletin of Hispanic Studies* 42 (1965): 106–12.

Smith, Paul Julian. "The Rhetoric of Presence in Poets and Critics of Golden Age Lyric: Garcilaso, Herrera, Góngora." *Modern Language Notes* 100 (1985): 223–46.

Spitzer, Leo. "El barroco español." *Boletín del instituto de investigaciones históricas* [Buenos Aires] 28 (1943–44): 12–30.

Vilanova Andreu, Antonio. *Las fuentes y los temas del "Polifemo" de Góngora. Revista de filología española,* Anejo 66. Madrid: CSIC, 1957.

Worren, Arne. "Mort et fécondité: *Fábula de Polifemo y Galatea* de Góngora." *Orbis Litterarum* 27 (1977): 27–40.

Young, R. V. "Versions of Galatea: Renaissance and Baroque Imitation." *Renaissance Papers, 1984.* Ed. Dale B. J. Randall and Joseph A. Porter. Durham, N.C.: Southeastern Renaissance Conference, 1985.

Part IV

❧

Power Stratagems of the Feminine Word

Constraints of Silence and Authority of Discourse

10

De voz extremada

Cervantes's Women Characters Speak for Themselves

Sara A. Taddeo

If we define feminism simply as "paying attention to women" in both their speech and their silence (Austin 1), then Miguel de Cervantes's women characters offer a ripe subject for feminist analysis.[1] They range from personified abstractions (Fama [Fame] in the *Cerco de Numancia* [*Siege of Numantia*]), to literary types (Clori and Marfisa in *La casa de los celos* [*The House of Jealousy*]), to humbler stock figures we recognize from medieval folk tradition in the *entremeses* [interludes], and the more modern characters of the *novelas ejemplares* [exemplary novels]. Cervantes's early plays offer novelesque heroines, often literally Italian as well as italianate, and classically inspired heroic figures; the *entremeses* [interludes] present clever *malmaridadas* [unhappy wives] and urchins of the type common to popular and scholastic theater and tales. He uses literary conventions as a springboard for the creation of complex women who eventually learn to use their powerful, if not always truthful, speech to characterize themselves.

Cervantes chooses to make his women characters subjects,[2] in every sense of the word: these are women with a voice of their own,[3] even if they do not always command the spaces they inhabit. They incarnate the struggle between the classical and Pauline ideal of women's silence—the notion that only "public" women would speak in public—and the necessities of characterization, since without speech the internal self remains mysterious to the outside world. Cervantes is clearly conscious of the imbalance imposed by enforced silence, by the lack of a "persona," and grapples with this problem throughout his works: the voice of the "other half" is neither privileged nor ignored in Cervantes, but given equal time.[4]

Since a full study of Cervantes's women characters is beyond the scope of a brief essay, I shall concentrate on *El laberinto del amor* [*The Labyrinth of Love*], an early play, and *La española inglesa* [*The English Spanish Girl*], one of the exemplary novels. These two relatively neglected works offer crucial keys to understanding Cervantes's construction of women characters. Though they differ in style and period as well as genre, both are deeply concerned with women's self-formation. The heroines of *El laberinto del amor* and *La española inglesa* define themselves through skillful speech. In the broader context of Cervantes's work, their voices enable the author to produce masterful counterpoint. These women's shifting identities engender doubt and ambiguity in the minds of his readers and undercut many notions of idealized love, which nevertheless find sincere expression in these works. The title of the play provides the clue to the themes and strategies that link the two works: both *are* labyrinths, and both forge identity in the seething contradictions of love.

The essential metaphor of the labyrinth produces confusion as well as enlightenment; it figures life as well as love, and enfolds language and identity. Ellen Anderson clearly formulated this idea in her analysis of *El laberinto del amor,* and I would like to expand upon it here, particularly in its relevance to *La española inglesa.* As Penelope Doob has shown in *The Idea of the Labyrinth,* the maze is a constant presence in the literature of the Renaissance, as it was in the classical and medieval periods: pastoral love stories and pilgrimages of self discovery, like chivalric romances and their parodies, are labyrinthine in structure. The labyrinth compresses the infinite into a finite space, yet it offers the reader/listener the challenge of discovery and the pleasure of extending the experience. The labyrinth is both a frightening mirror of our experience of disordered existence, and a supreme example of human construction's attempt to imitate an ordered, divine creation.

The forest, as locus of both confusion and freedom, is a standard companion to the labyrinth. These intertwining metaphors clearly inform Ariosto's *Orlando Furioso*[5] and may be glimpsed in many of Cervantes's works, including *Don Quijote de la Mancha.* In the forest, that which is artificial is often more real than reality, and as spectators we watch with delight the *ingeniosos enredos* [intricate entanglements]—in Doobs's phrase the "difficult process" —that Cervantes concocts. The forest of error is not a sinful vale of tears but an enchanted wood where freedom from society's strictures, sometimes from literal imprisonment (as in *El laberinto*), enables both sexes to attain moral betterment and social advancement. This world offers an antidote to the tyranny of Fortune, so the twistings and turnings of the plot eventually conclude with a safe exit from the labyrinth. An almost infinite deferral of this ending prolongs the reader/spectator's pleasure (Parker), while the author challenges his audience to decipher the false leads.

Certainly, when Cervantes chooses to write a pastoral novel or play, he interrogates the chaotic Italian models he knew so well and inevitably introduces similar elements of ambiguity and creative confusion. Cervantes, like Ariosto before him, is exceptional in making women in these tales the protagonists rather than merely the muse or the temptress who leads men into a web of confusion. The blind god of love leads all those in the labyrinth, but while the men are drawn into comical error as a result of the women's scheming, and are thus doubly blind, the women's stratagems draw them out safely at the end. Though Cervantes's early comedies seem artificial by contrast with his better known works in prose, his theatrical heroines already display a distinctive voice, based in part on a reversal of the usual expectations of the woman's role.

While the rhetoric linking "woman" and "error" in most Golden Age comedy, and most labyrinth-related literature, refers back to Eve and the loss of Paradise, in Cervantes's work the woman who errs is engaged in a wandering process of self-definition. The labyrinth of love provides the necessary opportunity for knowing the self, so although both the labyrinth and the forest are designed to deceive, we enter them willingly. Disguises serve a similar function: superficially deceptive, they are vehicles for comical mistakes but can also reveal deeper truths. Error allows imagination to take flight, to envision a just solution. *Errar,* then, is errantry, the haphazard quest that leads to discovery of self and of truth, which can lead to true wisdom.

Language mirrors this preoccupation with error in many ways. Petrarchan conceits, long employed in love poetry, are full of contradiction, of error, and they wander from point to point. Puns, of which this play and its cousins are typically full, provide great opportunities for error and emphasize sexual differences, even as the characters try to deny them. We should not forget that Romance languages are permeated by gender, and to sexual masqueraders, like the doubly disguised women who abound in romances, this proves especially troublesome. At the same time, while it provides the author with a rich vein of comic misunderstanding, it also serves as fertile ground to interrogate arbitrary roles, a further extension of the *theatrum mundi* trope.[6]

Both *El laberinto* and *La española* speak of conversion, of translation, and, thus, of the possibilities inherent in the labyrinthine process of self-definition.

Woman learns to navigate the blind alleys that society tries to impose upon her and to escape from the Minotaur that threatens to devour her—a loveless future, for reasons of economics, religion, or politics—by learning the language needed to triumph in this public arena. Cervantes presents women who are able to rehearse several different voices and thus to escape the male constructions in which they are imprisoned: an educated woman can uncover meaning in the labyrinth of language and defeat stratagems for her undoing. Cervantes uses the woman's voice as a counternarration, to present two (or more) versions of the story at the same time, leading the reader/spectator through a maze analogous to the one that puzzles the heroine. While in *El laberinto* the alternative voices are separate characters who adopt the idiolects expected of them on the stage, in *La española* the *personnae* are more subtly distinguished and integrated into Isabela's character by means of her command of separate languages not presented to the reader. Confusion of identity, which threatens the reigning social order, is possible because of the essential (Platonic) equality of souls. Thus the plays may be read as "dress-rehearsals" for later works, including the *novelas ejemplares,* because they reveal Cervantes's fascination with the many roles and continual self-construction implicit in the human condition.

Despite this thematic continuity, Cervantes's theater has suffered until quite recently from a more or less benign neglect. Scholars have used the lens Cervantes himself provided in the prologue to the *Comedias* [Plays]: "[D]e mi prosa se podía esperar mucho, pero . . . del verso, nada" (9) [Much could be hoped for from my prose, but little from my poetry] (my translation). In our day, as in his own, Cervantes's theater suffers by comparison to Lope de Vega's more commercially successful offerings. While Cervantes's heroic drama may receive grudging admiration, the artificial complications and often pedestrian verse of his romantic comedies make a poor contrast with Lope's smoother rhetoric, flowing lyricism, and more polished plotting.[7] However, for the feminist spectator or critic, Cervantes is of greater interest than Lope because he, like Tirso de Molina, presents heroines who are fully conscious of the power of the word. Though not all are fully realized individuals, they are true subjects who use their power of narration—the most successful form of self-definition and disguise—to change their lives.

The varied women characters in *Don Quijote* and the *novelas ejemplares* are sui generis, but they follow in the footsteps of numerous predecessors.[8] Many can trace their ancestry quite directly to Ariosto's women warriors from the *Orlando Furioso;* others descend from the scheming heroines of Boccaccio's *novelle;* still others are modeled on a host of biblical, classical, and contemporary *exempla,* from both the literary and oral traditions. The exemplary women characters of the *novelas ejemplares* present models of language in the mouths of moral role models. They serve a greater purpose, however, than stylistic perfection. It is surely not accidental that those novellas in which a happy ending is achieved are those in which the women's words are valued. Like Melveena McKendrick, I believe in Cervantes's "acute awareness of the injustice of the traditional attitudes that governed relations between the sexes in literature as in life" (*Cervantes* 245). By giving equal weight to the voices of his women characters, he attempts to redress this long-standing imbalance.

Cervantes's heroines transcend the familiar Ave-Eva archetypes, which have been a literary commonplace since the time of the Arcipreste de Hita.[9] On stage, in fact, the exceptional women characters of the *comedia* completely overwhelm most of the story's heroes. Porcia, Julia, and Rosamira do not conform to shallow stage conventions for disguised women: the tragic Amazon, who suffers in the service of martial ideals, and the comic Page, who schemes in the toils of love. Cervantes's women characters merge the pathos of the former with the linguistic legerdemain of the latter to emerge as authors. They do not need to adopt a man's voice in order to be heard. The women's speech or song is superficially beguiling, but its deeper purpose is to reveal the truth hidden in the labyrinth of lies, permitting a safe exit. Speech, and silence, whether enforced or voluntary, clearly has the power to change or fix identity. Cervantes concretely links the "language question" and the "woman question" by creating very vocal women characters who will embody different positions in the debate and different possible styles of (self-)expression.

It should hardly be surprising to find self-reflexiveness at the heart of Cervantes's labyrinthine consideration of women's words, since language and identity are crucial themes in all his work. We are accustomed to his exploration of these themes in the confrontation between the fictive and the real: the idealized world meets the picaresque world, and in its turn must face the challenge of a more three-dimensional character. Long before Marcela and Dulcinea, Cervantes's piquantly disguised pages challenged male definitions of female identity. They are remarkable not for their mere physical or even vocal presence, but because of their *narrative* presence: these women weave their own identities by force of willpower. Later still, the peerless paragons of virtue of the *novelas ejemplares* continue to call into question the ideal of feminine silence. The long-suffering Cervantine heroines do not merely endure; their artful dominion of spoken and written language enables them to tell their own stories and thus triumph over their enemies. They determine the language to be used and its value: to err is human, to sing, or at least soliloquize, divine.

El laberinto del amor[10] is set in the forest of Ardennes and is based on the same romantic tales that inspired Shakespeare's *As You Like It.* Cervantes's *three* heroines are Rosamira, Julia, and Porcia, noble ladies intent on securing the husbands of their choice, despite parental, that is to say, paternal, opposition. They, along with their lovers, concoct stories and disguises to thwart the Duke of Novara's plan to wed his daughter Rosamira to Manfredo. Dagoberto, son of the Count of Utrino, concocts a false (or is it?) accusation of illicit love, while Anastasio, his cousin, who also pines for Rosamira, disguises himself as a laborer in order to spy on the lady. Meanwhile, Dagoberto's sister, Porcia, loves Anastasio; she joins his sister, Julia, in disguising herself as a shepherd because "Ingenio tienes y brío, / y ocasión tienes también / para procurar tu bien, / como yo procuro el mío" (2:7–10; 268) [You are spirited and clever, and now have the opportunity as well to obtain the object of your love just as I procure my happiness]. The confusion of identity is far greater than in the Shakespearean version and does become labyrinthine. Julia even turns herself into Manfredo's favorite page, Camilo. In the end, Porcia, disguised as Rosamira, chooses Anastasio, leaving Rosamira free to select Dagoberto, while Manfredo pairs off with Julia by default and is able to refute the charge that he abducted the two ladies—avoiding a threatened trial by combat.

The women characters of *El laberinto* overcome numerous obstacles through their artful dominion of the spoken word. At first timorous and over-awed by their own daring, they fear that the costumes they have assumed, originally intended for a "farsa o comedia / que querían mis doncellas / hacer" (1:28–30; 232) [farce or play that my damsels wanted to represent], will be turned to tragedy if they are discovered. The clue, they fear, is the richness of the apparel, which does not suit their humble station. Even when imprisoned, they create their own stories and refuse to be silenced. Indeed, Rosamira, the woman who appears most passive, a silent victim, is revealed to be an arch-plotter in her own right. Porcia, Julia, and Rosamira are by necessity deceiving others when they transform, yet because, as Porcia says, they are revealing their true selves—"la verdad de mi mentira" (3:14; 330) [the truth of my false-hood]—this deceit is not condemned. The numerous changes of dress that Porcia, Julia, and their lovers undertake display a remarkable fluidity of iden-tity: Porcia and Julia emerge first as little shepherds, then pages, then students, then farmhands, and finally as farm girls, with Porcia even masquerading as the wronged lady Rosamira, and then *pretending* to be herself. Julia also changes into her "mistress's" [Julia's] garb, only to be accused by Manfredo of playing a trick on him! These are the complications that lengthen our pleasant stay in the labyrinth and that prolong the confusion of the lovers.

Moreover, the male disguise is but a portion of the identity the noble-women create for themselves: their speech is far more important than their dress. Porcia, as a student, for example, outdoes the students around her in wrangling with words as well as in wrestling: "no la ha de derribar" (1:7; 251) [but she shall not be knocked down]. Their virtuosity assures their ultimate vindication. Their bewildered menfolk, like the audience, must admire it. Manfredo confesses to Julia "eres mi igual, y aun mejor" (3:3; 321) [You are my equal, and even my better]. This speech refers in part to the lady's station, but it also clearly alludes to her superior plotting. Anyone who doubts who is in control at the end of the play should look to Porcia's declaration of her identity: "Soy la que . . . en traje mudado . . . he mi gusto procurado" (3:6,9; 331) [I am she who . . . in altered clothing . . . has procured her pleasure].

The women's speech, even more than that of Anastasio and Manfredo, their noble lovers who have *also* disguised themselves, is used for comic effect and also to heighten the audience's awareness of *theatrum mundi*. Locals suspect Julia and Porcia are not what they seem because their manner of speaking seems too exalted for their humble station. At the same time, identity is shown as a deliberate, theatrical composition: Julia, speaking as Camilo, identifies herself in this way to Manfredo: "lloviendo perlas de sus bellos ojos (2:25; 277) Yo soy aquella . . . la sinventura . . . la hija / del duque de Dorlan" (2:21, 29–30; 278) [raining pearls from her beautiful eyes . . . I am that lady, the unfortunate one, the daughter of the Duke of Orleans]. This self-description, designed to enamor, succeeds; Manfredo admits "el modo de decirlo me enamora" (2:15; 277) [your way of telling it enamors me]. Julia meets the man's expectations, then presents to him the dramatic realization—the picture come to life. Despite Manfredo's criticism of Julia's "apetito sin freno" (2:28; 287) [unbridled appetite], his curiosity is piqued, and he is eager to see the lady. Cervantes clearly contrasts the alternate methods of showing and telling in self-creation and self-deception, and concludes that, on the stage at least, telling is more effective.

The overarching metaphor of the labyrinth of love follows many twists and turns after the initial transformation it occasions: "Ya en el ciego laberinto / te metió el amor cruel" (1:18; 230), "Muestra ser varón en todo" (1:2; 231) [Since cruel love has thrust you into the blind labyrinth . . . / Show yourself a man in all things]. Here all is contradictory, the harmony of nature is disrupted and the will is powerless: "¡O amor! ¡O confusión jamás oida! / ¡O vida muerta! ¡O libertad rendida!" (1:28–29; 228) [Oh love! Oh unheard of confusion! Oh lifeless life! Oh surrendered liberty!]. Love can also change outward appearances, but it is primarily a positive force, though still subject to considerations of position and proper "correspondence."

When Rosamira feigns faintness, seemingly fearing to answer the charge of immorality that her lover Dagoberto levels against her, the duke, her father, reproves her, "Mal correspondes, hija, a quien eres" (1:24; 224) [How little you suit your station, daughter]. All the characters concern themselves with this correspondence between the social and the essential, being "quien se es" [literally being who one is]. It is a matter of estate, however; class is more important in this equation than sex. Anastasio assures Porcia: "Soy otra persona que este hábito astroso muestra" (2:30; 276) [I am a different man than is shown by these filthy garments], allowing her to reverse the expected roles of lady and lover-servant.

Nonetheless, this concern with reputation and the *código de honor* [honor code], corresponding to one's proper place in the social hierarchy, clearly spawns a society where women can only avoid being besmirched by rumor through confinement. As McKendrick notes in her thoughtful biography of Cervantes, this generally optimistic play clearly shows that the repression of women "encourages not obedience but revolt" (244) because "freedom [is] the natural . . . the only true habitat of virtue and of love" (242–43). As we will see in numerous later Cervantine works, *el engaño a los ojos* [the eyes deceive one] remains the cautionary tale to accompany all these meditations on love and faith. This might be expected, since the classical tale of the labyrinth offers a warning to rebellious women and their lovers; we should not expect blind trust to be rewarded. Ariadne gives the clue of wool to Theseus to enable him to retrace his steps and exit safely, thus betraying her clan for the sake of love. Theseus eventually abandons her, and her retribution overtakes his entire house.

The *novelas ejemplares* may appear at first glance to provide exemplary models of normative language and sexual conduct, but they are frequently more unruly than they seem. Harry Sieber's authoritative summation of the critical history in the introduction to his edition of the *Novelas ejemplares* (13–30) makes clear the many shifts in fortune they have experienced. Contemporaries eyed them with wary respect and current readers focus most on a few famous novellas and ignore the others as relics of the Counter-Reformation. Sieber's prefatory remarks (19; 29) linking "free economic exchange" as studied by Levi-Strauss with poetry and song in *La gitanilla* [*Little Gypsy Girl*] and mercantile exchange with the exchange of women (that is, marriage) in *La española inglesa*, are some of the most insightful to have been dedicated to these novellas. This linkage of women, words, and money is already in evidence in the early plays, as discussed above, and is present in most of Cervantes's work, though not always in such an optimistic fashion. Isabela and Preciosa, the heroines of *La española inglesa* and *La gitanilla*, represent, in effect, the union of the three disparate heroines of *El laberinto del amor* into a single, more powerful woman. They learn the transforming lessons of love's labyrinth and emerge with a newly forged identity revealed in their speech.

La española inglesa has traditionally been considered a lesser *novela ejemplar* and "hastily written," even by such sympathetic critics as McKendrick (*Cervantes* 275).[11] Scholars unwilling to dismiss any of Cervantes's work seek a more serious core to the novella than the turns of fortune, marriage plot, and anagnorisis, those staples of romance, that dominate its plot. This has lead to *La española inglesa* frequently being discussed almost exclusively in terms of the fortunes—be they political, economic, or religious—of its *male* characters.[12] Though these analyses offer much convincing detail about the period and enlightening speculation about Cervantes's religious convictions, they completely ignore the central and title character, *la española inglesa* herself, Isabela.

Cervantes's supposed lapse in artistry, his descent to the conventions of the romance, is better comprehended when we recognize that it is Isabela's *voz extremada* (279) [consummate voice] that provides the thematic and structural unity of her story. Her voice is our guide to the dangerous world she inhabits: a world of enforced silence and voluntary withdrawal of speech. This novella clearly contrasts public confession and private speech; it explores the ways language can be a means of division, as it has been since Babel, or a means of greater understanding. While the position of *conversos* [converts] compared with recusants, and the diplomatic ups and downs of Spanish-English relations are instructive to a full appreciation of the story, they simply mirror the central meditation on language. Isabela is an exemplary heroine, above reproach, who thrives despite exile, imprisonment, and separation from loved ones, and even attempted murder, because her power to charm is equaled only by her power to narrate.

Carried off in an English raid on Cadiz, Isabela is adopted by a recusant family and favored by the English queen. Daughter of a merchant, she moves in humble and courtly circles with equal ease, and her doubling is not duplicity. She is poisoned by the mother of a rival and eventually returns to her native Cadiz, and then to Seville. Just as she is at home in different social settings, she is also at home in different languages, and is quite capable of telling and translating her story. From the beginning, Isabela is fitted for her task: "La enseñaron a leer y escribir más que medianamente; pero en lo que tuvo extremo fue en tañer todos los instrumentos que a una mujer son lícitos, y esto con toda perfección de música, acompañándola con una voz que le dio el Cielo tan extremada, que encantaba cuando cantaba" (244) [After having learned all kinds of work becoming a young lady of good birth, she was taught to read and write more than passably well; but what she excelled in above all was in playing all sorts of instruments suitable to her sex, with extraordinary perfection of musical taste and skill, and with the accompaniment of a voice which Heaven had endowed with such melody that when she chanted she enchanted] (279). This initial ascription of Isabela's gifts to the Almighty, and the rather biblical description of her power to enchant with song, emphasize the underlying moral of the triumph of virtue, which we will be asked to appreciate at the end of the story. At the same time, it is clearly human agency that is responsible for the evil that must be overcome: Isabela's labyrinth is not of divine design, it is man-made, begun with acts of violence, which must be expiated.

Like all labyrinths, this one is based on doubling. It begins in the title character's apparent dual nationality, which the translator goes so far as to connect with a hyphen. Isabela is left sick for *two* months after a rival poisons her; she waits for Ricaredo for *two* years in Seville. She is "adopted" *twice*, once by her captor, Clotaldo, and once by the queen; each time she fears to be kept from the practice of her religion. Isabela's illness mirrors that of Ricaredo when he pines for her. Ricaredo's confession of love, like Isabela's literal shedding of her skin, the stripping away of the outer self after the poisoning, are cases of "difficult process," leading to greater truth. Her inner beauty is revealed even as her outer beauty is for the time obscured. The illness is in fact the motivation for Isabela and her family being returned to Spain (and the free practice of their religion); without this "twist" they would remain prisoners of the queen's pleasure at Elizabeth's court, even though Isabela would have been allowed to marry Ricaredo.

The forced uncoupling of lovers, of parents and children, mirrors the division of churches and nations. Each violent action provokes a violent reaction, until the divisions are healed with the reunion of Ricaredo and Isabela. The denouement of the romance presents literal and figurative translation. The star-crossed lovers seek to escape the strictures (literal shackles) imposed by differing nationality, parents' fears and economic necessity; in order to do so, the Englishman, Ricaredo, must undo, step by step all his father's misdeeds. Ricaredo must rescue Isabela's parents and set other Spanish prisoners free, then suffer Isabela and her father's fate of shipwreck, captivity, near death, and silent incomprehension as he arrives in Seville, as ignorant of Spanish as she had at first been of English. When Ricaredo has retraced the necessary steps to exit the labyrinth where Isabela had first been forced to enter it, they are free to depart.

Her literal translation of Ricaredo's narration culminates in a figurative translation as well; her voice is heard by the powers of heaven and earth, and past injustices are undone: "[A]unque Ricaredo quiso tomar la mano en contar su historia, todavia le pareció que era mejor fiarlo de la lengua y discreción de Isabela y no de la suya, que no muy expertamente hablaba la lengua castellana" (279) [Though Richard would willingly have taken it upon himself to tell his story, yet he thought it better to trust it to Isabella's tongue than to his own, which was not very expert in speaking Spanish] (309).

Isabela's bilingualism unites the two warring factions here and at court, just as it has previously permitted her to conquer the hearts of Clotaldo and his family: "[S]in olvidar la suya, hablaba la lengua inglesa como si hubiera nacido en Londres" (244) [(W)ithout ceasing to speak Spanish, she became as proficient in English as if she had been born in London] (279). In both England and Spain, her knowledge of both languages enables her to interpret rightly, to obtain the key that unlocks the mysteries of identity. Isabela is able likewise to undo the imprisonment of her father and her lover by recognizing and naming them. Finally she puts all right with the Church and the larger society by translating, then writing down, their stories for the bishop.

Though the novella bears the trappings of fairy-tale, Cervantes conjures two very real queens to act as "fairy godmothers" to his poor heroine: the English Elizabeth and, by implication, Isabel *la Católica*. From the beginning, we expect that Isabela will be like that most famous Isabel, her namesake: Catholic, heroic, and queenly. These two other Isabels are both exemplary and exceptional, one married, the other unmarried. They give Isabela their "voices"; they are her models and a key historical element in studying the novella, which in the end hinges on Isabela's decision between the convent and marriage, between silent contemplation and vocal participation.

When she goes to court in London, Elizabeth I becomes her patroness, in part because of the similarity of name—"Hasta el nombre me contenta . . . no le faltaba más sino llamarse Isabela . . . para que no me quedase nada de perfección que desear en ella" (250) [I like her name too, . . . Nothing was wanting to the fullness of her perfection but that she should be called Isabella] (284)—but also in part because of Isabela's gift of speech. Elizabeth's interest in other languages, in words, makes her capable of seeing through falsehoods, and she is able to converse with Isabela in her native language: "Habladme en español, doncella, que yo le entiendo bien, y gustaré dello" (249) [Speak to me in Spanish, maiden, for I understand it well and shall like to hear it] (284). The English Elizabeth is portrayed as a clever woman, a strong ruler, and a just monarch, despite being a Protestant, though she never puts Isabela and her recusant adoptive family to any religious tests. Elizabeth, substituting for Isabela's real parents, restores balance between the two lovers, imposing tests on Ricaredo to force him to *earn* what his father had stolen: "[E]l por sí mismo se ha de disponer a servirme y a merecer por sí esta prenda, que yo la estimo como si fuese mi hija" (250) [He must prepare himself to serve me, and win by his own deserts this prize which I esteem as if she were my daughter] (284). Elizabeth also literally restores Isabela to her parents, then restores their fortunes when she indemnifies them handsomely for the kidnaping of Isabela.

Classically, discovery of one who can vouch for a woman's true family origins leads to a happy ending in romance, whereas for Porcia and Julia the declaration is made by themselves, and Isabela's recognition of Ricaredo is more important than her own by her parents. The happy endings are based on the women's own actions and narration, not passive recognition by another authoritative voice. Porcia and Julia choose their husbands first and justify it afterward, persuading the men to follow *their* judgment. Isabela chooses and waits for Ricaredo, in opposition to her adopted parents' wishes. It is she who *writes* the story of La española inglesa, becoming the actor, translator, and author whose vocal prowess creates peace, harmony, and prosperity for nations and individuals.

I have outlined one reading of two of Cervantes's lesser-known works, with an eye to tracing the continuity of the writer's concern with the woman's voice, and encouraging further study of other texts from a feminist perspective. Cervantes is inexhaustible; each new wave of scholarship seeks a different, definitive interpretation, but all methods can assist us in interpreting his infinitely complex work. The increasing body of knowledge about Early Modern women will provide excellent background for such studies, as we keep in mind Cervantes's sympathetic view of all human failings. His subversiveness and his

ironic interrogation of received maxims certainly extend to those used to define and govern women.

The search for context, for historical and autobiographical elements in Cervantes's works, can be self-defeating, however, when we look to the woman's
voice. It is dangerous to ascribe too modern a sensibility to the writer. While
his personal experiences caring for unmarried/widowed sisters, nieces of dubi-
ous legitimacy, and his own illegitimate daughter and granddaughter doubt-
less contributed to his knowledge of women and their struggles to maintain
even minimal autonomy, the repeated ill-advised liaisons of the Cervantes
women and his daughter's apparent mercenary qualities might easily have led
Cervantes to become a misogynistic moralizer or a detached aesthete. The
antiheroine of *El casamiento engañoso* [*Deceitful Marriage*] and the anti-
mother of the *Coloquio de los perros* [*Colloquy of the Dogs*] might easily have
predominated, yet Cervantes remains engaged with the problem of women's
expression in literature. The early *comedias* were revised for publication to
make them more commercially viable (McKendrick, *Cervantes* 289–90); this
makes the women characters all the more noteworthy in what are otherwise
extended pastorals, which could hardly be supposed to represent the current
popular taste.

Despite the disillusionment Cervantes may have suffered, his women characters do not undergo a radical reformation in his old age, as Boccaccio's did.
Some continue to take part in the hopeful dialogues of the Renaissance, while
others are consigned to the realm of baroque inversions, expressing no more
than the triumph of disorder, the world turned upside down. The author's
experiences in Italy and his experiences with his own womenfolk are, perhaps,
a necessary component of his approach to characterization, but they are not a
sufficient explanation. In the end, whether we argue that Cervantes drew primarily from life or from literature is immaterial: he creates women who did
not previously exist, and they are not expunged by postfacto moralizing, but
remain at the core of the exemplary novels. The morally exemplary character
of Isabela only makes her authorial voice more irresistible. Of humble, though
honorable birth, the heroine achieves nobility through well-chosen words.
The central quest for identity in *La española inglesa* moves through the adventures of romance and concludes with the establishment of a unique voice, one
that will be heard. Cervantes's women characters know "quien soy" (*Don
Quijote*, 5.62) and, as in Unamuno's reformulation by an act of will, "quien
puedo ser" [what I am and what I can be] (*Vida de Don Quijote y Sancho*,
5.39).

Notes

An earlier version of this paper was presented at the 1997 NEMLA Convention in Philadelphia.

1. In the extensive bibliography on *Don Quijote* and the somewhat smaller one on the *Novelas ejemplares,* there is very little mention of Cervantes's women characters, despite the wide variety they encompass and their crucial structural and thematic roles. Diana de Armas Wilson's essay is an insightful consideration of women's speech and presence that could well serve as a model for further studies. Wilson argues convincingly that the elusive thematic core of this wandering novel is a preoccupation with the legitimacy of women's words.

2. For an early and important exposition of the idea of women's subjectivity, especially on the stage, see Belsey.

3. Anita Stoll, Sharon Voros, Amy Wilson, and Ellen Anderson have done groundbreaking work on the ways in which Cervantes and later dramatists found the *comedia* the ideal vehicle for examining the trope of self-construction and of the masks imposed by gender roles. Several useful essays may be found in Mujica and Voros. These studies are particularly valuable in reminding us to read often-neglected texts, such as the early *comedias,* and in alerting us to the vital importance of women's language. Like Diana de Armas Wilson, they focus less on dress and more on voice in the creation of women characters.

4. Cervantes does not spare women from his biting irony. See Mazzucco-Than for an analysis of the inflated and untrustworthy rhetoric women use in these tales.

5. For a recent exposition of the labyrinth in Ariosto, see Donato.

6. Maravall's *La cultura del barroco* remains the best discussion of the *theatrum mundi* and "the world turned upside down" motifs in the *comedia.*

7. Canavaggio's 1977 study of Cervantes's theater, much of it subsumed in his 1986 biography (translated into English in 1990), began a serious reappraisal of these works.

8. Benson gives a thorough examination of the emergence of "new" types of women and shows the uses and meanings of exemplary vs. exceptional women in several English and Italian authors of the period. Cervantes's women characters form part of this literary tradition.

9. Miller offers many persuasive essays on this topic. Not surprisingly, McKendrick's "Women Against Wedlock" is of particular relevance to this essay.

10. Because this play is not widely available, all citations will provide the *jornada,* [act] followed by the line number and page from the Schevill and Bonilla edition of the *Comedias.* The English translations are my own.

11. All citations are from Sieber's edition of the *Novelas ejemplares;* English translations are from Kelly, except the first one of *voz extremada,* which is mine.

12. Ricapito's *Cervantes's "Novelas ejemplares": Between History and Creativity* is a recent example of this trend, and he gives a full bibliography in this vein.

Works Cited

Anderson, Ellen. "Refashioning the Maze: The Interplay of Gender and Rank in Cervantes' *El laberinto del amor.*" *Bulletin of the Comediantes* 46 (1994): 165–85.

Austin, Gayle. *Feminist Theories for Dramatic Criticism.* Ann Arbor: University of Michigan Press, 1990.

Belsey, Catherine. *The Subject of Tragedy.* London: Methuen, 1985.

Benson, Pamela. *The Invention of the Renaissance Woman.* University Park: Penn State University Press, 1992.

Canavaggio, Jean. *Cervantes.* 1986. Trans. J. R. Jones. New York: Norton, 1990.

Cervantes, Miguel de. *Don Quixote de la Mancha.* Ed. Martín de Riquer. 10th ed. Barcelona: Editorial Juventud, 1975.

———. *The Exemplary novels of Miguel de Cervantes Saavedra: to which are added "El Buscapié," or "The Serpent"; "La Tia Fingida," or "The Pretended Aunt."* Trans. Walter K. Kelly. London: Henry G. Bohn, 1855.

———. *El laberinto del amor. Obras completas de Miguel de Cervantes: Comedias y entremeses.* Ed. Rodolfo Schevill and Adolfo Bonilla. Vol. 2. Madrid: Bernardo Rodríguez, 1915. 219–333.

———. *Novelas ejemplares, I.* Ed. Harry Sieber. 11th ed. Madrid: Cátedra, 1989.

———. "Prólogo." *Obras completas de Miguel de Cervantes Saavedra: Comedias y entremeses.* Ed. Rodolfo Schevill and Adolfo Bonilla. Vol 1. Madrid: Bernardo Rodríguez, 1914. 5–10.

Donato, Eugenio. "'Per Selve e Boscherecci Labirinti': Desire and Narrative Structure in Ariosto's *Orlando Furioso.*" *Literary Theory/Renaissance Texts.* Ed. Patricia Parker and David Quint. Baltimore: Johns Hopkins University Press, 1986. 33–62.

Doob, Penelope. *The Idea of the Labyrinth.* Ithaca: Cornell University Press, 1990.

Maravall, José Antonio. *La cultura del barroco.* 4th ed. Barcelona: Ariel, 1986.

Mazzucco-Than, Cecile. "The Doorways to the Maelstrom of Discourse in Cervantes's *El casamiento engañoso* and *El coloquio de los perros.*" *Romance Languages Annual* (1992): 516–20.

McKendrick, Melveena. *Cervantes.* Boston: Little, 1980.

———. "Women Against Wedlock." *Women in Hispanic Literature: Icons and Fallen Idols.* Ed. Beth Miller. Berkeley and Los Angeles: University of California Press, 1983. 115–46.

Mujica, Barbara, and Sharon D. Voros, eds. *Looking at the Comedia in the Year of the Quincentennial: Proceedings of the 1992 Symposium on Golden Age Drama at the University of Texas, El Paso.* Lanham, Md.: University Press of America, 1992.

Parker, Patricia. "Deferral, Dilation, Difference: Shakespeare, Cervantes, Jonson." *Literary Theory/Renaissance Texts.* Ed. Patricia Parker and David Quint. Baltimore: Johns Hopkins University Press, 1986. 182–209.

Ricapito, Joseph. *Cervantes's "Novelas ejemplares": Between History and Creativity.* West Lafayette, Ind.: Purdue University Press, 1996.

Sieber, Harry. "Preliminar." *Novelas ejemplares, I.* By Miguel de Cervantes. Ed. Harry Sieber. Madrid: Cátedra, 1989. 13–30.

Unamuno, Miguel de. *Vida de Don Quijote y Sancho.* 16th ed. Madrid: Espasa-Calpe, 1975.

Wilson, Diana de Armas. "Cervantes' *Labors of Persiles:* Working (in) the In-Between." *Literary Theory/Renaissance Texts.* Ed. Patricia Parker and David Quint. Baltimore: Johns Hopkins University Press, 1986. 150–81.

11

Silence Is/As Golden . . . Age Device

Ana Caro's Eloquent Reticence in *Valor, agravio y mujer*

Monica Leoni

In attempting to define loosely the parameters of message conveyance and emotional impact in a well-staged dramatic performance, students in a recently given theater course considered the question of scenic display and special effects, both visual and auditory, and concluded that these were key elements of engagement with the receptors. The students who participated in this informal debate also identified the authority of the written script as the governing factor in any specific adaptation. This further stimulated discussion on how hierarchical consideration of "content" could nullify prospective visions of a dramatic text. We were intent on description, not prescription.

At this point I put forth the idea that all well-staged drama results in a certain assault on one or more of the senses. When this statement was asked to be qualified, there was a notable absence of engagement with factors that went beyond the seen and the spoken as stimuli to the senses and/or intellect. Silence, as a force in and of itself, capable of transmission of opinion or judgment, or even as challenge to belief systems, did not present itself. Evidently our own parameters with regard to stimuli is still quite often left to obvious binary and somewhat outdated perception.

Although it is indisputable that silence carries with it connotations of serenity, stillness, and peace, in the Western world it has come to be associated more commonly with notions of death, emptiness, and absence.[1] There is a need to fill the void and somehow control the space that silence occupies, even if in its place we simply inject inconsequential small talk. And yet, each of us has undoubtedly experienced another's reticent response to an event or an idea, only to be left wondering if that moment of voluntary abstention from communication was taken with the intent of showing approval, disapproval, understanding, misunderstanding, or utter indifference. We have also all experienced at some point in our lives forms of voluntary abstention from communication that certainly did not imply disengagement. Here I refer to the myriad occasions we are spoken of, about, and for, when our presence is negated, or when we are simply not present to literally "give voice." This is not necessarily a benign engagement with those who assume our input "in absentia," but certainly in a dramatic context it is a powerful force of prerecognition that stages the audience's reactions.

For the purposes of this essay, I will focus only on the communicative power of the silences found on the stage and the freedom of interpretation that such absences grant to those performing and viewing the production, using Ana Caro's *Valor, agravio y mujer* [*Valor, Offense, Woman*] as a critical base. In *Speechless Dialect: Shakespeare's Open Silences*, Philip C. McGuire analyzes the Bard's use of verbal absence and the numerous resulting interpretations that these theatrical blanks, carefully "written" for certain key characters, provide. McGuire distinguishes between lasting silences (the death of a character) and open silences (characters who live beyond the fall of the curtain) and writes: "Such silences [open silences] grant to those who perform and produce the plays the power to give them shape and coherence, thus ensuring that the plays will vary from production to production, even from performance to performance. Open silences are only one source of the freedom that Shakespeare's plays generate, but these silences serve especially well to illustrate that such freedom is not merely accidental and peripheral but extends to how major issues posed during a given play are resolved" (xxi). It is my contention that in *Valor, agravio y mujer,* Ana Caro similarly uses a rhetoric of reticence in order to quietly remark on the conditions and limitations facing the women of her time. With the character of Flora, the conspicuously absent *criada* [servant], Caro tacitly weaves into a traditional plot a rather subversive commentary that invites the audience to complete the message that she herself cannot frankly convey.

From the perspective of gender studies, reticence and absence have long been associated with all things female. Ann Rosalind Jones notes that since the Renaissance, the views held of the female sex placed upon women an injunction to silence, and that the degree of "success" in following this quiet mandate would determine a female's acceptance as a proper model of femininity: "In the discourses of humanism and bourgeois family theory, the proper woman is an absence: legally, she vanishes under the name and authority of her father and her husband; as daughter and wife, she is enclosed in the private household. She is silent and invisible: she does not speak, and she is not spoken about" (79). To impose such a silence upon another is to disempower that individual from the process of meaning-making. Women found themselves accepted and marginalized in one fell swoop: accepted because it was becoming for them to be reticent and retiring, and marginalized because by playing this silent role, they immediately forfeited any potential attempt to participate in the power plays of the speaking masses.

Contemporary feminist studies have identified those speaking masses to be male in gender. Because historically the access to knowledge and the creation and sharing of thoughts and ideas had been a male privilege, the inaccessibility to information has been a reality suffered essentially by the female sex. Yet to view silence as a purely female characteristic, and therefore as a debilitating reality purposely imposed on women, is to view it from the patriarchal perspective, where the spoken or written word is the only validated form of communication. In her analyses of the silent text in the works of Jane Austen, Charlotte Brontë, and Virginia Woolf, Patricia Laurence recognizes the value of the understated and concludes that the recourse to the silent text by female writers can indeed speak volumes. It simply depends on how carefully one is "listening": "Depending on one's definition of reality, silences woven into the fabric of a woman's text can be an absence or a presence. If reality is perceived according to established patriarchal values, then women's silence, viewed from the outside, is a mark of absence and powerlessness.... If, however, the same silence is viewed from the inside, and women's experience and disposition of mind inform the standard of what is real, then women's silence can be viewed as a presence, and as a text, waiting to be read" (157–58).

In terms of theatrical effect, the impact of silence on the stage is much more easily discussed than is the silence of the page. In the dramatic text, silent moments or reticent characters are often difficult to identify and assess because they are usually not referred to specifically in the text itself. Silent figures on the stage are a common theatrical convention, used to great effect by playwrights throughout the centuries. Indeed, it is argued that the silent character must be present, if for no other reason than to provide someone with whom the audience can relate: "A modern audience sitting silently at performance undergoes many of the same feelings that the silent characters on stage experience. We understand the emotions of the silent characters because we too are silent in the face of rhetoric.... At times, the mutual silence shared by character and audience enables us to supply emotions in situations where words are absent" (Rovine 97). In Caro's case, however, the use of the silent figure is curious because the character's reticence is not absolute, but rather selectively employed and carefully woven into the text, with Flora choosing to make her voice heard only to those most likely to be moved by it—her audience.

A Golden Age woman writing drama definitely ventured into uncharted territory. Elizabeth Ordóñez comments that "drama offers less room for overt code breaking or revision than the novella, for as a public text it reflects and reinforces dominant beliefs and virtues" (9). Lola Luna goes further stating that Caro "como los personajes femeninos de sus comedias, bajo el disfraz de mujer varonil[2] o como amante secreta y nocturna, parece existir sólo en la escritura, velando su identidad bajo los textos" (12) [like the female characters of her drama, beneath the disguise of the "manly woman" or as the nocturnal, secret lover, seems to exist only in her writing, her identity remaining veiled behind the text].[3] Because an overt code-breaking would have complicated and most likely dismantled Caro's efforts to have Leonor's story told, she, like her very heroine, realizes that a subtle, unassuming approach had to be employed: a strategically planned attack with silence as her only arm.[4]

In *Silence in Shakespeare: Drama, Power, and Gender*, Harvey Rovine marks a distinction between the impact of female and male reticence. Although he correctly observes silence to function as a possible expression of confrontation to a person or to a situation, he concludes that "[w]hen men choose silence, it is often a means to an end rather than an end in itself as the passive resignation of women's silence often implies" (64). In her appropriation of the silent subtext, however, Caro does not represent the patriarchal construct of verbal absence in a traditional manner. Rather, I find that the playwright's use of it in *Valor* is done so as if to challenge its limited scope. Stephanie Merrim comments on Caro's subversive dramatic techniques and similarly remarks that "her two *comedias* [dramas] present a veritable thesaurus of the Golden Age theatrical conventions that lent themselves either to contestatory inversion or to feminist exploitation," defining contestatory inversion to be "the manner in which Caro upends conventions and constructs, of the theatre or of the *querelle* [quarrel], denigratory to women" (84).

Deceived and abandoned by Don Juan, Doña Leonor travels to Flanders intent on regaining her lost honor and forcing her betrayer to fulfill his obligation to her. Disguised as a man, and traveling under the assumed identity of Don Leonardo, Leonor will not be deterred. Displaying an acute understanding of both sexes, Leonor cunningly manipulates all around her and ultimately achieves her goals, becoming by the play's end, Don Juan's betrothed. María José Delgado comments on Leonor's admirable skill and tenacity and notes that "[l]a propuesta que resalta en la voz del personaje femenino no va tanto en contra del hombre sino en contra de las construcciones sociales que fomentan la subyugación de la mujer frente al hombre" (13–14) [the suggestion that comes forth through the voice of the female character does not speak against men so much as it speaks against the social constructs that support the subjugation of the female before the male]. Teresa S. Soufas goes further and remarks that despite Caro's adaptation of a conventional "male" plot, "she actually conducts a subversion from within" (89). It is this subversion from "within" that will now be the focus of this discussion.

Leonor arrives in Flanders accompanied by her loyal servant, Ribete.[5] While chatting with his mistress, the faithful lackey quickly takes issue with the unfair stereotypes the members of his class suffer:

Estoy mal con enfadosos
que introducen los graciosos
muertos de hambre y gallinas.
El que ha nacido alentado
¿no lo ha de ser si no es noble? (1.529–33)[6]

[I am sick of irksome / Individuals who introduce the / Clowns starving to death and / Cowardly. He who has been / Born brave, isn't he so / Even if he isn't noble?][7]

This *gracioso* [comic figure] defends himself against the generalizations commonly associated with his character and social position. His complaint is telling and echoes the female writer's own troubled reality. Mercedes Maroto Camino observes this parallel and writes: "By presenting the possibility that women and servants may have '*valor*' Caro dissociates the assumption that nobility is a privilege of the upper classes" and that this association "emphasizes the liminarity they share" (41).

In a significant scene where the two comic figures, Ribete and Tomillo, discuss the recent scholarly activity of women in Madrid, the former explains the latest events and notes:

Ya es todo muy viejo allá;
sólo en esto de poetas
hay notable novedad
por innumerables, tanto

que quieren poetizar
las mujeres, y se atreven
a hacer comedias ya. (2.1164–70)

[Everything is old news there; / Only in the matter of poets / Is there real
novelty due to / Their great number, so much so, / In fact that even
women / Want to write poetry, and now dare to / Compose plays.]

To this Tomillo exclaims: "¡Válgame Dios! Pues, ¿no fuera / mejor coser e
hilar? / ¿Mujeres poetas?" (2.1171–73)[8] [Good God! Well, wouldn't it be /
Better to cook and to sew? / Women poets?].[9] The discussion comes to an
abrupt end and the *graciosos* leave the stage. Of this exchange, Amy Williamsen has written that "besides the obvious irony, Caro's inclusion of this metatheatrical aside might also be interpreted as her anticipation of resistance to her
intrusion into a centre of literary activity. She implicitly recognizes that society in general would perceive a woman writer as someone transgressing established boundaries. Thus the text posits the problematic relationship between
margin and centre" (28). I would add that at the same time, in naming the
conflict, the text partially diffuses the difficult connection existing between
these two positions.

Caro's challenging of her social and professional reality is therefore under-
taken in an apparently inconsequential manner. Certainly, the unresolved debate between the two comic figures is telling but with Flora, the *graciosa,* the
challenge is taken to a new level. If one accepts that Caro's relationship with
the *criado* [male servant] figure is a strong one and that she uses these harmless,
peripheral characters as inconspicuous *portavoces* [spokespersons], one must
also admit that Flora's inclusion in the play serves a purpose that goes beyond
the limited sphere of the decorative.

The position of Flora in the text is indeed typically peripheral, her first
appearance being deferred to the last act of the play. This quiet presence is, of
course, a common trait of the servant type, showing said servant to be deferen-
tial to or supportive of his or her master/mistress.[10] Here, however, Flora is not
only silent, but also absent from the stage. She is not known to the audience
until the last scenes of the play, but is rather *spoken of,* immediately establishing somewhat of an identity in crisis—a woman who has no voice but of whom
much is said. Ribete informs the audience that Tomillo wishes to be the one to
"deflower" Flora (2.1144–46). Aside from this reference the audience has neither seen nor heard from the young woman herself. The spectator is therefore
informed of her existence without being given significant detail or informa-

tion, leaving her very much a name without a face, a woman associated only to a man, as a sexual referent.

In act 3, Tomillo suddenly enters and informs the public that he has just had a drink prepared for him by Flora herself. With the concoction finally taking effect, he lies down in a deep sleep. At this point Flora finally makes her entrance and explains her presence, "Siguiendo vengo a Tomillo / por si ha obrado el chocolate" (3.2351–52) [I come in pursuit of Tomillo to see if the chocolate has taken effect]. It is clear that she addresses her audience here, thereby establishing her first independent communication. She begins her search for valuable belongings that the now unconscious *gracioso* keeps hidden beneath his clothing. They are alone on the stage, and yet Flora continues to speak as she conducts her search. It is interesting that she begins her "investigation" by saying "vamos al expolio" (3.2364) [let's to the loot],[11] making a direct appeal to her public. Her search is fruitful and she exclaims:

Uno, dos, tres, cuatro, cinco,
seis, siete, ocho; es imposible
contar; mas ¡oh dulce archivo
de escudos y de esperanza,
con reverencia te miro! (3.2401–7)

[One, two, three, four, five, / Six, seven, eight, it is impossible / To count; but, oh sweet archive / Of shields and of hope, / With reverence I look upon you!].[12]

However, before finding the jackpot, as it were, Flora makes some additional commentaries:

¿Qué es aquesto? Tabaquero
de cuerno. ¡Qué hermoso aliño,
parto al fin de su cosecha,
honor de su frontispicio!
Hombres, ¡que aquesto os dé gusto! (3.2382–86)

[What is this? A tobacco horn. / A charming ornament is this I reap, / the glory of his visage! Men, to think / this gives you pleasure!].[13]

In her analysis of this scene Williamsen has commented that "[t]he overt belittling of masculine anatomy ... subvert[s] the traditional derision of the female body in female *comedias*" (26), suggesting that what could be regarded as an inconsequential comical interlude, is actually infused with a deeper, politically charged meaning that was not intended to go unnoticed.[14]

Until this point, Flora has been invisible and, more important, silent. She is included in the cast of characters and has been referred to by Ribete as the object of Tomillo's desire, but her own voice has failed to be heard. In this, her first appearance, Flora not only speaks, she also simultaneously silences Tomillo. Her belittling of the horn and making reference to it as "aquesto" [this] is, quite plainly, a rejection of it, but more significant still is the fact that she has taken center stage, forced Tomillo, quite literally, into a submissive position, and has effected her first communication—with us, her public.

Through her *criada,* Caro continues to subtly question gender limitations and to challenge the silencing of the female sex, expressing these views through a predominantly silent subtext. The "horn" episode is indeed amusing and most certainly served to inject an episode of comic relief, but one must note that the playwright has indicated at various key points that what has remained unspoken by her characters should not be disregarded nor forgotten.

The significance of the "unfinished business" between Ribete and Tomillo regarding the recent scholarly activity of female writers in Madrid, for example, is pivotal. The lack of a final point being reached suggests that no conclusion is intended. The open-ended discussion reflects, instead, as Soufas points out, "the efforts of the female author to resist the categorization of inferiority and/or oddity and to express her recognition of a *female* tradition" while also expressing "the unresolved quality of that struggle" (91). However, this exchange also establishes the rivalry between imposed silence and the voice striving to be heard. Tomillo wishes immediately to silence the female attempts at literary creation, suggesting that these women remain in the quiet confines of the home—cooking and sewing. To Tomillo's dismay, Ribete silences these very attempts to quiet the female and dismisses his foolish companion rather impatiently. Although the more foolish *gracioso* is intent on questioning his new friend about the astonishing developments taking place in the literary circles of Madrid, Ribete exclaims, "¡Voto a Cristo, / que ése es mucho preguntar!" (2.1182–83) [Christ, that is a lot of questioning!].[15]

As a female writer Caro constantly faced silencing by her male peers and yet recognized the importance of not antagonizing them. With Flora, she challenges these same writers, quietly, using a rhetoric of reticence to undermine the ascendancy that had silenced her. Indeed, Caro seems to experiment with various communicative strategies and gives a clear enticement to use silence, as well as language, to define relationships. Deborah Tannen, almost echoing Caro's "quiet" endorsement of such a strategy, notes the delicate degree of understanding that must exist between the speaker and the listener in order to effectively partake in such an exchange: "The rapport [of silence] comes from being understood without putting one's meaning on record, so that understanding is seen not as a result of putting meaning into words—which presumably could be achieved with any two people who speak the same language—but rather as the greater understanding of shared perspective, experience and intimacy, the deeper sense of speaking the same language. This is the positive value of silence stemming from the existence of something positive underlying" (97).

If it is agreed that the scene in which Flora communicates with her public is significant in terms of revealing a criticism of the patriarchal system, then I would suggest that her reticence deepens this connection between *criada* and audience, to the extent that even in silence can her message be conveyed and understood. Indeed, her reticence transcends the boundaries of gender and goes beyond the simplicity of the spoken word—which can ultimately be uttered by anyone and consequently understood/misunderstood, interpreted/ misinterpreted in any number of ways.[16] Silence, on the other hand, is here a rhetoric of opposition, which permits the silenced one to create a space that she alone can control and to which she can choose to invite or from which to reject those around her. By speaking to us, her audience, we should consider ourselves part of the silenced, and therefore extended, discursive intent.

The only instance where Flora speaks to another character on the stage is in response to Tomillo's last attempt to retrieve his losses. When he turns to her and says, "Flora, vamos a la parte" (3.2694) [Flora, let's split the loot], she retorts, "¿A qué parte, majadero?" (3.2695) [Split what loot, you fool?], but this brief exchange is made in almost a freeze-frame aside that includes no others. Until this point her voice has not been heard by the other characters, and even here no indication is given that this impatient exchange is overheard by anyone else on stage. It seems clear that this repartee serves, instead, to remind the audience of Flora's feisty personality and to perhaps draw attention to her one last time before the curtain falls.[17]

As the final marriages are arranged, it is noteworthy that Ribete initially informs Flora that both he and Tomillo reject her as a possible spouse. Ultimately, upon hearing that Estela will give her "seis mil escudos" (3.2746) [six thousand escudos], Ribete has a change of heart and agrees to the nuptials. However, once again Flora is essentially absent from the proceedings. The use of the second person singular pronouns—"tú quedas para los dos, / y entrambos te dejaremos" (3.2742–43) [you remain for the two of us and we shall both reject you] and then "te doy seis mil escudos" (3.2746) [I will give you six thousand escudos]—clearly indicates that she is present on stage, but yet once more she is spoken to and not heard from.[18]

Should Flora's silence be viewed as a means to an end—that end being the reaching of a happy conclusion traditional to comic plots?[19] Perhaps, but to view it in this way is to ignore Caro's skillful attempts to "subvert from within." More important, we would be perhaps dismissing her silent appeal and ultimately failing her as responsible spectators. The theatrical impact of Flora's silence is not intended to be felt by the others on the stage, but rather by those of us at its peripheries. If we ignore her verbal absence from the final nuptial arrangements, so too then should we not find a great deal of significance in her one verbal appearance. If this is the case, the overt belittling of the male anatomy of which Williamsen writes would be nothing more than a charming *entremés* [comical interlude] included simply to entertain and delight. Because it seems clear that Flora's presence in this particular scene is charged with much more than comedic respite, I am inclined to think that her presence in the entire work is also significant, specifically because it is limited.

The marriages are settled and Flora's hand is given to Ribete. In the end, as one would suspect, all the couples are married off, and social, as well as dramatic, convention is appeased. Leonor reveals her true identity and accepts the man who had betrayed her. Estela arranges her own union and proposes marriage to Leonor's brother Fernando. Lisarda, who had fallen in love with Leonor when she was disguised as Leonardo, is obliged to take the hand of Ludovico, a man whose personality has been repugnant to all the others. Soufas[20] has commented on the less than ideal circumstances that form the base of the various unions and the lack of repentance shown by the male characters. She concludes that Caro "moves toward an open-ended structure that affirms a more profound questioning of the portrayed society in which the female author herself inevitably will continue to struggle with the issue of professional identity and in which the debate over woman's worth and her right to a public voice and social justice can be addressed effectively only by the woman herself" (100). I would take this one step further and suggest that the open-ended structure is effectuated by Flora's lack of interest in the plans being made for her own future. Although she does not openly refuse the arrangements prepared in her absence of voice (or would it be more precise to say her silent presence?), she does not openly accept them either. She merely functions within the social norms expected of her and finds herself bound to the system, much like the playwright herself.

It would seem incongruous to introduce a character like Flora, have her take center stage and make such a memorable impression on her audience, only to reduce her to the submissive maid servant who idly watches as her fate is decided for her. Certainly, Flora's silence is meant to be heard as it is quietly threaded through the carefully manipulated symbolic order of words. In the patriarchal text she is mostly absent, but in the space she herself creates and over which she has complete control, Flora is present for her audience. With her *criada,* one could argue that Caro subverts the sexist tradition of the silent female by first, allowing her to act and speak freely before her audience and, second, by infusing her eventual silence with a new form of meaning that the same public is expected to recognize. What remains in question, however, is the ability of the receptors to do so.

This character's seemingly voluntary absence, therefore, could be meant to have a particular effect on the audience's understanding of the final scene. The fact that Flora is silent at the end of the work would not strike the other characters as odd, since exchanges with her never took place. But that she should remain silent may reveal a great deal to her audience, her confidants, her co-conspirators, the people who have seen her in action.

As a female writer Caro displays a consciousness of the masculine control of the written word, and this understanding appears to have confined her to a complex, open-ended approach to the challenge she faced. It is therefore difficult to close this discussion when my argument relies on there being a lack of closure to the text itself, so I turn now to Ana Caro's own words that, given the aforementioned possibilities of a reticent strategy, seem to issue a warning to the audience of the playwright's quiet intentions. In act 2, Leonor, dressed as Leonardo, is forced to justify his/her silence while in the presence of the woman he is supposedly pursuing. A somewhat perturbed Estela asks:

Don Leonardo, ¿no me habláis?
¿Vos sin verme tantos días?
¡O, qué mal cumplís, qué mal,
la ley de la cortesía,
la obligación de galán! (2.948–52)

[Don Leonardo, will you not speak to me? You, who have not seen me in many days? Oh, how poorly you keep your promise, how poorly you respect the rules of courtesy, the obligations of a gentleman!]

To which Leonor/Leonardo cleverly responds, "Mi silencio, hermosa Estela, / Mucho os dice sin hablar" (2.959–60) [My silence, beautiful Estela, reveals much to you with no words].

Notes

1. In *The Power of Silence*, Jaworski outlines the various degrees of tolerance for silence in several non-Western cultures. Referring to such groups as the Western Apache Indians, the Igbo of Nigeria, and the Amish, Jaworski concludes, "All those sources emphasize the fact that in societies that display very extensive uses of communicative silences, the valuation of silence is more positive than in societies in which talk is expected to occur most of the time in interaction" (55).

2. It should be noted that McKendrick chose not to translate the term *mujer varonil* in her book *Women and Society in the Spanish Drama of the Golden Age* (1974). I use the phrase "manly woman" here for lack of a more precise English equivalent.

3. Unless otherwise noted, translations are my own.

4. Soufas points out that although Caro adopts the typical *comedia* [drama] conventions used to great effect by her male colleagues, she manipulates these same conventions to serve her own purposes: "Caro gives evidence of both overt and subtle efforts to examine and question such evaluations of women as authors and characters. . . . she uses the theatrical devices of masculine disguise, love intrigues, and the honor code's double standard to present a female protagonist whose feigned masculine role is not a means to supercede her own sex but a way to offer to the males around her a better model for their own emulation" (85).

5. It has been noted that Caro had a strong affiliation with the lower, marginalized characters, particularly because of her own peripheral position within social and literary circles (Maroto Camino 40; Soufas 91).

6. Parenthetical text references are to act and line numbers of *Valor, agravio y mujer*, edited by Soufas.

7. I have used Soufas's translation of this scene, as published in "Ana Caro's Reevaluation" (91–92).

8. Jones discusses the opposition faced by women of the Renaissance who wished to explore various cultural interests such as reading and writing. It is interesting that Tomillo seems to be echoing the thoughts of Giovanni Bruto in terms of the battle between needle and pen. Jones cites the following excerpt from Bruto's *L'institutione di una fanciulla nata nobilmente* [*The necessarie, fit, and convenient education of a young gentlewoman*]: "[H]ow far more convenient the Distaffe and Spindle, Needle and Thimble, [are] for [maids] with a good and honest reputation, than the skill of well using a pen or writing a lofty verse with diffame dishonor, if in the same there would be more erudition than virtue" (76).

9. I refer once more to Soufas's translation of this scene (90).

10. Rovine offers an interesting study on the use of "Silent Service" in the works of Shakespeare; see 72–90.

11. Translation taken from the edition included in Kaminsky's *Water Lilies*.

12. Here I have consulted the translation of *Valor* included in *Water Lilies*. I have, however, slightly changed the translation.

13. Ibid.

14. See Williamsen's article for further examples of derisive references to the male anatomy in this play.

15. Soufas's translation (91).

16. Jaworski also comments on the necessary "connection" between the listener and the silent communicator and writes that "communicating in silence may require from the participants more filling in, more completion, and higher participation than communicating in speech" (141).

17. Mujica details a clever approach to staging Caro's work and provides insightful considerations regarding the blocking and possible casting for the play's production. She makes the following suggestions: "The director undertaking a production of this work must deconstruct Caro's new model, experimenting with the diverse components and making sure that the linguistic signs encoded in the stage dialogue are easily decoded by the audience, so that the extrascenic dialogue will take place. . . . The dramatist herself facilitates the 'private communication' through the inclusion of a number of verbal asides aimed at the audience, which the director can enhance through visual asides (grimaces, winks, etc.), presumably 'imperceptible' to those on stage" (24). To intensify Flora's presence in this closing scene, one possibility could be to have the actress playing Flora stand at the edge of the stage, a short distance from the audience. She may also make some sort of gesture or grimace to those of us beyond the stage and therefore engage us one last time in her true but disguised feelings toward the marital arrangements.

18. Rovine limits female silence at a play's conclusion to reflect "the proverbial notion that silence gives consent" (57). I find that Flora's reticence at this point can significantly alter the experience of this last scene both for the reader and the spectator if her current "absence" is compared to her earlier "presence." It is the deeper, more intimate level of understanding between two or more confidants, that delicate rapport of which both Jaworski and Tannen speak that is called upon here.

19. Despite the common convention of ending a play with the celebration of multiple marriages, Soufas observes that Caro's unions are plagued with a certain degree of pessimism and resignation (98).

20. Luna also comments on Caro's decision to end the play in celebration and writes: "El final feliz de la boda elegido por Ana Caro para sus comedias es sumisión a una convención dramática y a una ley 'natural' española, de la época" (31) [The final unions chosen by Ana Caro in her plays reflect a submission that obeys a dramatic convention and the natural Spanish law of the time].

Works Cited

Caro de Mallén, Ana. *Valor, agravio y mujer. Women's Acts: Plays by Women Dramatists of Spain's Golden Age.* Ed. Teresa S. Soufas. Lexington: University Press of Kentucky, 1997.

Delgado, María José. Introduction. *Las comedias de Ana Caro: "Valor, agravio y mujer" y "El conde Partinuplés."* New York: Peter Lang, 1998.

Jaworski, Adam. *The Power of Silence: Social and Pragmatic Perspectives.* Language and Learning Behaviors. Vol. 1. Newbury Park, Calif.: Sage, 1993.

Jones, Ann Rosalind. "Surprising Fame: Renaissance Gender Ideologies and Women's Lyric." *The Poetics of Gender.* Ed. Nancy K. Miller. New York: Columbia University Press, 1986. 74–95.

Kaminsky, Amy Katz. *Water Lilies: An Anthology of Spanish Women Writers from the Fifteenth through the Nineteenth Centuries.* Minneapolis: University of Minnesota Press, 1996.

Laurence, Patricia. "Women's Silence as a Ritual of Truth: A Study of Literary Expressions in Austen, Brontë, and Woolf." *Listening to Silences: New Essays in Feminist Criticism.* Ed. Elaine Hedges and Shelley Fisher Fishkin. New York: Oxford University Press, 1994. 156–67.

Luna, Lola. Introduction. *Valor, agravio y mujer.* By Ana Caro. Madrid: Castalia, 1993. 9–46.

Maroto Camino, Mercedes. "Ficción, afición y seducción: Ana Caro's *Valor, agravio y mujer.*" *Bulletin of the Comediantes* 48.1 (Summer 1996): 37–50.

McGuire, Philip C. *Speechless Dialect: Shakespeare's Open Silences.* Berkeley and Los Angeles: University of California Press, 1985.

McKendrick, Melveena. *Women and Society in the Spanish Drama of the Golden Age.* Cambridge: Cambridge University Press, 1974.

Merrim, Stephanie. *Early Modern Women's Writing and Sor Juana Inés de la Cruz.* Nashville: Vanderbilt University Press, 1999.

Mujica, Barbara. "Women Directing Women: Ana Caro's *Valor, agravio y mujer* as Performance Text." *Engendering the Early Modern Stage: Women Playwrights in the Spanish Empire.* Ed. Valerie Hegstrom and Amy R. Williamsen. New Orleans: University Press of the South, 1999. 19–50.

Ordóñez, Elizabeth. "Women and Her Text in the Works of María de Zayas and Ana Caro." *Revista de Estudios Hispánicos* 19.1 (1985): 3–13.

Rovine, Harvey. *Silence in Shakespeare: Drama, Power and Gender.* Theatre and Dramatic Studies, No. 45. Ann Arbor, Mich.: UMI Research Press, 1987.

Soufas, Teresa S. "Ana Caro's Re-evaluation of the *Mujer varonil* and Her Theatrics in *Valor, agravio y mujer.*" *The Perception of Women in Spanish Theatre of the Golden Age.* Ed. Anita K. Stoll and Dawn L. Smith. Lewisburg: Bucknell University Press, 1991. 85–106.

Tannen, Deborah. "Silence: Anything But." *Perspectives on Silence.* Ed. Deborah Tannen and Muriel Saville-Traike. Norwood, N.J.: Ablex, 1985. 93–111.

Williamsen, Amy R. "Re-writing in the Margins: Caro's *Valor, agravio y mujer* as Challenge to Dominant Discourse." *Bulletin of the Comediantes* 44.1 (Summer 1992): 21–30.

12

Woman of the World and World of the Woman in the Narrative of Mariana de Caravajal

Louis Imperiale

Taking as a point of departure a collection of novellas by Mariana de Cara-vajal,[1] *Navidades de Madrid y noches entretenidas* [*Christmas in Madrid and Enjoyable Nights*] (1663), I propose to define in this essay the most subjective fundamentals of the poetic voice of a woman and mother that is unique to her gender. In the confines of these tales it communicates to us a new way of perceiving the intimate, complex and unfathomable universe of the woman (virgin, bride, lover, wife, mother, grandmother, and widow) during the seventeenth century. I compare and contrast the style and tone of narration with that which is outlined throughout the textual production and which stands out in the tradition of masculine Spanish literature. At no time does this study pretend to be an exhaustive review of all the facets that represent the woman in Golden Age Spanish literature, but it is offered as an attempt to attentively listen to a voice that expresses the inexpressible and that defines within itself the essence of an unequivocally feminine way of being.

The semantic field of the word "mother" occupies a considerable space, if not a virtually limitless space, in the history of Golden Age literature.[2] The denotation extends from the chaste and pure concept of the Virgin, celestial mother and mediator between God and mankind, to that which Mariana de Caravajal, an early widowed and exemplary mother of nine children, does not waiver in defining as "la Emperatriz de los cielos, María Señora Nuestra concebida sin pecado original que goza el título de la Virgen del Pilar, como poderoso Atlante, sustentando en los hombros de su caridad la máquina terrestre" ("El amante venturoso" ["Fortunate Lovers"] [85])[3] [the empress of heaven, Our Lady Mary, conceived without original sin, who enjoys the title of Virgin of the Pillar, as a mighty Atlantis, holding on her merciful shoulders this terrestrial machine]. In the most prosaic sense, we find the offensive and degrading "mother of the brothel" (Celestina), the "go-between" (Trotaconventos), the "prostitute" (Lozana, Antona Pérez, Justina, Aldonza de San Pedro), and the "matriz" or "cunnus" (Allaigre 86), such as we encounter in the erotic narrative. All the images and (de)gradations of femininity are disseminated throughout this enthralling, controversial, and thorny body of literature.

Very little, however, are we able to say about the theme of maternity, if we do not understand that no mother stops being a woman and that, living in the midst of a misogynous, homocentric, and intolerant society, the feminine Eros is plagued, dominated, and stigmatized by the enslaving and intolerant attitude of the opposite sex, to the point that Lucía Guerra-Cunningham justly observes: "[D]e la totalidad compleja que constituye ser mujer, la imaginación masculina, inicialmente seleccionó y abstrajo la maternidad para hacer de ella la esencia exclusiva de su identidad. El signo "madre," entonces, la mutiló y la fijó en una fertilidad que hizo de ella una Mujer-Matriz, un vientre" (6) [From the complex whole that is woman, male imagination initially selected and abstracted motherhood as the sole essence of her identity. The sign "mother," therefore, mutilated her and fixed her in a fertility that made her into a Woman-Matrix, into a womb]. In Francisco de Quevedo's "Infierno enmendado" ["Reformed Hell"], we see a sinner reject the offer to return to life in order to avoid the revulsion and nausea that the embryo produces in him during the months of pregnancy: "Yo he de estar aposentado en unos riñones, y dellos, con más vergüenza que gusto, diciendo que se hagan allá los orines, he de ir a ser vecino de la necesaria; nueve he de alimentarme del asco de los meses; y la regla, que es la fregona de las mujeres, que vacía sus inmundicias, será mi dispensera" (266) [I will be lodged in the kidneys, with more shame than pleasure, asking that urine be made there, and will have the bodily sewer as a neighbor; for nine months I will have to feed on the monthly nausea and menses, the scullery maid of women, who empties their filth, and who will be my larder maid].

It is timely to recall, moreover, that in the majority of the works of the Golden Age, feminine characters do not speak from a subjective condition or from an eminently feminine consciousness. Being invented and conceived by homocentric authors, they speak the way men like to hear women speak since the words and attitudes of these characters are filtered through a masculine consciousness. No one can forget the cynical attitude of Quevedo in the presence of the opposite sex. To say that Don Francisco hates woman is equivalent to saying that the sun heats up during the summer. Nonetheless, we want to remember some of his words that clearly indicate to us the horror that seventeenth-century man feels in the presence of the mystery of his origins, which generate, precisely, in the woman's womb.

Quevedo describes in "Providencia de Dios" ["Providence of God"] the existential anguish caused by the horror of our biological condition: "Fuiste engendrado del deleite del sueño y del sudor espumoso de la sustancia humana en el vientre de tu madre y amasado con el humor superfluo, veneno vestido de sangre, que médicos y auxiliares derraman los meses por la conservación de la salud del cuerpo de la mujer" (1210 b, 1211 a) [You were begotten from the delight of sleep and from the foamy sweat of human substance in your mother's womb and kneaded with the superfluous humor, a poison dressed as blood, which physicians and their assistants spill every month for the preservation of the health of women]. To finish this sweet, motivating, and compassionate illustration of the physiological world of the woman, we will recall the son's attitude when faced with the "errors" committed by his friend:

Díceme vuesa merced que está preñada, y lo creo, porque el ejercicio que vuesa merced tiene no es para menos. Quisiera ser comadre para ofrecerme al parto; que compadres sobrarán en el bautismo mil. Dame vuesa merced a entender que tiene prendas mías en su barriga, y podría ser, si no ha digerido los dulces que me ha merendado; que el hijo yo se lo dejo todo entero a quien lo quisiere, no podiendo ser todo entero de nadie. Señora mía, si yo quisiere ser padre, en mi mano ha estado hacerme frayle y ermitaño; no soy ambicioso de cría. . . . Lo que importa es empreñarse a destro y a siniestro, parir a troche y moche, y echarlo a Dios y a ventura. Vuesa merced dé con el muchacho en la Piedad; que allí se le criará un capellán, que en los niños de la doctrina sirva a chirriar a las calaveras. Y alumbre Dios a vuesa merced con bien. Y si se le antojara de algo, sea lo primero no acordarse de mí. ("Sacúdese de un hijo pegadizo" [78] ["He shakes off a sticky son"])

[Your Worship tells me that she is pregnant and I believe it because Your Worship's trade cannot but cause that condition. I would like to be a midwife in order to help with the delivery; because you will have over a thousand midhusbands at the baptism. Your Worship gives me to understand that she has certain tokens of mine in her belly, which might be true if you have not digested the sweets that I have given you; the child I will leave whole to whomever wants it, not being able to belong wholly to anybody. My lady, if I had wanted to be a father, it was in my power to become a friar and a hermit; I have no desire for a descendant.... what matters is to become pregnant right and left, to go spawning up and down and to trust the child to God and Fortune. Your Worship should send the child to La Piedad since there he will be raised like a chaplain who may make skulls screech in Sunday school. And may God's blessing be upon Your Worship. And if you had any whims, the first one should be not to remember me.]

When Quevedo barks furiously against femininity, he tells us of his misogynous hate; he does not communicate to us anything credible about feminine reality, which does not interest him even minimally. Quevedo caricatures the attitudes and values of the opposite sex. Here women occupy the place of the Other in the sense of the mounting hate of homocentric authority that sees them as their threatening opposites.

The feminine diegesis that Mariana de Caravajal y Saavedra notes in her *Navidades de Madrid y noches entretenidas* does not, in turn, contain attacks against the opposite sex, but rather a touch of falsely innocent and mockingly sweet irony. All of this prompts the author to narrate episodes that reflect her own home; even though, at the last moment, what unites the protagonist, Lucrecia de Haro, with the author, Mariana de Caravajal, is precisely this consciousness of the burden placed by society on the shoulders of women obliging them to consolidate their familial foundations. A burden that, in one moment or another, sooner or later, can convert itself into an unbearable weight or nightmare.

The eight novellas of the *Navidades de Madrid* gather in concentric circles, superimposing the biological dimension, the intimate feminine world, the familiar nucleus, the urban atmosphere; thus, gradually, the vision of seventeenth-century Spanish culture appears. One must not lose sight of the fact that *Navidades de Madrid* is first a novella of entertainment and that it forms a part of the ludic literature that comes to light during the early years of the seventeenth century. Caroline Bourland states that "doña Mariana de Caravajal es una escritora ingenua, y su misma ingenuidad contribuye a hacer que sus novelas reflejen con fidelidad la escena contemporánea. Ella no tiene teoría que probar ni causa que defender; sus sencillos relatos no llevan otro fin que el de entretener" (331) [Doña Mariana is a naive writer and her very naiveté makes her novellas faithfully reflect the contemporary scene. She has neither a theory to prove nor a cause to defend. Her uncomplicated tales have entertainment as their sole aim]. We believe, nonetheless, that Caravajal's writings go beyond the simple courtly pleasure that the author proclaims to provide "gustosos y honestos entretenimientos, en que [el lector] divierta las pereçosas noches del erizado invierno" ("Al lector" [32] ["To the reader"]) [pleasant and honest amusements, in which the reader may while away the lazy nights of prickly winter]. Still, it seems to us that when we say/write "woman," an immediate and involuntary reflex is produced that helps assimilate the word to the physical referent, even though in reality the generic identification assumes much more, which is the uniting of the sign with a predetermined social role. This role contains a series of obligations that historically have subjugated the identity of the feminine self, chained by society to preestablished norms of conduct considered innate.

It is true that in the Spain of the triumphant Counter-Reformation, physical enjoyment at an official level cannot but seem an intolerable manifestation of diabolic luxury. It provokes the repressive rebuff of the authorities, who, after the Council of Trent, have valued the seventh sacrament and emphasized that physical love, a sign of human corruption, would only be permitted within the framework of marriage and as a means of procreation. From this, the erotic theme appears overall in a hand-written literature, or, it appears in published works. There is preference for burlesque perspectives that make frequent use of a disseminated and allusive vocabulary inherited from Juan Ruiz and the *tradición cazurra* [churlish/cazurra tradition], that which apart from the literal sense supposes another semantic level attained thanks to the reader's active collaboration in deciphering the allusions in the text.

What Mariana de Caravajal inaugurates is, above all, a silent revolution from a typically feminine writing in a literature that, in essence, attests to male patrimony. The writer constructs within her discourse the Other of the discourse, but not an opposed, antagonistic discourse. The awakened conscience of woman must remain concealed. But not because of this, does it remain inactive. The otherness is the work of this absence, the noise of silence of a marginal discourse (used also by the *conversos* [converts]). It is the conversion of negativity to positivity, in the vision of a woman who sees herself as another, not because the view of a patriarchal society projects her as this other in the devalued sphere of the lesser being, but because in order to exist at all, on that awkward occasion she must necessarily exist as the Other. By being another and being the same, she is at the same time mirror and reflection.

With this new way of thinking about literature, a group of heterogeneous voices emanates, in which strident nonconformance and eloquent silences and hesitations before patriarchal thought are made known. We note a similar narrative polyphony, originating in Boccaccio, which establishes the dominant tone throughout Caravajal's text. Shifra Armon writes: "The frame-tale explains various motives for convening the storytelling party, introduces the company storytellers, and reveals each one's vested interest in excelling at the recitation. The frame-tale makes explicit the social parameters within which the narratives operate, develops intrinsically entertaining dynamics among the storytelling guests, describes the setting for the gathering as well as certain arrangements the guests make for amusing their companions" (74).

Doña Mariana's text proceeds from the physiology of the female body, from a consciousness that amplifies the concept of body by situating it in relation to the processes of significance like a praxis that corresponds to that which is not represented, to that which remains outside nomenclatures and ideologies. The space of the corporal discourse, as it is described in Mariana's work, does not refer to genitals or to dark private parts, but to the politics of the body, to the rediscovery of its sociability thanks to a consciousness of the forces that control and dominate it. In "El esclavo de su esclavo" ["The Slave of His Own Slave"], Matilde, illegitimate daughter of Felix and of the sweet Blanca, "dama de tan rara belleza" [lady of such a rare beauty], is not only able to marry Feliciano (despite having been conceived outside of marriage), she also will establish bonds of peace and harmony with the Moors, Audalia, and Xarifa. In the writing of our author, as in poetic speech, "la noción de significado resulta insuficiente por esa fuerza instintiva o afectiva que no logra ser significativa y que permanece latente en la invocación o el gesto de inscripción" (Guerra-Cunningham 28) [the idea of meaning is insufficient because of that instinctive or emotional force that does not succeed in becoming significant and that remains latent in the invocation or through the gesture of inscription].

Neither can we disregard the fact that every literary text, in greater or lesser measure, reveals the manifestation of a collective way of representing reality or a pseudoreality. All textual production contains a discourse that originates within a determined circumstance, and its author is converted into the transmitter of a discourse produced within a historical context that functions as an extratextual referent for said discourse. From this claim, it is essential to read the discourse of *Navidades de Madrid y noches entretenidas* according to the practical discourse exercised by a producer based on one of the active ideological forms of the time period in the emission of discourse. Said eminently feminine discourse of Doña Mariana carries within itself diverse ideological possibilities of its historical referent. As the mother of nine children, our writer lingers on the small details of daily life in order to suggest, for example, the best way to educate children, especially when the economic resources of the family cannot provide an adequate dowry to assure the future well-being of a daughter:

> Criáronse estas dos criaturas [Pedro y Jacinta], creciendo en ellos el amor al passo de la edad, y llegóse el tiempo de aprender las urbanidades que deven saber las personas principales. Les dieron maestros suficientes, y pareciéndole a don Fernando que no tenía dote igual a su calidad para casar a su hija, la enseñó todo el arte de la música para que a título de corista gozara en un convento las conveniencias acostumbradas. Don Pedro, con el uso de la razón, dio a entender a sus padres se inclinava a ser de la iglesia, y passados los primeros estudios le embió don Fernando a Salamanca a passar los cursos y estudiar la teología, para que por las letras se opusiera a las cátedras y ocupara los púlpitos. (135)[4]

> [Their two children (Pedro and Jacinta) grew up, love growing in them with the passing of the years, and the time came for them to learn the good manners that people of substance must know. They gave them some teachers, and as Don Fernando thought that he did not have enough to provide his daughter with a dowry appropriate to her station in life, he taught her music so that she could enjoy all the usual comforts in a convent as a member of the choir. Don Pedro, when he arrived at the age of reason, told his parents that he was leaning toward the Church as a way of life. And after his first years of study he was sent by his father to Salamanca to take the courses and study theology, so that through his knowledge of letters he could hold chairs and preach from pulpits.]

Once again, the difference between man and woman, brother and sister, establishes itself by means of sex. Such a division still contains a disadvantage for the woman, and in the way it is conceived we see the prejudice of male superiority begin to show. In "Quién bien obra siempre acierta" ["He Who Acts Well Is Always Right"], the birthright of Esperanza does not prevail when faced with the evil of her stepbrother Leonardo:

> Tengo por mi desdicha un hermano bastardo hijo de mi padre avido en una esclava. . . . Ha conocido mi padre en público a Leonardo dando a

entender que es de otra madre, cosa que le ha dado tanta sobervia, que no ay quien se averigüe con él por sus muchas trabesuras . . . arrebatada de la cólera le dixe que era un vil esclavo, hijo de una perra. Echó su mano a la cara jurando que se lo havía de pagar. (118)

[I have the misfortune of having a bastard brother, a son of my father and a slave woman. . . . My father has publicly acknowledged Leonardo, having it understood that he is from a different mother, which has made him so immediately proud that there is nobody who can deal with him in his many mischiefs. . . . Furiously mad at him, I told him that he was a vile slave, son of a whore. His hand went to his face, and he swore that I would pay for that.]

It is clear that we cannot rewrite history or change this feminine discourse by trying to explain the work through the subjectivity and emotions of the author. It is fitting to contextualize the function of historical circumstances in which utterance has been produced from its discourse. In the prologue, Catherine Soriano writes, very judiciously, that "las *Navidades* despliegan ante el lector una infinidad de conocimientos y detalles sobre la vida cotidiana en España en la segunda mitad del siglo XVII, describiéndose casamientos, servidumbre, trajes, alimentación, medicamentos y remedios, vivienda y mobiliario, diversiones y espectáculos públicos" (xvii) [*Navidades* lays out before the reader a multitude of details about everyday life in Spain in the second half of the seventeenth century, describing marriage ceremonies, servants, clothes, food, medicines and remedies, dwellings and furniture, amusements and public spectacles]. Without defining itself as a realistic work, unlike novels of chivalry, the novella of Doña Mariana connects prevailing customs with the everyday and evokes a familiar and domestic universe.

As Maria Grazia Profeti clearly emphasizes, the heroine of Mariana de Caravajal stands out for her unique presence in the midst of the text. It deals with a woman who is alone, "settled," of high social standing or "importance," who possesses the capacity for determination and self measure, free from the presence of all homocentric tutelary. In "La dicha de Doristea" ["Doristea's Bliss"] and "Zelos vengan desprecios" ["Scorn Avenged by Jealousy"] we are in the presence of orphans, while in "El esclavo de su esclavo" and "Amar sin saber a quien" ["Loving Without Knowing Whom"] the protagonist remains outside paternal influence. By contrast, in "La industria vence desdenes" ["Ingenuity Conquers Scorn"] we encounter two widows who, from a narrative point of view, serve as pendulum to the two widows (Doña Lupercia and Doña

Gertrudis) who live in the residence of Lucrecia de Haro.[5] The writings of Caravajal portray an intimate universe full of affection and tenderness that weakens with the intrusion of the masculine element. In connection with this last novella, Evangelina Rodríguez points out that the incipient bourgeois instinct receives significant emphasis. She connects it with a typical pattern, which she identifies as "paradigma iniciático de uno de los recursos de ascenso progresivamente sofocados por la reacción de las fuerzas sociales en el Barroco: la cultura o el ejercicio de un arte liberal" (46) [initiatory paradigm of one of the means of social ascent increasingly suppressed by the reaction of social forces during the baroque period: culture or the exercise of one of the liberal arts].

Although in novellas like "El amante venturoso" we have the presence of a patriarchal authority in the family nucleus, the father appears more as an indulgent and tolerant friend rather than a tyrant and despot to his children. For example, Otavio Esforcia, Teodora's widower father declares that he is delaying his daughter's wedding "porque (Teodora) se muestra tan rebelde en tratándola de casamiento que, derramando lágrimas, me ha obligado a cerrar la puerta a todos los pretendientes. Quiérola tan tiernamente que no me atrevo a forzarla su voluntad" (87) [because (Teodora) is so intractable upon the subject of marriage that, shedding tears, she has made me close the door to all her suitors. I have such a tender love for her that I do not dare force her will].

Intuitively, in Mariana's *Navidades de Madrid,* a more serene, less angry, less distressed narrative discourse is noted than that of the textual production of the period. Caravajal's characters are polite, without being pedantic or affected, and they presume to be cheerful and "entertaining" like Pedro, Jacinto, the Raicionero, and the canons of "La industria vence desdenes." According to Armon: "Courtesy is a common thread which ties the frame tale of the *Navidades* to its eight *novelas.* Caravajal credits her noble characters with an aptitude for courtesy that includes the ability to master the art of courtly performance and an acumen for discerning the presence or absence of quality in others' actions. This aptitude, developed through instruction and realized in social rituals, informs a bilateral screening process through which courtiers identify and favor those of like standing" (201). What surprises us even more is that through this very normal and tranquil feminine voice, the woman emerges as the uncontested protagonist. It is true that, as Bourland reports, in Caravajal's novellas we cannot search for a penetrating study of the conditions that surround her, because the author lacks the critical and essential faculties for such a work. Mariana paints the work as it can be painted by a naturally kind woman, who possesses, thanks to a gift for observing details, an existential knowledge of the human heart. In her stories are manifest two characteristics (which the literature of the seventeenth century lacks almost absolutely): namely "the laughter and spirit of youth" (364).

With her calm and detailed prose, our writer operates an authentic silent revolution against the mental structures of her time. She eliminates, before anything else, abusive and inexpedient husbands, who can cause unfortunate setbacks. In these tales, various husbands die very early and they leave their widows to undertake deliberately new actions about which they had not even been able to think earlier. Premature death of the husband is a magnificent occasion for organizing parties and banquets:

> Passado el impetuoso torbellino de las repetidas penas y renovados llantos . . . Doña Juana deseosa de ganarle la voluntad [a Doña Lucrecia de Haro], dixo a los demás señores: "Ocho días nos quedan para llegar a la Pasqua, la Noche Buena siendo domingo . . . paréceme que estos cinco días de Pasqua no dexemos a nuestra viuda y que la festejemos entre toda. Y pues estamos libres de la murmuración de los vezino . . . tendremos un poco de música y otro poco de bayle." (40)

> [Once the impetuous whirlwind of repeated crisis and renewed lamentations had gone away . . . Doña Juana wishing to gain her goodwill (that of Doña Lucrecia de Haro), said to the other gentlemen: "There are still eight days to Christmas, and Christmas Eve falls on a Sunday . . . it seems to me that we should not leave our widow during these five days of Christmas and we should fête her above all others. And since we are free from our neighbors' gossip . . . we will have a bit of music and also some dancing."]

From Caravajal's humanistic prose, a very serene philosophy of existence stands out: there is nothing better than the death of a husband to inspire in the woman more confidence in life.

Nevertheless, the situation the author conjures up is opposed to what generally occurs with the existent conditions of widows. We will remember that widows, who are heads of family, are counted as "half a member," the same as minor children, and they appear on official registers under the headings of "widow" or "belonging to." In Spanish Golden Age society, one resident of every five is a widow: a social reality with certain economic weight. In general terms, the widow does not remarry and is burdened with children. Many do not have resources, and they declare themselves poor from a fiscal point of view. Some practice minor trades: spinning, weaving, selling spices, eggs, wood; they take care of lodgings or taverns that receive students or travelers. In the rural sector, widows support themselves with occupations of peasants; the most well-to-do have a yoke of oxen or a flock of sheep, and they are called "laboring widows." Some find themselves obligated to beg and they form a part of the group of the poor and aided. Nonetheless, a minority of widows have property: a house, land, and vineyards; they are considered well-to-do. In the Middle Ages as in the sixteenth century, the Church rejected remarriage, which it qualified as adultery in disguise—*honesta turpido*—and even bigamy (Molinié Bertrand, "Viuda," *Diccionario histórico* 82).

Now then, in this social cell created by Caravajal and controlled by feminine protagonists, the man acts in response to the directives of Doña Lucrecia, who is newly widowed and head of her household dominated by feminine presence. As an experienced hostess and acute observer, Doña Mariana presents a concise and effective description in order to establish the relationship between the boarders-renters, their respective rooms, and, perhaps, each other:

> Vivía doña Lucrecia en el cuarto de adentro por dar los que caían a la calle a sus nobles moradores. En los dos alinde al suyo vivían dos hermosas y principales damas, la una llamada doña Lupercia y la otra doña Gertrudis. En los del patio, en el uno habitaban dos cavalleros Vizcaínos, residentes en la Corte a pleitos y pretensiones. El uno llamado don Vicente, el otro don Enrique. Al cuarto frontero se mudó una viuda principal. . . ; tenía una hija de diez y siete años tan hermosa como honesta. (38)

> [Doña Lucrecia lived in an inner room in order to give those with windows to the street to her noble lodgers. In the two rooms next to hers, there lived two beautiful and noble ladies, Doña Lupercia and Doña Gertrudis. In those facing the courtyard there dwelled two Biscayan gentlemen, who were at the court engaged in lawsuits and other affairs. One of them was called Don Vicente and the other Don Enrique. A noble widow moved to the front room . . . ; she had a seventeen-year old daughter, who was as beautiful as she was modest.]

This introductory narrative frame, which functions as a ninth metanovella,[6] is traditionally Boccaccian in structure and previously used by innumerable writers, in particular by María de Zayas.[7] Caravajal evokes the reactions and commentaries of those present, thus creating a perceptual focus of multiple perspectives that recalls the narrative experiments imagined by Miguel de Cervantes. Without confusing the historical author with the first heterodiegetic narrator, we can affirm, nonetheless, that in the first *seuil* [threshold] of narration we encounter the writer-narrator who directs herself "To the reader" in order to present some characteristics of her book, to ask for *captatio bene-volentiae* [public sympathy], and to announce a collection of twelve comedies (32) that, unfortunately, we have never been able to find. Each novella will have its intradiegetic narrator who situates herself over two planes. On one hand, a character-narrator results from the frame of the eight novellas, and on the other, he or she is converted into the narrator of the novella.[8] The woman, narrator or character, becomes the dominant center of the stories referred to in the eight novellas. The emerging leadership assigned to the opposite sex converts her into an active character in all aspects of human duties, which transforms the writings of Caravajal, according to what has been said to date, into a look in the mirror, into the self-contemplation of an ahistoric literary model.

The *Navidades de Madrid* seems to evolve slowly toward the chronicle of historic social events, to the detriment of the fantastic, marvelous, or mythological that we found in the novels of chivalry. Nevertheless, the magic will continue to be a constant in her narrative prose. The presence of the mundane, the preoccupation of a mother worried about social well-being, or the equality of the rights for which she so yearned, lead the narrators to limit themselves more to the reality that is lived. In effect, Lucrecia de Haro, newly widowed, lives with her son Antonio; one of the tenants, Juana de Ayala, is a widow and she takes charge of the education of her daughter Leonor; also remaining alone are two "hermosas y principales damas, doña Lupercia y doña Gertrudis" [pretty and important ladies, Doña Lupercia and Doña Gertrudis]; later we meet two other narrator-tenants, Vicente and Enrique, future husbands of Gertrudis and Lupercia, also narrators of great talent. Finally, Antonio and Leonor, the two children of the widows, will marry at the end of these novellas (after the *Navidades*). The reader perceives that the marriage stratagem becomes the main coil of the action of all these *Noches entretenidas*.

As glimpsed through this early information, Caravajal's heroine finds herself alone in the middle of the text. She appears as a well-adjusted woman of good social standing with the capacity for making decisions and controlling herself. The familiar ties that unite the protagonist to the rest of the family are very tenuous, almost nonexistent, or they create false familiar relationships in light of the direct contribution to the central intrigue. The advantage of this system is supported by the fact that the heroine has the possibility of selecting her false father, and, moreover, we have the inversion of roles since the daughter socially controls the supposed father, as occurs in "La Venus de Ferrara" ["The Venus of Ferrara"]. In "La dicha de Doristea" the protagonist, upon the death of her father, "quedó en poder de una tía, hermana de su madre . . . de mucha edad" (63) [was left in the hands of an aunt, her mother's sister . . . who was very old]. A similar plan repeats itself in "El esclavo de su esclavo," where Matilde, born from a secret relationship between the Earl of Barcelona's sister and Felix, lives hidden in the country, cared for by a "faithful servant" that the child considers as her father. A similar situation reappears within the extradiegetic frame and we find out that Lucrecia, one of the narrators of the novellas, "no tenía padre, avíala criado una tía que al presente vivía enferma y deseosa de verla en estado" (39) [had no father, she was raised by an aunt who at the time was sick and eager to see her niece married].

Caravajal's world is very different if compared to the imaginary world of María de Zayas, where the family is transformed into a rigid mechanism, perfect and inclined toward the destruction of the woman, and where intolerant fathers give their daughters to husband-executioners who will humble them until they die. At times, the brother converts himself into the merciless executioner of his sister. We will remember as examples Zayas's "La inocencia castigada" ["Punished Innocence"], "El traidor contra su sangre" ["The Traitor to His Blood"], and "Mal presagio casar lejos" ["Marriage Abroad: Portent of Doom"].[9] By contrast, Caravajal rejects the system of enslavement and writes in favor of the liberty of each individual. In "Quien bien obra siempre acierta," Álvaro announces to his slave: "Ya Juliana se cumple vuestro deseo que tantas vezes me avéis pedido que os dé libertad. . . . Mañana os daré la libertad y demás de lo que avéis adquirido en mi casa, os daré quinientos ducados . . . y llamando al mayordomo, le dixo que truxera un cirujano para quitarla el clavo" (121) [Juliana, your desire, that you have so many times expressed, to be given your freedom . . . is about to be fulfilled. Tomorrow, I will give you your freedom and, besides what you have acquired in my house, I will give you five hundred ducats . . . and calling the butler, he told him to bring a surgeon so that he would remove the pin from the shackle].

If we compare such an attitude with that of Beatriz, the young nymphomaniac widow of "El prevenido engañado" ["The Deceptively Forewarned"] of María de Zayas, we find ourselves faced with two diametrically opposed situations. In this last case, Fadrique, pledged to Beatriz, discovers that the motive for the mysterious nighttime excursions of this woman "por encima de toda sospecha" [above any suspicion] is a black slave "tan feo y abominable, que no sé si fue la pasión o si era la verdad, le pareció que el demonio no podía serlo tanto" (148) [so ugly and abominable, and I do not know whether it was emotion or reason, it seemed to him that the very devil couldn't be as much]. And with this point, we can recall the prodigious and pathetic words of this wretched slave:

> Estando en esto, abrió los ojos, y mirando a su ama, con voz debilitada y flaca, le dijo, apartándola con las manos el rostro, que tenía junto con el suyo:
> —¿Qué me quieres, señora? ¡Déjame ya, por Dios! ¿Qué es esto, que aun estando yo acabado la vida me persigues? No basta que tu viciosa condición me tiene como estoy, sino que quieres que cuando ya estoy en el fin de mi vida, acuda a cumplir tus viciosos apetitos. Cásate señora, cásate, y déjame ya a mí, que ni te quiero ver, ni comer lo que me das; morir quiero, pues ya no estoy para otra cosa. (149)

[At this, he opened his eyes and looking at his mistress, he told her in a weak voice while he pushed her face away with his own hand:
—What do you want of me my lady? Leave me alone, please! What is this, that even when my life is ending you harass me? It is not enough that your perverse condition has lead me to this state, but you also want me to attend to your last fool desires when I am at the end of my life. Get married, my lady, get married, and leave me alone once and for all, that I neither want to see you nor eat what you give me; I want to die, since I am no longer good for anything else.]

And all this is due to the carnal demands of the supposedly exemplary and devout widow who has squeezed out the virile essence of the slave as if dealing with a lemon. The vision of the family that we have in the work of Zayas is obliterating. Profeti observes that in the "sistema-Zayas . . . la famiglia è un meccanismo perfetto teso alla distruzione della donna" (15) [family is a perfect mechanism whose purpose is the destruction of the woman].

In Doña Mariana's feminine world, tolerance is a quality that prevails in daily practice. The life shared between master and slave also has a pleasant and jovial character since, during the excursion to the *cigarral* [rural estate near Toledo], Jacinto dares to execute an African dance with Antonia:

> No tenga vuesa merced pena, que yo traeré el sol de Guinea para que nos alumbre. Y llamando a Antonia, le mandó trajese su adufe, diciéndole:
> —Señora morena, los dos hemos de bailar un baile mandingo a lo negro, con todas sus circunstancias.

Respondióle la despejada negra:

—No quedará por mí si vuesa merced le sabe bailar.

Y traído el adufe, lo bailaron, con tantos gestos y ademanes que hizo el mancebo remedando a su negra, que ya les dolían los cuerpos de risa. ("La industria vence desdenes" 152)

[Do not be sad, Your Worship, because I would bring the sun from Guinea to give us light.

And calling Antonia he asked her to bring her tambourine, saying to her:

—My Dark Lady, we both are to dance a *mandingo* dance in the African manner with all that it entails.

Thus answered the smart Negress:

—I would do it willingly if Your Worship knows how to dance.

Once they have the tambourine, they dance and so many gestures did the young man make in imitation of his Negress that they ached all over on account of having laughed so much.]

Said spectacle functions as a true antilanguage in the lap of the narrative discourse since it is defined as a counterdance (originating from a pagan indigenous culture, prohibited in many cases by the Church) if we compare it to the *capona,* or the Spanish traditional music, that had previously been interpreted, and that Jacinto and Beatriz had danced.[10]

In another context, it is suitable to note that in the *Navidades de Madrid,* the errors of youth are not irrevocable or fatal as they are in many comedies that unconditionally defend the paternal bulwark of dignity and honor. Even Doristea, the most unfortunate of the heroines, who had run away with her seducer, succeeds in emerging from the depths of her wretchedness and transforms her unlucky womanly condition into a happy final resolution. It is not the ending of a happy story with an insipid moral. It deals, rather, with a reflection about the feminine condition that offers alternative solutions to the woman in order for her to be able to reintegrate herself into society without suffering the stigmas that similar recovery brings with it.

To further escape the image of the father, Caravajal selects another place, capable of pointing out the difference between house and palace, symbols of power and captivity, of injustice and moral degradation, and center of abusive patriarchal authority. On the contrary, the villa, the garden, the country are *actants* that contribute to the loss of formal relationships, to the damage of the father/daughter binomial in order to inaugurate and institute renewed and diverse kinship through marriages freely chosen, and not imposed by the familiar code. In "La Venus de Ferrara" Floripa lives alone "en un castillo en una aldea ocho leguas de la Corte" (45) [in a castle close by a hamlet eight leagues away from the court] under the tutelage of a false father. In the novella "Amar sin saber a quien," Lisena lives far from the paternal court under the control of the admiral and she is able to create new relationships with Enrique in the serene paradise of the "Isla," a separate and privileged place, painted with Arcadian theatrical tones where we encounter make-believe peasants acting in a pastoral setting:

> Tenía Ludovico a doze leguas de su corte una bien fabricada ciudad en tan ameno sitio que la podemos llamar hermoso pénsil de la naturaleza, pues era un abreviado paraíso. . . . Sus moradores . . . vivían ricos y contentos; vestían galas a lo labrador, los mancebos de lustre, baqueros, guarnecidos de vistosos passamanos, las donzellas sayuelos y abantales, corales y patenas. (175–76)

> [Twelve leagues from his seat Ludovico had a well laid out city in such a pleasant place that could be considered a veritable garden, an abbreviated paradise. . . . its dwellers were wealthy and happy; they dressed in the country manner, the young men of the nobility, wore smocks with colorful sashes, the young girls, gowns and petticoats, coral necklaces and lockets.]

In another novella "Zelos vengan desprecio," Narcisa retreats "a una quinta a un quarto de legua de Milán, sitio de mucho recreo por sus amenos jardines y por estar cerca de un hermoso coto donde avía mucha caça" (124) [to an estate a quarter league away from Milan, a place of a great enjoyment because of its peaceful gardens and because of its nearness to a beautiful and plentiful game reserve]. Narcisa lives withdrawn from the court in order to avoid the visits of Duke Arnaldo "feo de rostro y sobervio de condición" [with an ugly face and haughty condition] who boasts that "nadie avía de gozar su hermosura sino era él, porque todos sus amantes eran unos pobres escuderos, indignos de merecerla" (123) [nobody was going to enjoy her beauty but him because all her lovers were poor squires unworthy of her]. Count Leonido, another arrogant suitor with little expertise with the opposite sex, "no se descuidava en vengar sus desprecios, hablando mal de la honesta dama con intento de desluzir su honor" (123) [was not remiss in avenging her rebuffs, speaking ill of the honorable lady trying to damage her reputation]. In her villa, Narcisa, our heroine, lives happily with her friends and her cousin. Here, Duarte, Leonido's rival, disguised as a humble peasant is able to meet with his lady and protect her on various occasions. Profeti postulates shrewdly that:

Le protagoniste (de la Caravajal) hanno esatta contezza che questo luogo(-altro) è funzionale al cambiamento di potere ed all'istituzione del patto matrimoniale alternativo. . . . È la donna insomma che finge protezioni parentali, ma di fatto esercita il potere, combina incontri, predisponendo luoghi non formali, mette in atto strategie interrelazionali, contratta il suo status. (17)

[The protagonists (Caravajal's) are fully conscious of the fact that this place(-other) is appropriate for a change of power and for the institution of an alternative marriage. . . . It is finally woman who feigns parental protection but in reality she exerts power, arranges encounters, by choosing unusual places, sets in motion interrelational strategies, negotiates her own status.]

Far from Francisco de Quevedo's distressed and intolerant attacks, beyond María de Zayas's extreme situations with her women vampires, Mariana de Caravajal observes, analyzes, judges, reviews, evokes, and describes a society in the height of mutation—a society that is evolving because the patriarchal family has been substituted by a cultural project that permits the woman a new freedom and the possibility of negotiating her marriage more through individual affinity than through collective imposition. In the case of Doña Mariana, we could discuss feminine "bourgeois" literature, in which the importance that is granted to courting, dance, refinement, elegance of fashion, good manners, musical aesthetics, pleasure of cuisine, etiquette, and good taste signals to us that the rites and privileges reserved for the nobility were being extended to the middle class.

With regard to the study of Golden Age feminine writing, modern criticism has multiple tasks, principal among them being to survey, precisely, the role of the woman in the redefinition of national culture, considered through her direct authorial contributions, and, next, to provide objective studies of marginal writings, accompanied by the analysis of sociocultural factors that impose censored expression or silence. In the Spain of the dark years of the seventeenth century, Caravajal's vindicating poetic and social voice introduces a risky and brave accent in the panorama of the novella of her time. Her motherhood, present throughout the eight novellas (as well as in the introductory frame), is a catalyst that blends the characteristic ambiguity of fantasy with a clean prose, a magic of *claroscuros* and *aguafuertes*. In this prose, feminine sensibility reappears, as well as the sharp observation of an artist who dared to transmit through *Navidades de Madrid* an act of conscientious intellectual rejuvenation, a vibrant womanly sensibility in a field that until then had been the favorite and exclusive terrain of phallogocentric power.

Doña Mariana's eight novellas cast new light on still little- known aspects of the feminine work of fiction, which, in some cases, documents certain socio-political problems more fully than do historical archives; poetic-literary production permits us access to the sociopsychological mechanisms that mobilized the dominated groups, or their eulogists. Archival investigation cannot provide us with this mental clue, mainly because the documents are generated by power entrenched in patriarchal codes and values. I sincerely believe that, in many cases, social sources frequently alter reality. Caravajal's work presents an alternative vision of women to that found in patriarchal texts, since literary images can liberate the multiplicity of women's lives and characters in ways that the power-based language and assumptions of official records cannot, and would not do.

Notes

1. I am very aware that in her edition of *Navidades de Madrid* (1993) Catherine Soriano writes the last name of the author as "Carvajal" instead of "Caravajal" and we ask ourselves why. In all the bibliographical references (including manuscripts and the first edition), as well as in literary studies, we find Caravajal and not Carvajal (Serrano y Sanz; Bourland; Valis; Armon; the annotated edition of *Navidades de Madrid y noches entretenidas* by Prato). In Soriano's edition, the Licencia del Ordinario says, "[D]amos licencia para que se imprima un libro intitulado Novelas, de Doña Mariana de Caravajal y Saavedra, por cuanto de nuestro mandado ha sido visto y examinado" (7) [We authorize the printing of the book entitled Novelas, by Doña Mariana de Caravajal, as it has been seen and examined under our charge]. Throughout the essay, all English translations from the original Spanish are my own.

2. Besides the basic reference dictionaries (Correas, Corominas, and *Diccionario de la Real Academia* [*Dictionary of the Royal Academy*]), see Cela, s.v. "mother" (604) and Criado de Val.

3. All textual citations are from the edition of *Navidades de Madrid y noches entretenidas* by Prato.

4. Armon wisely perceives: "Marriage was a means of assuring a family's fortune, but it could also be a means of improving it. While marriage tended to be contracted among members of the same social status (*hidalgos, caballeros, titulados* [gentlemen, knights, persons of rank], etc.) enrichment of an impoverished line could be accomplished by marrying 'down,' that is, by marrying into a wealthier but less prestigious family. By the same token, wealthy but lesser nobility could hope to gain status by marrying 'up'" (120). We know that, using the same process, many new Christian families could establish familiar ties with nobles of high *alcurnia*

[lineage], causing a serious problem with respect to the obsession of the Church toward pure blood.

5. On the first diegetic level, we find two widowers in "El amante venturoso," Ricardo Milanés and Otavio Esforcia.

6. Armon suggests that the narrative frame can be considered as "a ninth meta-novela or background story that surrounds each novela" (76).

7. See Zayas's *Novelas amorosas y ejemplares* [*Enchantments of Love*] and *Desengaños amorosos* [*Disenchantments of Love*].

8. For a study of the different levels of narrative, see Armon (92–95).

9. See Zayas's *Desengaños amorosos*. The theme of violence is not totally absent in the work of Caravajal. In "La dicha de Doristea," Claudio, an ungrateful man, brutal and unscrupulous of conscience, seduces and abandons Doristea, revealing to her his well-planned misdeed: "[Y]o no os saqué de vuestra casa para casarme con vos, sino para vengarme de vuestra caduca tía pues quien se atrevió a ponerse en mis manos no es buena para ser mi muger" (65) [I did not take you out of your home to marry you but to take vengeance on your doddering aunt because someone who gave herself to me is not good enough to be my wife].

10. The notion of "antilanguage" (in fiction), applied to a literary text, stems from the "functional" and "sociological" linguistics of Halliday, which Fowler conceptualizes in the following way: "The term 'anti-language' was coined by Halliday to refer to the special jargons or canting slang, or secret languages, spoken by the members of what he calls 'anti-societies.' For Halliday, anti-language is the extreme case of social dialect. Its speakers are not simply special groups contained *within* a society but sub-communities in an *antagonistic* relationship to the dominant culture: people categorized as 'deviant' or 'criminal' or 'deficient'—thieves, junkies, sexual perverts, convicts, political terrorists, street vandals, etc. Because they are antithetical to the norm of society, Halliday argues, their language structure will involve systematic inversion and negation of the structures and semantics of the norm languages. Halliday illustrates this sociolinguistic antithesis from Elizabethan rogues' cant, and the special languages of the underworld of Calcutta and of inmates of Polish prisons. The interest of such special languages is not only their practical functions such as secrecy, solidarity and verbal play; their most important value is that they facilitate an alternative social and conceptual reality for their speakers. There is a Whorfian argument here: the anti-language creates an anti-world view" (146–47).

Works Cited

Allaigre, Claude. *Littérature et sémantique: Le Retrato de "La Loçana Andaluza" de Francisco Delicado*. Grenoble: Imprimerie du Néron, 1980.

Armon, Shifra. *Mariana de Caravajal's "Navidades de Madrid y noches entretenidas": An Anatomy of Courtesy*. Ph.D. diss. Johns Hopkins University, 1993. Ann Arbor, Mich.: UMI Dissertation Services, 1998.

Bourland, Caroline. "Aspectos de la vida del hogar en el siglo XVII según las novelas de doña Mariana de Caravajal y Saavedra." *Homenaje ofrecido a Menéndez Pidal.* Ed. Federico Saínz. Vol. 2. Madrid: Hernando, 1925. 331–68.

Cela, Camilo José. *Diccionario del erotismo.* Barcelona: Grijalbo, 1988.

Corominas, Joan. *Diccionario crítico etimológico castellano o hispánico.* 5 vols. Madrid: Gredos, 1980–1991.

Correas, Gonzalo. *Vocabulario de refranes y frases proverbiales y otras fórmulas comunes de la lengua castellana.* Madrid: Establecimiento Tipográfico de Jaime Ratés, 1906.

Criado de Val, Manuel. *Diccionario de español equívoco.* Madrid: EDI, 1981.

Caravajal y Saavedra, Mariana. *Navidades de Madrid y noches entretenidas.* Ed. Antonella Prato. Verona: Franco Angeli, 1988.

Car[a]vajal y Saavedra, Mariana. *Navidades de Madrid.* Ed. Catherine Soriano. Madrid: Clásicos Madrileños, 1993.

Diccionario de la Real Academia. 21st ed. Madrid: Espasa Calpe, 1994.

Fowler, Roger. *Literature as Social Discourse.* London: Batsford, 1981.

Guerra-Cunningham, Lucía. "El personaje literario femenino y otras mutilaciones." *Hispamérica* 43 (1986): 3–19.

Halliday, Michael Alexander Kirkwood. *Language as Social Semiotics.* London: E. Arnold, 1978.

Molinié Bertrand, Annie. *Diccionario histórico de la España del Siglo de Oro.* Madrid: Acento, 1998.

Profeti, Maria Grazia. Introduction. *Navidades de Madrid.* By Mariana de Caravajal. Verona: Franco Angeli, 1988. 7–25.

Quevedo, Francisco de. *Obras completas: Prosa.* Ed. A. Marín. Madrid: Aguilar, 1962.

Rodríguez, Evangelina, ed. *Novelas amorosas de diversos ingenios del siglo XVII.* Madrid: Editorial Castalia, 1986.

Serrano y Sanz, Manuel. *Apuntes para una biblioteca de escritoras españolas desde el año de 1401 al 1833.* 2 vols. Madrid: Sucesores de Rivadeneyra, 1903–1905.

Valis, Noël. "The Spanish Storyteller: Mariana de Caravajal." *Women Writers of the Seventeenth Century.* Ed. Katharina M. Wilson and Frank J. Warnke. Athens: University of Georgia Press, 1989. 251–82.

Zayas, María de. *Novelas completas.* Ed. M. M. del Portal. Barcelona: Brughera, 1973.

Part V

Transforming Literary Conventions

Feminine Aesthetics and Gender Norms

13

A Cry in the Wilderness

Pastoral Female Discourse in María de Zayas

Deborah Compte

As a generation of feminist scholarship comes to full maturity, there is no doubt that over the past twenty-some years María de Zayas has received increasing critical attention, not only as one of Spain's first recognized women secular authors, but also as a complex writer whose texts generate continued debate. Highly acclaimed in her day, Zayas occupied a unique position in her society and was lauded by her contemporaries: Lope de Vega, Pérez de Montalbán, and Castillo Solórzano. Presumably a member of distinguished literary circles, whose poetic talent caught the ear of her fellow writers, her narrative gifts were captured in her two collections of novellas, *Novelas amorosas y ejemplares* [*The Enchantments of Love*] (1637) and *Desengaños amorosos* [*The Disenchantments of Love*] (1647). Both texts enjoyed numerous editions, were virtual best-sellers, and were subsequently translated abroad. Despite their popularity and acclaim, her works fell into disfavor, if not obscurity, in subsequent centuries largely due to their unconventional and scabrous nature. Vilified as a salacious storyteller given to excessive license in her tales,[1] Zayas was relegated to the very margins of scholarly attention.

Yet in her day, Zayas surely held sway in the public arena as her tales apparently reached both the highly literate as well as the nonliterate members of her society. Whether schooled or not, literate or not, her readers and listeners (for we can presume that her tales were narrated to a larger audience) were familiar with the narrative formulas and literary conventions marking distinguished literature. Indeed, I will argue that the interest generated by her tales was founded in the artful, creative innovations Zayas introduced as she both undermined and re-fashioned familiar formulas in crafting something new. It is her accomplishment in re-creating a malleable genre to present a distinctive female voice and perspective that I will examine in "Aventurarse perdiendo" ["Everything Ventured"], the subject of this essay. It is precisely in breaking the mold, pushing the boundaries of conventional narrative forms, that Zayas made her mark, while calling attention to the varied permutations that a female perspective could bring to enliven time-worn literary genres.

In treating Zayas, contemporary critics have often focused on her feminist ideological stance, slippery as it is, and this approach has engendered considerable debate.[2] Yet, I would argue within this debate, one must not lose sight of Zayas's considerable artistic merits. As a writer thoroughly familiar with literary convention and well aware of its inadequacy in addressing women's concerns and varied points of view, Zayas brings to her novellas an exemplarity that is remarkable in its inventiveness and ability to go beyond traditional modes in creating highly original works of art.

Zayas is typically identified as one of the most successful cultivators of the novella, following in the distinguished Spanish tradition of Miguel de Cervantes and Lope de Vega. The novella, particularly the *novela cortesana* [courtly romance] to which Zayas was drawn, is characteristically a hybrid genre, easily admitting the intrigue of the Byzantine novel, the emotional nuance of pastoral narrative, as well as the complexity of love relationships found in sentimental romance. Steeped in the traditions of earlier models, Zayas was undoubtedly drawn to the multifarious and protean nature of the novella. In addition, the novella's appeal among women readers and listeners provided Zayas access to a particular public receptive to the female-centered narrative and discourse she introduces in her works. Indeed, it is the artistic latitude inherent in the novella that Zayas so creatively exploits in giving women claim over the narrative and bringing their experiences to light.

Yet, while clearly situated within the novella tradition, Zayas quite deliberately distinguishes her works from their predecessors, noting their distinctive "wonderment," calling them "maravillas, que con este nombre quiso desempalagar al vulgo del de novelas, título tan enfadoso, que ya en todas partes le aborrecen" (31) ["enchantment." In using this term she wanted to avoid the common term "novella," so trite that it was now entirely out of fashion] (8).[3] As Margalida Pons notes, Zayas "propone la creación de un nuevo género. La palabra 'maravilla' remite a casos excepcionales, caracterizados por la extrañeza" (592) [proposes the creation of a new genre. The word "enchantment" recalls exceptional cases, characterized by wonderment] (my translation).

Thus, while working within the inherited frameworks that are the models that would be accessible and readily recognizable to her public, Zayas also gives them a twist, drawing attention to her own artistry in the process by underscoring her ingenuity. As the narrator of the "anonymous" prologue unabashedly proclaims:

> [E]ste libro te ofrece un claro ingenio de nuestra nación, un portento de nuestras edades, una admiración destos siglos, y un pasmo de los vivientes; . . . La señora doña María de Zayas, gloria de Manzanares y honra de nuestra España (a quien las doctas Academias de Madrid tanto han aplaudido y celebrado) por prueba de su pluma da a la estampa esos diez partos de su fecundo ingenio, con nombre de novelas; la moralidad que encierran, el artificio que tienen y la gracia con que están escritas, son rasgos de su vivo ingenio, que en mayores cosas sabrá salir de más grandes empeños. (25–26)

> [A brilliant talent in our country, a portent of our age, a wonder of all time, and a marvel among the living offers this book to you. . . . The lady doña Maria de Zayas, glory of the River Manzanares and honor of our Spain (whom the learned Madrid academies so applaud and celebrate), as proof of her pen, publishes these ten offspring of her rich mind called novellas. The moral they contain, the art they display, and the grace of their style are characteristic of her keen mind, as revealed in the ambitiousness of the undertaking.] (3)

Zayas's very deliberate design is both conventional and innovative, and at times quite radical in exploring new ways to articulate perspectives not usually treated in, or excluded from, the dominant modes of literary experience, while also highlighting the marvels of her literary enterprise.

If, in fact, the *novela cortesana* is principally suited to exploring elaborate love intrigues and the related theme of honor in an urban, aristocratic setting, it is no wonder that Zayas was drawn to the genre in examining the peripetiae of male-female relations. Yet in opening her first collection, the *Novelas amorosas y ejemplares,* she introduces a quasi *novela cortesana,* heavily laden with pastoral overtones. The choice of the pastoral mode is far from fortuitous, particularly in a writer so keenly versed in literary tradition. Pastoral, from its inception, examined the casuistry and even pathology of love relationships, a theme so integral to Zayas. She very clearly situates her leading tale, "Aventurarse perdiendo," in a rural, pastoral setting where the protagonist Jacinta appears as a shepherd/shepherdess discoursing in the manner of conventional pastoral romance. Although in recounting her tale of woe, loss, and betrayal, the scene shifts back in time and place to a courtly, urban ambience in detailing the multilayered love intrigues, the location of Zayas's first story in a pastoral locus is striking. While it is hardly surprising that Zayas would consciously recall the narrative mode most closely associated with love and its problematics, it is indeed curious in a writer whose essential vision is at odds with the fundamental bucolic ethos of love, harmony, and tranquility.

In opening her collection by venturing into the traditionally "male" domain of pastoral narrative, Zayas in fact reveals her artistic intent to play with and thus transform literary modes. While it may be argued that during this time almost any literary genre—the epic, the tragedy, the chivalric—was a characteristically male province, pastoral is typically considered a "male" genre where woman plays a significant, although very secondary role in the projection of male desires and fantasies. In his landmark study, *The Oaten Flute,* Renato Poggioli notes, "The pastoral is a private, masculine world where woman is not a person but a sexual archetype. . . . The pastoral hero treats woman as an object" (16). Similarly, Andrew Ettin observes, "Pastoral society is predominantly male. Women, nymphs, and goddesses are frequently mentioned and they may be dramatically important, but they rarely speak. Even in the romances and in Renaissance pastoral drama, where shepherdesses appear fairly often, they are usually outnumbered. Also, women writers seldom use pastoral literary motifs in the literal, traditional ways in which male writers do" (146). Amadeu Solé–Leris goes on to affirm, "The number of individualized female characters is small. This world of gallantry and sentiment, of course, revolves around them, but their role, except for the heroine herself, is mainly a passive one. They are the desirable prizes, and the admiring audiences, for the young man to whom action and the display of poetic and intellectual gifts are reserved" (49). While these statements are very true in the general sense, they hardly speak for Zayas's very conscious experimentation with pastoral in which she presents a female-centered narrative where the heroine easily displaces the traditional male shepherd and becomes the primary focus of attention. Zayas offers us, and her seventeenth-century audience, a very pointed examination of pastoral through a gendered lens in which standard narrative patterns are inverted and conventional poetic devices are ironically altered.

Before entering into an analysis of the tale itself, it is necessary to note the artistic manipulations of the frame narrative in laying the groundwork for the presentation of this work within a pastoral framework in order to call into question its very foundations. In establishing a frame narrative independent of, yet intimately related to, the individual stories, Zayas re-creates the familiar Boccaccian model of a series of narrators who relate inventive tales for entertainment and edification. While ostensibly entertaining Lysis, the dominant figure of the frame who has been stricken ill with quartan fever, each male and female narrator alternately displays his/her artistic gifts in a sort of literary competition, plainly reminiscent of the poetic contests within pastoral. While the soiree is clearly set in a courtly environment, in Lysis's lavish home in Madrid, the gathering of friends with the attendant subtext of rivaled affections, jealousy, and the examination of the vagaries of love, evokes a decidedly pastoral tone. Lysis opens the soiree with a mournful ballad, lamenting her lover's faithlessness:

> Escuchad, selvas, mi llanto,
> oíd, que a quexarme vuelvo,
> que nunca a los desdichados
> les dura más el contento.
> Otra vez hice testigos
> a vuestros olmos y fresnos,
> y a vuestros puros cristales
> de la ingratitud de Celio.
> Oístes tiernas mis quexas,
> y entretuvistes mis celos,
> con la música amorosa
> destos mansos arroyuelos. (33)

> [Forests, hear my lament
> listen while I sing my plaints,
> for happiness never lasts
> for the unfortunate.
> Long ago I testified
> to your elm and ash trees,
> to your crystal springs,
> about Celio's faithlessness.
> Tenderly you heard my plaints
> and distracted me from my jealousy
> with the loving music
> of your gently flowing brooks.] (10)

Within this urbane gathering, Lysis virtually casts herself into the role of the pastoral shepherd by situating her song within a *locus amoenus* replete with verdant nature and crystalline springs. She, in effect, appropriates the male poetic voice so characteristic of pastoral in discoursing on the inconstancy of her beloved. In true pastoral fashion, her listeners marvel at the beauty and power of her verse, praising her artistry and the singular qualities of her voice. Following in the tradition of the bucolic poetic contest, Lisarda, Lysis's rival for Don Juan's affections, is chosen to present the first enchantment. In assuming her role as narrator, and thus the focus of attention, Lisarda engages in a literary and, by extension, amatory competition with Lysis. Zayas thus prepares the reader not only for a dazzling display of her and her characters' wit and skill, she also begins to imaginatively re-create the alternative literary world of pastoral, amply suited to the problematics of love relationships.

Indeed, in describing the rich adornments of Lysis's sitting room, the meeting ground for the festivities, Zayas highlights their Arcadian evocations:

[E]n una sala, que aderezada de unos costosos paños flamencos, cuyos boscajes, flores y arboledas parecían las selvas de Arcadia o los pensiles huertos de Babilonia.

Coronaba la sala un rico estrado, con almohadas de terciopelo verde, a quien las borlas y guarniciones de plata hermoseaban sobre manera, haciendo competencia a una vistosa camilla, que al lado del vario estrado había de ser trono, asiento y resguardo de la bella Lisis, que como enferma pudo gozar desta preeminencia, era asimismo de brocado verde, con fluecos y alamares de oro, que como tan ajena de esperanzas en lo interior, quiso en lo exterior mostrar tenerlas.

Estaba ya la sala cercada de muchas filas de terciopelo verde y de infinitos taburetes pequeños, para que sentados en ellos los caballeros, pudiesen gozar de un brasero de plata, que alimentado de fuego y diversos olores, cogía el estrado de parte a parte. (31–32)

[Her parlor was hung with heavy Flemish tapestries whose woods, groves and flowers depicted exotic landscapes like Arcadia and the hanging gardens of Babylon. The room was crowned by a rich dais piled high with mountains of green velvet cushions ornamented with splendid silver embroidery and tassels. To one side of the dais was a luxurious couch that was to serve as seat, sanctuary, and throne for the lovely Lisis who, because of her illness, could enjoy this distinction. It was green brocade with gold trimming and fringe, the green symbolizing a hope she did not

really feel. All around the hall were rows of green velvet chairs and numerous taborets for the gentlemen to sit on while enjoying the warmth
of a silver brazier where incense was burned to perfume the dais.] (9)

The transmutation of elegant, purely decorative details into a gardenlike
setting where even the rows of green velvet chairs suggest a succession of
verdant hills enhanced by the sensorial delights of the perfumed incense,
clearly displays Zayas's literary gifts in drawing her readers to contemplate
another literary world. The pastoral nuances developed within a courtly setting provide a recognized locus in which to echo the amatory entanglements
of the frame narrative, as well as signal the reader to her artistry in reworking
conventional formulas. In transforming an aristocratic interior space into a
welcoming "natural" exterior landscape presided over by women, Zayas already shows her intent to unravel and experiment with literary convention.
Throughout the ensuing collection of tales, Zayas will explore and explode
the narrative strictures of prescribed genres in crafting revisionist models,
highlighting in particular the ascendancy of a female voice.

After Lysis's woeful song, the frame listeners turn their attention to Lisarda
as she recounts the first evening's entertainment. Already attuned to the pastoral trappings suggested in the frame, the story opens in the "ásperas peñas de
Montserrat" (37) [the craggy peaks of Montserrat] (12), a forbidding wilderness noted for its isolation and mystery. Fabio, a handsome young nobleman
from Madrid has made a sojourn here after business in Barcelona to pay hom-
age to the Virgin. As he wanders through the rugged mountains, he hears the
plaintive voice of a shepherd lamenting the loss of love. Intrigued by the
beauty of the voice, he cautiously approaches the singer who sits beside a
crystalline brook. Although the singer is garbed in shepherd's clothes, Fabio
quickly discerns that she is a woman and marvels that a woman would venture
alone into these desolate parts. The shepherd/shepherdess then recounts her
dramatic tale of misfortune in love, liberally interspersing her story with verse.

Within this very basic plot structure of "Aventurarse perdiendo," it is quite
easy to detect the pastoral overtones: the journey of a young courtly hero into
a remote natural setting where he seeks solace; the plaintive tale of rejection in
love; the stylistic pattern of prose and verse combined, highlighting the power
of poetic song. Yet, despite these formulaic conventions, the story unfolds in
unexpected ways as Zayas crafts an alternative vision. Given the introduction,
one would quite naturally expect Fabio to be the protagonist of the work. He
is clearly a laudable figure, with all the characteristics of a hero. The narrator
notes that he is an "ilustre hijo de la noble villa de Madrid, lustre y adorno de

su grandeza; pues con su excelente entendimiento y conocida nobleza, amable condición y gallarda presencia, la adorna y enriquece tanto como cualquiera de sus valorosos fundadores, y de quien ella, como madre, se precia mucho" (38) [illustrious son of the noble city of Madrid, a splendid example of her greatness and a credit to her fame. With his keen intelligence, his renowned nobility, his good nature, and refined manners, he adorns and enriches Madrid's fame as much as any of her brave founders of whom, as their mother, she is justly proud] (12–13). Clearly he possesses the exemplary assets of a hero. Moreover, he is endowed with spiritual qualities as he seeks to renew his soul by visiting the refuges of the holy monks and receive sustenance through meditation. A more fitting character for a pastoral hero could hardly be found.

Despite the reader's expectations, however, it is Jacinta who assumes the primary role in the tale. While the male shepherd's story typically dominates in bucolic fiction (despite titles to the contrary—*La Diana, Diana enamorada, La Galatea*), here Jacinta occupies center stage throughout. Moreover, in displacing the male hero, Jacinta becomes not only protagonist but narrator as well. She narrates her own story, and she composes the poetic verses that embellish the tale. She achieves agency in becoming the subject, as opposed to the object of the action, and in so doing becomes also creator, artist, and poet. The psychological transformation of the male bucolic hero in achieving a more unified sense of self is here given a female perspective in the development of an autonomous self.

In crafting her revision of pastoral, Zayas, through her two female narrators Lisarda and Jacinta, consistently manipulates the conventions of a traditionally male dominated genre to accommodate a female voice as well as display her own artistic inventiveness. H. Patsy Boyer speaks of the "conscious feminization of a tremendous array of motifs taken from a highly refined, male-produced literature" (xx). The initial setting itself, in Montserrat, is striking as a case in point. If in the narrative frame, Zayas transposed a typically masculinized courtly setting to a feminized "natural" setting as noted above in establishing a restorative refuge where the female characters preside, in "Aventurarse perdiendo" she achieves the inverse. The pastoral retreat has long been associated with feminine characteristics.[4] Its lush, gardenlike ambience provides a welcome haven to the weary courtly sojourners in need of psychological and spiritual renewal. Here, however, the "ásperas peñas de Montserrat" [the craggy peaks of Montserrat], while certainly remote, are clearly not the inviting arbor offering an escape from a frenetic courtly environment, particularly for the female protagonist.

Far from the feminized *locus amoenus* with its gentle breezes, welcoming shade, and comforting meadows, the harsh, inhospitable landscape of "Aventurarse perdiendo" is fraught with potential danger. Wild beasts and bandits roam the hills, more suggestive of a threatening environment. The temporary oasis in a harmonious natural setting more typical of pastoral romance is here replaced by a landscape where the "ásperas malezas..., el calor del sol y la aspereza del camino" (38–39) [rugged terrain..., the harshness of the trail, and the warmth of the sun] (13) are accentuated to highlight not solace, but Jacinta's abandonment, despair, and total aloneness. In fact, Margaret R. Greer notes the masculinization of the Montserrat locale. She sees the solitary imposing peaks of Montserrat as suggestive erotic symbols denoting the "phallic jungle of desire in which she [Jacinta] was lost in more than a symbolic sense" (191).

In a work so centered on female desire, as Jacinta's tale so explicitly details, as well as the dangers of its consequences, the landscape is layered with special meaning. What is typically conceived of as a retreat in masculine versions of pastoral becomes an additional adversity, essentially blocking women from self-realization. The dangers inherent in a natural setting for women, where Jacinta has already been robbed of her material possessions, become even more psychologically and morally threatening as she must also protect her honor and bodily sanctity. Thus, Zayas portrays a hostile rural landscape for a female protagonist, so contrary to the restorative *locus amoenus* standardly depicted in pastoral.

In addition, Zayas similarly adopts a gendered perspective in treating customary bucolic themes to highlight the articulation of a female voice, one who authors her own authority and identity. Renaissance pastoral romance is centered on the prototypical shepherd's lament on the inconstancy and mutability of women. Women's fickleness is underscored as shepherd after shepherd poetizes the depth of his love and the pain of rejection at the hands of a capricious beloved. Sireno's song, the opening poem of Jorge de Montemayor's *Diana,* serves as a model for this motif:

¡Cabellos, quánta mudança
he visto después que os vi ... !
¿Quién vio tanta hermosura en
tan mudable sujeto
y en amada tan perfecto?
¿Quién vio tanta desventura? ...

Mira el amor lo que ordena
que os viene a hazer creer
cosas dichas por mujer y
escritas en el arena. (13–14)

[Hair, what changes
I have seen since I saw you . . .
Who has seen so much beauty
In such a mutable subject
And in so perfect a lover
Such misfortune? . . .
See what love ordains,
It makes us come to believe
Things said by women
And written in the sand.] (52–53)

As if responding almost directly to the characteristic inconstancy of women
where a woman's words and actions are untrustworthy and shifting, Jacinta's
story opens too with a poem on the same theme. Yet it is she, disguised as a
man, who authors the poetic text, drawing the sympathies of her listener,
Fabio, with her lyricism. She inverts the standard theme, discoursing on the
fickleness of her lover, while drawing attention to the constancy of her own
affections:

¿Quién pensara que mi amor
escarmentado en mis males,
cansado de mis desdichas,
no hubiera muerto cobarde?
¿Quién le vió escapar huyendo
de ingratitudes tan grandes,
que crea que en nuevas penas
vuelva de nuevo a enlozarme?
¡Mal hayan de mis finezas
tan descubiertas verdades,
y mal haya quien llamó
a las mujeres mudables!
Cuando de tus sinrazones
pudiera, Celio, quexarme,
quiere amor que no te olvide,
quiere amor que más te ame. (39)

[Who would think that my love,
seared by so many sorrows,
weary of such misfortune,
would die a coward's death?
Whoever saw it escape, fleeing
from such harsh faithlessness,
would believe it would come back
for new and greater sorrow?
Cursed be the naked truth
of all my misguided love,
and cursed be the one who called
all women fickle!
When I should, Celio,
complain of your mistreatment,
love will not let me forget you,
love wills for me to love you more.] (13–14)

While at this point in the text, the singer-poet is not yet identified as a woman, as the poem unfolds it becomes apparent to the listener/reader that a distinctive female voice is emerging. Throughout the entire tale, in fact, Zayas privileges the female voice quite deliberately. Lisarda, the female frame narrator, presents a "true" story narrated in the first person by Jacinta, who highlights a female's life experiences as well as her own poetic talents.

The inversion of conventional male poetic discourse is evident in the reversal of other classic themes. The standard bucolic topos of the poet's humility in composing verse is also articulated from a woman's perspective, underscoring however the accomplishment and artistry of women's literary skills. In addressing her audience, Lisarda ironically prefaces "Aventurarse perdiendo" with a classic reference to the "flacas fuerzas de las mujeres" (37) [frailty of women] (12) and "los claros y heroicos entendimientos de los hombres" (37) [the clear and heroic wisdom of men] (12). Yet, women emerge not only as able and admired storytellers, but as strong and active protagonists too. Jacinta draws attention to the fact that she is a female poet, humbly apologizing for any defects attributable to her sex, as does Zayas herself in her introduction to the *Novelas amorosas y ejemplares*.[5]

In narrating her story, Jacinta shifts from initial humility to outright confidence in her poetic ability. She begins rather modestly:

Llegó a tanto mi amor, que me acuerdo que hice a mi adorada sombra unos versos, que si no te cansases de oírlos te los diré, que aunque son de

mujer, tanto que más grandeza, porque a los hombres no es justo per-
donarles los yerros que hicieran en ellos, pues los están adornando y
purificando con arte y estudios; mas una mujer, que sólo se vale de su
natural, ¿quién duda que merece disculpa en lo malo y alabanza en lo
bueno? (46)

[My love grew and grew so great that I even composed poetry to my
beloved ghost. If it won't bore you, I'll recite a poem for you, for even
though it's written by a woman, it's all the better—it isn't right to excuse
the errors men make in their poetry because they are all taught in all their
studies how to refine and adorn their verses with art; but a woman, who
has only her own instinct, deserves praise for everything that's good and
pardon for any defects.] (19)

Later, however, she more boldly affirms her talent:

[C]omo yo también hacía versos, competía conmigo y me desafiaba en
ellos; admirándole, no el que yo los compusiese, pues no es milagro en
una mujer, cuya alma es la misma que la del hombre, o porque naturaleza
quiso hacer esta maravilla, o porque los hombres no se desvaneciesen,
siendo ellos solos los que gozan de sus grandezas, sino porque los hacía
con algún acierto. (69–70)

[Since I too composed poetry, he would challenge me and we would
enjoy the competition. It didn't amaze him that I composed poetry.
That's no miracle in a woman whose soul is just the same as a man's,
and maybe it pleases Nature to perform this wonder, or maybe men
shouldn't feel so vain, believing they're the only ones who enjoy great
talent. What did amaze Celio was that I composed so well.] (36–37)

The appropriation of poetic discourse by a self-consciously female poet is
also reflected in the gendered articulation of particular themes. In a sonnet
clearly echoing the baroque theme of *desengaño* [disillusionment] Jacinta
gazes into the clear mirror of *desengaño* and sees herself free, "descuidada . . .
contenta de no amar, ni ser amada" (70) [unconcerned . . . happy to be neither
loved nor in love] (37), fleeing from the entrapment of passion and, in the case
of her relationship with Celio, the desire to be desired. Yet, Celio, "sol desta
edad" [the sun of this our age], blinds her from the self-knowledge and detachment she had achieved earlier following the untimely death of her husband
Felix. *Desengaño* here is freedom from love and deception, and is put in a

specifically female context.[6] Jacinta moves toward such a liberation in her later retreat to the convent.

The most significant alteration of literary convention is Zayas's inversion of male and female patterns of heroic development within the pastoral tradition. In a very suggestive and convincing work entitled *Female Heroism in the Pastoral*, Gail David has isolated a distinct archetypal pattern of female development in pastoral narrative that inversely mirrors the more familiar male pattern. In examining a wide variety of pastoral novels from the Renaissance to the twentieth century, she affirms that the female pattern "is not a weak and displaced variant of some privileged male norm, but a pattern that is at least as old and assuredly of equal weight to its better known, because oft-canonized, male counterpart" (25).

The standard bucolic trajectory is retreat from the courtly world to a temporary sojourn in a natural space of renewal and restoration, and subsequent return to society or court. Through their accumulated adventures as they embark on this journey, most pastoral heroes "come of age." The transformative experiences gleaned from intimate contact with a "feminized" landscape allows them to mature psychologically and arrive at a more integrated sense of self, ready to re-enter the urban world. Indeed, this pattern can be readily applied to Fabio, who leaves Madrid, enters the restorative space of Montserrat, compassionately shares Jacinta's story, and returns to the courtly environment of Madrid as a better man. Despite Montserrat's harsh landscape and the masculinized elements noted earlier, for Fabio it represents a distinctive female locus, presided over by the Virgin Mary. He visits the "milagroso y sagrado templo, tan adornado de riquezas como de maravillas; tantos son los milagros que hay en él, y el mayor de todos aquel verdadero retrato de la serenísima Reina de los Ángeles y Señora nuestra" (37–38) [miraculous and holy church there, endowed with innumerable miracles and unbounded wealth. The greatest of these miracles is embodied in the true image of Our Lady Queen of Angels] (12). Fabio adores the Virgin's image and receives "sustento para el alma y cuerpo" (38) [nourishment for body and soul] (13). Spiritually renewed through his devotion in Montserrat and psychologically reawakend through listening to Jacinta's story, Fabio accompanies her back to Madrid. He "comes of age," like most pastoral heroes, through his contact with the feminine and emerges a more wholly developed heroic figure.

Yet, while Fabio's developmental passage is significant, it is Jacinta's experiential journey that acquires primacy. Her trajectory is radically different, and conforms very neatly to the inverted pattern described by David. The female variant begins in a rural or protected domestic space and carries the heroine into an alien "masculinized" or urban realm marked by aggression and deception. In confronting the adversities she encounters in this alien space, the female character also matures, developing a certain autonomy, and then returns to the "feminine" space of the home or country. It is important to note that this pattern is not exclusive to female-authored texts but rather applies to female heroes within male-authored texts as well, and David points to Felismena in Montemayor's *Diana*, as an example. The woman's journey, while often more challenging, is an alternate form of development, where the women characters achieve selfhood, but through a very different set of experiences.

In her symbolic journey of initiation and development, Jacinta ultimately moves toward psychic wholeness. As she recounts her life story, Jacinta initially appears as a protected young aristocratic woman, safely harbored within the domestic sphere of her home. At a critical moment in her adolescence, her mother dies: "Faltó mi madre al mejor tiempo, que no fué pequeña falta, pues su compañía, gobierno y vigilancia fuera más importante a mi honestidad, que los descuidos de mi padre" (44) [My mother died at the worst time for me. Her loss was great because her company, upbringing, and vigilance would have been better for my modesty than my father's negligence] (17). Lacking the protective and emotional guidance of a cherished female figure, and abandoned emotionally by her father, Jacinta begins her initiation into an alternate realm. At age sixteen, she enters the imperiled and alien courtly world that surrounds her and struggles within this unknown world of men, alternately trying to maintain her honor, her sexual integrity, and express her own very real desire. From the death of her mother to her abandonment in Montserrat, Jacinta discovers the obsession of desire, endures the ravages of jealousy, suffers the grief of betrayal by her father, feels the despair of the loss of her beloved Felix, and experiences the pain occasioned by Celio's scorn and rejection. She is ultimately abandoned by a disloyal servant in the wilderness of Montserrat. For Jacinta, Montserrat provides not the welcoming and restorative refuge it did for Fabio, but represents yet another inhospitable place in which she must confront adversity.

Alone in an antagonistic space where bandits and wild animals roam, Jacinta must fend for herself. Determined never to return home, she cuts her hair, dresses as a shepherd, and tends the priest's flocks. The adoption of male dress symbolizes her developmental journey in which she begins to assume the strength of character and subsequent autonomy stereotypically associated with male figures. Her cry in the wilderness, which opens the tale, expresses the accumulation of chastening experiences she has withstood, yet it also signals her ascendancy in achieving a degree of agency. Her slowly emerging independence, self-sufficiency, and emotional detachment are a result of her sojourn into a "masculine" world where she is forced to draw on her inner fortitude merely to survive.

Persuaded by Fabio, Jacinta finally returns to a domestic female space; not the home, however, but the convent. The convent functions symbolically as an enhanced version of her familial home. Here in the company of women she eventually achieves autonomy. Although facilitated by a male mentor, the empathetic Fabio, her movement toward selfhood is fulfilled. As Lisarda notes, this is the happiest ending possible: "[H]oy vive en un Monasterio della, tan contenta, que le parece que no tiene más bien que desear, ni más gusto que pedir" (79) [Today Jacinta lives in a convent. She is so happy that you'd think she desired to live no other way, that she could ask for no greater pleasure] (44). It is significant to point out that Jacinta's retreat to the convent is not motivated by religious devotion, as she refuses to take vows because she still harbors the hope that Celio will return to her. Nonetheless, she experiences fulfillment in the convent. Her withdrawal to the safe haven of the monastery constitutes an alternate integration into another sort of society, one in which women clearly assume authority and are renewed psychically and spiritually. This last leg of her developmental journey brings her to the final stage of David's trajectory, the *locus veritas,* the "uniquely female variant of the pastoral *locus amoenus*" (60). The one "true" home for female characters is one in which women guide and are guided by female models. Indeed, Jacinta assumes a status and authority in the convent that would have been impossible in the male-dominated realm of the court, as she is nurtured by other women and in turn tends to the needs of the younger Doña Guiomar, who has recently lost her mother.

Curiously, this very same pattern of retreat to a convent is mirrored in the frame narrative. Although "Aventurarse perdiendo" is the opening tale of the first collection of stories, *Novelas amorosas y ejemplares,* its conclusion anticipates the close of the entire frame narrative in the second collection, *Desengaños amorosos,* published ten years later. After telling and listening to each other's disenchantments in the *Desengaños,* the five female narrators retire from the world to lead a secular life in the convent. Although the emphasis in the *Desengaños* is much more pointedly directed at fleeing the deceptive world of men and their falsehood, the renewal and sense of wholeness afforded by the convent parallels the welcoming, nurturing atmosphere of the female religious sanctuary in "Aventurarse perdiendo" where Jacinta, the despairing woman left crying in the wilderness, now offers the vigilance and protection that she herself lacked as an adolescent to another young woman, Doña Guiomar.

Moreover, in the same way the female characters join together in creating their own haven, Zayas crafts her own space within literature by subverting conventions to open the way for a definitive female perspective. Zayas fashions a literary world in which women tell their own stories, thus validating the legitimacy of female experience. The female narrators reclaim textual authority, as Jacinta does, and the female protagonists assume agency over their lives. In reversing normative patterns such as those evident in pastoral, Zayas gives primacy to female discourse as she imaginatively explores multifarious variations of inherited literary models. The will to value women as both subjects and authors, capable of producing admirable life as well as literary texts, reflects perhaps Zayas's own desire to achieve recognition and be accepted on her own terms. As Ruth El Saffar notes, "In Jacinta's combination of pride, competitiveness, and defensiveness can be found an echo of the Zayas of the Prologue, who both knows her talent and the hostility with which it is likely to be received" (213). While the self-referentiality of Zayas in her texts is often debated, her will to establish a distinctive identity for her characters as well as for herself lies at the cornerstone of her fiction. In her re-formulation of conventional modes of discourse, she not only displays her rich inventiveness but also enhances the very models she so often subverts.

Notes

1. Pfandl's vitriolic condemnation of her works is well known: "¿Se puede dar algo más ordinario y grosero, más inestético, y repulsivo que una mujer que cuenta historias lascivas, sucias, de inspiración sádica y moralmente corrompidas?" (370) [Can there be anything more gross and obscene, more nonaesthetic and repulsive, than a woman who writes lascivious, dirty, sadistic, and morally corrupt stories?] (Boyer xii).

2. Boyer notes Zayas's "highly subtle feminism" (xviii) in the *Novelas amorosas y ejemplares* as well as her "feminization of Golden Age literature and . . . her resoundingly modern feminist message" (xxiv), while Chevalier underscores her "militant feminism" (31). Griswold cautions against labeling Zayas a feminist in claiming that the "feminism" evident in her work responds to a long-standing feminist-antifeminist literary debate: "Precisely because Zayas' work makes use of themes which are part of a recognized and vital literary tradition, one must regard her 'feminism' as a topos and be very wary about believing that feminism to be a

sincere expression of her personal beliefs on the subject" (100). Brownlee highlights Zayas's Renaissance feminism, "rather than the modern feminist project that has characterized much of the scholarship devoted to her in recent years" (165). Other scholars see her as a champion of women's rights in her undeniable defense of women, noting, "Zayas' transformation of feminine culture into literature is an implicit feminist act" (Kaminsky 391). While the definition of her feminism is contested, her deliberate treatment of the relation between the sexes with its focus on women is a commonality recognized by all.

3. All citations from Zayas are to the edition by Amezúa. The English citations are taken from Boyer's translation.

4. David notes the classic feminization of the natural landscape: "[I]n the male authored Renaissance pastoral romance, typified by Sannazaro's *Arcadia* (1509), Sidney's 'old' *Arcadia* (1580), Greene's *Menaphon* (1589), and Lodge's *Rosalynde* (1590), the rural setting signifies those ideas clustered around the stereotypically 'feminine,' equally expressed in its associative sense with nature, relatedness, sensibility, or the unconscious" (xvii). Greer highlights the Freudian suggestiveness of the "bosque amenísimo" [lush forest] in Zayas's texts as an erotically charged female space (98).

5. The irony of Zayas's introduction, "Al que leyere" [To the Reader], should not go unnoticed. First acknowledging the oddity of women's authorship and her audacity in publishing her "borrones" (21) [scribbles] (11), she goes on to defend the equality of the sexes, noting distinguished female writers of antiquity. She teasingly concludes by stating, "Te ofrezco este libro muy segura de su bizarría, y en confianza de que si te desagradare, podías disculparme con que nací mujer, no con obligaciones de hacer buenas novelas, sino con muchos deseos de acertar a servirte" (23) [I offer this book to you, trusting your generosity and knowing that if it displeases you, you will excuse me because I was born a woman, with no obligation to write good novellas but a great desire to serve you well] (2).

6. Foa notes that the baroque theme of *desengaño* as displayed in a distancing or detachment from the false values of the world takes a very different turn in Zayas, according her a distinctive position within the *desengañado* tradition: "Although the retreat from the world, typical of her heroines, is backed by a lengthy tradition of renunciation, the motivation of her women is different. Instead of renouncing the world to escape vice and temptation, they are motivated by a longing to escape the deceits, cruelties, and betrayals of men" (63).

Works Cited

Brownlee, Marina S. "Elusive Subjectivity in María de Zayas." *Journal of Interdisciplinary Literature Studies* 6.2 (1994): 163–83.

Chevalier, Maxine. "Un cuento, una comedia, cuatro novelas." *Essays on Narrative Fiction in the Iberian Peninsula in Honour of Frank Pierce*. Ed. R. B. Tate. Valencia: Dolphin, 1982. 27–38.

David, Gail. *Female Heroism in the Pastoral.* New York: Garland, 1991.

El Saffar, Ruth. "Ana/Lisis/Zayas: Reflections on Courtship and Literary Women in María de Zayas's *Novelas amorosas y ejemplares.*" *María de Zayas: The Dynamics of Discourse.* Ed. Amy R. Williamsen and Judith A. Whitenack. Madison, N.J.: Fairleigh Dickinson University Press, 1995. 192–216.

Ettin, Andrew. *Literature and the Pastoral.* New Haven: Yale University Press, 1984.

Foa, Sandra M. "María de Zayas y Sotomayor: Sibyl of Madrid (1590?–1661?)." *Female Scholars: A Tradition of Female Scholars before 1800.* Ed. J. R. Brink. Montreal: Eden, 1980. 54–87.

Greer, Margaret R. "The M(Other) Plot: Psychoanalytic Theory and Narrative Structure in María de Zayas." *María de Zayas: The Dynamics of Discourse.* Ed. Amy R. Williamsen and Judith A. Whitenack. Madison, N.J.: Fairleigh Dickinson University Press, 1995. 90–116.

Griswold, Susan. "*Topoi* and Rhetorical Distance: The 'Feminism' of María de Zayas." *Revista de Estudios Hispánicos* 14 (1980): 97–116.

Kaminsky, Amy. "Dress and Redress: Clothing in the *Desengaños amorosos* of María de Zayas y Sotomayor." *Romance Review* 79.2 (1988): 377–91.

Montemayor, Jorge de. *The Diana.* Trans. RoseAnna M. Mueller. Lewiston/Lampeter/Queenston: Edwin Mellen, 1989.

———. *Siete libros de la Diana.* Ed. Francisco López Estrada. Madrid: Espasa-Calpe, 1970.

Pfandl, Ludwig. *Historia de la literatura española de la edad de oro.* Trans. Jorge Rubió Balaguer. Barcelona: Sucesores de Juan Gili, 1933.

Poggioli, Renato. *The Oaten Flute.* Cambridge: Harvard University Press, 1975.

Pons, Margalida. "Extrañamiento e identidad en 'La fuerza del amor' de María de Zayas." *Romance Languages Annual* 7 (1995): 590–96.

Solé-Leris, Amadeu. *The Spanish Pastoral Novel.* Boston: Twayne, 1980.

Zayas, María de. *The Enchantments of Love: Amorous and Exemplary Novels.* Trans. and ed. H. Patsy Boyer. Berkeley and Los Angeles: University of California Press, 1990.

———. *Novelas amorosas y ejemplares.* Ed. Agustín G. de Amezúa. Madrid: Aldus, 1948.

14

Zayas's Ideal of the Masculine

Clothes Make the Man

Susan Paun de García

The 1640s in Spain saw disaster after disaster. The decline in power and prestige, ignored and unnoticed until Rocroi, sent the nation's elite into despair. The king fretted, his ministers plotted to remove his *valido* [favorite], *arbitristas* [armchair politicians] abounded, and the nobility, awash in denial, played at court and displayed their wealth. Among those who lamented the decline was a woman, a public literary personage. Armed with words, María de Zayas y Sotomayor sought to inspire, motivate, urge, or provoke a change of attitude and behavior at the highest levels of society, in which she saw the origins of the nation's sins. For some, such as Sor María de Agreda, the troubles stemmed from the king's behavior—especially his extramarital indulgences, which had brought down upon the Spaniards the wrath of God; his sinful soul must be purified before there could be any chance of victory. For María de Zayas, however, the problem was more generalized among and within the highest levels of nobility, and it manifested itself outwardly, in men's behavior toward war and women and, more specifically, in the clothes they wore.

While it is not unusual to view María de Zayas as a forerunner of feminism, and by extension as a critic of men's antifeminism, she is not usually thought of as a detractor of masculine fashion. However, the two—criticism of men's behavior and criticism of men's outerwear—go hand in hand, the evils of one symptomatic of the excesses of the other and vice versa. Her acerbic rhetoric points to the fragility of the moment in which she wrote, when the Spanish political ascendancy was giving way to the French, and the male paragon of warrior/protector was giving way to the unrepentant libertine. The exclusivity of rank and class was being eroded, the modalities and fashions of the nobility copied by the masses. The elite masculine sphere of action, already moved from battlefield to court, was extended to public parks and promenades. In the eyes of María de Zayas, men's dress, comportment, and attitudes toward war signaled a society in danger of extinction. In the mode of Don Quijote, she argues for a return to a social and political Golden Age, when men were men, acted like men, and dressed like men.

A remarkably famous and popular novelist in the early seventeenth century, María de Zayas y Sotomayor wrote two collections of short novellas, the first published in 1637, the second in 1647. In the latter, the *Desengaños amorosos* [*The Disenchantments of Love*], through her narrators, Zayas laments the altered state of Spain, denouncing her own Age of Iron and the men who epitomize it. She berates the nobles and knights who have sworn to defend Spain, deploring the wars in which they do not participate and the enemies they do not defeat. Her barbs are aimed at the highest ranks of society, knights entitled to wear the insignia of their military orders, and bound by vows and obligations to their rank and to their order:

> ¿Pues qué ley humana ni divina halláis, nobles caballeros, para precipitaros tanto contra las mujeres, que apenas se halla uno que las defienda, cuando veis tantos que las persiguen? Quisiera preguntaros si cumplís en esto con la obligación de serlo, y lo que prometéis cuando os ponéis en los pechos las insignias de serlo, y si es razón que lo que juráis cuando os las dan, no lo cumpláis. Mas pienso que ya no las deseáis y pretendéis, sino por gala, como las medias de pelo y las guedejas (504–5).[1]

> [What law human or divine enables you, noble gentlemen, to so hurl yourselves against women that you can hardly find a single man to defend them, that you see so many men persecute them? I'd like to ask you if this is the way you comply with your obligation to your nobility? When you pin the insignias of nobility to your chest, what do you swear? Is it right for you not to uphold the oath? I think you seek and desire nobility only as adornment, like silk stockings and curly locks.] (399–400)

While she is referring to a chivalric obligation to defend women, she also means to include the obligations implicit in all three vows sworn by members of the orders of Calatrava, Alcántara, and Santiago: chastity, poverty, and defense of the faith. She criticizes the nobles' licentious behavior, their conspicuous consumption, and their apathy in the face of external threats: "¿De qué pensáis que procede el poco ánimo que hoy todos tenéis, que sufrís que estén los enemigos dentro de España, y nuestro Rey en campaña, y vosotros en el Prado y en el río, llenos de galas y trajes femeniles y los pocos que le acompañan, suspirando por las ollas de Egipto?" (505) [Where do you think the lack of courage you all exhibit nowadays comes from? That let you tolerate the enemy within Spanish borders, and while our king is doing battle you sit in the park and stroll along the river all dolled up in feminine frippery? The few men who do accompany the king long only for the fleshpots of Egypt] (400).

For Zayas, the ideal of masculine identity is located in the past, in the times of Ferdinand of Aragon. Although she does not mention him by name, perhaps Zayas had a noble in mind like Rodrigo Ponce de León, Duke of Cádiz, who died on August 27, 1492, marking the end of a "legendary era of lance and sword, of heroism and courtly grace, of unequaled personal mettle that had inspired virtually every major victory of the war [of Granada]" (Rubin 306). The duke's gallantry, bravery, and dedication to the monarchs and their war efforts "had epitomized the medieval concept of vassalage and personal fidelity that was fast disappearing in a cooler age of gunpowder artillery and the bureaucratic nation-state" (Rubin 306). Under Ferdinand, audacity, tenacity, heroism, and glory were the national ideals that made possible the providential task of keeping the faith and uniting Christianity, qualities that were lost as the seventeenth century progressed.

Furthermore, these men of old were inspired in great part by their devotion to Isabel, whom Zayas does not mention explicitly but who is the unspoken motive behind Ferdinand and the nobles' gallantry and courage. It was their valuation and protection of women that inspired noble men to great and daring deeds; the lack of this fundamental attitude both causes and explains Spain's sorry state:

De la poca estimación que hacéis de las mujeres, que a fe que, si las estimarais y amárades, como en otros tiempos se hacía, por no verlas en poder de vuestros enemigos, vosotros mismos os ofreciérades, no digo yo a ir a la guerra, y a pelear, sino a la muerte, poniendo la garganta al cuchillo, como en otros tiempos, y en particular en el del rey don Fernando el Católico se hacía, donde no era menester llevar los hombres por fuerza, ni maniatados, como ahora (infelicidad y desdicha de nuestro católico Rey), sino que ellos mismos ofrecían sus haciendas y personas:

el padre, por defender la hija; el hermano, por la hermana; el esposo, por la esposa; y el galán por la dama. Y esto era por no verlas presas y cautivas, y, lo que peor es, deshonradas, como me parece que vendrá a ser si vosotros no os animáis a defenderlas. Mas como ya las tenéis por el alhaja más vil y de menos valor que hay en vuestra casa, no se os da nada de que vayan a ser esclavas de otros y en otros reinos; que a fe que, si los plebeyos os vieran a vosotros con valor para defendernos, a vuestra imitación lo hicieran todos. (505)

[It comes from your low regard for women. I swear if you did love and cherish women as was the way in former times, you'd volunteer not just to go to war and fight but to die, exposing your throat to the knife to keep them from falling into the hands of the enemy. This is the way it was in earlier days, particularly under King Fernando the Catholic. Then it wasn't necessary to conscript men, forcing them into service almost with their hands tied, the way it is today (causing our Catholic king unhappiness and great misfortune). Men used to offer up their possessions and their lives, the father to defend his daughter, the brother to defend his sister, the husband to defend his wife, the suitor to defend his lady. They did so to keep their women from being captured, taken prisoner or, worse of all, being dishonored. I feel sure this is what will come to pass if you men don't gather the courage to defend women. Because you seem to consider women as the tawdriest and least valuable jewel among all your possessions, you care nothing about the fact that they may be enslaved and sent off to other countries. I swear, if common men could see your courage in defending us, they would all follow after you and do the same.] (400)

As if anticipating a rebuttal, Zayas acknowledges the inevitable and fundamental anxiety of the male—that women left alone and unguarded will fall prey to poachers of virtue and honor. However, her point is that the honor of king and country must take precedence over the individual, whether male or female. For their part, the women left behind will not only guard and protect their own honor, but also will, through their prayers, add strength to the soldiers' arms. They will, with the sound of their prayers, make the walls of the enemy come tumbling down: "Y si os parece que en yéndoos a pelear os han de agraviar y ofender, idos todos, seguid a vuestro rey a defendernos, que quedando solas, seremos Moisenes, que, orando, vencerá Josué" (505) [If you think that in going away to fight, you will be aggrieved or dishonored in your absence, then all of you go follow your king and defend us, and we, being left alone, will be like Moses who by praying will enable Joshua to conquer] (400). By not honoring and defending women, Spanish nobles have become "womanized," "feminized," or "effeminate."

What Makes a Man a Man? The Models: *Caballeros* [Knights/ Gentlemen]

As Andrew Williams demonstrates, the construction of masculine identity is derived from the cultural importance a society attaches to the public behavior of its male members. As such, society and personal identity are connected; individual selfhood remains, in the words of Rom Harre, "symbolic of social practices, not of empirical experiences" (quoted in Williams 96). In other words, there is a connection between gender identity and social identity. Similarly, although any cultural moment contains competing versions of masculinity, one version of the masculine ideal "invariably assumes the hegemonic position where it wields an inordinate degree of social and political power" (Williams 98). In fact, Michael Kimmel defines manhood as "a man in power, a man with power, and a man of power" (228). In Zayas's Golden Age, these men in power were ostensibly the knights of the military orders. They used this power to respect and protect not only their faith and their land but also their treasure and their honor. In María de Zayas's view, these last two are ostensibly equivalent to and indicative of their attitude and behavior toward women. The failure of men to protect women signals a shift in the paradigm of masculinity once defined, established, and exemplified by the members of established military orders.

It is well known that the military orders in Spain were founded during the Reconquest to serve as protectors of the faith and of the faithful. However, it is important here to remember that these warriors, under the command of their respective grand masters, participated in the Castilian civil wars of the fourteenth and fifteenth centuries, during which time the war against the infidel—their original raison d'être—was put into the background and their primary activities became political, their battles now against Christians. After the fall of Granada at the end of the fifteenth century, Ferdinand of Aragon, by authority of a Bull of Pope Innocent VIII, became the grand master of all of Spain's military orders, thereby terminating their political autonomy. With the end of the Reconquest, a knight's military service was reduced to a six-month stint in the galleys, which could be circumvented by payment of a sum of money. By Zayas's time, any service at all was nominal. New *caballeros* were admitted not on the basis of their military merits but on the status of their noble birth.

Although one of their three vows was to defend the faith against the infidel, the military spirit of these orders had long since declined into "a state of utter inactivity. . . . The last attempt to employ the knights of the three orders for a military purpose was that of Philip IV, in quelling the rebellion of the Catalans (1640–50)" (Moeller 152). In this endeavor, taking place as Zayas wrote and published her *Desengaños amorosos,* those members of the military orders who participated equipped a single regiment known as the Regiment of the Orders.

The completion of the Reconquest coincided with the beginning of the Conquest of the New World, prolonging the long, uninterrupted period of essentially victorious military elitism. As defenders of the faith, the Spaniards had fought infidels and had won—until the Protestant rebellions. By the time Zayas published her novellas, Spain's military dominance was no longer undisputed, the Christian world no longer exclusively Catholic. France's direct intervention in the Thirty Years War in May 1635 was for Spain a betrayal to the Catholic cause, but for France it amounted to a political decision destined to end Spanish exclusivity. In 1643 the Spanish troops suffered their first defeat since the union of the crowns at Rocroi, followed by another in Lens in 1646, leading up to the Peace of Westphalia in 1648, which marked the end of Spanish hegemony and the beginning of a new world order. The Holy Roman Emperor's hope of restoring both his own power and the Catholic faith throughout the empire was dashed with its fragmentation into a number of independent states and the isolation of Hapsburg Spain. The French war against Spain continued until the Treaty of the Pyrenees in 1659, when Spain lost part of the Netherlands and some territory in the north of Spain to France. The two treaties—Westphalia and the Pyrenees—established France as the predominant European power (Payne 315–17). Throughout these efforts, new Spanish military units were recruited from Spanish Italy, supplemented by German and Irish mercenaries. According to Stanley Payne, "The militarily skilled, valiant, and patriotic elements of the aristocracy had themselves been thinned by casualties. They no longer provided leadership, and most of the nobility simply dodged the call of duty" (317).

Was it a case of changing values? Or was it also the changing nature of warfare? In 1648, Fabricio Pons de Castelvi, in his *Gustavo Adolfo, rey de Suecia, vencedor y vencido en Alemania* [*Gustavus Adolphus, King of Sweden,*

Victor and Vanquished in Germany] writes with profound nostalgia of the past, of a Golden Age when the world was governed by more noble sentiments and a better order. The new world eschews the old values, even in battle: "¡Oh, Dicha, cómo te aventajas al Valor en las maliciosas batallas de nuestros tiempos! ¿Qué vale la Fortaleza? ¿Qué el Brío? ¿Qué la Reputación? Si por los apartados tiros de la artillería y mosquetería muere igualmente el cobarde y el valeroso" (Palacio Atard 109) [O Luck! How you exceed Valor in the malicious battles of our times! What use is Fortitude? Manliness? Reputation? If the distant shots of artillery and musketry kill both the coward and the hero equally] (my translation).

The old-fashioned virtues of honor and valor were now replaced by brute strength, wealth, and lack of scruples. The ruling class had degenerated, beginning at the top. The Hapsburgs, physically degenerate as the result of consanguinity, reigned over a politically degenerate governing bureaucracy composed of not the best and brightest but rather the mediocre and the favorites, and the nation as a whole felt the moral decadence and *desengaño* [disenchantment, disillusionment] of ideals and virtues. Philip IV's court was one of intrigue and expenditure, courtiers and cavalcades, and plays and masques in the new palace of the Buen Retiro. The *caballeros* of the military orders preferred feasting at palace to fighting at the front; the king had to threaten a fine of 2,000 *ducados* for *caballeros* of the military orders who refused to join him at the border of Aragon. The organization of the nobles into an army that was to accompany Philip to Catalonia was so reluctant that the nobles were generally called "eunuchs." These were the defenders of their faith, their *patria* [homeland], their honor, and their women.

The military had become "soft." Not only were the orders no longer essentially military but also their religious nature had vanished by Zayas's time. Originally sworn to poverty and celibacy ("marital chastity"[2] in the Order of Santiago [Sainty]), the latter vow was commuted to conjugal fidelity in 1540. Members of Calatrava were allowed to have families and to make free use of their personal property. The ideal male in Zayas's time was no longer the chaste warrior but rather the unrepentant libertine, as ostentatious in his sexual conquests and transgressions as in his "feminine" dress, a metaphor for the "muliebris" military male.

How Did the Fashions Change?

While Zayas does not criticize her own king, Philip IV—theoretically the origin and setter of standards and styles—she does chastise and deride the contemporary aristocratic male as being far from her ideal in comportment and attitude. An obvious manifestation of this objectionable masculinity is, for her, male fashion, which has drifted toward a feminized or "afeminado" French style: "Bien dice un héroe bien entendido que los franceses os han hurtado el valor, y vosotros a ellos, los trajes" (506) [Some clever writer has said that the French have stolen Spanish courage and you have stolen French fashion] (401).

"Masculine" dress refers to a gendered appearance. For Judith Lorber, gender is a social structure, an institution whose history can be traced, whose structure can be examined, and whose changing effects can be researched. Gender establishes patterns of expectations for individuals, and orders the social processes of everyday life. It is built into the major social organizations of society (for example, economy, ideology, family, politics), but it is also an entity in and of itself. Being feminine or masculine in a male body and being feminine or masculine in a female body are not the same thing. In María de Zayas's time, the terms "masculine" and "feminine" indicate that gender was centered less in the Freudian sexual construct and more in the attitudes of Heroic (masculine) and Defenseless (feminine). The "galas y trajes femeniles" [feminine frippery] both cause and explain the "poco ánimo" [lack of courage] of Spain's bravest and best.

Zayas appreciates the fact that the clothes we wear make clear reference to who we are and how we wish to be perceived. We also appreciate that the evolving masculine dress to which she refers clearly marks a moment of shift in historical context. At the collective level, clothes function as identifiers and signifiers, situating both the clothes and their wearers "symbolically in some structured universe of status claims and life-style attachments" (Davis 4). Codes of meaning in clothing are linked to design, occasions, and to historical frames of reference, as well as to place and society. That is, clothing is context-dependent. While the signifiers or markers are materially the same for everyone, what is signified can be quite different for different publics, and will vary between different social strata and taste subcultures (Davis 9). As well, meanings change over time, so that, for example, what was once considered masculine can later appear feminine, what was once considered informal can later appear formal, and so on. More to the point of this discussion, what was once the prerogative of feminine fashion can be adapted and adopted by males and vice versa. For Zayas, the change in style is symptomatic of the change in Spain's military status. Victory is motivated by duty, honor, and a desire to protect the weak; but now those whose duty it is to protect are adorned to look like the weak they are supposed to defend. At issue here is fashion, essentially reflecting sociopolitical changes, but also changing performative gender norms, as I will discuss later.

Men and women did not always dress extremely differently from one another. According to Anne Hollander, this began to happen around the fourteenth century, although things had been heading in that direction for a couple hundred years before. Whereas before clothing linked the two genders, now it divided them. And, says Hollander, the male dress has always had something about it that has made it inherently more desirable than female dress: "It is not just the sign of power in the world, or of potency in the head, nor has it ever generally been more physically comfortable; but since the late Middle Ages, male dress also has had a certain fundamental esthetic superiority, a more advanced seriousness of visual form not suggested by the inventors of fashion for women in the past" (39–40). It is significant that the "femininity" of male fashion decried by María de Zayas is indicative of just such a lack of power, seriousness, and superiority. As Hollander shows, the first revolutionary advances in European fashion were connected to the development of plate armor, which male fashion later imitated. In contrast to classical armor, which imitated the musculature of the body, plate armor created a new shape, new lines, highlighting the male shape. From then on, clothes for men and clothes for women took on very different looks.

In the sixteenth century, the typical male costume borrowed elements from military uniforms. The beauty and prestige of the armor influenced fashion well into the seventeenth century. Men's clothing consisted of stiff shapes—short coats over fitted tights and padded codpieces—culminating in the starched neck ruff. The slit sleeves and breeches of the Swiss uniforms were adopted; the codpiece (which disappeared toward the end of the century) probably derived from a gusset in mail armor; the doublet was curved and padded in the fashion of a cuirass; sleeves were padded to indicate strength, as were hose. In both male and female costume, the increasing slenderness of the waist was offset by exaggerated padding in the sleeves and the hips. However, the focus of the masculine form of dress was undoubtedly below the waist, exposing the leg. Attention was inevitably drawn to the genitalia, whether enlarged by a codpiece or substituted by a sword.

Women's clothes, on the other hand, copied only suggestions and elements from this model until the sixteenth century, when "certain styles of bodice, hat, collar, shoe, and sleeve were simply stolen from men, to add a new whiff of sexual daring to women's clothes without recourse either to forbidden pants or to excessive exposure" (Hollander 45). Hollander maintains that these gestures show a desire to look "erotically imaginative without looking too feminine"—to mimic male sexual freedom, instead of exaggerating the look of female compliance (45). Women still wore variations of the dress, but it became more constructed, with bodice and skirt, sometimes consisting of underskirt and overskirt. The bodice became stiffened, in imitation of the armor, and the petticoat became the defining feminine garment. In order to dress like a woman, all a man needed was a petticoat, which is true even today. The original aim was certainly modesty, with variations manifesting themselves generally above the waist: the lowered neckline exposing the breasts was the feminine answer to the masculine exposure of shapely legs. Masculine dress emphasized the body while feminine dress concealed and disguised it (Hollander 48).

In the seventeenth century, after 1620, the stiffness of costume gradually gave way to a greater softness. After the expulsion of the Moors, the textile industry was in a state of disarray, which resulted in a prohibition of the use of brocades, the lack of which was filled by increased use of braids and passementeries (Boucher 278). The feminine bodice exposed more shoulder, and the cape shrank to a *mantilla* [shawl]. Around 1640–48, the farthingale was replaced by the *guardainfante* [wide farthingale], a style which later spread to other Hapsburg courts. The ruff disappeared, allowing the hair to flow freely over the shoulders, a hair style not worn elsewhere in Europe, and which closely approximated the masculine coiffure. A striking fashion element for women was the use of large jewelry, perhaps to balance the enormous outline of the skirt.

James Laver points to the rigidity and austerity of the Spanish style of the sixteenth century as an indicator not of personality but rather membership in a caste—aristocracy. The molded padding, the stiff ruff, the constricted waist, all indicated an elevated position in a hierarchy that disdained work (90–91). Colors, fabrics, and decorations were more similar for both genders than for varying social strata. Highly constructed and ornamented clothes would indicate privilege and the civilized pleasures concomitant with conspicuous consumption. The tightness of the clothes paralleled the discipline that went with rank, while the material and the richness of adornment used indicated social degree. Indeed, the mark of the Spanish costume was its elegance and sobriety. Usually dark in tone, the Spanish tailor used rich materials—silks, satins, brocades, and velvets—embroidered in silver and gold, provoking repeated but generally ineffective prohibitions (1515, 1520, 1523, 1534, et cetera). François

Boucher quotes an eighteenth-century Spanish author who ponders the significance of so many sumptuary prohibitions: "This series of laws presents a phenomenon worthy of our reflection: the most rich and powerful nation in the universe, the land which added new immensities to the vast territories acquired in Europe, the nation with the finest craftsmen and manufacturers of all in gold, silver and silk . . . this nation limits or forbids her subjects the greater part of these materials" (227). Rather than forbid the use of the materials themselves, however, these laws prescribed the wearing of specific styles by certain classes of people, thus clearly distinguishing between noble and bourgeois.

In this way, the Spanish gentleman's sartorial language bespoke his chivalry, virility, and courtliness. As well, it symbolized the power and influence of Spain, which was to decline in the seventeenth century, while at the same time France reached her military zenith, paralleled by a growth in the spread of French fashion throughout Europe, with increasingly frequent changes of style, the result of which María de Zayas bemoaned. The Spanish nobles imitated the fashion of the French, throwing themselves into a pursuit of elegance that took precedence over the pursuit of enemies. By 1635, Spanish fashion had virtually disappeared from France; instead the French look was being exported to Spain.

At midcentury, the French fashion was refined and elegant, with a trend to increasing simplicity, which was, however, quickly replaced by exaggerated manifestations such as petticoat breeches. Extremely wide and short, with folds so full that they resembled skirts with no apparent division at the legs, these breeches were trimmed with lace or ribbon, or with deep flounces attached. The accompanying doublet was short at the waist and in the sleeves, allowing the shirt beneath to show. The entire ensemble was loaded with ribbons or bows, creating a decidedly "feminine" effect enormously popular in France, Germany, and England, but evidently not in Spain, according to Boucher (258). Nonetheless, some articulation of this trend evidently had been assimilated into the Spanish fashion vocabulary, evidenced by María de Zayas's denunciation of the "effeminate" style popular in Madrid.

The Spanish nobles of the sixteenth century that Zayas remembers and admires did not appear in such trappings. The less fashionable Spaniards in the early seventeenth century still wore much tighter breeches than the French petticoat breeches, with doublets with rounded or slightly pointed waists, and epaulettes or wings at the shoulders, and maintained certain basic elements that had come to be identified as "Spanish": the *golilla* [ruff], the *ropilla* [short over-doublet] with bouffant sleeves, and straight-cut breeches. Unchanged from the previous century were the small beard, the *ferreruelo* [small cloak], the plumeless hat, and the absence of wigs. In the second half of the century, the changes in military uniforms began to creep into the male fashion vocabulary, and the appearance of a French-style full-tunic shaped coat worn over a similarly shaped waistcoat began to appear. Not only was the coat looser, but it also covered and hid the genitalia in the manner of a skirt, and in so doing understated this marker of male identity and power.

According to Abigail Solomon-Godeau, this need not necessarily indicate any such diminution of male power (the phallus). As a matter of fact, in art, there is a marked difference in representation of male nudes between the phallus and the penis: "[t]he diminutive scale of the genitalia on the male nude in its classical, Renaissance or post-Renaissance incarnations announces this non-equivalence, as does the frequent counterpoint of large swords, bulky scabbards, and bunched masses of drapery" (36). It would seem that Zayas marks no such difference. The "femininity" of the French-inspired costume hides the genitalia and minimizes the sword, clear indications of concomitant and/or resulting loss of heroism, power, and therefore masculinity. As the fashion shifted away from armor as its basic vocabulary, so too did the heroic cease to define the masculine. Once the sole masculine model, the knight becomes an anachronism, a vestige of a golden age, replaced by an urban, courtly assortment of masculinities.

The Unrepentant Libertine

For María de Zayas, clothes do indeed make the man. Wearing "manly" clothes will make men behave like men, and by extension, Spanish men wearing the Spanish style will be treated in the manner that is their due. The military inspiration of the Spanish style has been a *cause* of vigilance and victory, not a *coincidence* of power. Similarly, the relaxed and feminine French style heralds a new male attitude toward war and toward women. As Zayas protests, these men dress up, parade around, and gossip about their sexual conquests, real or imagined, all to the detriment of God, country, and women:

> ¿Es posible que nos veis ya casi en poder de los contrarios, pues desde donde están adonde estamos no hay más defensa que vuestros heroicos corazones y valerosos brazos, y que no os corréis de estaros en la Corte, ajando galas y criando cabellos, hollando coches y paseando prados, y que en lugar de defendernos, nos quitéis la opinión y el honor, contando cuentos que os suceden con damas, que creo que son más invenciones de

malicia que verdades; alabándoos de cosas que es imposible sea verdad que lo puedan hacer, ni aun las públicas rameras, sólo por llevar al cabo vuestra dañada intención, todos efecto de la ociosidad en que gastáis el tiempo en ofensa de Dios y de vuestra nobleza? ¡Qué esto hagan pechos españoles! ¡Qué esto sufran ánimos castellanos! (505–6)

[How can you sit back and see us almost in the power of the enemy? From where the enemy is to where we are, the only defense is your heroic heart and your brave arm! Aren't you ashamed to be here at court, donning your gala outfits and curling your hair, strolling through parks and gallivanting in carriages instead of defending us? On top of that, you ruin our good name and our honor by telling tales about your love affairs, which I think are more malicious fiction than fact! You boast of exploits impossible even with a common whore, simply to prove your prejudiced ideas which are the product of the idleness you spend offending against God and against your nobility. So this is Spanish valor! How can the Castilian spirit tolerate this!] (400–401)

The code of behavior that renders dying in battle "heroic" is a part of a gender code. It valuates a masculinity that is egocentric (its agents must think themselves worthy of fame and glory) and at the same time altruistic (through the sacrificial deaths of its heroic men, society will persevere). Yet heroic masculinity, like any other, is wholly dependent upon its cultural moment. Masculinity is changeable, adaptive, reconfigurable; it is constructed rather than inherent. Furthermore, gender must be taken as a plurality, not as the binaries it deceptively presents. Masculinity becomes a spectrum of acceptable gender behaviors, with the "weak" man subordinate, and the powerful/heroic figure responsible for maintaining the hierarchy and the culture-specific formulation of male-to-male and male-to-female relationships.

In María de Zayas's construction of masculinity, that which is foreign becomes that which is deficient and (by a familiar leap of logic) that which is feminine. The loathsome French become a nation of eunuchs, missing a vital signifier or marker of power and authority that Spain, no matter how beleaguered, always confidently possesses. The essence of true manhood resides for Zayas at home. In her rhetoric of representation, the knights and the aristocracy ("los hombres" [men]) slip from the feminine into the monstrous.

Zayas's narrative mixes national, personal, and gender identity into a potent concoction that yields a rhetorically effective narrative. Spanish (male) identity is defined by opposition to "foreign" monstrosity, as seen most notably in

"Mal presagio casarse lejos" ["Marriage Abroad: Portent of Doom"], in which the Flemish husband is caught in bed with his page. The allusion to and depiction of the homosexual activity represents the feminized foreign as a violation of the norm (the heterosexual relationship). Here, the men are so feminized that they have no need of women, and, as a consequence, they certainly will not love, honor, and protect them. The threat posed to the nation is that of the monster, whose existence is defined by the disruption of boundaries, by the obviation of the female body, and by the blurring of the crucial division between masculine and feminine. The monstrous other disrupts the "Spanish" universe and produces its limits.

The problem with the heroic masculine is that it is performative, an identity derived from feats of arms or of love, always needing to be proven in action. The signifiers of this masculinity (and others) are not limited to (or by) the anatomy of particular bodies, but extend into almost every realm of human experience, from where one is born to how one dresses, carries oneself, speaks. For example, for the *caballero* the horse signifies and marks its rider. The presence or absence of a beard is a visual signal that the text of the body should be read against a particular set of gendered norms. Material signifiers, further, are essential: it is impossible to say if a man makes his clothing, or if clothes have made the man. By identifying Spain with the weak/passive/feminized French fashion, France ironically becomes the masculine/strong force.

Sebastián de Covarrubias Orozco defines "afeminado" [effeminate] in physical as well as social senses. It can refer to a man who is of a delicate constitution, even if he might be manly in spirit ("aunque tenga ánimo varonil"), but the first definition is related to performance: "El hombre de condición mujeril, inclinado a ocuparse en lo que ellas tratan y hablar su lenguaje y en su tono delicado" [The man of womanly condition, inclined to their occupations and their language, and their delicate tone] (22). As Gary Spear's study of Shakespeare shows, the term "effeminate" could signal and signify widely divergent phenomena, from male physical weakness to love of excessive pleasure (especially sexual pleasure with women), or an antiheroic military ethos. Used as a verb, it signified a weakening, a corruption, a generation, not only of men but also "entire social institutions and structures identified with male (or as later feminist criticism would have it, 'patriarchal') power" (411).

While the heroic/military masculine both excluded and involved women, the emerging new model of masculinity both incorporated and vilified the feminine. Women were subordinate but also powerful; they could control men through sex, and men were effeminated by excessive desire. The rejection of the manly venture of national defense and the championing of excessive sexual desire signaled a rejection of the manly self-discipline, the valuation of the individual above the national imperative.

Essential to this "effeminacy" is a debasement of the feminine, which can threaten to become "virile." The preponderance of plots revolving around the preservation of a woman's honor or the restoration of her lost honor allude to the vestigial appeal of this code, although in more than one of her tales, Zayas's heroines do indeed defend their own honor. The woman's honor is sullied by him who should protect it in both deed and word. On countless occasions, Zayas and her narrators decry the opposite practice, that of "composing and making public obscene and often misogynistic verse" (Williams 97) or of making public a sexual conquest—real or imagined, for the evident social solidification of the libertine as masculine ideal. Whether by word or by deed, the fashionable gentleman was sexually free, probably promiscuous, and eager to be recognized as such.

If the "Don Juan" is the triumph of the phallus, then the libertine substitutes "the actual phallus with logos, the word, which functions as a socially permissible, symbolic phallus" (Williams 100). Rather than make sexual conquests, he tells tales of them, boasting of feats that are, according to Zayas, "más invenciones de malicia que verdades" (505–6) [more malicious fiction than fact] (401). Yet, without the phallus, all is feminine; that is, when men only speak like men but do not act like men, they are in essence like women. The courtiers criticized by Zayas spend their time in the company of women and in the social space permitted to them: the promenades of the Prado. Rather than take their armies into battle, they take their carriages to the river.

Once the paragon of chivalry, the knight ("caballero") has become the unrepentant libertine, a sexual presence instead of a military might. Rather than wear the symbolic cross of the military order that previously defined a true gentleman, the courtier now manifests his identity in meaningless ornamentation and unproductive ostentation. Rather than a performance of heroism, masculinity becomes a "spectacle," both sartorial and sexual.

In this essay I have attempted a small exploration of one aspect of the representation of masculinity at a particular moment in history—one that amounted to a crisis in Spain and Spanish identity. The crisis of the Thirty Years War seems to have manifested an anxiety about masculinity, much like the "constant evocation of the menace of 'effeminacy'" after the French Revolution remarked by Solomon-Godeau (33). Whereas the latter crisis can be explained by the threat of popular female power, "whereby men ultimately deal with the threat of female power by incorporating it" (38), the threat to the Spanish aristocratic male is from without; it is the threat of French power that is being incorporated. The Spanish masculine ideal is determined and characterized through and by a series of differentiations: from the female and from the French.

As we have seen, although masculine and feminine dress shared many elements throughout the sixteenth century and the first part of the seventeenth, the fashion trend operating at the time of the *Desengaños amorosos* confounds these differences and differentiations. Ironically, the identification of the French dress with the feminine—indicating weakness—places the French in a position of strength and superiority. Elements of dress that might be markers of display are read and interpreted by Zayas as markers of gender difference. The exhibitionism and display of the masculine occupies a position of object of desire. "Effeminate" is Zayas's term for the dandy, whose display is the equivalent of the feminine, drawing attention to various parts of the body, while remaining nominally within the bounds of the new requirements for male costume. It would seem, according to Solomon-Godeau, that dandyism often serves as "the last gasp of an archaic model of masculinity, already marginalized and headed for (official) cultural extinction" (219–22).

The promise of Charles V—the new glorious age in which the world would be ruled by "one monarch, one Empire, and one sword"—was dimmed by constant wars, revolts, and defeats. Spain's struggle to maintain her vast overseas empire, confounded by repeated economic crises, eroded earlier optimism and led to *desengaño* [disenchantment], an obsessive and pervasive theme in political as well as literary discourse. The Spaniard's, especially the Castilian's, identity as invincible and fearless warrior and conqueror, maintained in practice and principle since the beginnings of Reconquest in the eighth century, now became less a reality than a memory, a source of nostalgia and gloomy comparisons to the "good old days." Zayas rails against the present, urging a return to the ideals of such a "Golden Age."

As Anthony Smith explains, the Golden Age "defined the 'true character' of a people, or even humanity, what it would and should be if only the people had been 'true to themselves' and had been left alone" (41). It marks not only the origin of a people but also its difference from the "outsider," both in character and in territory. It establishes a sense of continuity in the face of social change, even proclaiming an "imminent status reversal" from the undesirable present to the former glory, pointing toward a "glorious *destiny*, stemming from the true nature revealed in and by that golden past" (48–51).

In the passages cited above and in others, María de Zayas (sometimes through the voice of her narrators, sometimes in direct didactic commentary) condemns the lack of combative inclinations of the nobility of her day, asserting that they are not worthy of the insignias they wear on their breasts (the crosses of military orders established during the Reconquest). It is evident that for Zayas, the Spaniard of the Golden Age was first and foremost a gentleman, who demonstrated his qualities as such by willingly going to battle in order to defend the women of Spain, thus setting an example for his peers and his inferiors. Now it seems, the military trappings—the insignia—are a fashion statement, much the same as stockings or hair extensions. The once-fearless fighter now avoids the field of battle, even though the enemy is within the borders of the country; rather, the "gentleman" is concerned with appearing in places of fashion to promenade and to gossip, festooned in "feminine" attire. For Zayas, the changes of fashion indicate a change of heart, of mind-set, of identity, all of which, for her, are bound up in the way men value—or devalue—women. It would seem that women are no longer worth fighting for, or, even more significant, no longer worth dying for. Put bluntly, men who are like women endanger the national interest.

It is evident that for Zayas the qualities of "Spanishness" are being polluted and mutated through changes in fashion. The "feminization" of the male costume is seen to bring about the "feminization" of the male in general, a blurring of gender boundaries which, for Zayas as well as for the government, as manifested in official proclamations, might well result in the downfall of the nation. It is quite clear that what made Spain great was her essential "Spanishness": a warrior nation whose identity involved valor and chivalry on the battlefield, and self-restraint and temperance in the court. The knight is the model, whose insignia and whose costume is worn as an external sign of his nobility, valor, and virtue.

In the passages cited above, María de Zayas in effect reaffirms and revalidates the fast-disappearing masculine role model, and thus by extension, the institutionalized social order that had been in place theretofore. Myths of identity as empire built by a warrior nation, fused with ideals of romances of chivalry and concomitant courtly love, are at odds with the attitudes of her contemporaries, which she despises. She seeks an idealization of women, which, ironically, will come about in centuries to follow and will, in its protectionism, deny to women the very fundamental rights and liberties that Zayas elsewhere expounds as natural for her sex.

Notes

1. All citations in Spanish of Zayas's *Desengaños amorosos* are from the edition prepared by Yllera. Citations in English are taken from Boyer's translation.

2. "As part of their vow of marital chastity the knights were required to abstain from carnal relations on the feast of the Virgin, of Saint John the Baptist, the feasts of the Apostles, and on every fast day required by the rule of Saint Augustine, namely every Friday from the first of September through Pentecost and for the entire period from . . . 8th November until Christmas. Pope Innocent IV dispensed them from the full rigours of the latter rule by lifting the fasting requirement from the 8th November to the first Sunday of Advent if they were at war, and Pope Martin V made voluntary the requirement that they spend those days when they were required to abstain from carnal relations in the convent of the Order. Pope Innocent VIII in 1486 relieved them of all fasting obligations at time of war and also declared that other breaches of the rule would not be considered mortal sin" (Sainty).

Works Cited

Boucher, François. *20,000 Years of Fashion: The History of Costume and Personal Adornment.* New York: Abrams, 1987.

Covarrubias Orozco, Sebastián de. *Tesoro de la lengua castellana o española.* Ed. Felipe C. R. Maldonado and Manuel Camarero. Madrid: Castalia, 1994.

Davis, Fred. *Fashion, Culture, and Identity.* Chicago: University of Chicago Press, 1992.

Harre, Rom. "Identity Projects." *Threatened Identities.* Ed. Glynis M. Breakwell. New York: Wiley, 1983. 31–51.

Hollander, Anne. *Sex and Suits: The Evolution of Modern Dress.* New York: Kodansha International, 1995.

Kimmel, Michael. "Masculinity as Homophobia." *Toward a New Psychology of Gender.* Ed. Mary M. Gergen and Sara N. Davis. New York: Routledge, 1997. 223–44.

Laver, James. *Costume and Fashion: A Concise History.* New York: Thames and Hudson, 1985.

Lorber, Judith. *Paradoxes of Gender.* New Haven: Yale University Press, 1994.

Moeller, Charles. "Military Order of Calatrava." *The Catholic Encyclopedia.* Vol. 3. New York: Encyclopedia Press, 1913. 149–52.

Palacio Atard, Vicente. *Derrota, agotamiento, decadencia, en la España del siglo XVI.* Madrid: Rialp, 1956.

Payne, Stanley G. *A History of Spain and Portugal.* Madison: University of Wisconsin Press, 1973.

Rubin, Nancy. *Isabella of Castille: The First Renaissance Queen.* New York: St. Martin's, 1991.

Sainty, Guy Stair. "The Military Order of Santiago" *Almanach de la cour: Chivalric Orders.* March 17, 2000. <http://www.chivalricorders.org/orders/spanish/santiago.htm >.

Smith, Anthony. "The 'Golden Age' and National Renewal." *Myths and Nationhood.* Ed. Geoffrey Hosking and George Schöpflin. New York: Routledge, 1997. 36–59.

Solomon-Godeau, Abigail. *Male Trouble: A Crisis in Representation.* London: Thames and Hudson, 1997.

Spear, Gary. "Shakespeare's Manly Parts: Masculinity and Effeminacy in *Troilus and Cressida.*" *Shakespeare Quarterly* 44 (1993): 409–22.

Williams, Andrew P. "Soft Women and Softer Men: The Libertine Maintenance of Masculine Identity." *The Image of Manhood in Early Modern Literature: Viewing the Male.* Ed. Andrew P. Williams. Westport: Greenwood, 1999. 95–118.

Zayas y Sotomayor, María. *Desengaños amorosos.* Ed. Alicia Yllera. Madrid: Cátedra, 1983.

———. *The Disenchantments of Love.* Trans. H. Patsy Boyer. Albany: State University of New York Press, 1997.

15

Desire Unbound

Women's Theater of Spain's Golden Age

Lisa Vollendorf

The proliferation of available dramatic texts by Spanish women has confirmed once again that Spain *is* different. In contrast to women's production of closet drama in England and to the sometimes jocular sacred plays written by nuns on the Continent, for example, at least a handful of women dramatists in Spain wrote texts that seem destined for the stage. These plays challenge many fundamental assumptions scholars have made for years about Spanish literature: rather than evoke the seemingly irrational violence of the honor code and articulate male characters' preoccupations with love and honor, the texts deal with women's circumvention and awareness of societal restrictions.

The surge of critical attention to women's drama has given urgency to the task of reevaluating the literary canon, for it serves as a reminder that we need to widen our collective critical lens to incorporate the large body of Spanish women's writing that, to this day, remains understudied and undertaught.[1] The renewed interest in this drama also reminds us that Spain remains on the margins of Early Modern women's studies. In addition to increasing the numbers of Early Modern women's texts taught and studied, we need to embrace theories that will continue to effect a shift in the way that we think about women's cultural production in Early Modern Europe. A sharper focus on women writers and a revision of our critical apparati will necessitate a re-evaluation of all artistic production—by men and women—of the period. As the following analysis of secular women's drama suggests, the integration of Spanish women into the larger field of Early Modern feminist studies promises to enrich our understanding of literature and society in the Renaissance.

The Boundaries of Desire in *Comedia*

So far, very little is known about the Spanish female dramatists themselves, and no evidence has emerged that any female-authored play [*comedia*] was performed as public theater in the *corrales* [theaters]. As Teresa Soufas's engaging "gender-centered reading" of eight plays by women analyzed in *Dramas of Distinction* confirms, women's texts are rich in detail about gender relations (1). Readings of friendship, gender, and love in these gynocentric texts have shown that the patterns and codes of female desire can be read as feminized interventions into the masculinist perspectives of canonical Spanish drama. If we pause to remember that *comedia* itself often is based on the exploration of desire, it becomes immediately clear that plays written by and centered on women offer fascinating material for the consideration of female desire. Unlike many celebrated female characters, the protagonists of female-authored texts often have a choice. In making choices about their erotic pursuits, the characters demonstrate a gynocentrism that privileges women's desire.

An approach that allows for an integration of pertinent critical issues—performance, intertextuality, and difference—might be found by building on current feminist strategies by incorporating queer theory into our analyses.[2] A queer approach oriented toward same-sex relationships highlights the nuances of homosocialism and homoeroticism. It does not require that we claim lesbianism as an identity marker for the Early Modern period; and the choice of the term "homoerotic" (rather than "homosexual") aims to avoid such a collapse of connotations. Many excellent studies on homoeroticism in Early Modern England have shown that a queer approach encourages us to examine same-sex desire and interaction and to read for ways in which women's writing expands what we have heretofore understood to be the limitations placed on female sexuality in the period.

Critics of the English Renaissance have taken up the question of homoeroticism, but less has been written on the topic in Spanish studies. A group of scholars has worked to decipher the codes of male homoeroticism in England (cf. Alan Bray, Mario DiGangi, Jonathan Goldberg, Jeffrey Masten, Alan Sinfield, and Bruce Smith, among others), still fewer have taken on the task of understanding female homoeroticism.[3] Bruce Smith has pinpointed the difficulties inherent in studying female-female desire in a body of literature "written by men to men about men," saying, "If, in these texts, female sexuality in general has only a peripheral place, lesbianism seems almost beyond notice" (28). The reified representation of women's sexuality applies to the Spanish canon as well: nearly all of the texts are written by men and nearly all offer a male perspective on women's sexuality.[4] However, if we examine women-authored texts and follow DiGangi's recommendation to "acknowledge the homoerotic possibilities within the language of friendship" (10), we can untangle the differences between men's and women's representations of these issues and define the configurations of female sexuality in Early Modern Spain.

Women's texts afford us the opportunity to focus on women's self-representation, particularly on women's relationships with each other. In *El muerto disimulado* [*The Feigned Death*], *La traición en la amistad* [*Friendship Betrayed*], and *Valor, agravio y mujer* [*Valor, Offense, Woman*], such a reading shows that these plays' erotic codes can be read as displacing the masculine and violating the norms of male-female relations. These plays do not completely surrender their gynocentrism. In contrast to most male-authored texts, they cling to a woman-centered discourse that undermines dominant codes informing both gender and eroticism. Seeking to decipher the boundaries of female desire, this analysis suggests a framework for reading other women's writing in the period, for it points to the ways in which three women—Angela de Azevedo, María de Zayas, and Ana Caro—present and sometimes sustain alternative, feminized conceptualizations of desire and sexuality.

The genre of comedy follows the predictable path from disorder to apparent order, from the messiness of singledom to the purported stability of marriage. Dawn Smith notes the reassuring quality of this formula, in which audiences know that the plays "will end in marriages, the laws of society will be reimposed" (26). Whether or not we take the final marital pairings as a definitive restoration of order is certainly up for debate. Does the audience (and do we as readers) really believe, at the end of *La dama boba* [*The Foolish Lady*], that the clever women have learned their proper submissive roles and will never speak out again? Does Angela's marriage in *La dama duende* [*The Phantom Lady*] convince us that this heretofore active woman will step easily into the role of passive wife? Dawn Smith addresses the surface simplicity and underlying tensions of the genre: "Today, we appreciate the rich ironies of these plots and suspect that at least some members of the seventeenth-century audience looked beyond the diverting entertainment and conventional happy endings to a more sobering truth" (26). While most obviously found in the restoration of patriarchal hierarchy in the marriage endings, the "sobering truth" about cultural restraints on individuals also can be found in the many subversions and inversions of this hierarchy before the predictable final scenes.[5]

The overriding structures of *comedia* are tied inexorably to the sexual and social conventions of patriarchy. In this very fundamental sense, *comedia* plots and themes comply with traditional Western narrative structures, which have been described as compulsively heterosexual by queer theorist Judith Roof.[6] No matter what the first acts bring in terms of gender transgression, standard plots culminate with heterosexual (that is, male-female) pairings or, at the very least, they present heterosexual ideology as normative and desirable. In *Come as You Are,* Roof seeks a queer or perverse space in traditional narrative. Theorizing the imbrication of narrative with sexuality, she notes that we tend to read "toward the satisfaction of the end" (7). In an effort to explain this propulsion toward heteroideological endings, Roof tries to define the organizing structures of standard plots and locate the moments that are most propitious for deviance.

Like scholars of Early Modern theater, Roof seeks alterity in the middle of the action. She observes that the imposition of patriarchal principles of social organization in narrative endings "both forces *and* enables multiple sexual possibilities in the middle" (16). Elaborating on a strategy that looks to the unfolding of desire as a way to understand social organization, Sally O'Driscoll advocates analyses that "question the closed narrative system of heterosexual desire and read the text for what it can reveal about the construction of normative sexuality" (41).[7] These theoretical perspectives guide my analysis, in which I claim that the focus on women and women's desire in Azevedo, Zayas, and Caro challenges the stability of the heteroideologically bound endings by shifting our eye to the sacrifices demanded of women in the sexual economy.

Pinning Down Sexuality: Angela de Azevedo

These three women's plays pointedly "question the closed narrative system of heterosexual desire" by laying bare the structures of competition and the limitations on women that constitute the underpinnings of the sexual economy. While Angela de Azevedo's *El muerto disimulado* does not deal with female homoeroticism, it challenges the limitations placed on women in the arena of desire. Azevedo's social critique is read here as crossing gender boundaries and criticizing patriarchy; this reading establishes a baseline of social criticism that can be found in women's *comedia* and sets the stage for substantive queer readings of sexual border crossings in Zayas's and Caro's plays.

El muerto disimulado is based on various coincidences that result in the cross-dressed female protagonist falling in love with her brother's putative murderer. The play exploits the themes of competition and violence, pitting daughter against father, brother against sister, and women against each other. Jacinta, whose father threatens to kill her because she refuses to marry the man of his choice, faces violence at the beginning of the play. The cross-dressed protagonist Lisarda, who seeks revenge for the deaths of her father and brother, also must deal with men's violent ways. Soon after appearing on stage dressed as a man, Lisarda/Lisardo has found her brother's killer and, much to her surprise, fallen in love with him. Since the killer, Alvaro, is in love with another woman, she agrees to say that it was she who killed her brother so that Alvaro can go through with his marriage to Jacinta. The third primary conflict of the play also stems from the violent nature of sexuality under patriarchy: the ever-rash Alvaro spends a good part of the play discussing his wish to kill his sister, Beatriz, and her purported lover.

The first act pairs force and competition with sexuality on several levels. Jacinta almost has marriage imposed upon her by her father, love has Lisarda in its hold, and Beatriz claims that sexual desire reigns above all other concerns.[8] All three women put their lives on the line for desire: they encounter serious, even violent, resistance to their valuation of sexual love over familial obligation. Act 1 thus highlights the consequences faced by women who dare to challenge the lack of freedom afforded them by existing social structures. Several dicta can be surmised from these initial scenes: women must marry, even if it is against their will; men rely on violence in matters of honor; and competition governs all relationships. By showing feminized interventions into these familiar patterns of behavior—all of which appear in countless other Golden Age plays—Azevedo exposes the workings of a social structure that denies women a voice and leaves little room for nonviolent reconciliation.

The rest of *El muerto disimulado* works through the basic themes of competition, violence, and desire presented in the first act. All of these issues put into relief the constraints placed on women. Lisarda's brother Clarindo returns home alive and well. Dressed as a woman, he has the two-fold mission of avenging his attempted murder and testing Jacinta's love for him (l. 1426). Cross-dressed characters and resistant women progressively disrupt the social order in the play. Moreover, the authority figures—Rodrigo (Jacinta's father) and Alvaro—continually misjudge and underestimate the women around them. Alvaro's anger over Beatriz's relationship with Alberto reveals the extent to which men control, but fail to understand, women's sexuality. While Rodrigo advocates the marriage between Beatriz and Alberto because "muchos casan por amores" (l. 2002) [many marry for love], Alvaro opposes the match because of supposed improprieties and because of Alberto's lesser fortunes.

The conflicts between women and their male protectors in *El muerto disimulado* point to men's desire to control women. However, this is a female-focused play. As in *La dama duende, No hay burlas con el amor* [*Love Is No Laughing Matter*], and other *comedias,* women's loyalty and ingenuity allow them to achieve their desired matches at the end. Successfully stopping the cycle of violence, Lisarda reveals her identity and her love, begging her brother not to kill Alvaro. Facing death if he refuses to comply, Alvaro accepts the match. Clarindo offers his hand to Jacinta. Finally, Rodrigo steps in to make the match that he has advocated all along: he asks Alvaro to approve of Alberto's marriage to Beatriz. The men previously showed a complete misunderstanding of women's capacity for desire, as both Alvaro and Rodrigo misinterpret their charges' emotions.[9] By the end, however, the women are paired with the men they love, and the men successfully assert their authority by approving the marriages.

Azevedo's representation of the male protectors' failure to understand women articulates a strong critique of the limitations placed on women under patriarchy and of the failings of patriarchy to accommodate women's concerns. The success with which the strong-willed female characters resist male control and influence the outcome of the play validates women's intellectual, physical, and emotional strength. Finally, the forceful nature of marriage matches, the violence associated with gender relations, and the subjection of women to masculinist concerns denaturalize the male-orientation of the structures and values informing sexuality in the Early Modern period.

What Women Want: María de Zayas and Ana Caro

Revealing the structural underpinnings of gender and sexuality, *El muerto disimulado* shows female subjects working in isolation from each other and struggling independently against the sexual economy to achieve their desired matches. This pattern of the isolated feminine stands in stark contrast to the intermingling of women's lives in Zayas's *La traición en la amistad* and Caro's *Valor, agravio y mujer.* Just as competition informs nearly every relationship in Azevedo's text, characters in *La traición* and *Valor, agravio* struggle, often against each other, to gain the objects of their desire. Both Zayas's and Caro's plays constitute feminized responses to the Don Juan myth, so it comes as no surprise that they center on desire and that the heroes obtain their erotic objects. These patterns might go unremarked save for one difference: the heroes are women, and their erotic objects are men. Azevedo reveals the ways in which the sexual economy subordinates and manipulates women; Zayas and Caro flesh out this theme by portraying women characters whose resistance to men's machinations causes them to interact with other women. This glance into a feminized environment creates space for female homoeroticism in both of these plays. While *El muerto disimulado* offers up a decisive critique of gender and desire under patriarchy, *La traición en la amistad* and *Valor, agravio y mujer* beg a queer reading—one that pays attention to the ways women's interactions with each other undermine normative paradigms of female sexuality and desire.

In Zayas's feminized world of friendship and betrayal in *La traición en la amistad,* cooperation among women is validated while competition among them is discouraged. *La traición* deals with the gendered codes of eroticism by focusing on Fenisa, a female Don Juan with an insatiable appetite for love and sex. Fenisa's uncontained and unchecked desire leads her to seduce or attempt to seduce almost every male character in the play. She is every woman's rival, and her betrayal of female friends gives title to the play. In the first scene, when the protagonist Marcia tells Fenisa of her new-found love for Liseo, she also puts Fenisa's friendship to the test, insisting that a real friend would not urge her to stop loving this man (ll. 39–43). Fenisa's defense of friendship is entirely superficial, as her interaction with Marcia reveals. Rather than support Marcia in her "guerra de amor" (l. 37) [war of love], Fenisa attempts to dissuade her because, as she reveals to the audience, she, too, has fallen in love with Liseo after looking at his portrait.

Contemplating her choice of love over friendship, Fenisa actually experiences a twinge of guilt (ll. 163–65). Within moments, the guilt dissipates and Fenisa decides that, in the battle between friendship and love, "cayó la amistad en tierra / y amor victoria apellida" (ll. 173–74) [friendship is defeated and love emerges victorious]. The dichotomy between friendship and desire is established in this first scene, in which Fenisa initiates a series of betrayals. As the play unfolds, Fenisa devises schemes to court Liseo and the other men, while other women—Marcia, Belisa, and Laura—try to maintain their hold on the men of their choice.

It is unusual for a Golden Age play to focus so sharply on women's desire. As Catherine Larson states about Zayas's women characters, they "are proactive and dynamic, challenging the traditional view of women in the *comedia*" ("Reforming" 122). Add to these gripping characterizations the cooperation seen among all the women except Fenisa and we have an exception in the

Golden Age canon: this is a truly feminized play, one in which structures of competition and desire are presented from the female perspective, and in which the audience glimpses the workings of women's friendships. To my knowledge, every critic who has written about *La traición en la amistad* has commented on the importance of women's cooperation and on women's influence on the outcome of the play.[10] More important, these readings flesh out different aspects of gender relations while emphasizing the success with which female characters work together to attain their desired matches in marriage. Indeed, the world is topsy-turvy in Zayas's play, and this is due in large part to the various gender-role switches that occur: women act, men often only react, and even Don Juan himself is manipulated. Explaining the many ways critics have dealt with this complexity, Larson indicates, "It may well be that the most important element of *La traición en la amistad* is that it asks us to ask questions about the nature of relationships between men and women" ("Gender" 134).

La traición en la amistad provides richly suggestive detail about female-female interaction. If we consider women's relationships with each other, the play clearly "asks us to ask questions" about the nature of female homosocialism which, in act 2, expands to include homoeroticism. As mentioned, the opening scene of *La traición* pits female friendship against sexual desire as Fenisa consciously casts Marcia aside so as to pursue Liseo, her chosen man of the moment. The first scene in act 2 contrasts sharply with this exposition, for here we see Marcia ruminating over the intangibility and instability of desire immediately before she is confronted with what seems to be—and could easily be performed as—a highly charged attraction to another woman.

As the second act opens, Marcia delivers a soliloquy about the intense contradictions of love, which makes one love and hate both day and night, seek and fear relief from pain, and desire without knowing what one desires (ll. 863–76). Based on the tension created by opposing terms (love/hate, night/day, reason/daring, et cetera), Marcia's language is typically baroque in its awareness of the unreliability of emotion and language. By fleshing out the unpredictable, elusive nature of desire, this sonnet anticipates the homoerotic scene that follows when Marcia and Belisa receive an unidentified female visitor.

Although the subsequent scene revolves around the visitor's intention of repairing her relationship with a man, the interaction among the three women is marked by eroticized language. Belisa escorts the trembling woman, whose head and face are covered, into her cousin's quarters. Both Marcia and Laura are impressed by the other's appearance. Indeed, they take time to size each other up before speaking directly to each other. Marcia, for example, speaks to Belisa about the woman: "¿No sale, prima, el aurora / con tan grande presunción?" (ll. 891–92) [Cousin, does the day dawn with such presumption?]. Equally courteous and even, perhaps, taken with her hostess, Laura responds that Marcia's beauty is so extreme that she can barely speak: "es vuestro talle extremado; / me ha turbado, y casi estoy / muerta de amores en veros" (ll. 900–902) [Your beauty has disturbed me so much that I could almost fall in love with you myself].[11] Laura's unease is explained by her revelation that Marcia is her rival in love. As Laura explains, Liseo had promised to marry her and now she has come to make the weighty request that Marcia stop returning his favors so that he will comply with his marriage obligation.

If Laura's reaction to Marcia can be explained in terms of rivalry and competition, Marcia and her cousin's charged rhetoric cannot be untangled quite so easily. The fact that Marcia speaks *of* Laura twice before speaking *to* her directly establishes a curious dynamic that continues when the women deliver more asides after addressing each other directly. While Laura continues to muse aloud about her own cowardice, Marcia comments on Laura to her cousin ("Confusa, Belisa, está" [l. 908] [Belisa, she looks positively confused]). Further exchanges about the women's beauty raise our awareness about the power that lies in one's physical appearance and recall the descriptions in act 1, scene 1, of Fenisa and Marcia's experiences of falling in love at first sight with a man.

If Marcia and Laura merely compliment each other, Belisa raises the stakes considerably by employing the rhetoric of courtship: "No hay más bien / que ver, cuando viendo estoy / tal belleza. ¡El cielo os dé / la ventura cual la cara!" (ll. 915–18) [There is nothing better than the sense of sight, since it allows us to witness such beauty. Heaven gave you this face; may it also grant you good fortune]. Laura responds courteously, kissing Belisa's hand in gratitude. However, Marcia interrupts this interaction between the others by abruptly changing the subject back to Laura's visit and demanding that Laura tell her why she has come.

In spite of Marcia's attempt to draw Laura's attention to herself and/or her need to intervene in the overt homoeroticism, Belisa continues to express adulation for Laura. She praises Laura extensively and even goes so far as to cast her admiration in chivalric terms: "Soy vuestra servidora, / y a fe que desde esta hora, / cautiváis mi voluntad" (ll. 938–40) [At your service, and I promise that from this moment on, you can count on my good will]. This is the second time in the scene that Belisa puts herself in the position of a man; she has already said to Laura, "si hombre fuera, yo empleara / en vuestra afición mi fe" (ll. 919–20) [If I were a man, I would put my faith in your love]. Belisa's evident interest in (and even attraction to) Laura highlights the constraints placed on sexuality. By declaring herself Laura's servant and, in terms of courtly love, her deliverer, Belisa simultaneously points both to the boundaries of acceptable desire and of gender roles: it is impossible for her to act publicly on Laura's behalf, an active role reserved for men. Hence the women must develop a covert scheme by which Liseo will make good on his marriage promise to Laura.

The eroticized interaction among the women has provoked different comments from critics. Soufas notes a "brief erotic attraction among" the women (*Dramas* 143) and Susan Paun de García validates the strong feelings among the women as "love in the sense of friendship" (387). However, the homosocial and homoerotic interaction can be seen as having a cumulative effect, one in which the boundaries of women's desire expand to include the possibility of female-female eroticism. Coming on the heels of Marcia's sonnet about the unpredictability of love, and following a first act that revolves around male-female matches, this scene stands out for its feminized eroticism, for its possible homoerotic competition between two women for another woman, and for its almost hyperbolic cooperation among women in the quest to remedy the wrongs of a male-female relationship. This scene breaks down the dichotomy between homosocial friendship and heterosexual love by adding homoeroticism to the erotic choices already present in the play. Indeed, Belisa's declaration—"from this moment on, you can count on my good will"—can be read as sealing the homoeroticism with a pact, suggesting that it will survive beyond an initial scene among the women.

It is clear, however, that homoeroticism does not figure among the permanent erotic choices. The heterosexual impulse inevitably moves the plot and provides its resolution. The subsequent scene between Juan and Belisa restores the primacy of heteroeroticism as Belisa renews her love for Juan. Yet if we consider the homoerotic element as we look at Fenisa, the character who has refused allegiance with women in favor of alliances with as many men as possible, we see that the first scene of act 2 adds an important dimension to Fenisa's exclusion at the end of the play.

Demonized for her sexual choices as well as for her refusal to make sacrifices that other women have been shown making for each other, Fenisa stands alone at the end. The comic figure León goes so far as to offer Fenisa up to the public: "Señores míos, Fenisa, / cual ven sin amantes queda. / Si alguno la quiere, avise / para que su casa sepa" (ll. 2911–14) [Dear Sirs, Fenisa remains without lovers as you can see. If anybody wants her, ask her address of me]. Fenisa's solitude has been variously interpreted as a punishment (for she is not paired with a man and has no female friends), as well as an affirmation of her challenge to the dominant order.[12]

I would suggest that if we consider the homoerotic interaction, we can see that Fenisa is being punished in three fundamental ways: she is excluded from a match with a man, from friendship with women, *and* from the homoerotic possibilities that the scene among Marcia, Belisa, and Laura allows us to imagine. Inasmuch as Fenisa rejects female friendship and opts for heterosexual courtship and sex, she finds herself excluded from the many possibilities of women's friendship and desire. Through its validation of female homosocialism, *La traición en la amistad* expands the boundaries of desire by including female homoeroticism as a legitimate facet of women's relationships with each other. Ultimately, the fleeting homoeroticism in *La traición* is betrayed by the heterosexual imperative that drives the play toward its marriage resolution.

With a plot dependent on female cross-dressing, Ana Caro's *Valor, agravio y mujer* allows for a sustained queer reading that comes undone when the cross-dressed character reveals her female identity. The familiar story lends itself to an exploration of female homoeroticism: seeking to force Don Juan to comply with his promise to marry her, Leonor has cross-dressed and traveled to Brussels, where she finds Juan in love with Estela. The remainder of the play revolves around Leonor/Leonardo's courtship of Estela, a courtship aimed at releasing Juan from the clutches of another woman's love. The end brings several marriages, including the expected match between Leonor and Juan.

The representation of gender and gender relations in *Valor, agravio y mujer* intervenes in dominant codes of conduct, particularly those related to masculinity and heterosexuality. From the beginning, Caro exposes the reliance of masculinity on violence and aggression. The opening scene—in which Estela and her cousin Lisarda are lost in the wilderness during a terrific storm—anticipates the violent actions of the men who will soon enter the stage. While nature is discussed in feminine terms (for example, Estela mentions maternal entrails [l. 43], pregnant clouds [l. 47], and aborted lightning bolts [l. 50]), Mother Nature's violence pales in comparison to the three bandits who tie up the women, rob them, and prepare to do worse damage. Juan's well-timed entrance saves the women from further aggression, and his valiant fighting drives the men away and causes Estela to fall for him.

By presenting women in distress and men as rescuers, the opening scene evokes several gender stereotypes. It is worth noting, however, that the forest scene undermines these stereotypes at the same time that it sets them up. Estela mistakenly assumes that all men are reliable, for when she sees three men approaching, she thanks God for her good fortune (ll. 86–91). Indeed, the very presence of the women (who are dressed as hunters) in the forest during such a storm initially suggests that the women are more adventurous than one might expect. However, the bandits prove dangerous and the women, particularly Estela, need other men to come to the rescue. Expectations are established and upset here, and this gender instability directly relates to the gender play of Leonor's cross-dressing throughout the *comedia*.

Following up on the violence exhibited by several men in the first scene, Leonor explicitly equates masculinity with violence when explaining the existential change effected by Juan's abandonment of her. Clinging to her masculine identity, Leonor denies that it is merely her appearance that has changed: "Yo soy quien soy. / Engañaste si imaginas, / Ribete, que soy mujer; / mi agravio mudó mi ser" (ll. 507–10) [I am who I am. You were fooling yourself if you imagine me to be a woman, Ribete; the offense against me changed my very being]. Leonor demands that her servant Ribete think of her as a man because she has undergone a violent transformation. Having been deceived by a man, Leonor is now a new person. With this new identity she will stop at nothing—including violence (l. 517) and the deception of another woman—to right the wrongs done to her. Leonor is aware of the reliance of masculinity on violence and trickery. She sees herself as having been forced into performing an active, possibly violent masculine role in order to exact revenge.

The fervor with which Leonor goes on to woo Juan's new-found love, Estela, can be read as an equally intense performance of gender. Like the rest of Leonor's performance of masculinity, the courtship of Estela leaves aside aggression and emphasizes the intellect. Aware of Juan's love for Estela, Leonor determines that her salvation lies in an expert performance of courtship. Estela, who refuses all wooers, falls almost immediately for the intriguing new arrival, Leonor/Leonardo. While three men love Estela, Leonor/Leonardo is the only character able to capture and maintain Estela's affection. Immediately following Estela's rejection of Juan and Ludovico ("que ni estoy enamorada, / ni me pretendo casar" [ll. 957–58] [I am not in love, nor do I plan to marry]), Leonor/Leonardo delivers a flowery speech that will accomplish what the men have failed to do: secure Estela's love. After showing some initial resistance to Leonor/Leonardo's rhetoric, Estela proclaims, "¡Qué bien sabéis persuadir!" (l. 1073) [How well you know how to persuade!]. Finally, Leonor/Leonardo becomes the first man whom Estela invites into her life.

This interaction between the women brims with multiple possibilities and problems. To begin with, Leonor's conscious manipulation of another woman is done in the service of heterosexuality, for Leonor's primary goal is to find a way to force Juan to marry her. In this way, Caro uses Leonor's machinations to expose the sacrifices made by women in the sexual economy. Another problem rests with the depiction of Estela as fickle in love. In a short time, she falls in love with Juan, purports to reject him along with the prince, and then falls for Leonor/Leonardo. In short, she is not portrayed as the most trustworthy character.

But Estela's fervent and continued interest in Leonor/Leonardo should give us pause. In terms of the dynamics between women in this particular scene, two interpretations present themselves. As Soufas has noted, the scene can be read as women's "mutual recognition of what is truly appealing to them with regard to love and devotion" (*Dramas* 120). That is, it can be read as a scene in which two women model their notion of ideal heterosexual courtship. Or, if we continue to read for homoeroticism, this scene, and Estela's expressions of love that follow, can be read as women's expansion of the boundaries of desire, as women's expression of what they want *from each other* in love. The instability and unreliability of gender presented in the initial scenes sets up this expansive representation of women's desire. As I will argue, the final scene rests uneasily on the trope of the instability of desire.

Soufas's interpretation of modeling heterosexuality leads her to the conclusion that "Caro does not build into her plot any overt homoerotic substructure for Estela and Leonor" (*Dramas* 120). The pairings of Juan and Leonor, Fernando and Estela, and Prince Ludovico and Lisarda at the end of the play certainly support this conclusion. However, if we keep our eye on the homoerotic dimension, it is possible to locate a sustained homoeroticism that culminates in an awkward interaction between Estela and Leonor/Leonardo in the final moments of the play. While Estela remains a devoted lover until the very end, Leonor devotes herself to getting Juan to marry her and to helping Prince Ludovico court Estela.[13] This uneven dynamic—by which Estela's desire increases and Leonor's is increasingly displaced—creates the final tension of the play. With Juan's marriage promise secured through trickery and with broken promises now mended, Leonor gains access to femininity once again. To the surprise of the others, she exits the stage as a man and enters dressed as a beautiful woman ("dama bizarra" [p. 193]). Leonor pardons the men for their precipitous and unfounded claims about her fickleness in love. Then she explains her situation and verbally reclaims her female self: "Leonardo fui, mas ya vuelvo / a ser Leonor" (ll. 2723–24) [I was Leonardo, but now I return to being Leonor].

This proclamation of identity sets up a key moment. While Juan and the men are able to recognize the change (an obvious one given Leonor's garments and the explanation of her actions), Estela remains unconvinced. In the first and final overtly homoerotic interaction—the first time that both women know the biological sex of the other, Estela asks poignantly, "Leonardo, ¿así me engañabas?" (l. 2730) [Leonardo, you were deceiving me so?]. Leonor responds, "Fue fuerza, Estela" (l. 2731) [It was necessary, Estela]. In other words, Leonor justifies the betrayal in terms of the very violence ("fuerza") that, by her own account, changed her very being ("mudó mi ser"). This exchange makes room for Estela's match with another man. This male-female pairing is couched in terms of the relationship between the two women. Estela answers Leonor with a decision to marry Leonor's brother Fernando. Rather than direct her declaration to Fernando himself, Estela continues to speak to Leonor: "Quedemos / hermanas, Leonor hermosa" (ll. 2732–33) [Let us remain sisters, lovely Leonor]. With this, she asks Leonor's brother for his hand.

Fraught with tension, this final scene leaves much room for interpretation. The sacrifice of the homoerotic bond can be said to coincide with the rapid heterosexual pairings that often occur at the end of *comedia*. Equally important is the success with which Leonor's machinations obscure the homoerotic tension: pleased with Leonor's tight control of her own fate, the audience or the reader responds by applauding her ingenuity. However, what are we to make of Estela's choice of Fernando, a man in whom she has expressed no interest whatsoever, as a marriage partner? Like Estela's refusal to recognize Leonor/Leonardo's feminine identity, the choice of Fernando as a husband is a sign of resistance, an attempt to convert the temporary bond between the two women into a permanent one. The imminent disappearance of the female-female erotic bond suggests that, like Leonor's own abrupt gender transformations, eroticism itself is changeable.

Female homoeroticism is the least stable element in the play, for it necessarily must disappear for the text to come to a close. This absorption of unconventional desire can be explained, as Roof's study demonstrates, by the drive toward heterosexual endings. For the Early Modern context, Valerie Traub describes the tendency to represent female-female eroticism as fleeting: "Female homoeroticism is thus figurable not only in terms of the always already lost, but the always about to be betrayed" (72).[14] The erotic bond between Leonor/Leonardo and Estela is forfeited to the heterosexual relationship between Leonor and Juan. By lingering on the very moment of forfeiture, the text prolongs the eroticism and highlights the act of betrayal. *Valor, agravio y mujer* thus sustains female homoeroticism until the final moments of the play, and shows women securing a sororal relationship with each other as a permanent substitute for their fleeting homoerotic bond.

Desire Unbound: Reading Women's Texts

In these plays, Angela de Azevedo, María de Zayas, and Ana Caro push the boundaries of social criticism usually found in *comedia* by re-orienting our attention toward women. *El muerto disimulado* exposes the ways in which women are pinned down by patriarchal structures informing sexuality. Azevedo's play also shows that men fail to understand women's compromised position within these structures. Zayas and Caro focus on the variations of women's desire: *La traición en la amistad* and *Valor, agravio y mujer* explore various possibilities of women's relationships with each other. All of the plays show women's understanding of the behavior and sacrifices demanded of them in the marriage market. If Azevedo exposes men's failings and women's limited options in desire, Zayas gives us a glimpse into the cooperative and occasionally erotic aspects of women's homosocialism. Caro offers the most expansive vision of female sexuality by exploiting homoeroticism until the final moment and by lingering on the forfeiture of the female-female bond. We can speculate on the potential for performative subversion in these plays, each of which offers up moments that ostensibly or in point of fact explore same-sex eroticism: Lisarda/Lisardo gazes lovingly at Alvaro; Marcia, Belisa, and Laura praise each other extensively; and Estela pledges her love to Leonor/Leonardo. While we cannot precisely know the intelligibility of such desire from a seventeenth-century audience member's perspective, it is clear that, like other disorderly conduct in *comedia*, homoeroticism is meant to be contained by the marriage ending.[15]

Read as a group, these texts delineate women's role in a heterosexual script that is both a literary tradition and a cultural reality. The pressures exerted on women by this script are made patent through the interworkings of competition, violence, and desire. Through strong female characters and a focus on female perspectives, the authors critique the tenuous position occupied by women in the sexual economy. If we read these plays heterosexually—that is, toward the expected marriage ending and toward understanding the relationships between men and women—we gloss over the multiple manifestations of women's desire and the various expressions of women's sexuality.

We also miss the shifts that occur in the structures of competition and substitution as women who seek to fulfill their own desire assist, deceive, and even court each other. Free from the filter of the male author's pen, these women-authored texts offer up nuanced depictions of women's friendship and expansive representations of female desire. Such tantalizing, sometimes daring depictions point to numerous possibilities—of the existence of intelligible female homoerotic codes and of women's protest against cultural bias—that promise to enrich our current perceptions of gender, sexuality, and creative production in Early Modern Europe.

Notes

This project was completed with the support of a summer research grant from Wayne State University and the helpful input of Patsy Boyer, Denise Buell, Sidney Donnell, Kate Regan, and Alison Weber.

1. Modern editions of women's poetry and prose include *Tras el espejo la musa escribe* (Olivares and Boyce); *Untold Sisters* (Arenal and Schlau); and *Zayas and Her Sisters I* (Campbell and Whitenack). For editions of female-authored plays, see Arenal and Schlau, Teresa Soufas, and Hegstrom and Larson's Zayas edition. In spite of such availability, Brown and Johnson found that women's texts remain nearly absent from Ph.D. reading lists in the United States. For more on the challenges of women's literary history, see Cruz ("Feminism"), Gorfkle ("Re-Staging"), Larson ("Reforming"), Vollendorf, and Williamsen.

2. I gesture to the theorists I refer to here by using the term "queer studies," but I want to emphasize that I agree with Butler's refutation of the argument (made in such high profile publications as the *Lesbian and Gay Studies Reader*) that sex is the domain of queer studies and gender the domain of feminism. As Butler asserts, feminism is directly concerned with "contest(ing) the heterosexual matrix" (10).

3. Callaghan has noted the difficulty of deciphering women's desire (278). Traub's *The Renaissance of Lesbianism* stands out as the most comprehensive study on the topic to date.

4. Analyses of Iberian homoeroticism usually treat male-male relations (cf. Cruz "'Homo ex Machina'"; Heiple; Quiñones Vélez). Bravo-Villasante, Donnell, Gorfkle ("Re-Constituting"), *Lesbianism and Homosexuality* (Delgado and Saint-Saëns), and *Queer Iberia* (Blackmore and Hutcheson) consider same-sex pairings and women's eroticism.

5. See Blue and Friedman for more on *comedia* endings.

6. I use the term "heterosexual" as a way to describe male-female pairings (and the quest for consummation of male-female desire) that occur repeatedly in *comedia*.

7. O'Driscoll has also pointed to "the fiction of normal sexuality, the happy companionate marriage, . . . [which is] established in opposition to the chaotic 'rich

stew' of sexual choices that must be pushed into the margins and labeled as deviant" (39). Like scholars of the Renaissance (cf. DiGangi; Traub; Bruce Smith), Farwell focuses on textual instability (3).

8. Beatriz says: "siempre obligan más / que la sangre amantes veras" (ll. 1200–1201) [True lovers always oblige more than mere blood]. Quotes from Azevedo and Caro are taken from Soufas's *Women's Acts*. Quotes from Zayas come from Hegstrom and Larson's bilingual critical edition. All other translations from the Spanish are my own.

9. Rodrigo sees Jacinta as deceptive, when in fact she is loyal to her lover (ll. 2046–48). Alvaro makes a similar mistake when he asserts that Beatriz has no preferences of her own (ll. 3056–57).

10. Larson ("Gender"), Maroto Camino, Hegstrom Oakey, Stroud ("Love"), Rodríguez Garrido, Soufas (*Dramas* and "María de Zayas's [Un]Conventional Play"), Wilkins, and Wyszynski have commented on women's cooperation, friendship, and influence in the play.

11. I have followed Soufas's punctuation in lines 900–902.

12. Wilkins and Stroud ("Love") see the ending as a punishment, while Soufas ("María de Zayas's [Un]Conventional Play" 51) and Hegstrom Oakey (60) suggest that Zayas uses Fenisa to show that independent women have no place in *comedia*. Larson attributes the possibility for these different interpretations to the play's uncertain closure ("Gender" 133–37). The translation for lines 2911–14 is mine.

13. For discussions on metatheatricality and performance in *Valor, agravio y mujer*, see Cortez, Gorfkle ("Re-Staging"), Mujica, and Soufas ("Ana Caro's Re-Evaluation").

14. Also see Castle's *The Apparitional Lesbian* for more on homoeroticism's fleeting appearances in literature.

15. Traub has suggested that the existence of erotic interactions between women characters on the English stage was possible because female homoeroticism "did not signify" (80).

Works Cited

Arenal, Electa, and Stacey Schlau, eds. *Untold Sisters: Hispanic Nuns in Their Own Works*. Trans. Amanda Powell. Albuquerque: University of New Mexico Press, 1989.

Azevedo, Angela de. *El muerto disimulado. Women's Acts: Plays by Women Dramatists of the Golden Age*. Ed. Teresa Soufas. Lexington: University of Kentucky Press, 1997. 91–132.

Blackmore, Josiah, and Gregory Hutcheson, eds. *Queer Iberia. Sexualities, Cultures, and Crossings from the Middle Ages to the Renaissance*. Durham, N.C.: Duke University Press, 1999.

Blue, William R. *Spanish Comedies and Historical Contexts in the 1620s*. University Park: Pennsylvania State University Press, 1996.

Bravo-Villasante, Carmen. *La mujer vestida de hombre en el teatro español: siglos XVI-XVII.* 1955. Reprint, Madrid: Mayo de Oro, 1988.

Bray, Alan. *Homosexuality in Renaissance England.* New York: Columbia University Press, 1982.

Brown, Joan L., and Crista Johnson. "Required Readings: The Canon in Spanish and Spanish American Literature." *Hispania* 81.1 (March 1998): 1–9.

Butler, Judith. "Against Proper Objects." *Differences* 6.2–3 (1994): 1–26.

Callaghan, Dympna. "The Terms of Gender: 'Gay' and Feminist Edward II." *Feminist Readings of Early Modern Culture: Emerging Subjects.* Ed. Valerie Traub, M. Lindsay Kaplan, and Dympna Callaghan. Cambridge: Cambridge University Press, 1996. 275–301.

Campbell, Gwyn, and Judith A. Whitenack, eds. *Zayas and Her Sisters, 1: An Anthology of Novelas by Seventeenth-Century Spanish Women.* Asheville, N.C.: Pegasus, 2000.

Caro Mallén de Soto, Ana. *Valor, agravio y mujer. Women's Acts: Plays by Women Dramatists of the Golden Age.* Ed. Teresa Soufas. Lexington: University of Kentucky Press, 1997. 163–94.

Castle, Terry. *The Apparitional Lesbian.* New York: Columbia University Press, 1993.

Cortez, Beatriz. "El travestismo de Rosaura en *La vida es sueño* y de Leonor en *Valor, agravio y mujer:* el surgimiento de la agencialidad femenina y la desnaturalización del binarismo del género." *Bulletin of the Comediantes* 52.2 (1998): 371– 85.

Cruz, Anne. "Feminism, Psychoanalysis, and the Search for the (M)other in Early Modern Spain." *Indiana Journal of Hispanic Literature* 8 (Spring 1996): 31–54.

———. "'Homo ex Machina?': Male bonding in Calderón's *A secreto agravio, secreta venganza.*" *Forum for Modern Language Studies* 25.2 (1989): 154–66.

Delgado, María José, and Alain Saint-Saëns, eds. *Lesbianism and Homosexuality in Spanish Golden Age Literature and Society.* New Orleans: University Press of the South, 1999.

DiGangi, Mario. *The Homoerotics of Early Modern Drama.* Cambridge: Cambridge University Press, 1997.

Donnell, Sidney. "Between Night and Day: Aurora or the Transvestite Achilles in Monroy y Silva's *El caballero dama.*" *Romance Language Annual* 7 (1995): 450–55.

Farwell, Marilyn. *Heterosexual Plots and Lesbian Narratives.* New York: New York University Press, 1996.

Friedman, Edward. "'Girl Gets Boy?': A Note on the Value of Exchange in the *Comedia.*" *Bulletin of the Comediantes* 39.1 (Summer 1987): 75–83.

Goldberg, Jonathan, ed. *Queering the Renaissance.* Durham, N.C.: Duke University Press, 1994.

———. *Sodometries: Renaissance Texts, Modern Sexualities.* Stanford: Stanford University Press, 1992.

Gorfkle, Laura. "Re-Constituting the Feminine in 'Amar sólo por vencer.'" *María de Zayas: The Dynamics of Discourse*. Ed. Amy Williamsen and Judith Whitenack. Madison, N.J.: Farleigh Dickinson University Press, 1995. 75–89.

————. "Re-Staging Femininity in Ana Caro's *Valor, agravio y mujer.*" *Bulletin of the Comediantes* 48.1 (Summer 1996): 25–36.

Hegstrom Oakey, Valerie. "The Fallacy of False Dichotomy in María de Zayas's *Traición en la amistad.*" *Bulletin of the Comediantes* 46.1 (Summer 1994): 59–70.

Hegstrom, Valerie, ed., and Catherine Larson, trans. *La traición en la amistad/ Friendship Betrayed.* María de Zayas y Sotomayor. Lewisburg, Pa.: Bucknell University Press, 1999.

Hegstrom, Valerie, and Amy Williamsen, eds. *Engendering the Early Modern Stage*. New Orleans: University Press of the South, 1999.

Heiple, Daniel. "Lope de Vega Explores Homoerotic Desire." *Selected Proceedings: Louisiana Conference on Hispanic Languages and Literatures*. Ed. Joseph Ricapito. Baton Rouge: Louisiana State University Press, 1994. 121–31.

Larson, Catherine. "Gender, Reading, and Intertextuality: Don Juan's Legacy in María de Zayas's *La traición en la amistad.*" *Inti: Revista de literatura hispánica* 40–41 (Fall 1994–Spring 1995): 129–38.

————. "Reforming the Golden Age Dramatic Canon: Women's Writing, Women's Voice, and the Question of Value." *Gestos* 7.14 (November 1992): 117–25.

Maroto Camino, Mercedes. "María de Zayas and Ana Caro: The Space of Woman's Solidarity in the Spanish Golden Age." *Hispanic Review* 67.1 (Winter 1999): 1–16.

Masten, Jeffrey. *Textual Intercourse: Collaboration, Authorship, and Sexualities in Renaissance Drama*. Cambridge: Cambridge University Press, 1997.

Mujica, Barbara. "Women Directing Women: Ana Caro's *Valor, agravio y mujer* as Performance Text." *Engendering the Early Modern Stage*. Ed. Valerie Hegstrom and Amy Williamsen. New Orleans: University Press of the South, 1999. 19–50.

O'Driscoll, Sally. "Outlaw Readings: Beyond Queer Theory." *Signs* 22.1 (Autumn 1996): 30–51.

Olivares, Julián, and Elizabeth S. Boyce, eds. *Tras el espejo la musa escribe*. México, D.F.: Siglo Veintiuno, 1993.

Paun de García, Susan. "*Traición en la amistad de María de Zayas.*" *Anales de literatura española* 6 (1988): 377–90.

Quiñones Vélez, Harry. "Monstrous Friendship: The Dynamics of Homosocialism." *Journal of Interdisciplinary Studies* 7.1 (1995): 45–56.

Rodríguez Garrido, José A. "El ingenio en la mujer: *La traición en la amistad* de María de Zayas entre Lope de Vega y Huarte de San Juan." *Bulletin of the Comediantes* 49.2 (Winter 1997): 357–73.

Roof, Judith. *Come as You Are*. New York: Routledge, 1996.

Sinfield, Alan. *Cultural Politics, Queer Readings*. Philadelphia: University of Pennsylvania Press, 1994.

Smith, Bruce. *Homosexual Desire in Shakespeare's England*. Chicago: University of Chicago Press, 1991.

Smith, Dawn. "Introduction: The Perception of Women in the Spanish *Comedia.*" *The Perception of Women in Spanish Theater of the Golden Age.* Ed. Anita Stoll and Dawn Smith. Lewisburg, Pa.: Bucknell University Press, 1991. 17–29.

Soufas, Teresa. "Ana Caro's Re-Evaluation of the *mujer varonil.*" *The Perception of Women in Spanish Theater of the Golden Age.* Ed. Anita Stoll and Dawn Smith. Lewisburg, Pa.: Bucknell University Press, 1991. 85–106.

———. *Dramas of Distinction.* Lexington: University of Kentucky Press, 1997.

———. "María de Zayas's (Un)Conventional Play, *La traición en la amistad.*" *The Golden Age Comedia: Text, Theory, and Performance.* Ed. Charles Ganelin and Howard Mancing. West Lafayette, Ind.: Purdue University Press, 1994. 148–64.

———, ed. *Women's Acts: Plays by Women Dramatists of the Golden Age.* Lexington: University of Kentucky Press, 1997.

Stoll, Anita, and Dawn Smith, eds. *The Perception of Women in Spanish Theater of the Golden Age.* Lewisburg, Pa.: Bucknell University Press, 1991.

Stroud, Matthew. "La literatura y la mujer en el Barroco: *Valor, agravio y mujer* de Ana Caro." *Actas del VIII Congreso de la Asociación Internacional de Hispanistas.* Ed. A. David Kossoff, et al. Madrid: Ediciones Istmo, 1986. 605–12.

———. "Love, Friendship, and Deceit in *La traición en la amistad* by María de Zayas." *Neophilologus* 69 (1985): 539–47.

Traub, Valerie. "The (In)Significance of Lesbian Desire in Early Modern England." *Queering the Renaissance.* Ed. Jonathan Goldberg. Durham, N.C.: Duke University Press, 1994. 62–83.

———. *The Renaissance of Lesbianism in Early Modern England.* Cambridge: Cambridge University Press, forthcoming.

Vollendorf, Lisa. "The Future of Early Modern Women's Studies: The Case of Same-Sex Friendship and Desire in Zayas and Carvajal." *Arizona Journal of Hispanic Cultural Studies* 4 (2000): 265–84.

Wilkins, Constance. "Subversion through Comedy?: Two Plays by Sor Juana Inés de la Cruz and María de Zayas." *The Perception of Women in Spanish Theater of the Golden Age.* Ed. Anita Stoll and Dawn Smith. Lewisburg, Pa.: Bucknell University Press, 1991. 107–20.

Williamsen, Amy. "Re-Writing in the Margins: Caro's *Valor, agravio y mujer* as Challenge to Dominant Discourse." *Bulletin of the Comediantes* 44.1 (Summer 1992): 21–30.

Wyszynski, Matthew. "Friendship in María de Zayas's *La traición en la amistad.*" *Bulletin of the Comediantes* 50.1 (Summer 1998): 21–33.

Zayas y Sotomayor, María de. *La traición en la amistad / Friendship Betrayed.* Ed. Valerie Hegstrom. Trans. Catherine Larson. Lewisburg, Pa.: Bucknell University Press, 1999.

Contributors

Joan F. Cammarata is professor of Spanish at Manhattan College. Specializing in the literature of Early Modern Spain, she has authored the book *Mythological Themes in the Works of Garcilaso de la Vega* and has published articles on Teresa de Cartagena, St. Teresa of Ávila, Garcilaso de la Vega, and Cervantes. She is currently preparing a manuscript on the epistolary production of St. Teresa. She is past president of the Northeast Modern Language Association.

William H. Clamurro is Roe R. Cross Distinguished Professor at Emporia State University in Kansas where he is professor of Spanish and chair of foreign languages. He is the author of two books, *Language and Ideology in the Prose of Quevedo* and *Beneath the Fiction: The Contrary Worlds of Cervantes's "Novelas ejemplares,"* as well as several articles on Quevedo, Cervantes, and other Spanish Golden Age writers. He is currently working on a study of the picaresque.

Deborah Compte joined the faculty at the College of New Jersey in 1990 and is currently acting dean of the School of Culture and Society, after serving as chair of the Department of Modern Languages. She has published studies on Lope de Vega's pastoral drama, pastoral elements in his *Novelas a Marcia Leonarda,* and on Tirso de Molina's *La fingida Arcadia.* Her current research interests include María de Zayas's articulation of a female pastoral voice, as well as cross-dressing as an emblem of transcultural problematics in seventeenth-century Spain.

Frederick A. de Armas, formerly Edwin Erle Sparks Professor of Spanish and Comparative Literature and fellow of the Institute for the Arts and Humanistic Studies at the Pennsylvania State University, where he served as co-editor of *Penn State Studies in Romance Literatures* and associate editor of *Com-*

parative Literature Studies, is now Andrew W. Mellon Professor in Humanities in the Department of Romance Languages and Literatures at the University of Chicago. His books and edited collections on Golden Age Spanish theater include *The Invisible Mistress: Aspects of Feminism and Fantasy in the Golden Age, The Return of Astraea: An Astral-Imperial Myth in Calderón, The Prince in the Tower: Perceptions of "La vida es sueño," Heavenly Bodies: The Realms of "La estrella de Sevilla,"* and *Cervantes, Raphael and the Classics.*

Susan Paun de García, associate professor of Spanish at Denison University, specializes in Spanish seventeenth-century prose fiction and the theater of seventeenth- and eighteenth-century Spain. Her recent publications have focused on the novelas of María de Zayas and the *comedia,* including a critical edition of two plays by José de Cañizares. Her current research examines gender performativity and ventriloquism in the *comedias* of Cañizares.

Rainer H. Goetz is associate professor of Spanish in the Department of Foreign Languages and Literatures and assistant dean of the College of Arts and Sciences at Appalachian State University. His research interests revolve around the prose literature of the Spanish Golden Age, specifically autobiography and the picaresque genre. His publications in that field include several articles and a monograph, *Spanish Golden Age Autobiography in Its Context.*

Louis Imperiale is professor of Spanish literature at the University of Missouri-Kansas City. In addition to several essays published on Cervantes, Lope de Vega, Gutierre de Cetina, Francisco López de Ubeda, and Cristóbal de Villalón, he has written *El contexto dramático de "La Lozana andaluza," La Roma clandestina de Francisco Delicado y Pietro Aretino,* and *"La Lozana andaluza" a través de los siglos.*

Monica Leoni is assistant professor of Spanish language and literature in the Department of Spanish and Latin American Studies, University of Waterloo, Ontario, Canada. She is the author of *Outside, Inside, Aside: Dialoguing with the Gracioso in Spanish Golden Age Theatre.* Her research has focused on the politics of laughter in the Early Modern theater of Spain, but her attention has recently turned to rhetorical devices found in the works of Early Modern women writers. Leoni's articles have appeared in *Scripta Mediterranea* and *Bulletin of the Comediantes.*

Barbara Mujica is professor of Spanish at Georgetown University, where she teaches Early Modern Spanish literature. Her books include *Sophia's Daughters: Women Writers of Early Modern Spain* (forthcoming); *El texto puesto en escena,* edited with Anita Stoll; *Texto y espectáculo; Looking at the Comedia in the Year of the Quincentennial,* edited with Sharon Voros; *Et in Arcadia Ego,* authored with Bruno Damiani; *Iberian Pastoral Characters* and *Calderón's Characters: An Existential Point of View.* She has published eight literary anthologies and her articles have appeared in numerous journals and anthologies. She is also author of four novels, *The Deaths of Don Bernardo, Affirmative Actions!, Frida,* and *The Other Sister* (forthcoming) as well as two collections of short stories, *Sanchez across the Street* and *Far from My Mother's Home.* She has won several awards, including the E. L. Doctorow International Fiction Competition, the Pangolin Prize, and the Theodore Christian Hoepfner Award.

Carolyn Nadeau is associate professor of Spanish at Illinois Wesleyan University, where she specializes in Golden Age literature and culture. Her research interests include feminist readings on classical figures in *Don Quijote,* the role of the mother in sixteenth-century prose, and food presentation in Golden Age theater. In addition to articles on Cervantes, Antonio de Guevara, and Lope de Rueda, she is the author of *Women of the Prologue: Imitation, Myth and Magic in "Don Quixote I."*

John C. Parrack is assistant professor of Spanish at the University of Central Arkansas where he specializes in medieval and Golden Age Spanish literature and culture. His research interests include medieval hermeneutics, the emergence of female subjectivity, and the development of picaresque discourse. He is currently working on the relationship between Mateo Alemán's *Ortografía castellana* and the *Guzmán de Alfarache.*

Joseph V. Ricapito is the Joseph S. Yenni Distinguished Professor of Italian Studies at Louisiana State University, where he teaches Spanish, Italian, and comparative literature. He has published widely on the Spanish picaresque genre, and the picaresque in a comparative context. His edition of the *Lazarillo de Tormes* is very much in use. He has published on spiritual literature in Spain in the sixteenth century, especially on Alfonso de Valdés. Most recently, he has published two books on Cervantes's *Novelas ejemplares* and is currently doing research on a book on Cervantes's *Don Quijote.*

Anita K. Stoll is professor of Spanish and chair of the Department of Modern Languages at Cleveland State University. Her major research interests are the Spanish Golden Age and contemporary Mexican literature. She has published articles on pedagogy, twentieth-century Mexican literature, Tirso de Molina, and Lope de Vega. Her books include a critical edition of Lope's *La noche de San Juan; The Perception of Women in the Spanish Theater of the Golden Age,* with Dawn L. Smith; *A Different Reality: Studies on the Work of Elena Garro; Vidas paralelas: El teatro español y el teatro isabelino: 1580–1680;* and *El texto puesto en escena,* edited with Barbara Mujica.

Sara A. Taddeo is an independent scholar whose research focuses on women's voices in theater from the fifteenth through the early twentieth century. She received her B.A. in Spanish and Latin American Studies from Barnard College, an M.A. in Spanish from the University of Texas/Austin, and an M.A. and Ph.D. in comparative literature from the University of Pennsylvania.

Lisa Vollendorf is assistant professor of Spanish at Wayne State University. A specialist in women's writing and feminist theory, she is the author of *Reclaiming the Body: María de Zayas's Early Modern Feminism* and the editor of *Recovering Spain's Feminist Tradition,* a volume on feminism from medieval times to the present. Recipient of the Newberry Library's Monticello Fellowship and an Ahmanson/Getty Postdoctoral Fellowship at UCLA's Clark Library, she is preparing a manuscript on women's culture in Spain.

Sharon D. Voros is professor in the Language Studies Department at the United States Naval Academy and author of *Petrarch and Garcilaso: A Linguistic Approach to Style* (under the name Ghertman) and *Looking at the Comedia in the Year of the Quincentennial,* edited with Barbara Mujica. Her most recent publications include studies on Leonor de la Cueva y Silva, Lope de Vega, and Pedro Calderón. She is also treasurer for the Association of Hispanic Classical Theater and a member of the Modern Language Association Divisional Executive Committee on Sixteenth- and Seventeenth-Century Spanish Drama.

Index

Admiratio, 111–12

Aercke, Kristiaan, 115, 120

Ágreda, Sor María de Jesús de, 121, 253

Alonso, Dámaso, 160, 164, 171, 174

Amplificatio, 122, 128

Apophaticism, 59–60, 66–67

Arenal, Electa, 119, 123

Ariosto, Ludovico: *Orlando furioso*, 184–86

Aristophanes: *Lysistrata*, 143

Aristotle, 2, 28, 42, 58, 109

Artemidorus, Daldianus: *Oneirocritica [The Interpretation of Dreams]*, 4, 9, 148–49

Augustine, Saint: *Confessions*, 62, 64, 95

Avila, Juan de, 57

Avila, Julián de, 57

Azevedo, Angela de

—Works: *Dicha y desdicha del juego [Good and Ill Fortune in Gaming]* (arranged marriages in, 10, 146–47, 150; astrology in, 153–54, 156; devil in, 149–50, 154, 156; dowry in, 10, 147; dreams in, 10, 147–50, 152, 154–55; feminine desire in, 10, 147, 149–50, 152; kledonomancy in, 10, 147, 152–53, 155–56; physiognomy in, 147, 150, 151, 156; signatures in, 10, 147, 152–53, 156; Virgin Mary in, 148–51, 154–56); *El muerto disimulado [The Feigned Death]* (cross-dressing in, 146, 275–76; marriage in, 274, 276–77; patriarchal structures in, 14, 276, 278, 286; sexuality in, 15, 276); *La margarita del Tajo que dio nombre a Santarén [The Pearl of the Tagus River Who Gave Her Name to Santaren]*, 147

Baltasar Carlos, Prince, 118

Baroque, 108–10, 115, 117, 120, 128, 139, 141, 164, 166, 195. *See also* Góngora, Luis de

Boccaccio, Giovanni, 186, 195, 218, 223, 239; *Corbaccio*, 36

Breast-feeding. *See* Mother

Bruto, Giovanni, 210n.8

Buesso, Eugenia, 110, 128

Butler, Judith, 287n.2

Calderón de la Barca, Pedro, 115, 126, 153; *tapada* [veiled woman], 9, 136, 139–42. *See also* Molina, Tirso de

—Works: *Casa con dos puertas [House with Two Doors]*, 136, 139; *Don Quijote*, 111; *El escondido y la tapada [The Hidden Man and the Veiled Woman]*, 136, 140; *El galán fantasma [The Phantom Lover]*, 155; *La dama duende [The Phantom Lady]*, 136, 139–40, 274, 277; *Mañanas de abril y mayo [Mornings of April and May]*, 9, 136, 140; *No hay burlas con el amor [Love Is No Laughing Matter]*, 277

Calvin, John, 56–57

Cammarata, Joan, 61, 70, 105n.18, 129n.7

Caravajal y Saavedra, Mariana de: *Navidades de Madrid y noches entretenidas*

Caravajal y Saavedra—*continued*
[*Christmas in Madrid and Enjoyable
Nights*]: "Amar sin saber a quien" ["Loving Without Knowing Whom"], 220,
228 (bourgeois class in, 12, 221, 229); "El
amante venturoso" ["Fortunate Lovers"],
213, 221; "El esclavo de su esclavo"
["The Slave of His Own Slave"] (enclosure in, 12; everyday life in, 220, 229;
frame-tale in, 218, 221, 223–25; husbands
in, 12, 222); "La dicha de Doristea"
["Doristea's Bliss"], 220, 225; "La industria vence desdenes" ["Ingenuity Conquers Scorn"], 220–21, 227; "La Venus de
Ferrara" ["The Venus of Ferrara"], 225,
227 (marriage in, 12, 221, 224, 229,
230n.4; mother in, 213–15, 219, 224, 229;
narrative voice in, 219–21, 224; Other in,
12, 216–17; phallogocentric power in, 12,
230); "Quién bien obra siempre acierta"
["He Who Acts Well Is Always Right"],
219, 225 (self-referentiality in, 12; widows in, 220, 222–24, 226); "Zelos vengan
desprecios" ["Scorn Avenged by Jealousy"], 220, 228
Caro Mallén de Soto, Ana: *décima musa*
[tenth muse], 116; imperialism, 8, 113–15,
117, 119, 128; patronage, 8, 115–16, 119,
122, 124, 128; propaganda, 8, 128; Seville,
109, 112–14, 119–20, 124, 126
—Works: *Contexto de las reales fiestas que
se hizieron en palacio del Buen Retiro*
[*Text of the Royal Festivities Held in the
Palace of the Buen Retiro*], 110, 117 (authorship of, 8, 122; costs of festivities,
121; dedications in, 118–20, mythological
allusions in, 118–19, 122–23, 27;
regimiento de príncipes [advice to
princes] in, 120–21, 124; self-effacing
rhetoric in, 116, 127); *El conde
Partinuplés* [*The Count of Partinuples*],
109, 111–12; *Fiesta y octava con motivo
de los sucesos en Flandes* [*Festival and
Octave Celebrated for the Events in
Flanders*], 110; *Relación de fiestas por los
mártires del Japón* [*Account of the Commemoration for the Martyrs of Japan*],
110, 112; *Romance por la victoria de
Tetuán* [*Ballad for the Victory in Tetuan*],
110, 113; *Valor, agravio y mujer* [*Valor,
Offense, Woman*], 14, 111–12, 126, 274,
277 (absence in, 12, 200–202, 204, 207–9;
cross-dressing in, 202, 282–83; desire in,
284–86; Flora, 11, 202, 204–9; *gracioso*
[comic figure] in, 203–6; homoeroticism
in, 15, 278, 282, 284–86; honor in, 11;
marriage in, 207–8, 282, 284, 286; rhetoric of opposition in, 7; rhetoric of reticence in, 11, 200–202, 206–7, 209; Ribete,
203–4, 206, 208, 283; silence in, 11, 199–
202, 204, 206–9; Tomillo, 203–7; violence
in, 282–83, 286; women writers, 203–4,
206, 209)
Castiglione, Baldassare: *Il cortegiano* [*The
Book of the Courtier*], 2, 41
Castillo Solorzano, Alonso de, 120
Catholics, 54–55
Celestina. *See* Rojas, Fernando de
Cervantes Saavedra, Miguel de
—*Works: Cerco de Numancia* [*Siege of
Numantia*] (*Fama* [Fame], 183);
Coloquio de los perros [*Colloquy of the
Dogs*], 195; *Don Quijote*, 63, 96, 153–54,
184, 186, 195, 154; *El amante liberal* [*The
Generous Lover*], 80; *El casamiento
engañoso* [*Deceitful Marriage*], 195; *El
laberinto del amor* [*The Labyrinth of
Love*], 11, 186 (disguise in, 187–88;
feminine identity in, 184, 187–88; honor
in, 109; labyrinth in, 184–85, 188–91;
language in, 187–89, 191; *theatrum
mundi* in, 185, 189); *El licenciado
Vidriera* [*The Glass Graduate*], 83;
Entremeses [Interludes], 183; *Exemplary
Novels* (See individual novels); *La casa
de los celos* [*The House of Jealousy*]: autonomy in, 195; love in, 191; material
value in, 191; self-definition in, 185–86;

silence in, 183, 187; *La española inglesa* [*The English Spanish Girl*], 80, 185 (bilingualism in, 11, 186, 192–94; Isabela, 11, 186, 191–92, 195; labyrinth in, 11, 184, 192–94; violence in, 192; *voz extremada* [consummate voice] in, 11, 191); *La fuerza de la sangre* [*The Power of Blood*], 80; *La Galatea*, 242; *La gitanilla*, 79, 89, 191 (Andrés Caballero/ Don Juan de Cárcamo, 81, 84–88; economies in, 6–7, 81, 87; gypsy in, 7, 81–87, 88n.8; love in, 6, 80–85, 87; money in, 6–7, 80–86; *paje-poeta* [page-poet], 82–84; Preciosa/Costanza, 6–7, 80–83, 85, 87–88, 191; social class in, 6–7, 80, 82, 84–85, 87; theft in, 6, 81); *La ilustre fregona* [*The Illustrious Kitchen-Maid*], 80

Charles I (Charles V), 4, 20, 268
Charles III, 136
Cheronense, Sextus, 27
Cicero, 59
Ciruelo, Pedro, 149, 153
Claramonte, Andrés de, 147, 153, 156n.2
Conversos [converts to Catholicism], 57, 60, 191, 217
Cos, Claudio de, 127
Cross-dressing. *See* Azevedo, Angela de; Caro, Ana; Erauso, Catalina de; Women
Cueva y Silva, Leonor de la, 110, 128

David, Gail, 247–48
Davila, Juan Francisco, 110
Daza, Gaspar, 57
Deleito y Piñuela, José, 121, 135
Delicado, Francisco: *La Lozana andaluza* [*Portrait of Lozana*] (conduct hand-books/manuals, 41–42; didacticism of, 41; dreams in, 5, 49–50; eroticism in, 5, 35, 46; feminine discourse in, 48; literary references in, 39; love in, 38–39; phallogocentric order in, 5, 35; Rome in, 38, 40–44, 48, 50)
Derrida, Jacques, 2

Devotio moderna, 59–60, 67
DiGangi, Mario, 274
Dilatio [delay], 47

Enríquez, Leonor de Luna, Countess of Salvatierra, 115–16, 121
Enríquez de Guzmán, Alonso, 97
Erasmus, Desiderius, 5–6, 57, 61, 80
—Works: *De libero arbitrio* [*Discourse on Free Will*], 55–56; *De pueris* [*The Education of Children*], 20; *Enchiridion militis Christiani* [*Handbook of the Militant Christian*], 41; *Modus orandi Deum* [*Treatise on Prayer*], 60
Erauso, Catalina de (alias: Antonio de Erauso): *Vida i sucesos de la monja alférez* [*The Life and Adventures of the Lieutenant Nun*] (Americas in, 7, 91, 97–99, 102, 104; autobiography, 7–8, 91–100, 103; convent in, 7, 91, 97, 99, 101, 103; cross-dressing in, 7, 97, 99, 100; *encomienda* [land with Indian workers], 104; muleteer, 7, 99; sexual identity in, 7, 100, 103–4; violence in, 7, 97, 99, 101–3)
Espejo, Sánchez del, 117, 122

Father, 19, 25–26, 30–31, 43, 101, 103
Ferdinand II of Aragon, 255–57
Ferdinand III of Hungary, 117
Ficino, Marsilio, 55
Fideism, 56
Foucault, Michel, 62, 148, 152
Freud, Sigmund, 10, 100, 141

García de Toledo, Father, 71
Garcilaso de la Vega, 38
Gender, 1, 3, 5–8, 11, 12, 14–5, 36, 44, 91–92, 100–104, 108, 111, 185, 257, 260, 265, 274, 279, 282
Gilman, Stephen, 169, 172
Góngora y Argote, Luis de: *Fábula de Polifemo y Galatea* [*Polyphemus and Galatea*] (Acis, 10, 160, 169–75;

Góngora y Argote—*continued*
baroque style of, 10, 164, 166, 171, 175,
175–76n.1, 177n.20; cult of beauty in,
10, 170–72; Cyclops myth in, 163, 170;
the fall in, 10, 169–70, 172–73, 177n.12;
Galatea, 10, 160–61, 168–75; Garden of
Eden in, 10, 170, 173–74; images of
movement in, 161–62, 168–69; *locus
amoenus* in, 173–74; love in, 10, 170,
172–75; metrics in, 162; morality in,
10, 169–70, 172, 175; musicality in, 164,
166; Polifemo, 161–65, 167, 170–71,
175; sexuality in, 10, 171–75; Sicily
in, 164, 167, 171; theology in, 10,
169)
Guamanga, Bishop of, 91, 98, 103
Guevara, Antonio de
—*Works: Libro áureo de Marco Aurelio*
[*Golden Book of Marcus Aurelius*], 20–
22, 32, 33n.9; *Relox de Príncipes* [*Dial
of Princes*], 4, 19, 32 (animal imagery in,
23, 31; breast-feeding in [*see* Mother];
Christian prince in, 20–22; milk in, 26–
29; mother in [*see* Mother]; nursing in
[*see* Mother]; state in, 20–22, 24, 31; superstitions in, 20, 29–30; wet nurse in
[*see* Mother])

Haro, María de, 115
Hervet, Gentian, 57
Homoeroticism. *See* Caro, Ana; Zayas,
María de
Huarte de San Juan, Juan, 59

Ignatius of Loyola, Saint, 58, 61, 70, 73n.8
Innocent IV, Pope, 270n.2
Innocent VIII, Pope, 257
Inquisition, 55, 109
Isabel I of Castile, Queen (la Católica), 4,
35–36, 121, 193, 255
Isabel de Borbón, Queen (wife of Philip
IV), 117–18, 125, 146

Jesuits, 58, 73n.4

Jiménez de Cisneros, Cardinal Francisco,
56
Juana Inés de la Cruz, Sor, 109, 119, 127;
Los empeños de una casa [*The Cares of a
House*], 140, 142

Labyrinth. *See* Cervantes, *El laberinto del
amor; La española inglesa*
Lacan, Jacques, 10, 100, 141–43
Laudatio, 128
Laws of Toro, 1
Lazarillo de Tormes, 37
Lejeune, Philippe, 92
León Pinelo, Antonio de, 111, 117, 122, 125
López de Úbeda, Francisco: *La pícara
Justina*, 44, 214
López Estrada, Francisco, 108, 113–14
Lotti, Cosme, 115, 126
Luis de León, Fray: *La perfecta casada*
[*The Perfect Wife*], 4, 19, 21–22, 24–25,
29–32
Luján, Pedro de: *Coloquios matrimoniales*
[*Marriage Colloquia*], 4, 19, 21–22, 24–
25, 27–28, 30–32
Luna, Lola, 111, 113–14, 119, 202
Luther, Martin, 54, 56–57

Machiavelli, Niccolò, 41
Macrobius, 148–49
Maldonado, Juan, 57–58, 73n.3
María de Borbón, Princess of Carignano,
117–18, 126
Martin V, Pope, 270
Martínez de Toledo, Alfonso: *Arcipreste de
Talavera* (*Corbacho*), 36
Mediocritas, 61
Menéndez y Pelayo, Marcelino, 35, 46
Mesa, Juan de, 115
Misogyny, 4–5, 9, 11–13, 35–37, 44, 51, 146,
214, 216
Molina, Tirso de [Fray Gabriel Téllez]:
manto [shawl], 137–38; *mujer vestida de
hombre* [woman in male dress], 9, 135;
tapada [veiled woman], 9, 135–36, 138,

142 (*see also* Calderón de la Barca, Pedro)
—*Works: El amor médico [Love the Doctor]*, 9, 136, 138; *La celosa de sí misma [Jealous of Herself]*, 136
Montaigne, Michel de, 57–61, 65–66; *Apologie de Raimond Sebond [An Apology for Raymond Sebond]*, 56
Montalbán, Pérez de, 235
Montemayor, Jorge de, 242–43; *La Diana*, 248
Mother: authority of, 4, 19, 21; birthing by, 23–25; blood, 19–21; breast-feeding, 4, 19–24, 26–32; child rearing, 4, 19, 24; milk, 19–21; milk production, 27–28; - child relationship, 23–26, 29–30; nursing, 19–25, 27, 30; power and independence of, 4, 30; pregnancy, 19, 22, 24, 28; weaning child, 28, 30; wet nurse, 4, 19–30, 32n.4

Nebrija, Antonio de, 20, 37
Neoplatonists, 59, 73n.1
New Testament, 2, 67
Nueva Recopilación de las Leyes de España [New Recompilation of the Laws of Spain], 9

Old Testament, 2
Olivares, Don Gaspar, Count Duke of, 8, 111, 116–18, 120–22, 124, 126
Ortega Haro, Diego de, 115
Osuna, Francisco de, 60

Pacheco de la Vega, Gonzalo, 127
Palma, Ricardo, 137
Patriarchy, 4, 6–10, 12, 14, 79, 87, 101, 108, 110, 147, 156, 201–2, 207, 217, 227, 229, 274–75, 277. *See also* Azevedo, Angela de
Patrizi, Francesco, 20
Paul, Saint, 2
Pfandl, Ludwig, 250n.1
Philip II, 20, 135
Philip III, 59

Philip IV, 110, 115, 117–20, 122, 125, 258–60
Picaresque, 94, 104n.7
Pico della Mirandola, Gianfrancesco, 55–56
Pico della Mirandola, Giovanni, 55
Ponce de León, Rodrigo, Duke of Cádiz, 255
Pons de Castelvi, Fabricio, 258
Protestants, 54–57
Pseudo-Dionysius, 59
Pyrrhonism, 54, 56

Queer theory, 273, 275, 282, 287n.2
Quevedo, Francisco de, 12, 38, 111, 216, 229
—*Works*: "El mundo por de dentro" ["The World Inside Out"], 58; "Infierno enmendado" ["Reformed Hell"], 214; "Providencia de Dios" ["Providence of God"], 215

Reformation, 55
Relaciones de fiestas [accounts of festivals], 108–10
Rojas, Fernando de: *La Celestina*, 4, 36–40, 46, 214
Rousseau, Jean-Jacques, 92, 95
Ruiz, Juan (Arcipreste de Hita), 187, 217

Salcedo, Francisco, 57
Sanches, Francisco, 58, 60–61
San Pedro, Diego de: *Cárcel de amor*, 36–40
Savonarola, Girolamo, 55
Scripture, 56–58, 65
Serrano y Sanz, Manuel, 93–94
Sextus Empiricus, 54–57, 59, 60, 66
Shakespeare, William, 200, 266
Solórzano, Castillo, 235
Spain: Council of Trent, 217; Counter-Reformation, 217; Peace of Westphalia, 258; Reconquest, 257, 268–69; Thirty Years War, 258, 267; Treaty of the Pyrenees, 258
Spínola, Agustina, 8, 118–20, 122, 124

Spínola, Ambrosio, 118
Strata, Carlos, 8, 111, 117–19, 122, 125
Suárez, Francisco, 58

Teresa of Avila, Saint, 108, 111, 129n.7;
apophatic spirituality of, 59–60, 66–67,
72; confession, 61, 70; confessors, 57–58,
63, 68, 70; Erasmus, 6; humility of, 70;
intellect of, 62–67, 69, 71–72; kataphatic
spirituality of, 67; language of, 69–70;
letrados [learned men], 71, 73; on melancholia, 66; mental prayer, 6, 60; mystical marriage, 59, 63; obedience, 70; recollection, 60, 64, 67, 69; *retórica de la
abyección* [rhetoric of abjection], 61;
retórica de la incertidumbre [rhetoric of
incertitude], 61; rhetoric of self-deprecation, 5, 69, 71; skepticism, 5–6, 54, 59–
63, 66, 72; spiritual union, 6; visions of,
63–64, 67–69, 72
—*Works: Camino de perfección* [*Way of
Perfection*], 65, 72; *Fundaciones* [*Foundations*], 62, 65–66, 71–72; *Moradas* [*Interior Castle*], 63–64, 67, 73n.6; *Vida* [*Life*],
62, 64–66, 68–72, 95, 103–4
Tomás de Saboya, 117
Torquemada, Antonio de, 116
Tyndale, William, 41

Unamuno, Miguel de, 195
Urban VIII, Pope, 99

Valdés, Alfonso de, 40
Valencia, Pedro de, 59
Vega, Lope de, 116, 148, 153, 235–36
Vélez de Guevara, Luis, 109, 126
Vilanova, Antonio, 160
Vives, Juan Luis, 2, 57–58, 60; *Institutio
feminae christianae* [*The Instruction of a
Christian Woman*], 20
Vituperatio, 120, 126, 128

Women, 22, 35–36; adornment of, 9–10,
141; cross-dressing, 44, 140; defense of,
36; desire in, 9, 273–75, 287; feminine
identity, 1, 3, 5, 6–12, 14–15, 43–44, 103,
111, 217; *gynaceum*, 46; gynocentrism,
14, 273–74; inferiority of, 1–2, 5; legal
rights of, 1, 9; lesbianism, 273; moral
weakness of, 2, 9; as *mujer varonil*
[manly woman], 94, 202, 210n.2; as nun,
5; as Other, 5, 42, 50 (*see also* Caravajal,
Mariana de); passivity of, 2–3, private
sphere of, 2–3, 5–6; public sphere of, 2–3,
6–8, 15; silence of, 2–3, 11, 146, 183, 201,
229 (*see also* Caro, Ana); subordination
of, 2–3, 20; as wife, 5, 20–22, 24–25; as
writer, 5, 7–9, 11–13, 108, 110–12, 117,
122, 128, 229, 251n.5, 272. *See also*
Mother; Misogyny

Zayas, María de, 5, 108, 111, 223, 229;
criticism of men, 13–14, 253–55, 257–
60, 263–65, 269, 275; on effeminate
men, 257, 266–69; on feminine dress,
260–65, 266–68; feminism of, 250,
251n.2, 253; frame narrative, 238–39,
241, 245, 249; on men's fashion, 14, 253,
259–64, 266–67; military orders, 254, 257–
59, 267, 269, 270n.2; nation, 14, 255, 267,
269; *novela cortesana* [courtly romance],
236–37; pornography, 13, 250n.1; on treatment of women, 13, 266, 269
—*Works: Desengaños amorosos* [*The Disenchantments of Love*], 13, 235, 249,
254, 258, 268 ("El traidor contra su
sangre" ["The Traitor to His Blood"],
225; "La inocencia castigada" ["Punished Innocence"], 225; "Mal presagio
casarse lejos" ["Marriage Abroad: Portent of Doom"], 225, 266); *La traición
en la amistad* [*Friendship Betrayed*], 14,
274 (beauty in, 280; desire in, 277–82;
286; friendship in, 15, 278–79, 282;
homoeroticism in, 15, 273, 279–82;
homosocialism in, 279, 281–82, 286);
Novelas amorosas y ejemplares [*The
Enchantments of Love*]: "Aventurarse

perdiendo" ["Everything Ventured"] (bucolic themes in, 13, 238, 240, 243, 245; convent in, 13, 248; *desengaño* [disillusionment] in, 246, 251n.6; female voice in, 13, 236, 238, 242–43, 245, 250; *locus amoenus* in, 240, 243, 249; *locus veritas* in, 249; male disguise in, 244, 248; Montserrat in, 242–43, 247–49; pastoral genre in, 13, 236–43, 247, 250; poetic devices of, 13, 238; urban society in, 240, 247–48); "El prevenido enga-ñado" ["The Deceptively Forewarned"], 225

Zwingli, Ulrich, 57